THEY MOVED IN A WORLD WHERE A HEADLINE CAN MAKE A STAR, SHATTER A REPUTATION, DESTROY AN EMPIRE... WHERE ENEMIES COUNT FOR MORE THAN FRIENDS...

CAMPBELL HAIG—At twenty-five he had a small-town newspaper and a passion for justice. By forty he had an empire, fewer scruples than a tomcat, and more enemies than even a billionaire could afford.

ALEX NOYES—She grew up before the camera's merciless eye, her every move a potential headline. Haig inspired a hatred that shook her to the core—so intense, it was only a heartbeat from desire.

NORA NOYES—Making a career out of being a president's widow, she was the model of decorum, even when it came to destroying the man her daughter loved.

SISSY VALENTINE—*The New York Mail* should have been hers. Instead it went to the man who had already cost her her pride, her beliefs—and would soon cost her much, much more.

SEAN FARRELL—A firebrand, every word he wrote was an act of rebellion. But how could he rebel when Haig made him his editor? And how could he work beside the man who was his rival in love?

THE PRESS LORD

"A rousing story of a passionate newspaperman... recommended."
—*Library Journal*

"A never-before-seen look at the power and exploitation—the personal passions and hatreds—of the Fourth Estate."
—*Post-Gazette* (Boston)

Books by James Brady

SUPERCHIC
PARIS ONE
NIELSEN'S CHILDREN
THE PRESS LORD

The Press Lord
James Brady

A DELL BOOK

Published by
Dell Publishing Co., Inc.
1 Dag Hammarskjold Plaza
New York, New York 10017

Dell ® TM 681510, Dell Publishing Co., Inc.

ISBN: 0-440-17080-X

Reprinted by arrangement with Delacorte Press

Printed in the United States of America

First Dell printing—March 1983

For Fiona and Susan

The Press Lord

1949

The little boy loved the newspaper.

Before memory began he had loved it. The sound of the press, the vibrations he could feel through the soles of his shoes. The look and the feel of the office. The smell—the different smells.

Up front was the smell of stacked newspapers, some tidy, stacked, and fresh, others curled and yellowing. His father's place was in the window, in the very front of the office where anyone in the town could stand on the sidewalk to watch him work at his old rolltop desk. The three or four or six reporters, depending on whether it was a good year or hard times, were in the front with his father. A low burnished hardwood railing fenced off the back of the room. It had a hinged gate on which the boy, when he was really small, was permitted to swing. Behind the fence was where the advertising men sat and where his father's secretary typed and the table at which people wrote out their classified advertisements with the big sharpened pencils that also had their own smell. The railing was important, setting the advertising department apart from the news staff.

Behind the front room through a door was the press room, once a garage and before that a stable, with the big Goss press, dark and powerful and gleaming. The press room had a different smell en-

1

tirely, ink and oil and the fresh newsprint looking like huge toilet-paper rolls. Back here were two men, sometimes a third, who wore overalls and square paper hats that they taught the boy to make. He was allowed to wear a printer's hat in the press room but never in front where his father and the reporters sat. It was one of his father's rules.

Later, when he turned thirteen and wanted to deliver the paper on his bicycle, his father said no, that was for the Mexican boys who really needed after-school jobs. That was another of his father's rules.

The first words the boy ever learned to read, long before he had entered the first grade, he learned to read backward. They were in gilt on the big windows that fronted on Main Street, facing the bank across the proud, newly laid macadam that had finally gone down after his father had written a hundred editorials about the summer's dust and the winter's mud. *The New Mexico Advance.* Underneath in smaller print it said *Samuel Scotland Haig, Editor and Publisher.*

This was the boy's father.

Christmastime, the year the little boy was seven, he sat in his father's office in the late afternoon. It was the best time, with the office lighted and warm against the early winter dusk and the lights blinking on in the bank and in the shops along Main Street. The boy watched the pickup trucks and the old Chevies and Fords with their parking lights as they came up the street, driven by men in cowboy hats or by women wearing head scarves. He watched them through the big window, entertaining himself while his mother and sisters shopped for dinner and the holiday that was coming. His father sat at the rolltop desk in the black suit he wore always, the jacket buttoned as it would be even in the summer heat of the high desert. Beyond the low buildings lining Main Street the boy could just see the far mountains, gray clouds like tablecloths spread atop the snowy peaks.

His father was typing and the boy turned from the window to watch. He could not wait until he could type. His father's fingers moved swiftly over the keyboard of the heavy black Underwood upright. He was typing a letter. The boy knew this because if it were for the newspaper it could be on yellow copy paper. This was being written on his father's stiff, creamy stationery that had come all the way from Dallas, from Neiman-Marcus. To the left of the typewriter an envelope had already been addressed. The boy stared at it, trying to puzzle out the words.

"Papa?"

His father said, "Yes, boy?" and continued to type.

"Who are you writing to?"

"To whom?"

"To whom are you writing?"

Samuel Scotland Haig stopped typing and turned to regard the boy, small and slender and with his mother's fine brown hair and the long, girlish lashes under the strange green eyes. He took up the envelope and his fingers picked out the words. "Well, now, Campbell, this is a letter to a man I knew during the war. He owns some newspapers in England."

"Like the *Advance*, Papa?"

Haig smiled gently at the question, his gray eyes a long way off, across an ocean and the years.

"Well, like the *Advance*. And bigger. I write him every Christmas. And he writes to me. A great man, some people think. Look now, see if you can make out the words: 'The Right Honorable Lord . . .' Can you read that?"

"Only 'the,'" the boy said, sadly shaking his head. "That last word," he asked, "the long one. What does it say?"

"Why, that's his name," Sam Haig said. "Beaverbrook. His name is Lord Beaverbrook. More accurately, that's his title. I usually call him Max."

"Oh," the boy said. He knew about lords from stories his mother read him. And he was impressed that his father should know a lord and call him Max.

The little boy hoped that one day he too would know distant lords and be permitted to address them by their Christian names in letters he would write on typewriters in an office that smelled like this. It was in such a place, he firmly decided, that he would spend all the days of his life.

I

"Franklin Roosevelt sat in that chair," the old woman said, her rheumy eyes fixed fierce and disapproving on one of the three men who had come to counsel her. The man moved uneasily.

"People were mistaken about Franklin," the old woman went on, ransacking the attic of memory. "They thought because he used a wheelchair that he was helpless. Rubbish! He had tremendous strength. His arms, those shoulders!"

The three men listened politely. As if all this were new to them. The old woman, whose name was Meg Valentine, permitted her ferocity to soften in reminiscence.

"He'd come up here to the office and settle himself in that chair and proselytize. During the Depression it was for the NRA, the Tennessee Valley power plan. Later, when he tried to pack the Court. Then, when the war came, for lend lease and the overage destroyers and on helping the Russians. Finally, for the fourth term. Sometimes I'd go along with him. Sometimes I wouldn't."

She stared out at the river that flowed past her office, not seeing a river.

"It was difficult to say no to Franklin. He was so bright, so reasonable, so Goddamn . . . sexy. And that charm! He made it hard for a woman to say no. In the end I knew he was dying. He sat right

4

there and I could see death in his eyes and then I went ahead and backed the fourth term. I felt we owed him that," Meg Valentine said, her voice thoughtful and remembering. Shifting harshly into the present she demanded, "And now you come and sit in *his* chair and issue ultimatums?"

Only the man in the Roosevelt chair moved. He recrossed his legs. What bad luck to have chosen this particular chair. The most powerful, cranky, opinionated woman in New York and age had done nothing to erode her granite. Meg Valentine's face conveyed an amused contempt.

"Lawyer talk." She spat out the words. Then, sitting back in the swivel chair behind a barricade of a desk, she waved an imperious hand, signaling that she was at last prepared to listen.

The man in the Roosevelt chair *was* a lawyer; the others, a banker and a certified accountant. The lawyer said, "Mrs. Valentine, we are simply telling you what the tax law is and what will happen to your estate if you continue to hold the company in private ownership."

Meg Valentine rapped a bony hand on the polished surface of the desk. "You're telling me I can't afford to die."

The accountant smiled. "That is precisely what we are telling you."

The old woman gave a whoop of laughter. "The best news I've had in years," she said, "and I suppose your fee will so reflect."

The lawyer shook his head. "I'd waive my fee if I could guarantee immortality."

"*That* would set a precedent," she grumbled.

Shuffling some papers, the lawyer sat slightly forward in the Roosevelt chair and resumed. "Your tax man and your banker can elaborate, of course. But what I'm telling you is that the estate taxes are simply going to eat up everything. Not only won't your heirs have anything, there won't be operating funds sufficient to keep the newspaper running."

At the word "heirs" her face crinkled with disgust, but the lawyer continued smoothly. "You have got to divest now, while you're alive and well, and abandon this notion of passing on an entity after you're gone. We all understand how you hate the idea of selling *The New York Mail.* But as your advisers we have a fiduciary responsibility to tell you the new federal tax codes leave you no alternative."

Impatient, she again waved a hand so desiccated it seemed translucent.

"A foundation," she said shrewdly. "I could set up a foundation. Hearst did it, didn't he?"

"He did," the banker said quickly. "Two of them, in fact, one in California, the other here in New York. And until the seventies so could you. But this latest revision of the federal code changed all that. Today you can't assign more than five percent of the stock of a private corporation to a foundation."

Meg Valentine stopped listening. She was tempted to demand the names of the fools who had permitted such legislation to pass so that she could punish them in the *Mail*. But she was too tired. All this learned counsel was such a bore. A late-morning spring sun bounced off the river through tall windows to splatter on the golden carpets and soak into the liquid depths of fine old wood. How many thousands of hours had she sat in this room atop the *Mail* building, how many hundreds of significant conversations had taken place here, not with technocrats like these but with great men?

She could recall, in precise detail, where famous men had sat and what they had said and where she had lounged with her celebrated legs stretched out before her as she listened. Jack Kennedy had sat in *that* chair, LaGuardia had favored *that* hassock, Castro had sprawled over there. Adlai's favorite place was near one of those tall windows framing the East River and the bridge and beyond them, Brooklyn and the Heights. Poor Adlai, standing there, seeing every side of every question, lacking only answers. FDR had the answers. She could visualize where his wheelchair would be placed and how the tires bit into the deep carpet. She imagined even now she could still see the wheel marks. How foolish, she thought, forty years after he had last been in this room.

Her advisers, consulting impressive briefs, were still droning on. Now Meg Valentine stood up.

"Gentlemen, you have made your point. Painfully so. I'll consider your advice."

The men rose, shook hands, and left. As the door opened Meg Valentine could hear, a long way off and muted, the roar of the presses. Nearly noon. The third edition was being printed. As the door swung shut the sound was silenced and instead the words of her banker hung in the room like dust in the sunlight. "Consider your heirs, Mrs. Valentine."

Meg Valentine scowled. Her heirs. What a bad joke. Not Sissy. Not that girl. Meg's own spirit had leaped a generation to her granddaughter. A sunshine girl everyone liked, even the most sullen, burned-out rewrite man on the copy desk, even the grimy thugs who lived in the building's bowels, the hard-case unionists who operated the great brute presses that thundered and shook the building six floors below. She was not tough or aggressive enough but Sissy was all right.

Not so her father. Meg's only child, Junior Valentine. *Junior.* A retarded juvenile so inept she paid him to stay away from the newspaper. And rather than feeling shamed, Junior had gloried in the arrangement. It permitted him to pursue his only avocation: playing Broadway angel, casting pliable ingenues in dubious shows. He had married a Philadelphia girl his last year at Harvard. Five years later she was dead of leukemia, an easy out for Junior. Her sensuousness had only turned him more juvenile. Left with two small children, he abdicated responsibility for Willie and Sissy to an excellent nanny, one Jean Hughes, chosen by Meg. Jean did well with Sissy, less so with her brother. The children had the use of the East Hampton house and a duplex on Park Avenue, good schools and an occasional audience with their father. Junior had other interests. In the small bar downstairs at Sardi's it was said he was the sort who backs "actresses who run and plays that don't."

The comment had got back to Meg Valentine, and her rage was such that Junior exiled himself to Hollywood for a year rather than face her.

Her heirs!

There was her grandson, Sissy's brother, Willie. At first he had shown promise. A good space salesman. Damn good. And like all publishers Meg Valentine was properly respectful of a good space salesman. Publishers were permitted to laugh at reporters, at rewrite men, even at editors. They did not laugh at men who brought in the advertising contracts from Bloomingdale's, from Macy's, from GM, from American Airlines, from the A&P. Willie Valentine had brought in the revenue in the early flush of enthusiasm, but he hadn't gone on. There was something about the boy: too smooth, too ready to laugh. He switched his charm on and off; it was insubstantial and suspect. There was that trouble Willie had at Kent. Meg had closed off any possibility that he had stolen anything from his roommate; a Valentine might be flawed but could not steal. Never. But Meg still remembered Willie's smile, too ready and too winning, when the other boy was forced to apologize for having made the accusation. The memory of that smile kept her from ever truly warming to her grandson. Only Sissy was loved without reservation.

Meg Valentine did not exempt herself from criticism. She realized that to her lawyer she was a vain old woman living largely in years, in decades past. She knew she talked too much of FDR, suggesting more to their relationship than she should, more, perhaps, than there was. About some things—the indentations his wheelchair left in the carpet—memory was as keen as ever. On other matters, distressingly vague. She shook her old head. Too many years. She swiveled her chair to confront Brooklyn, to blot out thought, to rest and to think no more.

The office in which Meg Valentine now lazed, half dozing, was on the sixth and top floor of a long sandstone building on the Manhattan bank of the East River, a paranoid building owing as much to fear as to architecture. It had gone up at a time when the nation's press lords feared the mob their own screaming headlines and shrill editorials had created. At their base the walls were six feet thick. There were no windows on the lower floors and heavy bars on those on the upper; there were steel doors. Nothing on the facade indicated that this structure housed the country's oldest newspaper; no sign proclaimed *The New York Mail*.

Men like Hearst and Pulitzer and Gordon Bennett put up buildings like this one. Publishers who pandered to the mob and feared it. Such men ignited revolutions and then, trembling, demanded the authorities put them down, restore law and order, protect property. Such men fed their own voracious egos in contemplation of the powerful forces they had unleashed. Such men went mad. Bennett carried a derringer. Pulitzer passed his last days in a rubberized room resting on ball bearings, to shut out the vibrations of trolley cars and horse-drawn carriages. Hearst had wanted a new American revolution and then, in the Depression, he withdrew to San Simeon behind guards and gates and distance.

Meg Valentine shared their megalomania but not their fear. She loved this old building. Loved the building, loved the newspaper it housed, loved the stinking tidal stream New Yorkers called a river that flowed past, lapping against the foundations of the building, carrying the barges and yachts and container ships past the windows of her office. An office from which she had directed the fortunes of the newspaper since the death of her husband nearly fifty years before.

The *Mail* had been George Valentine's toy. He had purchased it on impulse, as a man might buy a necktie that caught his eye. It was the boom time of the twenties, there were a dozen newspapers in New York, he golfed with men who owned papers, this one was up for sale cheap, and he bought. "Why not?" he had responded when his young bride asked why. Two years later he was dead, the stock market had crashed, and the *Mail* was struggling to remain afloat in a market dominated by larger, richer, more professionally run papers. The sensible thing for the widowed Meg would have been to sell. Clear out, her advisers had urged, get out from under.

Instead, stubborn, still mourning her frivolous, impractical, wonderfully romantic husband, Meg said no. She would keep the *Mail.* It had been George's hobby; she would make it her monument to him. Knowing nothing about newspapers, never having worked or managed or hired or fired anyone but a maid or a cook, she had herself driven downtown, taken the elevator to the sixth floor, informed her late husband's secretary that she, Mrs. George Valentine, was now the publisher and editor of *The New York Mail* and would the girl please put out an announcement to that effect. The girl blinked, inquired politely if she shouldn't get someone's authorization first, and within fifteen minutes was out of the building, the first but not the last employee Meg Valentine would sack.

The *Mail* had not always been a plaything for dilettantes like George Valentine. It had an honorable history, dating back to a publication once edited by the legendary Peter Zenger. It had broken with Andy Jackson over the issue of national banks, supported Lincoln except on the draft, campaigned against the Spanish war on the sensible basis that it was Mr. Hearst's war. But by the time George Valentine bought it, the paper no longer thundered, was no longer a voice to which Washington or Albany or even City Hall harkened. It had lost readers to the brighter, racier *Daily News*

under Captain Joe Patterson, to the conservative *Herald Tribune,* to
the gossipy *Mirror,* to the flag-waving *Journal,* and, of course, to the
great *New York Times,* by then embarked on its campaign to become for America what London's *Times* was to Europe. And with
its lost readers went the advertising and the profits.

It had been willful of Meg to keep the *Mail;* it was willful of her
now to refuse to sell. She knew that. She never lied to herself. To
others, when it was important to do so, but never to herself. Today's
visitation by her counselors had conjured up memories of the lean,
stark Depression days when she had revived the *Mail,* restored its
glory, had herself become a force in the city, a strong woman wooed
by important politicians. It was in those years they had begun to
come to this room to lay out their proposals, their initiatives, their
ambitions. In this room she had listened, probed, pondered, decided.
No editorial boards to be consulted, not in those days, and not now.
No group journalism at the *Mail.* Meg Valentine *was* the editorial
board, Meg's the voice a million readers heard each day in her
unsigned editorials. Her judgments inclined to the erratic, enraging
statesmen who left this room aglow with her anticipated endorse-
ment only to cry "Sold!" when they read that the *Mail* had come
out for the opposition. Other men had limped away wounded by her
apparent contempt for their hopes, only to read a day or a week later
how ringingly the *Mail* was supporting them. Presidents, governors,
kings, dictators, mayors, reformers, and grafters, they all courted her,
here, on her own ground. Always one on one, never over cocktails
or at linened tables, no hint of the salon tolerated. Meg wanted no
distractions as she weighed, tasted, sniffed the essence of the man
seeking her favor. She was remembering some of those men now
when a tanker, riding as high as an apartment building, interrupted
her reverie with a rude blast of its horn.

Meg Valentine stood up, a bit shakily from having sat too long
in one position, silently cursed the long, still shapely legs that were
her trademark but that now, unsteadily, refused to do the things they
had always done. She rang for her secretary and the girl came in,
carrying tea and a sandwich and the third edition. Meg glanced at
the front page and then, quickly, at a change she had dictated in the
lead editorial. Satisfied that no enemy, no competitor, no traitorous
union saboteur had worked his mischief on her newspaper, she

relaxed and toyed with lunch. Her advisers had told her nothing she did not know already. She understood that the *Mail* must be sold while she was still alive. She owed it to Sissy, to the employees, to the newspaper itself. It had been amusing to give the impression that she was unalterably opposed to selling. It would be even more diverting to see their faces when next she summoned them and announced that the *Mail* was up for sale.

She swiveled her chair toward the window and the river, remembering the giants who had once run the city's newspapers, the press lords of the past. Hearst, Ochs, Adler, Gordon Bennett, Pulitzer, Dan Richards. . . .

Daniel Compton Richards, her contemporary, the only one of the titans still alive, confidant of the great, a man who made, and sometimes broke, presidents, heir to a great publishing empire, a man shrewd and hard, proud and intuitive, and now . . . Each morning Richards was dressed in this three-piece suit with the American flag inserted into his lapel and helped out onto the gravel driveway of his estate to await the limousine that would take him into the city. A limousine that would never come. After a few minutes his wife or a maid would come out and take him gently by the arm, announcing brightly that "The office just called. Today's a holiday." And the great Dan Richards would hobble back inside.

Meg shuddered. To become senile was unthinkable. In recent days that special dread had eased. Now there was another reason, beyond love for her grandchild, beyond the urging of solemn men, that she must sell the *Mail*. And soon.

Just a week ago her doctors had told Meg Valentine she was dying.

2

The night wind blew in off the Seine and across the Place de la Concorde to bank around Napoleon's column of melted-down cannon in the Place Vendôme. Campbell Haig stood by the open doors of his suite on the top floor of the Ritz, the breeze drying the sweat on his body, cooling him, clearing his head. The air smelled of the sea a hundred miles away to the west. In this season the sea wind blew across Flanders and northern France and into the Ile, fetching clouds and misty rain.

Behind him the girl stirred gently in her sleep. Her long hair and a bare arm lay still against the white sheets and the soft blanket, her lovely mouth opened slightly, her well-bred London face in repose. It had been silly, bringing her along to Paris. He was angry at himself. And at her.

Haig had built a life that was solid and would endure without women. His work was what he had. He understood that without love any life was incomplete. Eventually there would be a woman, the right one, and then everything would be in place. But that time had not yet come. Until it did he had the newspapers and his work and he was reasonably content, except when he permitted himself such foolishness as this trip to Paris, on the vague rumor *Paris-Match* might be for sale.

The girl was an accident. Nothing more. Haig had been in London on business, Lord Rothermere had given a dinner in Belgravia, and then, afterward, there was the urge to go on to someplace else and the someplace else had been Annabel's. A big table. Noise and smoke and drink and the usual florid Englishmen and oil sheikhs and chinless wonders. And, of course, any number of beautiful English girls with cheekbones and bare shoulders and honeyed skin and eyes that said more, much more, than reticent English mouths. He had danced with the girl. Then, at the table, from the way she sat and moved and touched his hand just once, had known what she was telling him. He was bored with the party, bored with London, bored with himself. He made one phone call and then in the gray dawn he and the girl had been driven to her flat and then to Gatwick and the chartered plane to Orly. That was yesterday. Now he was tired of her and annoyed with himself.

It wasn't the girl's fault. Not at all. But he didn't want the distraction of a girl of her kind. Not now.

In the evening they'd gone up to Pigalle, to a dingy theater where a death's-head blonde sang Nazi-tainted German songs that the French audience cheered ecstatically. Then to Castel's cellar. The English girl wanted to dance. At the next table Belmondo and two other men teased a girl and took turns trying on hats. The English girl danced very well. Haig did not. But she moved nicely against him and he did not mind. It was past two when they got back to the Ritz. The concierge on the Vendôme side handed him a message form. On it were a New York phone number and a name misspelled, that of a newspaper broker who worked for him, and a garbled message.

"What time did this come?"

The concierge was vague. Someone else had received it before he came on at midnight.

"What is it?" the girl asked in the elevator.

"Nothing," he said. The elevator operator looked straight ahead but Haig did not like to talk business in front of people he did not know.

He unlocked the door of their suite. Light from the Place filtered into the room. He started to turn on the lamps.

"No," she said, opening her arms to him.

For an instant he resisted, his back stiff.

"You're angry," she said. "It was that message, wasn't it?"

"Yes."

"Because you weren't here when they called."

"Yes."

She was not the sort of girl who took her moods from a man. She was a little drunk. "Rubbish," she said, and reached behind her back to undo her dress.

He knew she was right but his irritation lingered stubbornly. She overrode it. She tossed her dress toward a chair, her slip tumbled silkily to the rug. Her body gleamed in the soft light of the windows as she pulled off stockings and wisps of underwear.

"Now," she said, extending a hand to him, leading him to the bed.

Yes, he thought, now. She drew him to her, her bare body tight against his suit, her arm snaking upward to pull his head down toward her. They fell on the waiting bed.

There was something stirring back there in New York, something big. But here was this bed and this girl. She tore at his clothes and squirmed against him. "Yes, Campbell, yes."

The girl was still asleep when the first gray broke over the gardens of the hotel and, unable to resist, Campbell Haig picked up the phone to ask for the transatlantic operator. To hell with it. His people in New York would just have to wake up.

Campbell Haig was never happier than when he was buying a newspaper. Daily papers were the voices of great cities, of entire nations, the monitored pulse of millions. And a New York paper? Damn! It was frustrating to be three thousand miles away with such a possibility looming. His intelligence services were good. If the message said the thing was possible then it was the moment to strike. Buying newspapers and running them might be his way of making it up to his father for his failures. Partly. But for Haig the chase, the hunt, the final kill were their own justification; they provided their own nearly sensual fulfillment.

Over the phone he heard someone in New York pick up and then a voice, far away and sleepy. He began to talk. Behind him the girl stirred again in her sleep, a beautiful well-bred English girl in a large bed, mirrored in the open door of the armoire. And Campbell Haig did not bother to look at her, had forgotten she was there.

Much that would explain what Campbell Haig had become, and why he lived and worked and drove himself as he did, had happened twenty years before, in 1962.

Summer on the high desert of New Mexico is a hard time in a hard land. The country is as spare as the Gobi with low hills that do not cool as they rise out of the dry valleys but simply become hotter, dustier, closer to the angry sun. There is always a wind but it is hot and dry, crusting eyelids, parching throats, and drifting dust to grime the interiors of even the best-insulated house. Stringy cattle nudge against one another for position in the dubious shade of the few stunted trees that are the landscape's only relief. Along the valleys, at the confluence of dry streambeds, are the towns, dun, dull, sleepy. One of these towns is called McAllen.

McAllen as a county seat boasted a courthouse, a bank, a hotel, and a weekly newspaper, *The New Mexico Advance.* Like a thousand such papers across rural America, the *Advance* provided its subscribers with a predictable fare of local births, deaths, weddings, and school bond issues; it reported on the exotic journeys of local citizens who ventured as far afield as San Francisco or Denver, it carried a column of Washington chat written by the press secretary to the district's congressman, it sold advertising to the local supermarket, the dry goods store, the drive-in movie. Just another small-town paper.

Except for its editor and owner, Samuel Scotland Haig.

The Scots are the Chinese of Europe, the Jews of Christendom. They leave their homes young, they wander, they trade, they bargain, they sell, they work. They send money home and farm their sons out. The first Haig sent out to America from Scotland was destined for New York or Boston or Philadelphia but by some mishap landed instead at Galveston the year after the Civil War, narrowly escaped being lynched as a Yankee carpetbagger (*all* accents being suspect in those days), and set up in Dallas as a shopkeeper. Wherever the Scot settles becomes a bit of Scotland; whatever he does, he prospers. Haig prospered, found Dallas to his taste, married a local Presbyterian, sired four sons. One son, Sam's father, went west to New Mexico, worked for a job printer just long enough to learn the trade, founded a newspaper, married a rancher's daughter, and lived to eighty. His son in turn, Samuel Scotland Haig, broke the racial tradition by staying home, succeeding his father as editor and publisher of the newspaper. Sam had one son and three daughters. His wife, also a Presbyterian, was the daughter of a cattle rancher, a small-boned woman who doted on her husband, children, and horses, in that order. The children, as might be expected, grew up self-sufficient, abnormally close to their father, and horse lovers.

The Haigs lived well. Graciously, in fact, for small-town New Mexico. Sam's wife inherited a substantial spread south of the town when her parents died, the *Advance* prospered, the girls were sent off to private schools, and the one son, Campbell Haig, destined for the state university, was instead dispatched to a more sophisticated campus, to Tulane in New Orleans. It was his mother's notion.

"He'll learn French and manners," Delia Haig predicted hopefully, and when her husband protested that Campbell was a westerner and not one of your panty-waisted Creoles, she sniffed at his "provincialism" and proceeded to pack the boy's suitcases. Instead of wasting away, as his father feared, Campbell Haig flourished at Tulane. Following an uncomfortable first year (his roommates dubbed him "Cactus" Haig), old Sam's son shed his cowboy boots along with the hard edge of a regional twang, bought himself an ancient MG roadster, failed to make the varsity baseball team, and learned to drink. In the summer of 1962 he had finished his junior year and was taking summer courses in both literature and economics, two disciplines Sam Haig insisted a man needed if he were to run a family newspaper successfully. Campbell was bright, the courses were easy, and summer in New Orleans was soft, humid, pleasant. The night his father died young Haig was drinking bourbon and listening to the Assunto Brothers' Dixieland Band in a Vieux Carre bar with a blond coed named Sharon who had been a Sugar Bowl princess that year. They were at the bar.

"My God, it's hot," she said.

Campbell just grinned. "The music," he said, "listen to the music."

Around them the crowd pressed close, moving with the music.

One of the band stepped out on top of the bar itself from the raised bandstand behind. The bartenders, who knew the act, moved away deftly. The musician, blowing a muted horn, strutted the length of the long bar, spilling drinks, knocking over an ashtray, stepping on fingers. Haig grinned again. The music, the drinks, the whole feel of the place, it was right. The girl, well, she was fine. But the music and the crowd and the drinks came first.

When the Assuntos had finished their set Sharon took his arm. "Hey, let's go, huh?"

She was a year older than Campbell. They had made love once before and she shivered now, remembering the tan, lean body. When her roommate had asked later how it was Sharon had said, not critical at all, "He makes love with a Texas accent." She was vague on geography and perhaps he did. She knew she was not important to him. But no mind. She would work at it. At last she pried him away from the bar and they went down the street to an apartment she had borrowed and went upstairs and to bed.

Which was why there was such difficulty finding Campbell that night when his father died.

Campbell knew, as clearly as if he had been there, how it must have happened. His father's last hours were vivid as his own memories. He knew the office, how it would look at that time of day, where his father would have sat at the desk, reading, thinking, wondering. Campbell had gone over it all a thousand times and he knew just how it must have been that hot, dusty final evening of his father's life.

Sam Haig pushed at a letter that lay, opened, on the old rolltop desk that dominated the editor's office. Funny, he thought, it had been years since he'd received this sort of crude threat. These days angry special interests didn't issue dramatic death threats. They simply pulled their advertising when you took them on over a controversial issue. Death threats had gone out of style. He supposed he ought to take the letter along to the sheriff's office, see if Clayton made anything of it. Except the damn fool would probably laugh and have it all over town that Haig was behaving like an old woman, going feeble in his years. Still . . .

He got up and went to the old-fashioned safe in the corner of the room. He opened the unlocked door, reached inside, and came up with a soft chamois bag. He returned to the desk, set the bag on the writing surface with a solid thud. After staring at it for a few minutes he slipped open the drawstring and took out the Smith & Wesson .38, a Military & Police special with a four-inch barrel. He hefted the revolver, flipped open the chamber, spun it twice, slapped it shut, and shoved the revolver into the waistband of his trousers.

"What the hell," he said aloud. "Can't hurt."

He got up and stretched. The Seth Thomas clock on the wall said six fifteen. He pushed at the letter again with his finger, picked it up, shoved it into a pigeonhole, and rebuttoned his suit jacket, checking to see that the gun was hidden by the jacket's skirt. Of course the series the paper had been running on the land development scandal had caused talk, had irritated people, had forced the legislature down in Santa Fe to think again about a matter everyone thought had been foreclosed. That's what newspapers were supposed to do. "A newspaper's job is to print the news and raise hell." Roy Howard said that. And that was what the Advance was doing: telling readers that something smelled just godawful out there where the shopping center was planned, and raising hell with the developers for the way they'd rammed the deal through without reference to the town. Money had changed hands at the courthouse. Of that Sam Haig was sure. If only one of the so-called reporters he paid could come up with the names. Until now all he had to go on was instinct, a gut feeling that something was wrong and that if the paper didn't raise hell the bulldozers would be in there and McAllen presented with a fait accompli.

"Fait accompli," he repeated, liking the way the French sounded. He resolved to use the phrase in his next editorial attacking the land deal. Half his readers would suspect it was a typo, the other half that he was slipping an obscenity in on them.

The telephone rang. His wife.

"Yes," he said. "You can start dinner. Leaving now. Bye."

He put down the phone, turned off the light, and walked through the empty office. He locked the front door behind him and got into the old Buick out in front. Across the street the thermometer atop the bank building blinked on and off dimly in the brilliant light of early *evening. Ninety-four degrees . . . ninety-four degrees . . . ninety-four . . ."*

"Hot as hell," Samuel Scotland Haig muttered to himself as he blinked into the glare of a low and dying sun.

He turned the ignition key.

He did not actually feel or even hear the explosion.

Across the street the bank's thermometer continued to blink, its light fogged by the thin red spray that was what remained of Samuel Scotland Haig.

It was not until noon the day after his father died that Campbell Haig returned to McAllen. All the way home on the plane he punished himself for having been drunk and with the girl. He knew this was illogical. That if he had been in class or studying in the dorm or even right there in McAllen, the thing would still have happened. But being young, being Scots, and being Presbyterian, he roiled in guilt. His mother and his sisters got him through the next three days, and by the time the last spadeful of desert dust had been shoveled into Sam Haig's grave, Campbell's guilt and grief had become anger and a passion for revenge. On that day, the day of the funeral, Campbell Haig began his search for the killers.

He searched and then, stubborn but not stupid, he understood it was no good. Clayton had tried. Some of these old western sheriffs were good, and Clayton was honest. There was so little to go on, nothing left of the car or the bomb, no strangers had been seen in town, and the land grab boys, as Sam Haig had called them in his editorials, were all alibied. After the first, fruitless week of his search Campbell had gone to call on them. The man he saw seemed genuinely shocked at Sam's death.

"God, boy, a difference of opinion over land usage is one thing. Killing a man like your daddy is something else."

Campbell tried to read "lie" in the man's eyes, in his voice. "But there *was* a letter," he said. "There *was* a bomb." The words were more confident than he was.

The man only shook his head.

"A terrible thing," he commiserated. The boy could see nothing in his eyes, could hear nothing in his voice beyond sympathy.

His father would be better at such questioning. Men found it difficult to lie to Samuel Scotland Haig. But his father was not there. When his questions had run dry, the man stuck out his hand to the boy. For an instant, Campbell let it hang there in the air. Then, more in confusion than capitulation, he took it.

That night he drove out to the construction site alone. White-washed stakes marked out the ground; taut white string stretched from stake to stake. Campbell turned off the headlights and got out. Yellow bulldozers and levelers, heavy rollers and trucks were parked haphazardly over the tract of prairie. He walked out across the staked ground. There was a moon, turning the night desert into a lunar landscape haunted by pale shadows. A shopping center, a Goddamn shopping center! A banal excuse for murder. There was a nice geometric symmetry to the white string and the wood stakes, stark against the earth. Stark, and mute. Nothing here to tell him anything. He walked past the plotted area and out into the desert a few hundred yards, a boy burdened with a man's guilt.

He had never felt this helpless, not in all his twenty years. It was like running in sand, there was nothing he could get purchase on. Every face in which he sought murder softened to him in sympathy. The sheriff, his mother, his sisters urged him to give it up, to rest, to get ready for his last year at college, not to destroy himself as his father had been destroyed. Angrily, he shook his head, cursed the night sky and the marking stakes and the string, and stalked back to the car. He wrenched the steering wheel viciously as the old car lurched across the broken ground, snapping the string, splintering the stakes. Round and round it sped, the tired engine whining in low, tires complaining, tears of frustration running down the boy's face.

In the end young Haig tired of destruction. On the road back to town he stopped in a bar and heard a man in a hard hat talking to the barman about the shopping center. "Damned patch of dust. Hardly worth makin' a man work eight hours in the sun up on that Goddamn cat."

It was then Campbell Haig hit him.

The tractor driver put down his glass very carefully. Some of it had been spilled by Campbell's punch. He did not intend wasting any more of it now. "And what was that all about?"

Haig shrugged. It was silly. Men who drove tractors for a living and wore hard hats in workingman's bars didn't go around wiring explosives to the ignition keys of newspaper editors' cars. But how could Haig explain? How could he even speak of his father in a place like this?

The tractor driver hit him. And kept on hitting him. The man seemed more amused than angry but he proceeded nonetheless to break Haig's nose, two of his ribs, and one molar.

The next day, swollen, sore, embarrassed, and sullen, Haig sat silently before the great rolltop desk that had been brought down from the office to be stored in his father's study. He had been there for hours, the curtains drawn against the desert sun. He was frustrated and feeling more than a little sorry for himself. There was a tap on the door and when he said nothing it opened and his mother entered, small, erect, determined. She sat down in her late husband's big leather reading chair, folding her hands in her lap.

"Son, this isn't getting us anywhere. It isn't helping your father. And it's hurting you. Classes begin in three weeks and you ought to be thinking about that instead of brooding about him, about who . . . did it."

"I failed him by not being here when it happened," he said. "I've failed him ever since. Old Clayton could have done as much as I've done. I was going to solve this thing in a week and make it up to him. Instead . . ." He looked away from his mother, not wanting her to have to look at the marks of the beating.

His mother returned to the theme of Tulane, of study, of preparing himself to take over the newspaper.

"I have a duty to my father," Campbell said, "not to some small-town weekly paper."

Delia Haig got up. She stood barely five feet tall but in anger she looked taller.

"That small-town paper you're so contemptuous of, that little old paper *was* your father."

She turned and left the room. After a while Campbell cried. First he had failed his father, now he had saddened and angered his mother. Obsessed, he ransacked the rolltop desk again, delving through his father's papers, letters, receipts, memos, notes for future editorials. Anything that might provide a clue to his killers. There was nothing. Then, overlooked before, a beribboned sheaf of letters on wonderful stationery, heavy as cardboard.

They were from Lord Beaverbrook.

Campbell read and reread the great press lord's letters to his
father, proprietor of *The New Mexico Advance*. Sam Haig had met
Beaverbrook in England during the war. The two men, both Scots
colonials, shared common ground. The correspondence was sparse
but it continued through the years. Reading the letters for the first
time, Campbell saw that Beaverbrook, with the hardheaded
egalitarianism of the Scot, did not look down on Sam Haig. One
passage in the Beaverbrook letters stayed with Campbell Haig the
rest of his life.

Your great wild and barren New Mexico must be something
like my Canada—without all the snow, of course. I do not think
the English will ever understand us *or* our countries. The sheer
expanse is too much for their limited vision, too wild for their
drawing-room mentalities, too straight-spoken and blunt for their
tactful minds. But though they are too proud, too insular, too
Europe-looking ever to learn from us, never forget that we can
learn from thèm. It was here in this old and perhaps tired city that
I first learned how powerful a newspaper could be, how when all
the king's horses and all the king's men were unable to cope with
some vexing problem, a newspaper, speaking with clear and un-
cluttered voice, drawing upon the eternal verities and not trim-
ming or exaggerating, could do the job. Your own little paper,
Haig, would be laughable in London or, I suppose, in New York.
But in that great and empty land you tell me about, what other
voice have the people? What other source of truth? Where else
do they turn in the hour of need? Who else catalogues their
progress, mourns their dead, salutes their triumphs, avenges their
wrongs? A newspaper can do more than most men dream of.

The next day Haig wrote a short, carefully edited letter to London. Ten days later Beaverbrook's reply reached him. That September, instead of returning to Tulane for his senior year, Campbell
Haig sailed from New York to London.

He would learn how to run a newspaper.

Twenty years later, something of a great press lord himself, Campbell Haig could still recall the five days of that crossing in precise

detail, his moods, his hopes, his boyish doubts. He mulled over what Beaverbrook had written and, beyond that, implied. How childish of him to have played detective. There was only one way to reach his father's killers, to avenge his death, and that was to become as powerful as they. He knew that he was ignorant, naive, untutored. Beaverbrook, he hoped, would tutor the ignorance, the naiveté, out of him. But he was sure that the one essential element was already in him, in the bone—the professional instinct that more educated, more experienced men might never have. His father and his grandfather had run newspapers. And he was of their line.

Pretty girls made up to him during that first crossing but he shunned them. There had been too much of that already. He considered vows of celibacy, of temperance, to remain in force until his apprenticeship was completed. The vows were never taken; still, he was never drunk again as he had been the night of his father's death, not for a long, long time. And it would be years before he would give himself completely to a woman.

Now, in a Paris hotel room, with a girl asleep a few feet from him, Campbell Haig talked with men in New York about the possibility that the most important newspaper he would ever want might suddenly be attainable. When he had put down the phone he sat in a big chair staring out over the gardens of the Ritz. As dawn broke, he shivered, not from chill, but from anticipation more sensual than drink or passion.

3

Alexandra Noyes had the seat she wanted, far forward on the left side of the first-class cabin of the 747, a window with the seat next to it carefully kept vacant. Far forward so that she could stare at the bulkhead and not into the eyes of curious fellow passengers. On the left side of the plane so as to present her better profile. With self-mocking honesty she recognized the schizophrenia of her seat selection: privacy and recognition at the same time. Well, was she not her mother's daughter? Her mother, alternately crying out for relief from the pursuing paparazzi and having her secretary phone the papers with precise timetable details on her next appearance.

She was glad enough to have people see her; she had no doubts about the way she looked, even after her last night in L.A. Alex had the head and stomach of a lumberjack. The late hours and booze, the smoke, the dancing, the sniff of coke, had left no mark, no pallor. She looked, but for one thing, the way she wanted to look. The blond hair, chopped off short, framed her face uncompromisingly. On another woman the cut would have been cruel. On Alex Noyes it simply stayed out of the way of her extraordinary beauty. She had a broad but not a high forehead, a straight nose, a determined chin below strong white teeth that had never needed braces. A generous mouth. Blue eyes flecked with the same gold as her hair. Her body was sturdy, healthy; one saw her mother's exquisite delicacy crossed with peasant stock. Her legs worried her. They were why she exercised. Her breasts were the kind men turned to stare at. Alex had never minded that.

Alex paged idly through the copy of *Time* with its annoying cover and wondered why she ever went to Los Angeles. No hostess in New York would have sat her next to that dreadful little man at dinner, plump and ridiculous in a caftan he kept asking that she admire. She supposed he was taking mental notes of everything she said, her every gesture, for that awful celebrity column he wrote for the Haig newspapers. She shuddered, wondering if she had made one of her tactless remarks, to be retold around the Hollywood gossip circuit and end up garbled in a dozen tabloids. She had been relieved when the little man caught an eye and went off somewhere with a suntanned beach boy.

The press! Only last month one of the London rags had run a picture of her with the younger prince. A party at which three hundred people were present and a dozen women had danced with him! Yet their names were linked every time she visited England.

It did not occur to Alex Noyes to consider all the poor, drab women out there who read this sort of nonsense and who were vicariously thrilled by it. Neither did she pause to recall that her best friend was a journalist herself. She did not think of Sissy Valentine except as another wealthy, famous, beautiful girl from a great family, the right schools, and possessing infinite possibilities. Nor did Alex even consider that she herself might be one other thing: a snob.

The stewardess came by and Alex ordered a Stolichnaya on the rocks. She had a dinner date in New York that evening and it would help her snatch a few hours sleep before they landed.

A half-dozen rows behind her, on the other side of the first-class cabin, Sean Farrell watched Alex Noyes's right profile. He had never met the girl but he knew her face, her look, her haughty posture; that was part of his trade. Ten years earlier Farrell would have scurried up the aisle to bluster or cajole or beg an interview from her. Now he no longer needed to chase celebrities, but he was not past sensing glamour in them. Not entirely. Not past wonder at being in their world with them. Not bad, he thought, not bad at all for a kid from Brooklyn, same first-class cabin as a President's daughter. Especially one who looked like this. Thinking this, and remembering how Alex Noyes's breast had moved under the cashmere sweater when she took her drink, nearly wiped away the bad taste of his two weeks in Los Angeles.

Farrell wrote a column for *The New York Mail.* Three times a week, seven hundred words of tough Irish wit blended with sentiment, edged with anger, passionately crafted. Farrell was good. He was very good. The best police reporter they ever had, some said, wired into both the cops and the underworld and virtually libelproof. Mafia buttonmen he had profiled scathingly sought him out in courtrooms before being led away, wanting only to shake his hand gratefully.

One of those columns had taken him to California. A major movie studio had thought there was a film in it. They had taken a year's option for $10,000, paid him another fifteen for a treatment, and had now, with abrupt and lunatic solemnity, informed him that he was mistaken if he thought a movie could ever be made from such material. But he still had some of the twenty-five, he had had the bungalow at the Beverly Hills Hotel for a fortnight, he had a West Coast tan, and now he had a first-class seat just to the right and to the rear of Alexandra Noyes. I wonder, Sean Farrell asked himself, I wonder who she's sleeping with.

Jesus, Farrell told himself, this is a long way from Gerritsen Beach. A really long way. Exhilaration took him and, then, an idea. What the hell, Farrell thought, she can only say no. He cleared his lap of newspapers, tugged his tie snug, and got up. He took the carpeted aisle to her seat, put his hand on the armrest of the empty seat, leaned down. "You're Alexandra Noyes, aren't you."

She looked up without surprise, with no change of expression, no expression at all. "Yes?"

"I'm Sean Farrell."

She shook her head. The heavy blond hair moved.

"I'm a writer."

"I'm sure you are," she said, sarcasm slipping into her voice.

Farrell had a temper. "You always this gracious to your fans?" It was out before he knew it, sounding as nasty as he now feared it had.

"Mr. Farrell, I didn't ask you to come up here."

"Journalists rarely get invitations," Sean said, smiling. He had smiled down a thousand snubs.

"I'm not surprised."

He was accustomed to shoving his foot into doorways. He was not discouraged easily, but across the aisle a middle-aged couple was obviously eavesdropping. "Well," he said, "see you in New York."

She smiled without warmth. "Won't that be nice."

Farrell retreated, feeling the heat in his face. Women usually welcomed him. But by the time he was at his seat again, he was beginning to recover. A hundred heartbeats later, the pink of his face having paled to its normal rosiness, Farrell laughed. He'd phone Alexandra Noyes in New York. Let her see the futility of snubbing him. And let her wonder how he got hold of her unlisted number.

Farrell shoved the matter out of mind as just an episode in a reporter's curious tour of duty. Why worry about it? He had a more serious irritation in the persistent rumors that Meg Valentine was going to sell his newspaper out from under him.

Alex Noyes resisted the temptation to turn and watch him go. Angrily, she shoved the copy of *Time* deeper into the pouch on the bulkhead until it was completely out of sight.

When she had first looked up to see Farrell smiling down at her from his great height and bulk, genuine friendliness shining from a clever, openly confident face, rosily fair and a bit battered under coarsely wavy reddish hair of a kind she always liked, she had supposed she had met him somewhere, that he had a right to speak to her. At the word "writer" she'd recoiled. But how could he know he was hitting on sore spots? Her anger was partly at herself for overreacting. I really am a bitch, she thought. I really am Nora's daughter.

In New York Alex Noyes's mother was collecting copies of that same issue of *Time*. Nora Noyes laughed. My God, not again! Secretly she was pleased, though of course it would not do to show it. After all, it was not the first time she had been on the cover of a magazine, it was not the first adulatory profile. Still, *Time*! And all because she had contributed money to something worth supporting and had been named to something again. And was still the legendary Nora Noyes, widow of a gallant young President, heroine of an entire generation.

Nora was not all that pleased about the cover portrait. A photograph by Hiro. She would have preferred a painting. Or perhaps Avedon. This Hiro photo: stark, terribly stark. It showed the years and the pain and the loneliness. The loneliness, that at least had been by choice. How they'd queued up after Matt died! How they'd wooed and beckoned and begged! The old rich from Europe, the young American rich, the socially well placed, the trimmers and the owners of baseball franchises. And after all these years of loneliness she was sure she had been right to say no, to remain a widow, to keep the flame. Not for her the Jackie Kennedy merry-go-round.

Of course Nora had had her moments. Hadn't they christened her, in those first days with Matt, "No-No" Noyes, because she said no to nothing? That was the wild streak that was surfacing in Alex these days, that and not this later Nora, the woman of dignity, of presence, of substance.

The woman of piety and the church.

At first, after Matt died, there was only shock and then grief. There was no anchor, no sheltered cove, no safe harbor. No place to which she could retreat. The national sympathy, genuine and nosy at the same time, weighed on her, oppressive as a summer night. Without family, only Matt's associates and her admirers, she had nowhere to turn. Nora had not been raised in any church. She had never been religious. Nor had Matt. Far from it. To Matt, who through his parents was vaguely Protestant, religion was a garment gracefully worn when the weather called for it, hung neatly in closets when it didn't. He treated the church, all churches, as just another constituency, glad-handing political bishops and television preachers, being hugged by old women after Sunday services, calling upon the Deity in his inaugural address. Then he was dead and Nora was alone.

All around her people made clucking sounds and knotted damp handkerchiefs and were of no help at all. Then came Monsignor, socially impeccable, quietly sensible, dangling before her the consolation of a church, a faith that understood her ordeal and offered solace. All of it was new to her, had novelty value; the rubrics, the liturgy, the clergy. Nora rose up and grasped religion to her widow's weeds. And, almost as an afterthought, young Alex, who was not asked her opinion on the matter, was baptized along with her mother.

Later, as the initial shock numbed and gradually, so gradually, receded, friends began to suggest, in the subtlest of ways, that Nora's religious devotion was becoming obsessional. Well, what did they know about it? About anything? Did they think it was easy to lose a husband, burned to death on a hillside in the prime of life, hers as well as his, to try to raise a willful child like Alex, to put up with harrassment from the gutter press, the *Enquirer* and its supermarket imitators, or the New York tabloids, or provincial papers like Haig's? Let them try it, Nora told herself as the Monsignor nodded encouragement, just let them!

Thank God for religion, she thought, with the convert's passion. Even Alex became a little more tolerable if one had religion.

She did not know that her only child was flying home. And if someone had thought to inform her of the rumored sale of *The New York Mail,* she would have shrugged contemptuously. The *Mail* was the breed of newspaper Nora Noyes despised.

And with reason. For the *Mail* had helped drive Nora to a second Golgotha, in its way more painful even than the death of her husband in the crash on a Maryland mountainside.

The scandal prospered in the *Mail,* but it began in Congress. It was one of those slow seasons with the ambitious chairman of an obscure subcommittee probing into some dreary graft. Shocking even himself, he stumbled across a sometime actress who swore almost casually, through her chewing gum, that she had simultaneously been mistress to a minor mafia lordling and to the President of the United States. Of course the woman's claim was a cheap publicity stunt, a reckless attempt to divert the Congress from its pursuit of evil, a posthumous smear by political enemies. Or could it be . . . ? In confusion the committee retired into executive session to consider the position.

As was proper, the committee voted unanimously to hush it up. No one ever learned which of them was the first to get to a phone. The story broke in one of the less prestigious weeklies, and then the more prestigious weeklies and dailies and just about everyone else repeated and reprinted the tale, wringing their hands that such trash should be peddled and peddling it nonetheless and gleefully. One of Campbell Haig's companies, a small syndication outfit specializing in serialization, bought the wretched girl's story and sold it to "respectable" newspapers throughout the nation and abroad. It was a decision Haig did not make or even know about, but of which he would have approved.

The whole affair was a marvel of consistency. Matt Noyes had been a consistent cheat, it turned out, as other aging young women raced their own confessions into print. The press was consistently hypocritical, condemning sin and selling millions of papers on the promise of it. The congressmen were consistently venal, swearing one another to circumspection and negotiating talk show appearances to air their own highly privileged view of "the Noyes affair."

And Nora was consistent. She declined all comment, and on the very night one of the worst of the scandal stories hit the cover of *Newsweek* and the front pages of *The Washington Post* and *The New York Times,* she appeared at a gala opening of the Metropolitan Opera and with an implacably icy smile swept all before her into shamed murmurs of admiration.

It took a hardy cynic like young Sean Farrell to remark, "She's in her glory. She loves this. It makes her twice the heroine she was before, only this time she doesn't have to share the billing with a corpse."

And now, fifteen years after his death, Nora was again the gallant young widow of the President, risen serenely to her rightful place.

Alex, just seventeen, raged at the gutter press when classmates maliciously brought her copies of the papers.

"Lies, cheap, rotten, stinking lies! Just to sell papers!"

Later, when the evidence loomed too massively for even Alex to discount, she wept, silent and alone. When the first pain had numbed, she began to work out her own version of what Matt Noyes had done and found consolation in her father's wickedness. He had rebelled against the cloying confinement of Nora's loyal, gallant grasp. How gallant! How loyal! How . . . grasping . . .

It never occurred to the girl that her father, an admirable man in so many things, was one of those dashing fellows who simply could not keep his trousers on. And that Nora had not had much of a married life and, considering the circumstances, had behaved rather well. What she saw as her father's rebellion justified her in whatever she did. Whatever! For was she not Matt Noyes's daughter? Her father's sins, her mother's "hypocrisy," provided young Alex an excuse for doing whatever she liked. She had taken advantage of her opportunities. Much too eagerly.

4

Meg Valentine's decision to sell the *Mail* exploded in *The Wall Street Journal*. In the inbred, gossip-loving, clubby realm of big publishing it was rare for secrets to be kept. This one had been. The *Journal*'s story was brief, it was unconfirmed (Mrs. Valentine had been "unavailable for comment"), but it had the ring of revealed truth. *The Wall Street Journal* is a careful newspaper. It tends to bury rumors back among the tombstone advertising. This rumor was carried in the front-page summary of major news.

Newspaper publishing sources reported yesterday that Margaret Olcott Valentine, owner, publisher, and editor of *The New York Mail*, has decided to sell the newspaper, a continuously published daily since 1805, a weekly before that, one of whose earliest editors was Peter Zenger.

Mrs. Valentine, 78, is the widow of George Breed Valentine, who purchased it in 1928 and who was its publisher until his death. Mrs. Valentine, known throughout the newspaper business as "Meg," named herself publisher succeeding her late husband.

There followed a brief history of the *Mail* and details about other significant newspaper deals in recent years. There was no hint as to who might buy Meg Valentine's paper.

Across the country, across the oceans, news that the *Mail* was on the market set in motion Meg Valentine's peers, the press lords of the English-speaking world. They began to counsel, to calculate, to take advice, to muse. None of them had precise information, of course, the *Mail* being a privately held company not required to publish its figures. But people like Walter Annenberg, Rupert Murdoch, Otis Chandler, Lord Rothermere, and Katharine Graham tend to know what the other fellow is doing. They had accurate circulation figures, the Audit Bureau of Circulation being what it was. They knew the *Mail*'s advertising rates and could count the number of pages sold and then multiply. They knew how many employees Meg had and, suffering under similar union pay scales, could reckon her payroll. They knew the price of newsprint and ink and truck rental and flashbulbs and paperclips. They also knew, as everyone did and only Meg would not admit, that the great days of the *Mail* were behind it.

There was one other concern, beyond profitability or readership or risk or potential. If they could not or would not buy the *Mail* themselves, they wanted to be certain Meg did not sell to the wrong party, to an outsider, to someone not in the club. The press lords did not want a weak competitor who might buy the paper and fail quickly. Newspaper failures depress stocks everywhere. Neither, and this was perhaps even more important, did they want too strong a competitor who might prove . . . difficult. Better that Meg sell to someone who would keep the old paper going but just barely. And the one thing on which all the press lords would have agreed, had they caucused, was that the *Mail* must not be sold to a maverick, to some publishing buccaneer who ignored the rules, who was not in the lodge.

Someone like Campbell Haig.

Haig was in his Dallas office when he got the news off the Dow-Jones wire, confirmation of the rumor that had so tantalized him in Paris. It was not yet eight in the morning but his secretary was there too. He got her on the intercom and asked, "Where's Gideon?"

By a happy fluke he was in New York, on the scene. Gideon

Benaud could have been anywhere on Haig service. In less than a minute Haig was talking to him on the phone.

"The New York Mail is up for sale," Gideon said. "Just as you predicted. I don't suppose I can talk you out of this?"

"That's why I called you. What do you think she'll ask for it?"

"Fifty million? Hard to say, Campbell. The *Mail* is no raving success these days."

"She'll ask seventy-five," Campbell said.

"Seventy-five? You think she's dotty?"

"No. But her pride will inflate the price. At the start, anyhow."

"And you're bidding, Campbell?"

"Of course I'm bidding. How often does a New York paper come on the market?"

"How much?"

Haig paused. "We'll bid thirty and go to forty. Somewhere between there and fifty she'll deal."

Gideon cleared his throat. It was an impressive sound.

Haig waited. Although he tended to bully Gideon verbally, he respected his acumen. Gideon was one of the few who could say no to Campbell Haig. Haig waited now, his hand tightening on the phone.

Finally Gideon spoke, his calculations completed. "It's doable, Campbell. Under fifty million it's doable."

Haig spoke quickly. "Gideon, I'm flying up tonight. Get me the suite at the Carlyle. Meanwhile, no contact with Meg Valentine whatever, no statements. But get over to Chemical Bank, Chase, Marine Midland. See what our line of credit on this deal looks like. Be at the hotel tonight. Late. We'll powwow."

"Ugh," Benaud said, mocking Haig's Indian jargon.

Haig hung up.

Gideon Benaud, once considered Lord Beaverbrook's hatchet man, was now thought Haig's. He was twenty years older than his employer, a French-Canadian with a touch of Scots. A huge, barrel-chested man with a trim red beard, powerful, astute, considered one of the keenest financial brains in publishing, he was also, to use one of his own favorite expressions, loyal unto the death. Haig was a boy learning his craft when Benaud first came across him in London.

Then Benaud was the master, Haig the protégé. After the Beaver's death the boy, who had lost his real father and now the surrogate, turned eagerly to Benaud. "A regular plague of locusts he was," the older man would cheerfully complain, "questions, always questions. Are sex and violence the only sure front-page sellers? At what point do you compromise with the unions and at what point do you take a strike? How much money should a newspaper have in hand and what should its indebtedness be? Why? Is it more economical to own forests and paper mills or to buy newsprint? Should the comics be all on one page or spread out? Should editorials be signed? How much expense-account padding do you permit a foreign correspondent to get away with? Is eight-point type large enough when you consider the growing population of older readers?" And, always, "How do we sell more papers?"

While Haig had returned to America, hoisted the McAllen paper out of debt and barely begun his empire-building, Benaud stayed in touch, first informally, later more regularly, advising the young man on the more arcane financial and commercial aspects of operating a successful chain of newspapers. Eventually Gideon succumbed and came to America as Haig's chairman. And, by now, Gideon was admitting to himself, if to no one else, Haig knew more about the business than he did.

Gideon's admiration for Haig was as great as his fidelity. And when the younger man seemed stubbornly to be blundering into waters beyond his depth, as he occasionally did, it was Gideon Benaud who was inevitably there on the shore to toss the lifeline.

Haig showed audacity in bidding on the *Mail.* Audacity was his trademark, but this was audacity of a new magnitude. There was shrewdness in the move as well. Gideon knew him better than any man. Once, when one of Haig's executives had questioned one of his business judgments, Gideon had snarled:

"If you want to understand Haig, go to the races with him one afternoon. He backs every horse in the race. Of course he loses money. But he has the winner. Every time!"

There were rivals in the game, but only Haig could move on his own without intricate, time-consuming consultation. He had a board of directors but there was no need to convene it. The board was a rubber stamp.

Others who coveted Meg Valentine's newspaper had boards that were not. In Los Angeles, two days after *The Wall Street Journal* story had appeared, one day after *The New York Times* had, belatedly and somewhat ponderously, added its imprimatur to the first rumor, Otis Chandler summoned the elders of his Times-Mirror Company to counsel with him about possible purchase of the *Mail*. In Washington Kay Graham sat with certain directors of her company in the wood-paneled boardroom of *The Washington Post*. On the Avenue of the Americas, Henry Grunwald and other great men of Time, Inc., wondered what Henry Luce would have done. Punch Sulzberger did not even bother to call the board; there was no chance the Justice Department would smile on the acquisition of another New York paper by the great *New York Times*. In London Rothermere spent hours on the phone with Clay Felker in New York, wondering, out loud, whether the *Mail* was worth trying to acquire and to salvage. And in Berlin Herr Springer and his colleagues fussed with dollar–mark exchange rates and considered possible courses of action.

Meg Valentine lurked in her office over the East River, reading the news stories, accepting phone calls from the right people, reading her mail, and reveling in the attention. Flirtatious, teasing, again a young coquette, she fobbed off the less ardent suitors with an arch "But whatever made you think I'd sell the *Mail*?" and lured on the more assiduous with a practical "But if the price is right *everything* is for sale, don't you agree?"

Powerful men who had ignored her and her newspaper in recent years again came calling. The office was a revolving door of the great. I should have played this little game years ago, she told herself. I didn't know how popular I could be. And she laughed harshly.

The Roosevelt chair was rarely empty these days. Her callers suffered her reminiscences gladly.

"This chair?" a famous Chicago publisher demanded incredulously. "FDR actually sat here?"

All of them got the Valentine smile, the Valentine charm, the Valentine memories of boon times past. And little more. To a favored few Meg actually talked business. Girlishly, she refused to have her advisers in the room.

"Plenty of time for you later," she told them firmly. "When we get to price, to terms, to timing. I'll handle the preliminaries. Plumb their intentions. Have you heavy-handed fellows in the room and you'll fall to cheapjack niggling. When I've narrowed it down to the serious suitors, you can come in with your lawyer talk and sharper tricks. Until then, stay away!"

Others came calling on Meg besides the suitors.

The unions came. Wanting assurances. With them Meg pleaded poverty and an inability to understand such complex matters as pensions and overtime and unit-manning and redundancy payments. The shop stewards, fearful the old lady might one day simply close down the paper, lock the door, and go home to die, did not press her. Better that she should sell. They could always negotiate with the new proprietor. The unions got little from their audience with her. But then, they always did.

Lyman came. The editor or rather, since Meg herself held that title, the managing editor. Old Lyman knew he held the job on sufferance, that Meg did not really want a stronger man. Now, racked by insecurity, he asked if the stories were true about her decision to sell. "Now, Mr. Lyman," she lectured him, "leave such matters to those who understand them and go back and make me a nice front page for tomorrow." Lyman, smiling gratitude, backed out of her office as from an Oriental despot's presence.

Sean Farrell came. With Farrell she was as direct and honest as she was capable of being. As he slouched where Adlai used to stand, Meg Valentine sat squarely behind the great desk and tried to imagine Farrell's reaction when he first heard the rumor. Loud? Angry? Obscene?

"I'm surprised your famous bush-telegraph failed you, Farrell. I'd expected to have you bursting in here even before the *Journal* printed that extraordinary nonsense."

Farrell grunted. "That's what comes of being out of town for a couple of weeks. You pull a caper like this."

"If you'd been here where you belong, working, and not romancing actresses in Beverly Hills, I might have consulted you. You know how high an opinion I hold of you."

Farrell grinned. "Now let's leave the charm school in recess, Meg," he said. "And I know damn well the story's true. Or else you've floated a trial balloon to get an appraisal of what the old rag is worth."

Meg started to lecture him about calling her newspaper a rag. But she didn't. Farrell had her rising to bait like that too often. The only man these days who could. The way Franklin used to. . . .

Farrell was still talking. "Not that the *Mail* couldn't use a fix. There are so damn many things we're just not covering, Meg, cheap as you are. We're understaffed and underpaid and overworked and—"

She cut in. "Strong young buck like you, three columns a week? Too much work? Ha!"

Farrell got more out of her than Lyman or the unions. Not much, but something. And he left her with a small threat. The *News* had been after him for years. The *Times* had made whinnying sounds. If she sold to someone he didn't fancy, well, his loyalty was to her and not to the new owners. She scowled at him and then, as he left, smiled. Back in the city room Farrell fobbed off the questioning of less favored men and began to tap out his column for the next day, an evocative essay on loyalty. Up *and* down.

Sissy Valentine did *not* come calling. Meg sent for her grand-daughter. "I won't bother your brother with this," she said when the girl was seated in Jack Kennedy's chair. "He'll just blab it out among the salesmen, and you and I both know salesmen can't grasp more than one idea a week and I don't want any of them to take a strain."

Sissy smiled. She wished her grandmother liked Willie more but she had lost that battle too often. Besides, she was as curious as everyone else about the rumored sale.

"I may sell. I may not sell," Meg began. "You own a little stock and I trust your judgment. You're entitled to know the situation." When she had finished her exposition Meg sat back. "Well, Sissy, and what do you have to say?"

The girl looked solemn. "Well, Grandma, I'd hate to see the *Mail* owned by anyone else but I understand. It's your paper. You're the one who's kept it going all these years. I'll vote my stock as you vote yours. If you sell, I'll sell. If you don't, then I won't."

A good girl. Sensible, faithful, and no nonsense.

"And really, Grandma, I'm still just learning the trade. I'm just happy to have a job here. I love the paper and I'll do anything that's right for the *Mail*. And for you." She stopped then and her face darkened uncharacteristically. "I don't suppose that if you sell it means I lose my job," she said.

Meg slapped her hand on the big desk. "A condition of sale, love, an absolute condition of sale is that you stay on as a reporter."

Sissy's face brightened. "I mean," she said, "no free rides. Only if I'm good enough."

Meg got up and went to her. The girl stood and the old woman embraced her.

"Good enough? Why, you're as good as I was when I started. Almost, anyway."

After a fortnight there were five serious bidders for the *Mail* and three that Meg felt she could accept. The question now was which would win. As she pondered her choice, Junior Valentine, overcoming his fear of his mother, burst into her outer office. The secretary, who was new, looked up. "Yes?" she said, and Junior said he wished to see his mother.

"Your mother?" the young woman asked, perplexed.

"Yes, my mother. She owns the damn paper!"

Once inside Meg's office Junior put on his manners. "Why, Mother, how well you're looking. We really should see one another more often. It must be . . ."

"Eight months," Meg said dryly, "and it seems like just yesterday."

He came around the big desk and kissed a cheek she only marginally offered. Then, carefully avoiding the Roosevelt chair, he sat down, smiled at his mother, and wondered how he was to begin.

"You've heard about my selling," she said. "That's what brings you."

Ever since Harvard Junior Valentine had affected a modest stutter and he retreated into it now. "B-b-but not at all. I-I-I heard the r-rumors, of course, but I wanted t-to see you in any ev-v-vent. Nothing s-s-sinister about that, is there?"

She ignored the question. "Well, I *am* selling. If I get my price. And it looks as if I will. Haig seems to mean business. And if he falls apart there are others. Everyone says the *Mail* isn't the paper it once was, but just give them a chance to buy it."

"But to Haig?" The distaste in Junior's voice overcame the stammer.

"Why not? He has the money, he has the will. He's a newspaper-man. Comes from a newspaper family."

"The man's a smut peddler!"

"Was it Haig sold you your last play?" she asked brightly.

Junior looked hurt. "Just because there was a bit of language and one bedroom scene certainly didn't make *Harvests* smut," he said. "Clive Barnes called it 'significant American theater.' "

"There hasn't been a drama critic I could read since Alec Woollcott," she said.

"Haig," her son muttered.

Meg Valentine said, more gently now, "Why this sudden concern for the *Mail*? Years go by without your even reading it. What is it to you if I sell to Haig or to Katharine Graham?"

Junior sat up. "K-K-Kay Graham is a l-l-lady."

"And Haig isn't." Meg laughed. "He's a roughneck out of New Mexico. And I know what his papers are. I get them flown in each day."

"How can you bring yourself to read them?"

Meg Valentine swiveled her chair to stare at the river. If Farrell had asked the question she would have answered, explained, justified even. But not Junior.

Her silence emboldened him.

"And forgetting the q-q-quality of his p-p-papers, don't you feel you have a responsibility to me . . . to my ch-children, to c-c-consult with us before you d-d-do anything definitive?"

She stood, then, the pale old eyes icing over, her face cold, her thin lips taut. "How dare you even use the word 'responsibility'? What do you know of responsibility? As for your children, you've never given them a thought. Thank God Sissy is what she is, a stranger to you and everything you are. I only hope your son displays the strength of character to disown you as I have. Now get out of here, and go to whatever playpen has attracted you this semester and romp with your toys. The *Mail* is mine. I shall do with it as I choose."

Her son stifled a reply. He rose and turned to leave the room.

In her fury Meg could not resist a final lash. "And don't fret about your allowance. It will continue to be paid. A parent does, after all, have a certain responsibility to a retarded child."

That evening in a smoky corner of the season's trendiest saloon Junior Valentine took comfort in the ministrations of the headwaiter and the sympathetic ear of his current protégée. She had a small role off Broadway. He had promised her great things. Now her beautiful empty face and bare brown shoulders consoled him as he reported, without a single stutter, his own version of that day's unpleasantness. Sympathetically she pressed a long brown leg against his.

"People that old and mean ought to be put away," she said.

"It's what comes of being too understanding, too ready to forgive."

The girl patted his knees, promising further solace.

Junior neglected to tell the girl the true reason for his hatred of Campbell Haig.

JUNIOR VALENTINE BARES ALL

Two years earlier one of Haig's more colorful tabloids had gleefully reported how a young girl had been locked out of Junior's hotel suite and had attracted attention by marching naked into the lobby to demand a second key. The girl was high on drugs. Thanks to the UPI news wire the item had reached the East Coast and his mother's eye. Meg Valentine remembered the incident, but she had never realized that one of Haig's papers had first printed it. Haig himself had forgotten. But Junior Valentine remembered and now, as the negotiations continued, he told himself he would never forget. *Never.*

5

On the lower jaw of the crocodile's mouth that forms the eastern
end of Long Island is the village of East Hampton. East Hampton
is a blend of discreet old money, serious artists and writers, Polish
potato farmers grown rich from having sold off their golden ground
to builders or grown resentful and sulky because, in the face of all
this wealth, they had not. It was in East Hampton that Sissy Valentine had spent every summer she could remember. And now she was
weekending in the great house her father owned, but rarely visited,
on the margin of the ninth fairway of the Maidstone Country Club,
a long iron shot from the grassy dunes that held back the Atlantic
Ocean. It was a glorious June day, and Sissy and her best friend,
Alexandra Noyes, lay on the lawn tanning, Sissy face down, Alex
watching a young man do laps at impressive speed in a turquoise
pool. At last the young man heaved himself out of the water with
a conscious display of pectorals and stood, toweling himself, over the
two girls.

"Hey," Sissy called out, "don't block my sun."

The young man did not move. Addressing himself to Alex he said
glumly, "I love that girl. Trouble is, so does everyone else." He
continued to towel, gazing dolefully at the linear beauty of Sissy, all

long limbs already turning tan, long chestnut hair spread to dry.

Sissy's voice, slightly muffled, came up from the huge beach towel. "The water's gotten to the man's brain."

But what the young man said was true. Alex knew it and, sometimes, was envious. Sissy had a better nature and a better summer place. Alex had a summer place of her own, of course, one of the great Newport "cottages," a house so huge, with a garden so "bright with sinuous rills," that David Merrick had wanted to film *Gatsby* there. Nora Noyes had said no through her secretary. Privately she had expressed shock that Merrick had even bothered to ask.

Alex preferred this house of Sissy's. Alex and her mother did not get on. She and Sissy did.

Now, on this summer day, bored with their young man, heedless of the power struggle being fought over the *Mail* in Manhattan and Washington and London and other places, Sissy and Alex would go "slumming." It was Alex's word. "To the scuzzy Hamptons!" she cried.

"Snob," retorted Sissy.

Their young man, whose name was Gordon, was permitted to go along. They could always strand him somewhere if his devotion became unbearable.

Sissy drove. Well, as she did most things. The car was a four-wheel-drive Jeep. In East Hampton there are, of course, Rolls-Royces and Mercedes and Cadillacs. But among the old East Hampton families pickups and Jeeps are *de rigueur.* Sissy shifted gears smoothly and wheeled onto the Montauk Highway heading west. Alex sat next to her in the front seat, studying her friend's perfect profile, which, unlike Alex's, had no better side. And if it had, Alex realized, Sissy would not have cared. The young man, banished to the rear of the car, sat windblown and breathless, whipped sharply at times by Sissy's hair, content to be aboard, a man of wealth and potential power reduced by infatuation to eager lap-dog.

Sissy enjoyed the feel of the wheel under her slender, already brown hands. She liked the hard springing and the solid thump of the tires as the Jeep wheeled west across the tarred concrete sections of the road. Driving occupied her completely. It was as if she were alone. Much as she felt when she rode her horse in the early morning down the margin of the roads that wound through Maidstone, up over the dune and down to the beach. She had the ability to block out thought, to turn a physical activity, driving or riding, into a mind-cleansing moment or hour.

Alex envied that too. She wished she could be as open, as tolerant, as buoyant, as uncomplicated. Alex was aware of her own faults. Simple enough to slough them off as the inevitable consequence of family, of history. She barely remembered the White House, was unsure if she remembered her father or simply the photos, the films. How young he had seemed. How ridiculous a man so young should have been President, should have died, should have been her father. Now, in her twenties, she sometimes felt she was older than he had been when he died.

The "scuzzy" part of the Hamptons was a great barrier dune separated from the island proper by a broad, shallow bay. Rickety bridges arched the bay. People put up beach houses on stilts along the narrow strip of dune and prayed against the inevitable hurricane. And a few canny operators threw up cardboard shacks with open decks, rented elaborate musical amplification systems, hired brawny Irish bartenders, titled themselves discotheques, and for four months of the year got rich.

Sissy Valentine turned the Jeep neatly into a parking lot and bounced across dirt ruts to park nimbly between a pickup truck and a VW bus. Gordon looked dubious at what he saw about him.

"Hell, don't be so stuffy," Sissy said.

It was late afternoon now, not quite six, the sun still high over the bay. Hundreds of people swarmed through the place and over its open deck. Amplified music boomed out over the parking lot and the dunes. Gordon stared at the young people drinking beer, smoking, laughing, dancing. "This is why my secretary can't type Mondays," he said. "Places like this."

Sissy plunged into the mass of young people, happily became part of it, pulling Alex along behind. The two were quickly swallowed up in the jam of the dance floor. The music drummed insistently around Gordon, the beat heavy, fast, undeniable. Gordon looked around the room perplexed. It is odd, he thought, how soon Sissy Valentine and Alex Noyes, two of the most famous young women in the country, can so totally lose their identities. He could not see them anywhere.

How could he? Just two more in a blur of suntanned girls in T-shirts, unbound hair, bare feet, sunglasses.

Soon it was eight thirty and the sun hung just over the edge of the bay, a red ball over the blue-green sheen of still water. A sign above the bar said "Light Show Courtesy of the Lord."

"How do you feel about your family's selling the *Mail*?" Alex asked.

Sissy shrugged. "My grandmother's, really. It's her paper. And she's getting old. I dunno. Sometimes I wish someone else *would* buy it so if I get a byline or a front-page story there aren't those amused looks, you know, 'cause my family own it."

The two young women were standing on the deck of the discotheque looking west across the bay. They had cans of beer. Gordon was gone.

"Oh, Gordon, just flee, will you?" Alex had snapped at him.

"And leave you two here?" he asked incredulously.

"Yes, Gordon, it's okay. We know our way home," Sissy said, more gently.

When he was gone Alex said, "There are so many guys like him. Wet."

"I know," Sissy said. "Yet he can be so sweet."

They danced with some farm boys and a man who worked for an ad agency and a fisherman and a couple of lawyers.

"I don't believe they were lawyers at all," Alex said.

Sissy laughed.

Someone came over with fresh beers. They took them and smiled promises they had no intention of keeping.

"Do you know this Sean Farrell?" Alex asked.

"Sure, do you read his stuff?"

She shook her head. "I met him on a plane the other day. He tried to pick me up, I think."

"You *think?* I wouldn't exactly call Sean Farrell subtle. If he tried to pick you up I guess you'd know it."

"What's he like?"

Sissy thought for a moment. "I don't know him except around the office. I've had a drink with him. He's a terrific writer, the best thing we have on the paper. Self-taught. Tough. Honest, I guess."

"Whatever that means," Alex said. "I was sure he wanted to get me talking and splat it all over his cheap rag." She stopped. "Hey, I'm sorry, it's your paper. I didn't really mean . . ."

"Okay," Sissy said. "It certainly isn't the *Times*. Once when I was still a copy kid on a slow news day I remember how a school bus crashed in Westchester and everyone on the city desk got so excited and then someone said in a loud voice, very disgusted, 'Oh, shit! Nobody killed.' "

"Ugh," Alex responded, screwing up her face.

Sissy went on. "But Farrell's okay. He wouldn't pull that on you. If he wanted to do a piece, he'd tell you. Then if you said no he'd tell you to go to hell and he'd just write it around you, interview your friends and people who hate your guts, and it would turn out worse in the long run. That's why it's better to do the interview." She stopped and looked at her friend. "But what am I telling you all this for? I guess you've been interviewed as much as anyone in the world."

Alex gave a short, bitter laugh. "Not like my mother," she said. "No one's as popular with the press as dear Nora." Alex felt a pang of shame for deriding Nora to Sissy. Sissy never mentioned her own mother except to identify her in a photograph, or to say of some trinket or piece of furniture, here in East Hampton or in the Central Park West apartment, "that was my mother's." It was Miffy that Sissy spoke of often, easily, fondly. "Miffy" was a baby name for Jean Hughes, the nice woman Meg had gotten Junior to hire to bring up Sissy and Willie. Miffy, married now to a professor and living in Santa Barbara and raising *his* children. Sissy's silence about her mother always awed Alex, who was not easily awed. Of course Sissy had been tiny when she died, three or four. . . .

A couple of young men with grimy hands bought them fresh beers and they danced, and the subject of Nora Noyes did not come up again. Nor that of Sean Farrell. Alex had not told Sissy that Farrell had called. Or that she had cut him cold, once again.

The young men had become pushy now, wanting them to go somewhere driving in their pickup.

"You may not believe this," Sissy said, laughing, "but I've been in a pickup before. It really isn't that big a treat."

"Yeah?" one of the men said.

There was a cheerful exchange of insults then and the girls went

down off the deck and got into Sissy's Jeep. One of the men wore
a painter's cap with the brim pushed up. Now he raised a finger in
obscene tribute as the other disappeared in the direction of the bar.
The man in the cap glowered down at them.

"I don't like the look of that sportsman at all," Alex said, shudder-
ing slightly. "He's got a mean streak."

Sissy laughed. "A Bonacker."

"Bonacker?"

"Local type. Inbred as hell. Don't worry, he'll find some zaftig
Brooklyn girl and forget us."

Alex looked back as the Jeep spun its wheels in the sand, got
traction, and jounced its way through the crowded parking lot. The
Bonacker was still standing there, staring after them; memorizing
the license plate, perhaps. Alex felt a chill but now they were on the
highway and she said nothing.

They had dinner at the Lobster Inn where they split a liter of
Frascati. While they waited for the check, Sissy said, "I'm surprised
you scared Sean off that easily."

"Sean?"

"Farrell, the reporter on the plane. He's usually more persistent."

"The word is obnoxious," Alex said.

Sissy shrugged. "That's just Sean. If you snub him, he'll keep after
you just to prove he's unsnubbable. I'll bet he calls you just to prove
something."

Alex was within an eyeblink of saying "but he did!" and adding
that she had cut him cold once again.

But there was something about the look on Sissy's face when she
mentioned the reporter that held her tongue.

"He'll call," Sissy said stubbornly. "I bet he will."

It was midnight. They'd gone home at last and stabled the Jeep
in the big garage. Now the two girls walked barefoot down the lawn
to the dunes, one brave yellow flag dimly fluttering on the links. The
moonlight bounced off the ocean as the measured rollers came in,
crashed, and slid back from the sloping sand. They had had wine
with dinner and they were slightly, pleasantly drunk. They had heard
a Streisand record and now they tried to mimic her slow tempo:

> Happy days are here again,
> The skies above are clear again.
> Let us sing a song of cheer again,
> Happy days are here again. . . .

The grass was spiky beneath their bare feet, the smack of the waves metronomic. The fresh damp breeze off the ocean, the darkness in front of them and the lighted house behind, the smell of salt, the wine very much with her, Alex felt a heightened sensitivity to the night, to the evening and the afternoon that had gone before, and to the dark loom of Sissy at her side. Suddenly Sissy raised her arms to the sea in mute tribute. Perhaps reaching for something that was not there. Or was and Alex could not see it. Tanned, slender arms reaching. Lifted.

The words of the song still echoed in Sissy's head but she was quickly asleep.

Alex, in a bedroom down the long hallway, thought for a while about her friend and how fortunate she was to have her. Then, presently, of Newport townies she'd had trouble with in her teens, and then the hard face of the man on the deck of the discotheque was there clearly and she remembered how he had stared at Sissy. She wondered what "Bonacker" meant and just how being inbred affected a person. Sissy said they were harmless, but Sissy was so open and generous, so . . . vulnerable. While she, Alex, had all the tough resilience of both father and mother. And was nothing near as . . . good.

She was remembering Sissy's slender, suntanned arms reaching, reaching, when she too slept.

6

Campbell Haig's first approach to Meg Valentine was typical. While Gideon Benaud roamed the banks and argued ferociously for a quarter of a point less interest, Haig buried himself in a suite at the Carlyle or in a branch of the public library in Hell's Kitchen, devouring back issues of *The New York Mail.*

In financial circles and in the press Haig's name was mentioned among others as a possible buyer. But he was not listed among the probables. Too young, too rustic, too poor.

In the great boardrooms men in decent gray sniffed when the name of "that cowboy" came up. His college nickname was resuscitated by a writer in *The Village Voice.* Cactus Haig! Could anyone called Cactus Haig succeed to the ownership of a major New York daily? Haig ignored the rumors, the sniping, the patronizing. The New York bankers had a greater respect for Haig than his fellow publishers. The banks were impressed by Gideon Benaud. They had been for years. They were more impressed when Benaud laid out the balance sheets for them. In less than twenty years, starting with a dust-bowl paper in debt, Haig had built a smooth-running, prosperous little empire. While the publishers sniffed haughtily, the bankers' eyes widened. Within a week Benaud was able to report to Haig that, if the deal could be made, the money would be there.

"Don't you worry about the deal being made, Gideon. Now that you've got the money it's my turn to play."

His opening gambit was a letter, handwritten on oyster-white Tiffany Bond he'd paid $200 to have engraved over a weekend and that he would never use except for this one brief letter. It went out to Meg Valentine on a Tuesday.

"Dear Mrs. Valentine," it read. "I would like to come see you about buying your fine newspaper. Sincerely, Campbell Haig."

Meg Valentine's letter came a week later. "Please phone to set a mutually convenient appointment."

They met in Meg Valentine's office. She sat erect behind the great desk. He was not what she had expected. Like most New Yorkers she held to stereotypes about the provinces. Georgians would be slow and tricky; Bostonians close-mouthed and grasping; Californians lazy and self-indulgent. And New Mexicans, of course, would be huge, arrogant, boisterous, and display dreadful manners. Campbell Haig was compact, neat, soft-spoken. And he remained standing until she had ushered him to Roosevelt's chair.

"Franklin . . ." she only started to say and then, instinctively knowing he would not squirm and be impressed, she abandoned the ritual phrase and decided not to fence but to go to the matter.

"What makes you think I'd sell you the *Mail*, Mr. Haig?" she asked.

"Because," Haig said quietly, looking into her pale eyes, "you want to leave a great newspaper behind as your monument and you know I can do that for you."

For an uncharacteristic several seconds she was silent, angry at his impertinence, his presumption; then she recognized how cleverly he had melded the clear suggestion of her mortality with an appeal to ego. Yes, she thought, that is precisely what I want. But when she broke her silence it was not to say this but to pose questions about his newspaper philosophy to which he responded more articulately than she would have expected a few moments earlier. They were fencing now, his bluntness having forced her onto the defensive, and although they came to no agreement that morning, Meg Valentine knew, from the instant of his first reply, that if the dollars were right, this was a man to whom she could sell her newspaper.

She swiveled her chair toward the window, toward the Brooklyn Bridge. "A man called Roebling built that bridge. A hundred years ago. He built that bridge. It makes me feel good just to look at it," she said.

Haig listened, waiting.

Meg Valentine went on. "Roebling was an engineer and a good one. But they didn't know then what we know now. When they sank the caissons his men kept toppling over, being dragged out paralyzed. It was the bends, but they didn't know that. They only knew that something terrible happened when a man worked under pressure down there for a whole shift, that when he came up again it would hit him.

"Roebling had no answers. But these were his men who were being hurt, his men who were dying or being paralyzed. And since he was a good engineer he figured the only way to find out was to go down there himself."

She paused. Haig watched her face.

"The bends got poor Roebling as well. Paralyzed him. Never walked again. But he didn't quit. He rented himself a room over there in Brooklyn and he supervised the job until it was finished, watching the work progress from his bed, through a telescope he rigged up."

Haig nodded now. And Meg went on, not so much talking to him as to the river and the bridge and the past, to old Roebling over there in Brooklyn, lying in his bed.

"Whenever I wanted to give up, whenever things here at the *Mail* became really bad, I remembered Roebling over there with his telescope." She focused again on Haig. "He believed in that bridge, Mr. Haig. As I believe in the *Mail.*"

They shook hands after that, and when he left, the old woman turned her chair again toward the river and the bridge.

Gideon raged and quoted the Old Testament. Haig listened patiently and riffled through ponderous computer readouts.

"I know the *Mail* isn't worth fifty million in book value," he said. "I can read a balance sheet as well as you."

"Well, then?"

Haig got up from the bed in his suite at the Carlyle and stood by the window, looking out at Madison Avenue and Fifth beyond it and Central Park beyond that.

"I'll pay sixty if I have to," he said quietly.

"Sixty?" Gideon exploded. "Campbell, by the great god Jehovah, *why?*"

Campbell turned back from the window with a small, shy smile. "Because I want it."

Others wanted it as well.

Time Inc. had been bitten by the newspaper bug even when it had to close *The Washington Star*. Kay Graham wanted a New York paper to create a power axis between the capital of the country and the capital of the world. Otis Chandler wanted it but his lawyers warned of antitrust ramifications, that he would have to shed himself of the extraordinarily profitable *Newsday* to make the deal. The television networks lusted but feared the courts would never permit such a concentration of power. Hearst had never quite reconciled itself to the death of the *Journal-American* and the *Mirror*, and Frank Bennack looked longingly at the *Mail*. Then there was the richest of them all, Capital Petroleum, battered by ecological class-action suits and anti-oil editorials in the *Times* and on *60 Minutes*, badly in need of a powerful public relations image-builder. Robert Anderson had bought London's *Observer* for Arco. Why couldn't Capital buy the *Mail*?

All of them had the money, all wanted Meg Valentine's newspaper. Only none of them wanted it as much as Campbell Haig.

"It's like buying New York itself," he would tell the protesting Gideon. "We own Texas and Indiana and Oregon and central California. New York would be the flagship. The jewel in the crown."

Gideon would moan and produce computer printouts and Haig would wave an impatient hand. Instinct ruled Haig. He *knew*, as Gideon did not, that his newspaper empire, that he himself, would never be complete until a New York daily had been slid into place as the keystone.

Capital Petroleum was the first of his rivals to capitulate. A terse statement was issued by its board chairman. "Capital Petroleum has been unable to reach an agreement on terms of purchase of Mrs. Margaret Valentine's stock in The New York Mail Company and has withdrawn from the bidding."

Behind the statement there were a few who could discern the hand of Campbell Haig. From coast to coast his newspapers had editorially warned of the danger of the oil lobby's "reaching its tentacles into the very heart of free expression in America, the editorial offices of a great daily newspaper." There were syndicated columnists and men on other papers and in radio and television who owed Haig favors. He called in his tickets now. And to millions of Americans, reading or listening or viewing, for more than a week it must have seemed that Capital Petroleum combined the worst features of Hitler, organized crime, and Jack the Ripper.

A newspaper chain that owned a profitable radio station in New Jersey bowed out seemingly without any pressure from Haig. A quiet query to the Federal Communications Commission drew the informal but adamant reply that the chain would have to surrender its radio license to win the *Mail* and the chain's senior men unanimously refused. What they did not know was that three days before Haig had flown to Washington to dine with the FCC commissioner who made the informal reply.

In Los Angeles the Chandlers threw in their cards early. Acquisition of the *Mail*, with its parlous financial future, wasn't worth losing *Newsday*. The Knight-Ridder group stayed in the hunt only long enough to read Meg Valentine's balance sheet. In London Rothermere reluctantly abandoned his dream of competing again with Rupert Murdoch in the New York market and, as if to make up for his disappointment, announced the purchase of a half-dozen provincial weeklies in the Midlands and Yorkshire.

Another competitor was scared away when Benaud, acting for Haig, dropped the casual threat that if Haig were thwarted in New York, he would launch dailies in three Midwest cities where the rival now enjoyed a prosperous monopoly. Cramped by New York, Gideon delighted in the flight west, the confrontation, the veiled hint, and the swift capitulation.

"By the great Jehovah, Campbell," he telephoned in triumph from an airport phone booth, "it's like having the Beaver alive again and knocking Roy Thompson for six in the final over."

Haig, to whom cricket remained a mystery, missed the allusion but not the tone of elation.

"Come home then, Gideon. There's one more, you know."

Amalgamated Communications owned radio and television and

newspaper properties in six of the top fifteen markets. Charles Messenger, founder and board chairman of Amalgamated, lusted for a New York outlet as Haig did. The *Mail* seemed to have all the requisites: a great tradition; a sorry present (meaning the price would be reasonable); and, under Messenger's direction, a brilliant future.

Haig's first stratagem failed. "Go calling on Mr. Messenger, Gideon," Haig instructed. "Tell him if he drops out of the bidding I won't open another paper in California for five years. No, make it ten if you have to. But if he stays in the race I'll open three papers a year for the next decade."

Gideon Benaud grinned broadly. "That's a combination in restraint of trade, Campbell."

Haig smiled just as broadly.

But Charles Messenger wouldn't bite. "You go back and tell him I have a better idea," he told Benaud. "Tell him to get the hell out of New York or I'll open *six* papers a year, every one of them in his markets, and I'll operate them as loss leaders just to run that cowboy out of town."

Benaud took the threat seriously. Charlie's older brother, Warren, was one of the most powerful Republicans in the nation. There was still talk of his running once again for the presidency. Whatever connections, whatever subtlety young Charlie may have lacked, brother Warren could supply. In surplus. Benaud reported all this by phone. Haig did not seem depressed. He had never expected Charlie Messenger to cave in tamely.

"Okay, Gideon, go back to Charlie tonight. Do what you have to to make an appointment. Suggest that he's got me scared. That I'll do damn near anything to protect monopoly situations in our markets. Tell him I'll leave New York and the *Mail* to him."

Gideon exploded. "Quit now? When you've got them all beat but him?"

"Yeah, but tell him I don't trust him and he's got to put it on paper. I want a piece of paper and he can have the *Mail.*"

Benaud's rage became jubilation. "And you'll leak his letter to the antitrust division."

"Nothing that subtle, Gideon. I'll call a press conference and demand the federal government do something about this robber baron."

Charlie Messenger turned Benaud down flat. "Gideon, you've been around too long to expect me to put even a sentence on paper."

What Meg Valentine had expected had come about. Two powerful rivals bidding for her nearly bankrupt company, pride and ambition and strength butting head on, and with the price rising each time they did. In her riverside office she rubbed her hands and told herself how proud FDR would have been.

No one, and certainly not Charlie Messenger, suspected the depth of Haig's resources. His commitments from the banks, so carefully constructed by Benaud, held. The bidding was no auction room affair. The bids were phoned or conveyed by bonded courier from the suite at the Carlyle and from Messenger's command post in Rockefeller Center to Meg's banker. Now her professional advisers began to earn their retainers. They kept her informed by telephone and she sat grumbling on the sidelines, at the same time gleefully multiplying each bid, down to its fraction of a dollar, against the number of outstanding shares.

Once, late on a Wednesday night, when Messenger went to the equivalent of $56 million, Benaud actually gave up. "That's it, Campbell. Let him have the bloody sheet."

He'd been pacing the sitting room with the long phone cord snaking behind him. Haig, shirtsleeved, a half-eaten sandwich and some milk beside him, sprawled full length on a couch, his stockinged feet over the arm. On the walls were six or seven famous paintings, virtually the only things Haig owned, bar newspapers.

"Go up fifty cents a share," Haig said quietly.

Benaud whirled on him. "By the saints, Campbell, you can't. We don't have the money. Do you want to wreck the company? Do you want to be back where you were twenty years ago just for a mad dream about New York?"

"Fifty cents more, Gideon."

His face as red as his beard, Benaud went to the desk and sat down, rapidly punching keys on his calculator. Getting up again he crossed the room and shoved the calculator in Haig's face. "Fifty cents more means fifty-eight million two hundred thousand dollars, Campbell. That's eight million more than the banks agreed, and it's forty million more than we have. You still want to continue this insanity?"

Haig held up one hand, its fingers extended.

"Five-oh," he said slowly, articulating the words precisely. "Fifty cents. One half of a Yankee dollar."

Benaud groaned and sank into a chair, the calculator showing eerie green light in his great hand.

"Now get it on paper and ring for the messenger, Gideon, and we'll resume the bidding. You know, I'm sort of glad Charlie Messenger sat in. This'd be a damn dull takeover if he hadn't decided to play."

At noon the next day Messenger had gone to a fraction under sixty million. Benaud, more businesslike now, took a new tack with his employer.

"You'll be selling off some papers pretty soon, Campbell. No other avenue as I can see."

Haig nodded. "I agree."

His calm drove Benaud once more into fury. "Sell the newspapers? But that's something you've never done, Campbell. Not ever. Not since the start. Buy, yes. But sell, never! Like cutting off your hand, you said. You can't sell our newspapers, lad. You can't."

Haig looked at Gideon coldly. *"My* newspapers, Gideon. And I'll sell every one of them but McAllen, if I have to, to get *The New York Mail."*

At ten the next morning, with the price at sixty-two million dollars, Messenger quit.

Haig's phone rang.

"Campbell, Charlie Messenger. You can have the son of a bitch and I hope it runs you right into Chapter Eleven." He slammed down the phone without waiting for a reply.

Haig grinned at Benaud. "Seems I must have done something to annoy Mr. Messenger," he said. "Anyway"—he paused now—"anyway, he's out. We win."

"Win what?" Benaud asked quietly.

7

They had met in Meg Valentine's office at ten o'clock of a hazy July day to negotiate final terms of sale. For a time, around noon, it looked as if there might not be a deal. Meg had held out for two last concessions: an employment contract for her key workers and an advisory role for herself. Haig accepted the second stipulation so quickly she wondered, suspiciously, whether he knew what her doctors had told her. On the employment contracts he threw up his hands.

"Mrs. Valentine, I assure you I didn't bid for the *Mail* just to clean house. I can promise you any employee who does his job will not only have secure employment but will prosper. At the same time I don't want to have my hands tied before I even come in here. You've complained yourself about featherbedding on New York newspapers. I read your speech to the ANPA four years ago. Until I come in here and go to work I have only a vague idea how many people it takes to put out the *Mail.* Maybe I'll need everyone you have and then some. Maybe I can do it with less. You're asking me to limit my flexibility before I know how much flexibility the situation calls for. Is that fair?"

Meg Valentine shrugged. It might be unfair but it was what she wanted. "Job security may not mean much to thee and me, Mr. Haig. I assure you it means a great deal to salaried employees."

Benaud asked smoothly, "Just how many *key* employees are there, Mrs. Valentine?"

She waved her delicate hands vaguely. Haig had withdrawn to a window and was staring at a tugboat on the river.

"Perhaps a hundred," Meg said.

Gideon's eyebrows lifted.

"But it's well known," he said shrewdly, "that you were running a one-man show here. That all decisions, that every significant news judgment, every business negotiation, was handled by you and you alone. Were we mistaken as to that, Mrs. Valentine? Did others help you run the *Mail*?"

Meg made a small gesture. Gideon had said the right thing. "A few key executives, of course," she conceded. "No one person can do it alone. There were a few others."

"How many?" Benaud echoed, pressing her now.

"Oh, perhaps . . . eight or ten. Say ten."

Gideon looked around at Haig. Without taking his eyes from the tug Haig nodded so slightly it was imperceptible except to Benaud.

Gideon turned back to Meg Valentine. Of course, he said smoothly, they would be pleased to guarantee employment to her ten key people. If she would simply supply their names . . .

It went easily after that. They put the announcement out on both the AP and UPI wires and over Dow Jones: "Agreement has been reached in principle for the purchase of *The New York Mail* by newspaper chain owner Campbell Haig for an unspecified amount of cash, *Mail* proprietor Margaret Olcott Valentine announced today."

At the press conference hastily assembled that afternoon Haig deferred to Meg.

"I think until the final papers are signed I'd better leave that question to Mrs. Valentine," he said diffidently, over and over again. "After all, it's her newspaper. Not mine."

Her old face wrinkled in a grin. "Not yet, he means, gentlemen. And I'll wager he's counting the days."

There was a little laugh in which Haig joined. Why not? he thought. Let this be Meg's day. His would come.

Sean Farrell stared through the smoke at his new employer. He had been told that Haig neither smoked nor drank, yet here was Haig with a large wine glass before him and a dark Havana jutting rakishly from the side of his mouth.

There may be, Farrell told himself, any number of things about Mr. Haig on which we were misinformed. Perhaps it was untrue that Haig's passion for work crowded out all interest in women. At that moment he noticed Haig looking at him as if he were listening to Farrell's thoughts, and Farrell smiled and lifted his glass in fractional tribute.

Haig was giving a party in an upstairs room at the 21 Club. Gideon Benaud was there, of course, and for diplomatic reasons several of Meg Valentine's advisers. Lyman and Sean Farrell were there as the most visible of Haig's new employees, and there were Haig's banker and lawyer, and several lean, hard-faced men from other Haig newspapers. Meg had been invited and had declined. The waiters fetched drinks and lobsters, drinks and steaks, drinks and coffee, drinks. It was all splendidly male and clubby.

When dinner was over Haig's men were drunk and so was one of Meg's. Haig's lawyer begged off when the survivors descended the stairs to close the bar. At some point the governor joined them. People kept coming up to their little group to introduce themselves to Haig or ask to be introduced. Blessedly the bar closed and they were all out in the street and someone declared they must go to Elaine's for breakfast. A limousine was standing at the curb and the driver, in livery, said he would take them uptown for ten dollars. Farrell said okay and climbed in. Haig was hesitating on the sidewalk.

"Come on," Farrell said.

"We can get a couple of cabs," Haig said. "Ten is a bit steep." The man had just spent sixty million to buy the *Mail*.

Farrell said to forget it, that he'd pay, and Haig got in but first they went by to pick up the early edition of the *Times*.

"The *Times* will play it down," Haig predicted dourly. "Way inside."

"No way," Farrell said. "It's front-page news. You'll see." He was right. On page one there was not only the story but stock photos of Meg and Haig.

"God, I take a lousy photo," Haig said. But he said it pleasantly. Farrell wondered if he was drunk.

At Elaine's the front room had been abandoned to the backgammon players and the serious drinkers and two writers telling one another the plots of novels they would never write and Elaine, kibitzing one of the matches, got up from the table and came forward and hugged Farrell.

"So you went and got yourself a new boss."

He introduced Haig. Elaine knew who he was, of course, but she was maintaining control of her own room, saluting a friend before recognizing the friend's superior. Haig understood.

"Eggs," Gideon cried, "if there be such in Sodom."

The cook had gone home. Elaine went into the kitchen and fried bacon and scrambled eggs and brought out hot bread and pots of coffee, and at six in the morning the party was over.

Now in the half-light of dawn Campbell Haig and Sean Farrell stood in Second Avenue in front of the restaurant. Gideon Benaud and the others had taken cabs and left. Farrell had one at the curb.

"Can I give you a lift?" Farrell asked.

Haig shook his head. Somewhat unsteadily he held out a hand.

"I want to thank you for being with us tonight, Farrell. It was good of you to give us the time."

Farrell took the hand. A formal little speech, he thought. And unexpected. "Well," he said.

Haig nodded. Farrell got into the cab and when he looked back Haig had started to walk south. Then Haig was out of sight and Farrell, lazing in the back of the cab, neither totally sober nor completely drunk, wondered what a man like Haig was thinking on this dawn after his great triumph.

Haig thought of a woman. A nice climax to a momentous twenty-four hours. He walked south, breathing deeply, trying to clear his head. The last time he'd been drunk was the night his father was killed. There'd been a girl that night. Sharon, he could recall now, twenty years later, the pale sheen of her body, the texture of her hair, the feel of her against him. No, he would not compound the error. This night belonged to no woman. Only to himself.

He was in the seventies now, within a few blocks of the Carlyle. But when another cab approached he whistled, and it slid to a halt and he got in.

Sean Farrell was home now in his apartment in Turtle Bay. Just before he slept he thought again of Haig.

Was there a woman? Where had he gone? What sort of man was he, really? For better or for worse we now belong to this man and none of us knows a damn thing about him.

As Farrell was thinking this Campbell Haig was standing on a rotten pier jutting out into the East River. It had begun to rain, obscuring a thin sun newly risen, and he stood there, hands in pockets, coat collar up, staring across the cobblestoned street, at a squat building that looked more like a fortress than the offices of *The New York Mail.*

Haig was drunk but more on fatigue and elation than on wine. He knew that the simple pleasure of victory would not last long. All were pals now. The unions and Meg and the governor and that pugnacious-looking giant Farrell. Haig wondered how chummy they would be a year from now, when he had begun to run the *Mail* as his own paper. The paper they all thought of as theirs. Well, it wasn't their $62 million and it wasn't their paper. Not anymore, regardless of what he had said in that little speech in Meg's office. That was Cactus Haig's fortress across the street. His crowning acquisition, his piece of New York. As little as they wanted Haig and his kind of paper, as little as they were going to like it, Haig had fought his way in. Would stay in, and rub their noses in it. This was Haig's revenge, his ruling passion, and would be so. He had sworn that to himself and to a grave in the high desert country of New Mexico.

8

Alexandra Noyes scarcely remembered the White House. Her memories of her father himself were only slightly less blurred: a tall, dashing man with a wonderful voice and a lap that was for her alone. She missed her father, not the dead President. She remembered the strong arms lifting her rather than gesturing in oration. Still, that was twenty years ago and she was tired of ghosts, of her father's legend, of her mother's perpetual mourning.

Now Alex was again at Newport in July, the high season, summoned not because Nora wanted to see her but because society demanded that mothers and daughters acknowledge the niceties and lay cool cheeks against one another.

To Nora's right at table a sunburnt man who was the skipper of the current America's Cup defender. Then an eighty-year-old woman sculptor. Then the governor of Rhode Island next to an aging actress, and beyond them a male Rockefeller and a female Whitney. A minor Austrian graf and a celebrated feminist completed that side of the table of eighteen.

At the foot of the table, facing Nora at the head, was the most presentable of the contemporary crop of fashion designers. To his right a young actress, all the rage that past season on Broadway; a local senator; Alex Noyes; a brilliant filmmaker; a lady who owned department stores; a TV anchorman; a tame Jesuit; the governor's wife; and to Nora's left, an astronaut who had walked on the moon.

Alexandra Noyes was grateful for the filmmaker. Sulkily she remembered a good line she had once got off to Sissy Valentine, describing her mother's "little" parties. "It's like having dinner at Madame Tussaud's," Alex had said.

She liked it that the filmmaker was wearing sneakers with his dinner jacket.

"Do you do that to shock?" she whispered.

Behind his glasses his frightened eyes darted around the table. "No, yes. I mean, they feel good. Did your mother *say* something?"

Alex felt less grateful. Even he seemed awed by Nora.

The candles flickered, the courses were served, the wines poured, beyond them in the warm night the sea lapped gently at the shore, great cities throbbed, stars blazed, Asians starved, Africans made war, thieves plotted, men and woman made love. None of it mattered. In this room, in this house, and to a great extent in Newport itself, Nora Noyes reigned. Brittle, informed, lucid, her conversation, her laugh, her gaze dominated the party. Another triumph for Nora. Except that Alex was there, mocking her with her youth, her beauty. Claiming a share in the Noyes mystique.

It isn't, Nora told herself, as if the girl truly represents competition. Not with those sturdy legs, those unfashionable breasts, that heavy blond hair hacked short as if with a garden shears. It is simply that she too is a Noyes, she too a remnant of the dead President.

And, least forgivable of all, she is young.

The time when Nora could still intimidate Alex had long passed. Why then, Alex wondered as she strained to hear the filmmaker's whispered *mots*, did she attend? She supposed it was loyalty. She and her mother had no one else, no other close relations, and it was not all that bad an idea to present a united front to the world, if anyone really cared, and so long as she was not called on too often. The designer was saying something now and Alex watched Nora's face as her mother watched him.

Fifty years old and still lovely! Even Alex marveled at her mother's beauty. The good bones enhanced by the light summer tan, by the hair being just so, by the several pilgrimages to Dr. Pitanguy over a decade. But there was no way to enhance or diminish those eyes. Deep, placid, wide, haunting. Alex knew she would never be the beauty her mother was.

The sailor was describing, by moving silverware and salt cellars, how the America's Cup would be retained, when Nora, sensing that precise moment when expertise becomes a bore, stood up and declared coffee and brandy would be served in the round room. Chatting amiably, her guests drifted through the great house, Alex with them. No one noticed Nora's brief absence.

Upstairs, in the huge bathroom fully contained within her bedroom and dressing suite, the former First Lady carefully swathed a towel around her shoulders and bosom, leaned over the toilet, inserted a finger into her throat, and methodically vomited her dinner. A moment later, mouthwash gargled, a damp cloth patted lightly over her face, a stray lock of hair anchored, the mirror consulted, she was ready to rejoin her guests, once more grateful to dear Nan who had taught her, so many years before, the secret of remaining slim without all that tacky dieting.

The next day their guests had departed, all but the Austrian. He and Nora went riding, Alex lay by the side of the pool. She was nearly asleep when her mother's shadow fell across her. She looked up. Despite the heat, Nora was in full English riding costume.

"Ugh," Alex said, "I don't know how you can ride in this weather. Just the body heat from the horse . . ."

Nora looked at her daughter. "A little exercise wouldn't hurt you, my sweet."

Alex instinctively glanced at herself, solid, filling out the bikini, and then grinned. "Well, I never claimed to look like you, did I?"

Nora liked that. She smiled. "Curt rides beautifully. I wonder why it is American men just don't have the same ease. His seat is marvelous. So controlled. So . . ."

Alex gave a short laugh. "European aristocrats have nothing else to do but learn to ride. How many Americans get all that practice galloping around playing Cossack and sabering the odd peasant?"

Nora drew herself up even straighter and taller. "The Graf von Kroma does not saber peasants. During the war his father was a famous anti-Nazi, and Curt himself is a serious *homme d'affaires* who rarely gets a chance to ride anymore at all."

"Okay, let's not fight. I'm sure he's sensational."

Nora's face relaxed. She continued to stand. Her riding clothes were cut too severely for her to sink into one of the poolside chairs. Alex rolled over on her stomach. She sensed her mother had more to say.

"Alexandra . . ." Nora began, sending a shiver through the girl despite the heat. "Alexandra" was never good. ". . . don't you feel that by your age [she never actually stated her daughter's age since it too precisely emphasized her own] you might have some idea of just what you're going to do with yourself? Is there some boy you're interested in? Some sort of career? I don't mean a job, of course, but something useful you might enjoy doing? Service work, one of the more appropriate charities? Instead of this drifting, this rootless existence?"

Alex half listened, knowing the scenario. When her mother had finished she said, "No, I don't think so" without looking up.

Her mother inhaled sharply as if struck.

Alex looked up then. "Hey, I'm sorry. I didn't mean to be snippy. It's just, no, I don't have any ideas. I'm not hung up on anyone. And, yes, I kind of like hanging around New York and having my own apartment and flying to Europe or L.A. once in a while. Why shouldn't I? We've got the money. I don't have any marketable skills. I'm twenty-five. Don't worry so much. Something will hit me one day and I'll know it and then I'll go out and become a loving wife or a useful citizen or whatever it is we're supposed to be in America."

The graf joined them then and Nora turned her attention to him. He was a smooth number, Alex had to admit, very fine in his riding clothes. She didn't like the way he looked at her mother all the time rather than at the ripe young daughter. That isn't jealousy, Alex told herself, simply suspicion. It wasn't normal for a man like von Kroma to gaze with such fascination on a fully-clothed fifty-year-old woman and to ignore a suntanned girl in a bikini. Suddenly Alex thought, Oh, Jesus, she isn't going to get married? Not to *this?* Not after all the years playing the Virgin Nora?

Alex made her excuses that afternoon, and the chauffeur drove her to the airport for the seven o'clock plane to LaGuardia. Nora kissed her on both cheeks but did not seem sorry to have her go.

Intermittently Nora Noyes took time to think about her only child. In the beginning there was the consolation that Alex showed little promise of becoming the beauty her mother was. Then, resentment that a child of hers would *not* be beautiful. When Alex turned nine or ten and suddenly sprouted skyward at the same time that her features began to fall into place, resentment gave way to jealousy. But why? They weren't rivals. Or were they?

A year or two earlier they'd fought.

"I'm me, not you, Mother," Alex had blurted out in instinctive answer.

"I'm quite aware of that."

"And I'm not your damn rival. We aren't in competition."

Nora was arch. "I hope not," she said coolly.

Alex tossed her head, the hair still long then, whipping angrily through the air.

"Well, we're not. And I wish to hell I knew what you resent in me."

Nora had not answered then. How could she admit regretting that her own daughter, her only child, had grown into a beauty? Instead, she ended the brief spat with a silent retreat into a very Catholic contemplation of her own virtues and the ingratitude of children.

Alex was still not her mother. Not with those field-hockey legs, those breasts. Nora looked down instinctively at her own fashionably small, high bosom whenever she thought of Alex's bust. But there were other things about the girl Nora found threatening. She was not the child she and Matt Noyes should have had, the child she deserved, the child his memory called for. Even as an infant Alex had been rebellious. Nora could still remember the surprising strength in her pudgy arms as Alex pushed away from her whenever Nora held her daughter. In the end Nora solved the struggle as she solved most problems: swiftly, coolly. She turned Alex over to a nanny and limited their contacts to brief, reserved morning greetings and evening farewells.

Then there was school. First there were the convent schools and Foxcroft and then Miss Porter's, and then Miss Somebody Else's.

Alex was not especially mischievous, certainly not stupid. At first Nora took Alex's school problems personally. "It reflects on your upbringing. And since your father is no longer here, people blame me."

And at first Alex was wide-eyed and repentant, vowing to do better at the next school. But as she came to understand that it was her own life being spoiled and not her mother's, she worried less about Nora's reaction.

The trouble was, as Alex saw it, the spotlight that picked out her every step, especially every false step, at whatever exclusive girls' school she was attending. Her classmates had wealthy parents, some quite well known. But none of them had a father who had been a dashing young President, dead tragically and prematurely, or a mother widely accepted as one of the most beautiful and fascinating women in the world. By twelve or thirteen Alex was carrying, in addition to the usual adolescent burdens, the weight of both parents on her young shoulders.

But by then Nora had rather despaired. "I just don't know, Father," she dejectedly informed that season's pet cleric. "Alex must have been sent me as a cross. It doesn't seem right or fair that with the parents she had, there'd be all this difficulty."

"There *are* wicked children," the priest said soothingly, "and we must honor their parents for bearing with them with Christian patience."

In the beginning Alex's sins were decidedly venial: ignoring lights out, smoking, exchanging notes in class, being taken in possession of an unauthorized (read "dirty") book. Then boys became aware of her.

At thirteen Alexandra was already a beauty, lacking the slender elegance of her mother but with long yellow hair, the bluishly golden eyes, the glowing skin faintly suffused with freckles. In all respects but one it was still a child's body, the legs pudgy, the waist still straight and unformed, the arms youthfully plump. The exception was her bosom. By the time the Thanksgiving parties and dances of her freshman year had come around, Alex Noyes's bosom was already a legend in half the prep schools of the East. Boys attended the usually despised girls' school mixers simply to gaze upon it. An Andover football hero owed his fame less to three touchdowns against Exeter than to his claim (true, in fact) that he had once slipped his hand up under Alex's Fair Isle sweater and touched, actually *touched*, one of her breasts!

At fourteen during a father-daughter dinner dance, her roommate's father, carried away by the punchbowl or by Alex's beauty or both, danced with her closer than he should have and suggested she visit their home in the Christmas holidays. At fifteen a Harvard senior drove her down to the Cape in a car that broke down in Truro and she spent the night keeping him out of her motel bed. At sixteen she had considered it was time to stop fighting off the inevitable.

He was a red-haired Dartmouth senior. She'd gone up to Hanover for a spring dance, suitably chaperoned, suitably accompanied by a dozen other girls her age. Even Nora would have approved. The redhead had been attending such dances for four years. Neither chaperone nor companions inhibited him at all. He'd chosen Alex the moment he saw her, at the first glimpse of her breasts riding under the short angora sweater that grazed her bare midriff above a long cotton skirt. After their third dance he said, "Come on," taking her hand firmly and leading her through a side door of the gym.

Outside, standing on the lawn, the stars of a New Hampshire spring riding above them, skimming the mountains, Alex looked back. A little girl still, in a woman's body. She could hear the music, see the colored lights of the gym, smell the punch and the cigarette smoke and the pot, remember that her friends were still safely inside, other little girls playing grown-up. The boy held her close. She could feel him against her. She liked the feel of his hand as it stole up under her sweater against the flat of her back, still damp from the dancing and the sweaty gym.

Beyond the noise of the dance was the rush of the White River swollen with the mountain snow melt, beyond the lawn the lights of old Dartmouth, of Hanover, of the Vermont hills looming dark across the river. Everything crystallized. It was an instant of passage for Alexandra.

"Okay," she said. He hadn't asked anything.

They went to his room in a fraternity house. He locked the door from the inside, turned to look at her. She smiled. She wasn't sure smiling was appropriate. Suspected she ought to look pouty and inflamed.

"Beer?" he asked, trying to be cool.

"Yeah."

He got two cans out of a small refrigerator near his bed. She switched on a stereo. Barry Manilow shook the room, the strings pounding heavy as metal. The redhead whose name was going into the yearbook as Loring Dodge (Red) Mason, flopped on the bed, his back against the wall. He patted the blanket beside him, lit a joint.

"I used to hate Barry Manilow," she said, still standing, still just that millimeter unsure.

"Yeah, me too."

"Yeah," she said.

"Hell, everyone hates Barry in the beginning," Mason said, with the assurance of men who have reached twenty. "Now, c'mere."

She sat down close to him, letting his arm snake behind her.

"What'd you say your last name was?" he asked, sipping the beer.

She told him. It didn't seem to register. She liked that, being just a girl in a Dartmouth bedroom. She drank some beer. It was very cold and she liked the smooth way it went down. Mason put down his beer and turned her upper body toward him. She tilted her head so they could kiss. His tongue pushed at her mouth and she let it slide past her lips. Behind them Manilow boomed in the night.

Mason had her sweater off and she was lying next to him on the bed, his leg shoved between hers, one hand playing with her hair, the other cupping one buttock. She could feel his erection.

"Hey," she said, pulling her head back so she could speak, "you want me to change the record?"

Mason shrugged. "Sure, why not."

She walked across the room, straightening the long skirt, aware of her breasts moving in the stale air. They were cold where his tongue had touched them. She picked through a stack of records, leaning over, sensing that he was watching them hang and move, liking it. When she'd positioned a new record and adjusted the volume, she turned back. Mason still lounged on the bed, his eyes on her body.

"Let's not get that skirt all wrinkled," he said, voice flat.

"Okay."

Her hands went to the snap and the zip closure. He did not move until she was naked. Then he stood and began to tear off his own clothes. She watched. He had a nice body. When his penis came free with its fringe of red it was larger than she'd expected. Then they

were in bed, under a coarse sheet, and his hand was pressed against
her mound, his thumb searching for her clitoris. Alex knew the terms
and she knew what he was doing.

"You take the pill?" he said, his voice thick with excitement.

"No," she said, "but it's okay."

He was four years older than she and he knew what to do when
they weren't on the pill. He worked on her breasts and her clitoris
with his hands and then he dove down to use his tongue. Alex
moaned and writhed. If she'd known it was to be like this she
wouldn't have waited so long.

"Come on," he said, pulling her up and rolling over on his back,
kicking the covers off.

First she didn't understand and then she did. She knelt over him
on all fours, and while he continued to handle her he pulled her head
gently down.

As her lips opened to him he arched toward her and his hand, no
longer gentle, tangled in her hair and jerked her head down. Now
she could taste him, the whole pulsing, swollen thickness of him, and
her head, guided by his hand, began to bob slowly up and down. And
then not as slowly.

Beneath her, Mason groaned and then, mouthing obscenities,
told her what he would do to her.

Later that same night, more gently, prudence cast away, and to
the music of Donna Summer and the smell of pot, Alex Noyes
offered up her virginity to Red Mason, who entered her body more
obligingly, the way she wanted it.

Mason had some trouble, until the lower sheet was displayed in
evidence, persuading fraternity brothers that he had been the first
with her. By then he knew she was the daughter of a President of
whom he had some vague childish recollection.

Alex's triumph at Dartmouth got all over school. A sophomore girl
who liked to let her mother know what a cesspool this "nice" establishment really was wrote a letter home. The mother's sister-in-law
counted herself one of Nora's good friends, too good not to tell Nora
what a good friend should.

It was then Nora swooped, pulled her out of that particular school,
and packed her daughter off to Switzerland, to Le Rosay. The
stratagem boomeranged.

Alex's early guilt, the sense of being unworthy of her formidable mother, her dead father, a half-digested Catholicism, had given way to more complicated hangups. The Dartmouth boy had unleashed a drive so urgent it frightened the girl. Could she be one of those creatures one read about—a nymphomaniac? Mingled with the unfamiliar physical urge there grew new admiration for and resentment of Nora and the new conviction that being a President's daughter carried responsibilities, priorities, and duties that she could never meet.

Le Rosay was a very proper school with a very proper curriculum and a very proper enrollment. Precisely the environment, Nora reasoned, for a rebellious child whose family deserved better of her. This reasoning went aground on the shoals of adolescent lust. First, a brilliant Belgian boy whose family owned banks, then a young Danish giant who played soccer, finally an English boy with doelike eyes and a famous title. Alex had become the naughty schoolgirl of Victorian dirty novels. Or so it seemed to Nora when Le Rosay sent her daughter packing. The truth was, Alex had behaved with restraint, limiting her affairs to one "sweet" boy at a time and resisting the simultaneous promiscuity indulged in by her friends. At this stage Alex thought sex with more than one boy at a time was "really gross." And she always shrank from dormitory homosexuality. The trouble was, the other girls were clever about their transgressions and Alex, incapable of being sly, got caught.

Back in the States Bryn Mawr had her for a time, and when that didn't work out UCLA was given its chance. Finally she won a degree from a small country-club college in Virginia. Nora could not bring herself to utter its name.

But if school and college had been a trial, the worst, in Nora's view, was yet to come. Her only child, Matt Noyes's daughter, became a "playgirl."

It was not all Alex's fault. The publicity spotlight focused now even more fiercely on the most commonplace of her remarks, her actions, her flirtations, even her shrugs. Alex became, without having a say in the matter, the darling of the media. A women's magazine that could not find a new angle or yet another "exclusive" bit of tattle about Nora would settle happily for Alex. And while Nora was litigious, jealously battling for her privacy (except in those moods when she *wanted* publicity) in writs and courts, Alex seemed to capitulate to the gossip *apparat.* If they were determined to have her in their cheap sheets, then so be it. Why should she exhaust herself in the losing struggle to avoid them?

On the plane to New York Alex had two martinis, relaxed for the first time in nearly a week, and wondered whether it might not be amusing to phone Sean Farrell. Perhaps she'd agree to see him. Maybe the word would filter back to Newport that she was going out with a newspaperman.

The fact alone would be enough to disturb Nora's little idyll with the Goddamn graf and his wonderful "seat."

9

It was just before Labor Day that Campbell Haig took control of *The New York Mail*. He appeared at the front door of the building at ten minutes to three that morning.

"I'm the new owner," he informed the startled night watchman, and walked past him into the press room.

Later the watchman told his superiors he let Haig go unchallenged "because there ain't any other sons of bitches around here with Texas accents."

In the press room the lobster shift, which begins work at midnight, was even more startled. No one could recall any publisher, dating back to the late George Valentine, ever entering the press room at any hour. Haig introduced himself to each of the men in the press room, shaking their ink-stained hands and cheerfully accepting and clapping on his head a pressman's hat crafted of newsprint. He then picked up a telephone and had coffee and Danish for everyone sent down from the cafeteria. He sat on one of the safety railing pipes, dunked his Danish into the cardboard coffee cup, and joshed with the men for a few moments. Press rooms are noisy, dangerous places. One of the men had a hook in place of a hand; another had lost a ring finger. Their conversation was all shouts. The roar of the presses, silent now, damaged hearing. Haig was familiar with this. Cheerfully he shouted back.

His early coffee with the press-room gang was planned. He knew the pressmen had the most militant of the eight or nine newspaper craft unions. Uncharacteristically shy in his presence, no one thought to ask Haig anything about his plans for the *Mail*, his attitude toward their contract, or whether he planned any layoffs. Appearing among them as he did had disarmed the press-room gang.

An afternoon newspaper at three in the morning is a strange place. There is activity in the composing room, where they set the type, and in the city room, where a skeleton staff of reporters and editors are reading copy, writing stories, or using the telephone, but the pulse of the place is still. The great presses and the conveyors that carry bundled papers to the loading dock are silent, waiting.

A noted gangster had been shot in a Broadway restaurant the evening before and the police reporter on the story was in the city room, haggard, unshaven, smelling of whiskey. Haig sat on his desk and talked to him about the dead man, about what the police had to say. Then he called for the story, read its first two takes quickly and asked politely who the copy editor was. A lean man with the rounded shoulders of an office worker raised his hand. Haig introduced himself and asked what the headline would be and how many pictures they planned to run.

Whether he was satisfied or not, he nodded as each bit of information was conveyed, and after asking a few more questions, he left the floor and now, for the first time, went upstairs to Meg Valentine's old office. It was locked and there was a bit of a stir until someone found a key. When he was alone inside the office Campbell Haig sat down behind Meg's old desk. (The haunted chairs and sofa were gone, Meg had taken them; she had left the desk with its chair in the denuded room. He thought he might keep it.) In his own hand he wrote a brief memo to Lyman, asking the managing editor to see him that morning, "when convenient."

Then he flicked off the overhead lights, sat back in Meg's big swivel chair, and watched the eastern sky brighten until finally, around six, the sun popped up from behind a Brooklyn warehouse. At eight thirty the presses began to roll with the first edition and he made a second visit to the press room, not speaking this time, but only standing there as the metro edition's rolls of newsprint fed smoothly, swiftly, noisily into the presses.

Lyman arrived, as he customarily did, at eight, and by nine o'clock he was seated in Haig's office opposite his new employer.

"I plan to come in at three every morning for the time being," Haig informed him. "It would be good of you if you could do the same. I'd like to watch how you put the paper together."

Lyman, a small, frightened man, said that, yes, of course he could do that. Was there anything else?

"Yes," Haig said, "the editorials. I'd like to see those every day before they're set. I might try my hand at writing one occasionally."

Again Lyman agreed, once more avidly. Nothing special about such a request. Even Meg Valentine dictated the odd editorial. Anything else?

Haig smiled, almost bashfully.

"Would you have a copyboy wheel up a typewriter and table? Any old standard machine. And some copy books. I hate writing anything in longhand, even a memo."

The city room of *The New York Mail* through which Sean Farrell walked at eleven that morning owed nothing to the *Lou Grant* show. The walls were dun and covered with faded notices from management and the Guild. The furniture was as battered as a police reporter's sensibilities. The cleaning people stole the ashtrays every night and the floors were a mosaic of scorch marks, of cigarette butts and the relics of cheap cigars. People ate at their desks and colonies of roaches flourished in the old wooden drawers. The windows, grimed and streaked, framed a view that was undeniably Brooklyn. Only the eerie green screens of the video display terminals brightened the monochromatic landscape.

The men, the older ones, and some of the women, were pallid as men who work in mills or mines. A copy editor with psoriasis scratched himself through the sleeves of his shirt until blood showed. He blinked at Farrell through pale eyes as he walked by, lifting a hand in greeting. Farrell grinned back at the man. No one wanted to sit near him or use the same coat rack. Farrell knew what it cost the man to come to work each day.

Haig might own this newspaper, but Sean's name was on it too.

Had been for a lot longer. A copygirl in tight corduroy pants and sneakers flipped her long hair at him.

"Well, hello," he said, half to himself. He loosened his tie and sat down at his desk.

The City Hall man was on the phone at the next desk. "No," he was saying, "I don't want a copy of his speech to the widows and orphans."

A stack of mail leaned against his typewriter. Farrell stared at it. A man could spend the whole day opening his damned mail.

In one of the anterooms coffee brewed on a hot plate. You put a dollar a week in a kitty. For that you got as many cups of rotten coffee as you wanted. By noon everyone who came to the coffeepot, everyone in the city room, had his very own Campbell Haig story. Since Farrell was the paper's star turn, and popular besides, which was not always the same thing, they came to him with their stories. Farrell nodded, listened, and said nothing. Jesus, he thought to himself, you'd think the Holy Ghost had come among us, speaking with the gift of tongues. With Campbell Haig there was to be no gradual assumption of authority. From dawn on his very first day the man was there and making damn sure everyone knew it.

Farrell sat down behind his desk and began to slice open his mail. The press releases he threw unopened into the oversized wastebasket. A woman with a brain-damaged child urged that his column scream the outrage she felt about a certain medical facility in Queens. Farrell threw her letter out. He had done a brain-damaged child six months earlier and he didn't believe in boring his readers. A longshoreman wrote, anonymously, a screed about pilferage on the docks. An indicted judge in Brooklyn whined that a recent column had handled him unfairly and brought unwarranted abuse upon his family. There were two mash notes, one of them including a nude photo. And a royalty check for $67.40 for a book of his columns that had been published two years earlier and had quickly died. He tossed everything but the check and the letter from the judge into the wastebasket. If the judge felt that bad about his column perhaps he deserved another, even tougher.

All around him the city room hummed. Typewriters clattered, video display terminals glowed, copyboys fetched coffee and back issues of the paper, telephones rang; in the wire room just off the

main room the UPI and AP and Dow Jones machines spewed out
their simultaneous and differing versions of the day's events. Next
door, in the composing room, young women pasted strips of paper
on layout sheets as the replated third edition was made ready for the
noon press run. Everything was as it should be, Sean Farrell concluded happily. The coming of Campbell Haig in the predawn dark
had been an event to be noted. But now it had passed, superseded
by other events, and the men and women who worked there, and
the paper itself, went on, instinctively, on schedule, almost automati-
cally. What the hell, Farrell thought. After all, what was Haig?
Another proprietor, another boss.

He had his feet on the desk, a still-damp third edition on his lap.
He had been out the night before and he had a small headache. But
now, thinking about Haig, about bosses, he forgot his hangover.

In Rome, on *The Daily American,* he had been on the copy desk.
His slot man, an old foreign hand who claimed to have edited papers
in Cleveland and Denver, had weak kidneys. The office joke was that
you could always tell where he had gone, following the trickle along
the office floor. In Houston there had been Joynstone, a spindly man
who wore suits six or eight sizes too large for him, made for his late
father. And in San Francisco there had been Goeghan, the aesthete.
He invited young Farrell to his houseboat at Sausalito, and as they
listened to Shostakovich on the stereo his lean hand fell to rest on
Farrell's knee until the young man had said "I feel I should tell you
that, unfortunately, I'm not a homosexual." Goeghan had said
"Oh," in a small, hurt voice, and had invited Farrell to hear no more
music.

Now Farrell had a boss who came in at 3 A.M., probably to show
how energetic he was and to make people nervous. Would people
start coming in early and leaving late, acting jittery because Haig was
apt to pop in any time? Farrell felt the heat in his face, knew it was
going pink. Knowing that, he felt the heat rise again. He sat up
angrily, slammed his paper into his wastebasket, and put a sheet of
copy paper into his machine.

He was rounding off a paragraph when he saw Haig drifting into
the city room. The last edition with the closing stock market and
the afternoon baseball had gone. Farrell had the knack of concentrating on his work and seeing everything around him: an athlete's

peripheral awareness. He saw Haig buttoned up in a good suit, brown hair combed, tie in place, moving to the copy desk without looking right or left. Farrell went on typing until his paragraph was clean and done. Haig stood by the copy desk and cleared his throat and around him men and women stopped typing, turned away from terminals, whispered apologies into telephones and hung up. Lyman, seeing Haig through the clear window of the managing editor's office, scurried across the city room to his side, fearful of being left out. Haig greeted him solemnly as "Mr. Lyman." Then, turning to the editorial staff, perhaps thirty-five people at this time of day, he spoke.

There were no dramatics, no reminders he was the son of a crusading journalist blown to pieces by landgrabbers, no flowery tribute to previous management bar a courteous salute to old Meg, no soaring hymns to the greatness of New York.

"Unlike you," Campbell Haig said, speaking slowly and with the western accent softened by the accoustics of the large room, "I am not a New Yorker. I'm a stranger, both to you and to this city. But like you I am a professional newspaperman. Here in New York and across the country newspapers have been dying. Jobs have been lost. Readers have lost options in their daily opportunity to select between various media. Some of my publishing colleagues blame television. They fear it. I believe them to be wrong. Television exists. It has its strengths, its weaknesses. There are two hundred million Americans, half of them literate. In the New York trading area there are sixteen million people. We sell less than a million papers a day. The *Times,* the *Post,* also less than a million. The *News,* a million and a half. *Newsday* under a million. The North Jersey papers, say a half million.

"There are more people not reading newspapers than are reading them. I don't blame television. I blame bad newspapers. Dull newspapers, complacent newspapers. Give the reader something to react to, to chew on, something he didn't know an hour before, give it to him attractively packaged, and he will buy your newspaper. This is a newspaper with a great old history. I intend that it reach a younger reader, a reader who perhaps has forgotten the joy of a daily paper, who thinks television news gives him everything he wants in twenty-two minutes. And, considering the commercials, that's all it is. A newspaper is read and rumpled and clipped and saved. The ads are read, the puzzles done, the editorials argued over. No one watches John Chancellor more than once each evening. People go back to a paper. Again and again.

"Mrs. Valentine has given me a rare opportunity. I promised her a great newspaper. Whatever you have heard, I did not come in here to fire people. I have no plans to bring in outsiders to run the *Mail*. I want to revitalize and improve this newspaper with your help and collaboration. I will ask none of you to do anything I will not do myself."

The room was quiet. Haig paused and looked around.

"Thank you for your patience."

He did not offer to answer questions and there were none. Sean Farrell had the impression no one wanted to draw Haig's attention this early in the game.

Haig had nodded to no one coming in, caught no eye during his speech, but now he turned and walked directly to Farrell's desk, holding out his hand. "Missed you this morning." He smiled.

"I'm seldom here at three in the morning," said Farrell.

Haig said, "I may call on you at some odd hour for help," and he smiled slightly then. "Be forewarned." And he was gone.

Farrell was pleased that Haig had singled him out and then angry with himself for caring.

There were, Farrell knew, a lot of burned-out cases in the city room of *The New York Mail*. Men and women like that want only to be left alone, not to be noticed, to slip quietly through the seine unchallenged. Having thought this Farrell was annoyed at himself again. Was he already siding with Haig against his fellow employees?

Just before he left for the day a copyboy brought him an envelope. Inside was a copy of one of his columns clipped from a Pacific Northwest paper. The back slip attached to it said: *Hope we do better by you in the* Mail. *CH.* The column had been ridiculously cut and set up. Farrell shrugged. The guy sure reads the competition.

At seven that evening Haig dismissed his driver and his secretary, a gaunt, loyal, competent woman from McAllen, and left the building alone and on foot. He paused only once to look back at it, the sandstone pale in the September dusk. He walked up the hill toward Chinatown, losing himself once or twice in the narrow, bustling, winding streets, hearing the babel of dialects, the coarse, high-pitched chatter of the market women, the cries of the young children. He stopped in a store and bought three Punch cigars, smuggled in, the proprietor assured him, direct from Havana. Chinatown disappeared behind him and City Hall and the Federal Courthouse in Foley Square loomed. A black man stood at the entrance to the subway, playing a decent trumpet, muted, sweet, tempting in the night, and Haig threw a crumpled bill into the man's cap in front of him on the pavement. He ducked into the subway with the last of the secretaries and litigants and ward heelers of the government complex. At the change booth he bought his first subway token, had to be informed of its cost by a plump black woman who shook her head sadly at his ignorance, was given directions, and took the Lexington Avenue local (he was not yet sufficiently venturesome to dare the express) uptown.

Meg Valentine was giving a dinner for him that evening at the Metropolitan Club. They would all be there: Sulzberger of the *Times,* O'Neill of the *News,* Murdoch of the *Post,* Davidson of *Time,* Paley of CBS, Goodman of ABC, Kay Graham of *Newsweek,* Dolly Schiff and the governor and the mayor and Wriston of Citibank and Rockefeller of Chase and a score like them, the men and the women to whom this great city belonged, if it belonged to any of the seven million.

Meg Valentine, who no longer owned anything, no longer had political leverage or the power of a newspaper behind her, could still summon the great to table.

The Establishment! They hung together, the club members did. Well, perhaps it was just as well. The way he planned to run *The New York Mail* precluded the sort of chummy relationship on which the Old-Boy network thrived. He would remain an outsider. The paper would speak for him within the concentric circles of the city. It would be his voice, his lever, his instrument of power.

He was content.

The dinner, which turned out quite pleasant, with curiosity about him overcoming disdain for an alien, ended at midnight. He went back to the hotel and was immediately asleep.

And at three the next morning he was back in the city room of *The New York Mail.*

10

Campbell Haig, as he had so often done after buying a newspaper but never on so grand a scale, began the long ceremony of meeting his people one at a time.

"Trot 'em on up," he told Lyman. Meg Valentine, beaming at his elbow, said she'd be glad to sit in, to help in the transition. Haig looked at her.

"Let me make my own mistakes," he said. "Let me feel my way."

Meg, thus dismissed, went off muttering. Maybe she should have sold to Messenger after all.

The metropolitan editor came up first. Haig asked him how he conceived of his role, what guidelines he gave his staff.

"It's New York," the man said histrionically. "Greatest city in the world. All five boroughs, all seven million people. From Coney Island to Riverdale, from Jamaica to the Outerbridge Crossing. Whatever they do, whatever they say, when they laugh, when they cry—"

Haig stared. "I mean, specifically, what sort of instructions do you give your people?"

The metropolitan editor smiled blissfully. In orotund tones he said, "Bring me this city every day, triple-spaced and exclusive. With an angle."

Haig had Sean Farrell sent up.

"I have difficulty getting a straight answer from the metropolitan editor," he said. "You're a columnist. But from what I've read you seem to have a grasp of the city, of its pulse. Tell me, frankly, what you think of the *Mail*'s coverage of New York."

Farrell looked at the ceiling.

"Seriously," Haig said, his voice harder, "I'm not asking you to criticize a colleague. I'm asking you as a professional journalist, is our local coverage any good?"

Farrell's eyes moved to the new publisher. "It sucks," he said pleasantly.

Haig grunted. "What do you think of our political coverage? Anything there?"

Farrell shrugged. "The paper supports a candidate who last had dinner with Meg."

"The financial pages?" Haig probed.

"Sometimes we get the stock tables right two days in a row."

"Thank you, Mr. Farrell."

At his shoulder Gideon Benaud was taking notes. The two men were alone now, awaiting the next member of the staff.

"Bad, Gideon," Haig said, "pretty bad."

Gideon smiled beatifically. "Campbell, the worse it is the easier the change. And you just know that bad *or* good, you're going to change it."

Well, Haig thought, there was something in that. But there must be *something* on which they could build. Farrell had a nice touch as a columnist. Sports seemed sound.

"Let's see the sports editor next."

The sports editor was a sulfuric little man with a brush cut. "Glad to meet you, Mr. Haig," he announced without waiting, "because you may have to get me out of jail tomorrow and you ought to know me before you stand bail."

"Oh?"

The editor nodded vigorously. "Toronto. That's where I'll be. Whatever precinct is closest to Maple Leaf Gardens. That son of a bitch."

Gideon Benaud suggested gently that it might be helpful to know what the sports editor was talking about.

The little man's brow furrowed. "Oh, I'll tell you. It's no secret. I've sent the word ahead. They can't stick their fingers up the noses of *my* reporters and get away with it."

"*Who?*" Haig asked.

"Stasio!" the little man shouted. "On the Rangers. Hasn't taken a run at anyone in the league in years. Took a run at my man Slotnick in the locker room last night. Slotnick! A little guy! And Stasio put his finger up his nose and reamed it. Tonight, in Toronto, we'll see whose nose gets a finger up it!"

He looked triumphant. Haig thanked him for his contribution.

One by one they came up to talk to the new publisher. There were some great city room characters; any paper would have boasted of them. There was Treanor, a dauntless reporter when sober, Lyman said. Treanor was said to have punched press agents, thrown bar glasses at gentlemen he mistakenly thought to be ad men, screwed copygirls standing up in the city room toilet . . . Not everyone loved Treanor. Once he went wandering through a snowstorm with a drink from Costello's in his hand and a cab ran over his foot. A rival had said, "I hope it wasn't his writing foot." But no one denied that Treanor was a great leg man, in the old newspaper sense of the term.

There was Langton, the old-time left-wing columnist with a deft touch and a big heart. Haig asked Langton if any readers resented his outlook. "To the day she died," said Langton, "my own mother thought they got the wrong man when they arrested Alger Hiss."

Coyle—oh, God, Coyle, who exposed himself at press parties. A dreamer, Ratchet, who baked bread at home to soothe his jangled nerves.

One by one Haig saw them, checked on them with Lyman or Farrell, sometimes with Meg. They saw good things in all of them. Haig's green eyes grew narrower with each claim to redeeming talent. There had to be some holes in this broken-down daily, but Lyman, Farrell, and Meg—particularly Lyman and Meg—made out each pathetically passé staffer a genius, the sum of their talents a new age of Pericles.

Haig wanted to meet New York's power brokers, the men who ran the city. He needed a handle on the town, he needed to overcome local resentment of a Western claim-jumper. When he told Lyman of his wishes the managing editor offered to set up a series of appointments.

"No," Haig said, "I'll pick up a phone and call them. Play it one on one. Just give Miss Mayhew the phone numbers."

The editor went off, dazed by the whirlwind, wondering just when his pension rights might be exercised.

Ben Cork was one of the first to meet with Haig. Like Jimmy Carter, Haig had an easy way with blacks. Cork sensed it from the first. He was the most powerful New York black politician since Adam Clayton Powell and in his way just as flamboyant. He knew all about the white power game and how a black, if he were clever and ruthless, could play it, relying on white guilt, white fear, white greed, to carve out his own rich black fiefdom.

Cork, handsome, assured, more immaculately tailored than his host, laughed a deep baritone.

"But don't you know I'm a rascal, Mr. Haig? A dangerous demagogue? A hissing and a byword to the white establishment?"

"So I'm told, Congressman," Haig replied. "Just as there are those who say even worse about me."

"You?" Cork asked in mock surprise. "Nice white newspaper publisher like you?"

Haig nodded. "And *I* don't have congressional immunity," he said.

Ben Cork did not laugh. He was under investigation but it was still supposed to be a secret. He looked at Haig through narrower, less mocking eyes.

"I'm at your service," he said.

"Tell me what this newspaper can do to work with middle-class blacks."

Cork raised his eyes. "That's limiting the field. What about poor blacks? Welfare blacks? The unemployed?"

Haig lifted his hands. "I'm no redeemer, Congressman. I run a newspaper. There are limits to what the *Mail* can do. Middle-class blacks read newspapers and the poor don't. I want to encourage the middle-class blacks to stay here, not to go out to Long Island or up to Mount Vernon and White Plains. Just as I want the middle-class Italians and Jews to stay. If this city is ever going to get back on its feet the middle class is the key. Not the poor. As far as I'm con-

cerned New York would be better off if they went home to Ala-
bama."

Cork leaned back in his chair. He hadn't expected this. Either this
Haig was even more arrogant than he was portrayed or he was an
honest white man.

"You know," he said, sliding away from Haig's point, "the black
community has me and Charley Rangel and Shirley Chisholm and
a few others down in Washington. We make speeches and get paid
off with a little patronage, some summer jobs, with welfare, with
what's left of CETA. But these are crumbs from the table. The
white establishment runs things. I'm a realist. I know that. And I
know it's going to be like that for a while. And street blacks know
it too. Maybe they can't articulate it, but they know it.

"You ever see these kids walking around the streets carrying big
portable radios, maybe wearing those earphones with antennas?
They're shutting out the white sound all around them. Dark glasses
to turn everything dark, to pretend this isn't a white world. You
know, there are black motorcycle gangs. Leather jackets, crash helmets, Nazi decorations, all the rest of it. But they don't have motor-
cycles. They have bikes. Just plain old Schwinn bikes, with lots of
fancy mirrors and gear just like they were Harley-Davidsons. They
can't afford real irons. So they're playing make-believe." He paused.

"But you don't play make-believe," Haig said, "do you?"

Cork shook his big, handsome head. Then, signaling their talk had
ended, had been ended by *him,* he stood as he said, "Just don't be
so quick to forget about my *poor* blacks, Mr. Haig. They may not
read papers, they sure as hell don't vote very often, but . . ."

Haig remained seated. He was damned if he was going to be
bullied by Ben Cork.

"But what?" he asked.

Cork shrugged.

Then, looking into Haig's eyes as if to measure him, he said
quietly, "But they might decide to come downtown some day."

That night Campbell Haig entertained Peter Burke, the head of
the FBI, in his suite at the Carlyle. Burke was in New York to make
a luncheon speech that day to the City Club, and Haig lured him
uptown for a meal. Now the two men sat over cigars and brandy,

Burke noting that Haig barely touched his, and the publisher probed relentlessly, posing questions, picking brains, a sharpened pencil forming Pitman shorthand on a yellow legal pad.

"I wish organized crime at Kennedy Airport and on the docks were all we had on our plate," Burke said, fatigue in his voice.

Haig brightened. Dinner was off the record, Burke had stipulated, but surely there would be any number of news leads to follow. "Oh?" he said, putting down his pencil to encourage his man to talk more freely.

"Sure," Burke said. "How long do you think we're going to be immune to these European kidnap capers? Why should this country escape when there's more money here, more famous potential victims, more room to hide?"

"Do you have any firm leads?"

"A few vague reports. Nothing substantive yet. It isn't the occasional kidnap case that concerns me. There's no way to arm yourself against that. No, it's the organized European gangs that worry me. Three million Europeans a year visit this country. The Concorde puts Europe three hours away." He sipped his brandy and looked at Haig. "The Red Brigades gunman who shoots off a banker's kneecap in Turin tonight can be in Manhattan tomorrow."

"But you have no solid information as yet?"

Burke opened his hands, palms upward. "A chance remark here, a flash of intuition there. Nothing concrete." He looked at Haig steadily. "Please, I don't want to see in your newspapers any subtle reference to 'FBI Chief Fears Red Brigades Coming Here.'"

Haig laughed. "You write a good scare headline, you know."

"And scare headlines sell newspapers."

"Virtue and piety surely don't."

The FBI chief laughed and stood up. The two men shook hands. It was nearly midnight. When his guest had left, Haig phoned the office, as he did each night before he slept.

"Nothing doing, Mr. Haig," the night editor said. "Bomb threat about nine thirty."

"Against whom?"

The night man laughed. "Us. The paper. The usual crazy on the other end of a phone."

"Call the cops?"

"Nah. Do that and you'd miss a couple of editions with dogs and cops sniffing all over the place for hours."

The night editor had done the right thing. If you shut down a newspaper over every crank threat, every loonie wandering into the lobby, every rock thrown at a delivery truck, you'd never make an edition.

As he got ready for bed Haig thought about Red Brigades kidnappings in New York. Burke was no Hoover—no right-wing paranoia there. No doubt he had hold of something. But there was nothing in it for the *Mail* to check on. You just had to luck onto a story like that.

Four days earlier two men and a woman had sat in a kitchen out in Queens. The house they were in was on a quiet street of similar houses, each with its Madonna, small lawn and garden in front and an attached garage. It was an Italian neighborhood where these people did not stand out. They supposedly had special qualifications for this American operation. The woman, for instance, spoke fluent "American."

Benedetto was the leader. Now he was talking as the three sat around a kitchen table covered with lists and maps.

"A great deal of care has gone into the compilation of this roster," he said quietly, a manicured fingernail tapping a sheet of paper on the table before him.

"Here in America it would be nothing to kidnap Mr. David Rockefeller. Who would care? A robber baron and the son of robber barons. Similarly Mr. Ford. Or Mr. Ludwig. No, public opinion would not be outraged. There would be a spate of sensational newspaper headlines and the police and the FBI would issue portentous statements. Private investigators would be retained by the score from Pinkerton's. Then the money would be paid or it would not be paid. The subject would live or die. Simple commerce. No, one must use the American tools of television, the news magazines, the press to capture the imagination. Were we simple brigands I would say, yes, bring me Harvey Firestone or Mr. du Pont.

"But we are not brigands. The money is important, of course. It provides operational funds. But to succeed we must blend political action with the financial. Political terror. The shaking of society's complacency. We must strike at the heart of America as well as its purse.

"That is why this roster has been so painstakingly drawn. It limits itself to New York and the environs. New York is the most cosmopolitan of American cities. A foreigner in the streets of Denver or Houston draws attention. In New York half the population is foreign. And wherever their country homes, their pavilions, their great beach houses, the American rich all have apartments in New York, offices. So it is here in New York that we strike. And at the children."

He looked quickly at the faces around him, especially at the woman who spoke fluent "American." Satisfied that he caught no sign of softness, he continued. "Our reputation as Italians is that we dote on our children. But every research we have had done indicates that compared to the Americans Italians are ice cold. Take a child, the son or daughter of a great American dynasty, and you galvanize the entire communications *apparat* of the United States."

He looked around the table once more. He wanted to be sure. Again he saw no hint of reluctance. "Here," he said, holding up his sheet of paper. "Here is the list of children."

On the list of seventy-three children of great American families who lived in New York were the names of Alexandra Noyes and Sissy Valentine. Along with three other names on the list, these were underlined. Next to Sissy's name was a notation: New employer—Campbell Haig.

Sissy Valentine rarely saw her brother, Willie, outside of the office. Nor very often on the job, since ad people and editorial worked on different floors. His apartment was in Sutton Place, hers on Central Park West—a big, echoing flat once Ring Lardner's. He rang her at work. He had a date for dinner that evening but couldn't they meet for a drink? They really should, he said, to compare notes on the coming of Campbell Haig.

Sissy saw no point in this but she loved her brother. In her heart she supposed he was, as old Meg said, somehow lacking. But she hated herself for this secret disloyalty and tried to quell it.

Willie Valentine was a good space salesman but too fastidious to be the best. Great ad salesmen can absorb any abuse, any insult, any rejection, and any crudity, and still come back to ask for the order.

Willie's carapace was not that thick. He blew a major sale by stalking out of the office of the president of a big Brooklyn department store right in the middle of his pitch. Willie had been exuding all his vaunted Valentine charm when the eminent retailer stopped him in midsentence by picking his nose.

"Jesus," Willie had complained. "Some of these people are animals. Just animals!"

When she heard the story Sissy thought that she would not have shown any offense if she had been interviewing the executive. "Not everyone has been brought up by Miffy," she said mildly.

This September evening they met in the back room of Costello's, the newspaper hangout on East Forty-fourth Street. Willie was jubilant.

"Sissy, this is the greatest opportunity the *Mail* has ever had. Everyone agrees Campbell Haig is a real promoter, a P. T. Barnum, another Hearst. He'll shake this damn town up and he'll give us something to sell. The *Mail* has been asleep for so long it's embarrassing even trying to make a sales pitch. The whole town knows we're sucking hind tit behind the *Times* and the *News* and the *Post.* The department stores don't *use* the *Mail;* they throw us a bone out of sheer pity. Meg was too old or too proud to admit it. Campbell's going to show them. He'll spend some money too. TV commercials, I hear, lots of them, starting in prime time this fall. Maybe for once we'll have one of those big, old-fashioned Christmas seasons, hundred-and-sixty-page papers instead of ninety-six."

Sissy let her brother run on. When he paused for breath she asked, "Have you met Mr. Haig yet?"

"Why, no. Why?"

"You called him Campbell. I thought you and he must be on a first-name basis."

He missed the sarcasm. "Well, we will be. I can't wait to meet him. I've got some ideas those old fogies in sales wouldn't dare try. Not with Meg and her memos hanging over them."

They were drinking beer. Up in the front room, along the bar, reporters from the *Mail,* the *News,* and the *Post* clustered, talking shop, needling one another, complaining, flirting with girls. Down the bar, toward the entrance, the ad agency people and the public relations men had their little groupings. No one had arranged it that way, certainly not young Costello or Freddy the barman. It just happened, a caste system ritually observed. Maybe that is the trouble with Willie, Sissy concluded. He isn't a newspaperman at all but a salesman.

"It should mean more money," Willie said. "God knows, I could use a raise. The commissions we're earning these days wouldn't keep a dog alive."

Sissy resisted the temptation to mention his apartment in Sutton Place. She was working for Guild minimum. Willie, three years older, was certainly getting more, but not enough to rate Sutton Place. Junior hadn't given either of them a penny for years. Meg was always good for a Christmas check. But still, Sutton Place . . .

Neither of the grandchildren had as yet realized anything from the sale of the *Mail.* Sissy owned a few shares of stock. Her share would amount to, for a young girl, a small fortune. Unlike her father she had not yet bothered to do the multiplication. Willie held none. Meg had set aside an equal amount for him, but, still unsure of the boy, she held it in trust. One day soon, of course, she would have to sign it over or rescind. One day very soon.

The plump German waiter brought two more beers. From the bar a photographer from the *Mail* waved back to the booth.

"Hey, Sissy, don't hang around with them salesmen too long. You'll get a bad name."

She laughed and waved back. Across the table Willie's handsome face darkened.

"It's all such crap," he said, "this sophomoric rivalry between business and editorial. Who the hell do they think pays their salaries? Circulation loses money, no one ever made a nickel on news. Ad sales. That's what keeps the whole house of cards from collapsing. Maybe some day they'll realize how important we are."

Sissy studied her brother. Willie sulked so easily. She loved him, there were even times she liked him. And, God, he was good-looking.

"Who's this new girl?" Sissy asked, hoping to dispel Willie's pout. He brightened immediately.

"Sensational. Wait till you meet her. She's picking me up here and we're going to 'Twenty-One' for dinner. A model. She's on the cover of the new *Cosmopolitan.* You know," he said with a histrionic leer, "blouse opened down to here."

Sissy laughed. "But, Willie, that describes *every* girl who's ever been on the cover of *Cosmo*."

When the girl came in there were throat clearings the length of the bar. Willie could pick them. Sissy said the usual polite things and then, when they left, stopped to chat with a woman's page writer from the *News*. Just then Sean Farrell walked in.

"Hail the Hollywood screenwriter," someone said. Farrell growled back and squeezed his way up to the bar.

"Hello, Sean," Sissy said. Farrell was one of her heroes. "Buy me a beer?"

Farrell looked into her open, lovely face. "Sissy, even if you don't own the Goddamn paper anymore."

Freddy drew the beers.

That evening in Sutton Place, while the girl on the cover of *Cosmo* unpinned her hair and took off her eyelashes and showered and did whatever such girls do before they are capable of making love, Willie Valentine riffled through a sheaf of unpaid bills.

Jesus, he thought, more than twelve thousand dollars. Last year he had made thirty. Old Meg had better come through with something substantial in the way of stock or else. Haig better double his salary. He was pinning his hopes, he knew, on two situations over which he had absolutely no control. Yet could he afford to live less well? A Valentine was expected to maintain some sort of standard. Well, Willie thought, carefully stacking the bills atop the mantelpiece, there were always other ways to raise cash. He knew. He'd tried those other ways. Remembering, he shivered.

Then the bathroom door opened and the girl walked into his bedroom, naked except for a fine gold chain around her suntanned midriff.

"Hi," the girl said. She was not very bright, but she thought Willie was the best-looking boy she'd ever met and rich and important besides.

Willie didn't care about her lack of wit. All he knew was that her breasts looked even better in his bedroom than they did on the cover of *Cosmo*.

He would get the money. Whatever it took.

"Christ, no!" Farrell exploded. "How the hell am I to get out three columns a week shepherding him around?"

It seemed that Haig wanted a guide to the city. A privileged insider was to be privileged to tutor this invader in the ways of New York.

Lyman wheedled. "Sean, do this for me. He wants you. Says you know both sides of the tracks. Please, for me. Take him around. Take him anywhere. But get him out of the building. I've started shaving at night before I go to bed. My hands shake so badly in the morning, just knowing I've got to have my first meeting with him at three A.M."

Haig and Farrell. Farrell and Haig. They traveled together, through the city, through the day, through the pages of their newspaper. *Theirs!* As shared, Haig insisted, as the marriage bed. "No one can do it all. One man has to lead. You can't do it by committee. But you need a hundred other good men with you."

Farrell and Haig. Disparate. Antagonistic. Potential enemies, perhaps. Lovers of newspapers. Little in common and everything.

"I don't understand New York," Haig told Farrell, green eyes in lean face.

"Of course you don't. How could you?"

But Farrell did find it strange. Haig was at home in London, Milan, Paris. But New York was foreign to him. Too big and too unmanageable.

"And you don't really like it, do you?"

"I don't know. I'm learning."

And he *was*. Farrell had to give the bastard that. I'll bet you're learning, he thought. Learning so as to dominate. The power syndrome. Haig must be a hell of a fellow in one of his small towns.

Haig was a stickler for early starts. He was no longer going in at 3 A.M. but his car would pick up Farrell every morning in Turtle Bay. Sean hated early rising. He went to bed late; he liked to sleep late. Instead, Haig would be in the apartment lobby, buzzing impatiently, his voice croaking through the intercom. "It's after seven. Hurry."

"Hurry." That was the word Farrell most associated with Haig in those first months. "Hurry." To do what? To make the paper better, to make its authority felt by the powerful who ran the town, to learn about New York. He was hurrying, always, Haig was, impatient, carping, nagging, and learning. Always asking and learning. But with the prejudgments of the bright boy in class who *knows* the school-marm is wrong.

A distinguished black jurist had written a book. Farrell urged that it be serialized.

"He's a professional black," sneered Haig.

"Well, he's more than that. Besides, what black leaders aren't professional?"

"Let him buy space and mount his pulpit in the ad columns."

Sometime later Haig would meet the black at a fund-raising dinner in the Waldorf, argue vigorously with him throughout the evening, and next morning urge Farrell to devote a column to his black view of things.

"Why isn't Staten Island part of New Jersey?"

Farrell, for whom history began with the Depression and Roosevelt, did not know. The next morning, in their dawn drive south together, Haig lectured him for fifteen minutes on colonial New York and handed over a list of nine books Farrell should read. Farrell pocketed the list and groaned.

"Why did The Bronx go bad when most of Brooklyn didn't?"

"Bedford-Stuyvesant isn't exactly Grosse Pointe, you know," Farrell said sarcastically.

Haig ignored the tone. "Yes, but why so *much* of The Bronx? Bad politics, bad economics, bad race relations? What?"

The car was cruising through blighted little streets off the Hunts Point market, with Haig's chauffeur, a big beefy former policeman, looking warily from side to side as he drove.

"Look, Haig, I'm not a sociologist. I just don't know the answers to some of your questions. You ask me who runs The Bronx now, which Puerto Rican had the biggest drag at City Hall, who runs the numbers games in Harlem, which Irish judge can be bought cheapest, I'll tell you. Things like that a good newspaperman *knows*. He has to. But the whys and wherefores of why a borough goes rotten call for deeper study. A reporter has surface knowledge. Every morning he starts all over again. We don't keep our notes. We ask questions. I know where the reference books are and I may have screwed the librarian. But all knowledge is not within me, I promise you."

Haig nodded. "I'll find out. Someone will know." The car bounced uncomfortably. "Mark down that pothole, Dennis," he told the driver.

It wasn't only Sean Farrell that Haig was driving to distraction but City Hall and the various commissioners. Haig counted potholes and chimneys belching smoke and inoperative traffic lights and lounging garbagemen the way misers counted pearls. And at the end of every working day his secretary, Miss Mayhew, called in the infractions to the appropriate authority.

"I want to see Ben Cork again," Haig announced.

"Okay," Farrell said. That was one thing he could handle. "But why?"

"You say Cork is the most powerful crooked black in New York. I've met the honest ones. I met Cork once. Now I want to get to know him."

Farrell groaned and set it up.

One afternoon in Jamaica someone took a shot at the limousine. The bullet cracked a side window and showered glass into Farrell's lap.

"A local divertissement," Farrell said dryly.

Haig was delighted. "Dennis," he ordered, "get that fixed. Better have them put in bulletproof stuff. I don't want Mr. Farrell injured. His union wouldn't like it."

Gerry Brophy didn't like Farrell's new dinner companion. "Like going to bed with the Blessed Virgin," he drawled in his nasal South Boston voice.

In an unguarded moment Farrell had mentioned that he was going to dine with Alex Noyes. Brophy was Farrell's best friend on the *Mail*. He argued like a Jesuit, wrote like an angel, and had four children and eighty pounds on Farrell. It was a mistake telling him about Alex.

"I'm buying her a meal," Farrell said, "not marrying her."

Brophy waved a big hand at his friend in disgust. "Ah," he snarled, "you're getting above yourself!"

They met in one of that season's, or that week's, new places on the East Side. She had second thoughts before they met. Her phone call to him had been a reaction to Newport, to the flatterers who pranced around her mother. Whatever he was, crude, pushy, out for the main chance, Farrell would be a man.

They were both tense. As they pushed through the narrow front room of the bar toward their table, following a deferential fag in a floral caftan, Farrell could hear the whispers. "Isn't that Alex Noyes . . . Noyes . . . Noyes." Noise! She walked ahead of him, long-legged, broad-shouldered, a big girl who moved well, a woman you would notice across a room even if she had not been a President's daughter.

They ordered drinks. When Alex reached for hers her upper body moved in a way that made Farrell glad she had called. *My God, she has a body!*

But she also had a head. Before the first drink was finished Farrell was convinced she was as strong-minded, wrong-minded, and stubborn as any woman he had yet encountered. Alex Noyes's ferocity took his mind off her blue and golden eyes, her wide, sensual mouth, and the rest. The trouble began with his casual mention of Campbell Haig.

"Campbell Haig runs the sort of newspapers I've always despised. Tabloids!" Alex exclaimed.

"Tabloid just means it's a smaller-sized sheet, as opposed to a broadsheet. Nothing to do with the content."

Alex shrugged. "You know what I mean. Papers like his have been rotten about my father. About my family. Me."

"The history books will judge your father. Not Haig. Not me. None of us. As for your family, they should have developed a pretty thick hide by now."

"And me?"

Farrell smiled. "I don't know if you remember but I wrote a pretty bitchy piece about you three or four years ago. You did a dumb debutante stunt, got arrested for speeding, and I went all pious and lectured you in print."

"I didn't read it."

She had said this too quickly.

"Sure," he said smoothly. "How could you read everything?"

She leaned forward, suntanned arms crossed on the table under her breasts, chin firm, eyes staring into his. Jesus, Farrell thought, trying not to look at her breasts, I wish she wouldn't do that.

"What gave you the right to write about me anyway?" she asked. "Suppose I pulled some dumb teenage trick. Don't all teenagers? Do you sermonize over them?"

"Not all teenagers had fathers who were Presidents."

"How do you know so much about me anyhow? Do you study up on women you go out with?"

"No," he said. "You were different." This was turning out badly. How wonderful she looked. Yet she was intent on a fight.

"So I was different. A freak."

"Not at all. I just read up on you. I was curious. I pulled out the morgue folder and—"

"What a curious thing to do," she said. "Are you a necrophiliac?"

"Look," he said, "there are lots of things I *don't* know about you. That maybe I'd like to know."

"Oh?"

"Sure," he said, "like how do you spend your time, where do you go, does it bother you not to have a job, what do you do evenings when you aren't slumming with police reporters like tonight?"

The light tone didn't come off.

"I sit home and watch cable television."

She seemed curious about Haig. He tried to mine that vein.

"He's Goddamn exhausting," Farrell said. "He took a speed-reading course years ago and now he carps that all of us should. He retains everything. He takes shorthand. They insisted on it when he was a kid in Fleet Street and he sneers because we can't take it. And he gets me up at dawn every morning. The son of a bitch never sleeps."

"Why don't you say no?"

"No one says no to him."

"Maybe that's your problem."

When they had finished eating she refused coffee or brandy and got into a cab outside the restaurant. She would get herself home, thank you.

He watched the cab drive off, her profile determined, haughty.

Brophy needn't have worried.

When Sissy learned that Farrell had taken Alex to dinner there was a brief stab of jealousy. Sean was her *beau idéal*. She admired his writing, envied his range of acquaintance. No matter how she worked at it she would never possess the instinctive skeptical judgment Farrell called his built-in shit detector. And it went beyond professional admiration.

Alex said the evening had been disastrous. "I'd gotten myself into this terrible bitchy mood and he started being Irish and tough, and by the time the check came we were nearly squaring off."

Sissy's jealousy had lasted only a moment. "Gee," she said, really meaning her regret, "that doesn't sound like you *or* Sean."

"When I called him I thought it might be fun to date a reporter instead of running and shouting 'No comment!' And it would have been glorious to have seen Nora's reaction if she ever found out. She thinks the press is there to worship us, not to touch."

"Then what happened?" Sissy asked.

"Then the bitch in me came out. Even before I met him I was sorry I'd called. Men usually call me." She paused. "Then I went into my frigid Queen of the Nile number. I remembered how sincere you said he was and how interested and enthusiastic he'd sounded on the plane. So I picked up the phone and called him." She lit a cigarette.

Sissy said she would talk to Sean and assure him Alex was really not the monster she seemed.

Alex looked at her friend, the long hair, the tall, spare body, the long arms and legs, the lovely face.

"Hey, Sissy, forget it. I'm not sure I want to bother. Any guy stupid enough to be around you every day and not make even a tentative move . . ."

Sissy had wondered about that herself.

12

Gerry Brophy was, after Farrell, the best police reporter in town. He dined with mafiosi, drank with vice squad detectives, received requests from publicity-minded inmates of Attica.

"They keep scrapbooks on themselves," he told Farrell. "They like seeing their names in print."

"Sure," Farrell said. "They're just like the rest of us. A whole Goddamn population of publicity hounds."

They were drinking in an East River waterfront bar. It was February. Campbell Haig had owned the *Mail* for six months and the earth had not yet opened up nor comets collided. Circulation was up 50,000 a day but the professionals discounted that, knowing how much money Haig was spending on television commercials, on bonus coupons for housewives on Wednesday, the big day for supermarket advertising, and on newsboys.

"You've got to give him that, Sean," Brophy said. "There hasn't been a newsboy hawking papers in New York in my time. Haig brought 'em back."

Farrell grunted into his beer. So far Haig had lived down his reputation as a journalistic wild man. No topless beach bunnies had yet appeared on page three. His editorials seemed tempered by the realization that liberal New York was not conservative New Mexico.

There had been Haig "touches." A new logo, a change in the body type, additional pages of television news ("They're all out there watching television eight hours a day and we'd better not forget it!"), more racing news ("New York is one big OTB parlor!"), a "busier" front page. He hired away a distinguished movie critic from the *Times*, tried to lure Bill Buckley from the *News* ("There are too many liberals on our editorial page") and failed, promoted a young basketball writer who reported, as none of the "Establishment" sports writers had done, that one of the big stars on the Knicks had a serious, and sapping, cocaine habit.

And he had not fired anyone. That, to Farrell, and to Brophy as well, was a surprise.

The drama critic got into a fistfight with one of the five great Broadway producers. The press-room gang continued to work four-hour days for their $26,000 a year, still engineered an occasional web break to halt the presses, delay an edition, and permit them to pocket another $65 an hour overtime. One of the junior fashion writers, earning the minimum $528 a week, was seen flaunting her second mink coat. A baseball writer still picked up every Thursday his hundred-dollar "expense" money from the ball club. Men and women on the payroll of *The New York Mail* had love affairs, married, gave birth, divorced, took overdoses, borrowed money, saw their psychiatrists, lied to their wives/husbands, drank too much, chased girls/young men, cheated on their expense accounts, fought with their in-laws, died.

In spite of the well-known endangered species status of the trade, the *Mail* people, like the *News* and *Post* and *Times* people, were having, to their pleased surprise, a sort of heyday.

Not since the 1920s had there been a better time to be a newspaperman in New York. Murdoch had revived a moribund *Post*, both the *Times* and *News* were spending and promoting and stealing talent from one another in an attempt to retain their leadership. Now the *Mail* was giving signs of life. The city was ailing, but bad news sold papers. The country itself was prosperous and the national advertising poured in. The tobacco giants, banned from radio and television, swamped the papers with their millions. And there was even a new glamour about newspapers. Credit that to Woodward and Bernstein or to Redford and Hoffman. Watergate had been the best newspaper story of the century, lasting longer and with greater sustained interest than space spectaculars or sex scandals or mass murders. Watergate had not only sold papers; it surrounded journalists with an aura they had lost.

In the Lion's Head and a dozen other hangouts like it a new breed of newspaper groupies had sprung up. Girls hung around reporters the way they flocked to rock stars. And it wasn't only the young lions like Farrell or Pete Hamill or Steve Dunleavy who drew them. Fat Brophy, nearly three hundred pounds and happily married, had to shoo them away.

"Jesus, Sean," he told Farrell at the Lion's Head, "I hated to see that one go the other night. Those tight little jeans and the legs. Oh, God, my wife should look like that. She should *smell* like that."

The girl Brophy rejected had turned instead to a balding veteran of the night desk, a decent, self-deprecating fellow with false teeth who admitted the next day, "I was thirty years old and working on *The Sun* the first time I ever got a blow job. It was one of the girls in classified ads, and she had bad breath and a little mustache but I was drunk and when she got down there I swear to God I didn't know what she was doing until she did it. Anyway," he said, a blissful look on his middle-aged face, "last night was the second time!"

The girls came to the newspaper hangouts late. They tried to drink with the reporters, which was a mistake because they were usually high on pot or pills before they took their first drink and when it hit them, it hit hard. Farrell went to bed with a couple of them. The sex was fine, he had to admit that, but there was always guilt in the morning.

"Damn kids don't know the score," he grumbled. "They think we're all going to win the Pulitzer this year and go to Hollywood and write novels and become famous. They're looking for a taste of fame and we're the ticket. What they don't know is we're tired and broke and getting old, most of us will never have a thousand bucks in the bank. We've got bad livers. Most of us will die smoking in bed in some furnished room, working a couple hours a week on some half-ass copy desk for money to buy cheap booze."

Brophy looked at him. "You paint a pretty picture, Sean, all rosy-fingered optimism. You're why I fled South Boston. I was appalled by the local despair. I knew Manhattan would be a more cheerful place."

"Listen, Gerry, I'd love to be a hedonist, to wallow in pleasure. Trouble is I have this inconvenient conscience. More Puritan than Irish. Be damned if I can figure out where it came from."

Brophy reached over the bar without asking and grabbed a couple of bottles of beer. The barman was reading the *Racing Form.*

"Here, we'll drink to puritanism, to Cotton Mather and burning the Salem witches and Oliver Cromwell and—"

"No toasts to Cromwell, Brophy, you'll take *that* back."

Brophy bowed formally from the waist. "Your worship, forgive me. I knew not what I did."

"Mention another Puritan," Farrell said, "and we'll drink to him."

Brophy paused only briefly. Then, quietly, he said, "Campbell Haig?"

Farrell stared at Gerry Brophy. "Gerry, it may be pure accident but I think your nimble brain has hit on precisely why I'm uneasy about the guy. He *is* a Puritan. You're right."

Brophy looked narrowly at his friend. "But will you drink to him?"

Farrell thought for a moment. They'd been in the bar a long time but neither man was drunk. He spoke carefully now, weighing his words as carefully as a judge summing up.

"So long as Campbell Haig does nothing to hurt this newspaper I'll drink to him."

Brophy was solemn but only for a moment. Then his high-pitched Boston laugh rang out. "How in the hell could anyone damage this newspaper when you and I haven't succeeded?"

They got a cab and went over to another place but the evening ended, spoiled for Farrell, when a pretty girl smiled invitingly and said, "I've always wanted to meet you, Mr. Hamill."

Brophy exploded in glee. When his laughter died down Farrell had gone home.

Their Puritan was indulging in his favorite vice: He was reading newspapers. It was Sunday morning, the *Mail* published only six days a week, and Campbell Haig was atypically abed at eight in the morning in his bedroom at the Carlyle, surrounded by the Sunday editions of the *Times,* the *News,* the *Washington Post, Newsday,* two Philadelphia papers, and the *Jersey Record.* He had just finished his second pot of room service coffee. Outside the window Madison Avenue lay under a blanket of fresh snow. Haig had mixed emotions about snow. Blizzards made wonderful copy, great headlines, memorable photos. They sold papers. But if there was too much snow you couldn't get the papers out. You had absenteeism and stalled trucks and shut-down newsstands and commuters not bothering to struggle into the city, and circulation tumbled. A light snow like this one wasn't news yet there was enough of it to cut into the sale.

Haig was at home in hotel rooms. In London there had been a bed-sitter in Chelsea, and since then furnished apartments, hotel rooms, couches in offices. Not since McAllen had he really had a home, and he put off setting up in one. He had abandoned a half-hearted search for a Manhattan apartment. The industrious Miss Mayhew had finally given up. She would find what seemed a suitable place and her boss would refuse to go to see it, pleading other engagements, fatigue, or a growled dislike of a neighborhood, a building, a decorating plan he had never seen.

What he should really expend his time and money on was buying a good, big, comfortable house in the country, to which he could slip away for a weekend, and hang his pictures, where he could keep a horse, get in some riding, some tennis. Haig was lean and sinewy but around the middle he imagined the vaguest softening.

These musings were interrupted by the boisterous intrusion of Gideon Benaud.

"Stacked up an hour and twenty minutes over Kennedy," Gideon fumed, his choleric face as red as his beard. He had flown in on the red-eye from Los Angeles, and now, as he tossed coat and scarf and dripping galoshes to various corners of the bedroom, Haig asked:

"Galoshes? You had galoshes in Los Angeles?"

Benaud threw himself into a big chair and picked up the phone for room service.

"Winter months I always carry galoshes in my bag. Ever since I was in Miami and you insisted I fly up to Chicago and it was ten below and a foot of snow and I was wearing a Palm Beach suit and fairy Italian shoes, with no more sole to them than a sheet of newsprint."

He barked instructions for kippered herring, scones, and tea, and hung up the phone angrily. "No kippers," he roared, "and they call this a great city."

When Haig emerged from the bathroom, hair wet, tucking shirt-tails in, Benaud had covered the cocktail table with papers, computer readouts, scrawled notes from the plane.

"Sit down, Campbell," he said. "I'm about to shock and depress you."

Uncharacteristically docile, Haig pulled up a chair and sat down.

"Campbell," his business manager said quietly, "we're in trouble."

They were spending more than they were taking in. There was a cash-flow problem. Shuffling the papers, punctuating each bit of paper with a soft "Um," Haig nodded in agreement. Even without Gideon's evidence, Haig had known. He didn't need a computer to tell him. It was just that he had determined to concentrate his efforts this first year on *The New York Mail* and to let the rest of the chain limp along as best it could. He knew that Gideon Benaud would pull him up short of a real collapse.

"Um," he said again, and pushed his reading glasses to the top of his head.

"Got to sell something, Campbell. Sell off one of the papers. That or cut back drastically on what you're spending here in New York. One or t'other."

Haig got up from his chair and went to the window. Some kids were playing with sleds in the street below, now emptied of traffic by Sunday and the snow. A block away was Central Park, all very Currier & Ives. He spoke without turning from the window, his back to Benaud.

"Hate to sell a paper, Gid. Of course a couple of million would solve our short-term cash situation. But it's bound to have a depressing effect on the stock. Sell off one shopper's throwaway and Wall Street smells dissolution. 'Boy Wonder Haig Forced to Divest.' Can't you see the headlines?"

Benaud was silent. Haig turned to him and pulled off his glasses so he could run a lean hand through his brown hair.

"Look, Gid, I *know* there are economies we can make at the *Mail*. Damn shop is overstaffed by a third. People down there haven't pulled their weight in years. No automation. We could save millions by automating. That press room alone costs us four, maybe five million a year in featherbedding."

Gideon listened carefully. He knew Haig was not merely ranting.

"I wasn't in there a month before I could name you fifteen or eighteen people in that city room I'd pay off and have out of there. Lyman has no more notion of how to run a newspaper than a nursing child. The ad salesmen get no direction. Their expense accounts are the only thing impressive about them. The stereos, the engravers, the press room . . . I don't even like to think about them."

Benaud nodded. "Contract renewal time."

Haig grinned. It was not a friendly grin. "I can't wait!" he said. "But I really wanted to let things settle down this first year before I did anything drastic. I've had a couple of designers working on an entirely new look. There won't be a paper in this country looks anything like it. Did you get a price on those color presses?"

Benaud riffled through his files. "Four million and change. And it'll take nine months to build them, another six to get them into operation."

Haig crashed his fist into his palm. "Not good enough, Gid. I won't wait another fifteen months to make this paper look like today."

"It's academic anyway, Campbell," Benaud said quietly. "You don't have the four million and credit is tight as snare drums."

Haig calmed. "The Oregon paper. I've never been comfortable with that market. What would it fetch?"

"Six million, maybe eight. Charlie Messenger always had a yen for that area. Maybe he'd—"

"Messenger," Haig growled. "He hates my guts." He could still hear Messenger's growl on the phone the day Haig beat him out of the *Mail. You can have the son of a bitch and I hope it runs you into Chapter Eleven.*

"Isn't there anyone else?" Haig asked. "Knight-Ridder? Capital Cities? Time Inc.?"

Benaud said he would ask around.

"Quietly, Gid, quietly. I don't want it out that we've got a little trouble."

Maybe, Haig thought, six months is enough. Perhaps the resentment had died down sufficiently so that he could begin to make some of the hard decisions. Maybe New York had forgiven him for barging in on its private tea party.

He decided he would not wait a year. He would begin the next morning to recast Meg Valentine's old newspaper in his own image and likeness. He would start with Sean Farrell.

13

"I think it's absolutely essential that all of us rough it once in a while," Nora declared as she lay on a yellow chaise on the new-mown lawn that descended gently toward the canal and its passing pleasure craft.

There were appreciative nods from her audience, a half-dozen people ranged about her in lawn chairs of heavy wicker painted gleaming white. All but from her daughter, Alex, who lay flat on her stomach on a beach towel in the Palm Beach sun, her back and legs still wet from the pool, dramatically brown against the pastels of her bikini. Roughing it! Alex thought to herself.

An English Jesuit from Farm Street, uncanonical in boxer shorts and Lacoste shirt, shook his sunburned pate in tribute.

"Nora, I don't know how you do it. You cultivate the wilderness, you tame the aboriginals, you irrigate the desert with your charm."

Around her there rose a babble of agreement. The bearded Franciscan in his brown robe and sandals, a homosexual painter, three women her own age in Lily Pulitzer prints; all talking at once, all anxious to prove fealty. Nora, looking cool despite the afternoon heat in her Valentino caftan, smiled. How good it is to be surrounded by friends who know one's value.

The painter piped up. "And though she'll have me drawn and quartered for revealing her secret, she teaches Sunday school classes to pickaninnies on the other side of the tracks."

Nora broke the "ohs" and "ahs" of tribute. "Bascom, I won't have you refer to those darling children as 'pickaninnies.' I won't. I won't."

Alex thought for a moment her mother might stamp her foot.

The Franciscan went into a discourse on the responsibility of the leisure class. Alex got up, stretched blatantly, and said, "I've had enough sun. See you at dinner."

The Jesuit stared openly at her back and her long legs as she went.

"Alex is so lovely," one of the women murmured.

Nora threw up her hands. "But difficult. Nothing but play, play, play. No sense of responsibility. None at all."

"I'll bet she doesn't even teach Sunday school," Bascom said in a bitchy whine.

The Franciscan wondered if they might have some more of that chilled Pouilly Fuissé.

Nora Noyes rang a little golden bell. "But of course, Father, we owe it to those less fortunate, who depend so on us, to keep our strength up."

Alex Noyes stood naked on the thick carpet of her dressing room, half hearing the voices of her mother and her friends. She had a year-round suntan but even so she could feel the strong Florida sun's rays working on her shoulders, her shins, the insteps of her feet. It was good to get out of New York in February. She'd wanted Sissy to come with her but Sissy said no. She had a ton of terrific assignments and couldn't leave the job.

Alex came down alone, but it had not been fun. The voices from the lawn strengthened now in laughter. Bascom was demolishing a reputation.

Alex whirled away from the window and went into the shower. Fifteen minutes later she lay on her bed, drowsy, the sun, the swim, the softness of the silk bedspread lulling her nearly to sleep.

Wasn't she herself nearly as bad as her mother? she wondered drowsily. Neither of them really *did* anything. Well, at least she was honest about it. Her mother clothed herself in her mantle of sanctity. She, Alex, knew she contributed nothing and made no pretense. Suppose she wanted to do something. She'd been trained for nothing. What was she to do? Front for some socially ambitious new money as a P.R. adviser? Do charitable work for the Junior League? Read to old people in hospitals?

Sissy Valentine. Her best friend. She might not know what to do with men. Sissy should have grabbed that bastard Farrell and used her position, her name, her grandmother, used anything if she really wanted him. *I would have.* But at least Sissy had a profession. While Alex lay there disgruntled Sissy was working in New York, earning a wage, drawing satisfaction from her work, writing things that thousands of people read.

Now Alex was asleep in the tropic dusk, the sun falling toward the endless swamps and Everglades west of the canal. When she woke, briefly, it was dark. Later one of the servants rapped. No, Alex said. She was not hungry. Let them dine without her.

She was lying. She *was* hungry.

She slept again. Restlessly, her ripe body moving this way and that, naked atop the silk coverlet. At eleven she woke again, fully this time. She looked at her watch. Downstairs she could hear the murmur of brandy.

Alex bounced from the bed, opened the French armoire that dominated the room, pulled out a pale-blue French T-shirt, floral bikini pants, a pair of white duck trousers, espadrilles. She ran a comb through her thick short hair, a washcloth cool with fresh water across her face, brushed straight white teeth. She pushed money and keys and a driver's license into a pocket, glanced again at the mirror, and descended the back staircase.

"Miss?" a maid asked. Nothing, Alex mimed. Nothing at all. She went out through the back way, past the ten-speed bicycle and the garbage cans and the clothesline to find her car, a little Triumph. Inside they may have heard her gun the motor. It was unimportant. She crossed the bridge and drove toward West Palm.

Behind her were the chic *boîtes* of Palm Beach, the bars where she knew every bartender, the restaurants where the captains bowed. Ahead, West Palm, the "other" Palm Beach.

In a dark bar on a tropic night it was never difficult. The men found her, sought her out, pursued and wheeled and bought drinks and essayed their smoothest, most effective lines.

The man had begun with the usual line. "You know, you look exactly like the President's daughter, Matt Noyes's kid."

She gave the practiced laugh. "It's the short hair. And we're about the same age. Everyone says I look a lot like her." She gave him a phony name.

"That's a pretty name," the man said. He hitched his red vinyl bar stool closer to hers. Along the bar a couple of other men looked faintly sick as if regretting they'd not moved more quickly when she first came in alone. A jukebox played, the booths held half a dozen couples talking low or necking. There was the faint scent of marijuana. The man pretended to keep his eyes on her face but they kept straying down.

"What brings you to West Palm?" he asked. "You live around here?"

She was a schoolteacher from Connecticut, fed up with snow and children's runny noses, taking an unauthorized sabbatical. She was staying with an aunt who lived over near the airport.

That was all the line she needed. The man took it up from there, talking endlessly about himself, his ex-wife, the line of products he sold, about how freewheeling and independent he was, having the luxury of stopping work every so often, as he had now done, and just settling into a good motel for three or four days, unwinding, fishing, getting a little sun, having fun. This last with a knowing grin.

How wonderful, Alex thought, I'm bored already. And this boredom was driving out the deeper boredom of Nora and her circle.

Usually Alex was harsh in her judgment of men. They measured up or they were speedily discarded. As she'd done, perhaps unfairly, with Sean Farrell. But when these rare, frankly sensual hungers were on her, then her standards shrank to the merely physical. The man must be attractive, clean, not too drunk, no emanations of violence.

They went back to his motel. Her little Triumph followed the red tail lights of his outsized Chrysler through the streets, past the palm trees, by the shopping centers of the big town. At any corner she could have turned off, driven speedily home, been safely in bed in a few minutes. She did not turn off.

There was a bottle in the room and he poured straight drinks in plastic motel bathroom glasses and lay on the bed, glass in hand, head propped against the pillows, while she undressed to the background music of a television set somewhere along the corridor. His eyes widened when she tugged off the pale-blue T-shirt. When she was naked she had him refill her drink and she downed half of it in a swallow. Whatever her aching need there was always this one terrible moment of surrender. Being high, on alcohol or a joint, helped ease her over the momentary barrier.

He waited no longer but jumped up and grabbed her and took her then, quickly, harshly, and in a way, satisfactorily. Later, when he used more artful techniques and asked her to do this and to take that, she did so. But with less pleasure. He was asleep when she slipped from the room and ran to her car.

She drove home across the causeway toward dawn. Sober now, satiated, her guilt had begun to surface. Her sense of having once again betrayed herself and her lineage. A woman of sensibility and taste, selective in every other thing she did, except when it came to this infrequent but overwhelming hunger.

She knew there was something more out there than the pious masquerade of her mother's court and escaping from it through screwing salesmen in motel rooms. It was frustrating not to know just *what.*

14

Monday morning was cold and damp, a cutting wind off the river. Sean Farrell came downtown on the subway, lacking as he usually did on a Monday pocket money for a cab. Happily Haig had scheduled no tour for this morning and Farrell felt sybaritic arriving at the paper just before eleven. He'd gone to bed early Sunday night, he was not hung over, and despite the rotten weather there was an amiable languor about late rising and the realization that winter was nearly spent.

He went up in the big freight elevator at the back of the building and strolled into the city room, bustling now with the second edition just away with the opening market prices and replated pages sent through correcting the typos that marred each day's metro edition. One of the sportswriters had just engaged him in a discussion of a possible column on why New Yorkers were philosophically incapable of supporting a losing team, as they were once again being forced to do with the Rangers, when Farrell's eye caught the familiar sheet of copy paper tucked beneath the bar of his typewriter.

"Can you come see me if convenient this morning?" It was signed Haig.

Farrell absentmindedly told the sportswriter he'd consider his

thesis, took off his jacket and slung it over the back of his chair, and
went upstairs in his vest to listen for the thousandth time to what
he referred to privately as his master's voice.

Haig was standing. He did not bother to ask Farrell to sit. "I want
you to become managing editor," he said flatly.

"You've got an editor," Farrell said.

"I have a pleasant gentleman who carries that title. I don't have
an editor."

Farrell snorted. "So much for your great speech that first day.
'This newspaper staff can rest easy. I plan no changes.' Wouldn't you
say getting rid of Lyman was a change?"

Haig looked impatient. "You *always* say things like that the first
day. It's a convention. No one believes you."

"How many papers do you own?"

"Twenty. Twenty-one."

"And on each of them you've pledged to make no changes in the
staff and every time you've done so. That isn't a convention, Haig.
That's Goddamn *lying!*" He paused. "You really are a piece of
work."

Haig made a little bow with his head. "Thank you. Now, I need
an editor. Lyman won't do. Lyman's comfortable for the staff because he's weak. As the strongest man on the staff that probably suits
your purposes. You're the editor now, in fact if not in title. They all
look to you. Mrs. Valentine was aware of it. She told me she'd
offered you the job."

"I'm a writer, a reporter, a columnist. Find your editor somewhere
else."

"You're self-indulgent, Farrell. Lazy, self-indulgent, and a shirker.
Editing's the toughest job on the paper and you're the best man and
you won't take it."

Farrell had begun to bristle. Now he laughed. "So I'm lazy and
a shirker and the best man in the place. All in one sentence. Haig,
what the hell do you eat for breakfast?"

"Black coffee, if it means that much to you. Now, what about the
job? Taking over from Lyman?"

"Why don't you take the job yourself? They tell me you play
editor at all your papers anyway. You don't want a strong editor, you
want a first-rate clerk."

Haig looked thoughtful. "You're right. In most instances that's precisely what I want. Someone who takes orders and is bright enough to carry them out, energetic enough to follow through. The *Mail*'s different. New York's different."

There was something in his voice now that was new to Farrell. A subtle difference but it was there. "So you finally sense that," he said sarcastically.

Haig's narrow eyes seemed to zoom in on Farrell. "Really," he said, "you're too intelligent to underestimate me this way. I bought the *Mail* because I'm quite aware of how significant, how large, how unique New York is. Just why do you think I want you as my editor?" He paused. "Because I'm not a New Yorker. You are! I don't know much about the city. You do! And I want the *Mail* to be a great paper again. I can't do it with discards like Lyman. Maybe I can't do it with you. If I can't I'll pay you off and have you out of here the day I come to that conclusion. And I'll get someone else. And after him, someone else! But for now, you look like it. Lyman goes, whatever you say. Now, will you take it?"

"I'm a writer," Farrell said stubbornly.

Haig said nothing for a moment. Then, standing by the window, his back to the columnist, he said mildly, "You aren't quite correct about what I said that first day to the staff. I said I *planned* no changes. And I didn't. Had Lyman proved up to the task I wouldn't be talking to you this morning. I get no pleasure out of sacking people. It causes tensions, it hurts people, it costs money. Sometimes a great deal of money."

"Money," Farrell said bitterly, "it's always money, isn't it?"

Haig whirled. "Of course it's money. That stuff you get in a check every Thursday. The stuff people put down to pay for their *Mail* every afternoon. You know what I paid for the *Mail*, don't you?"

"Sixty million?"

"Sixty-two to be precise. And in six months I've lost another five or six. I'll be fortunate if I can keep the losses this first year alone to ten million. Next year could be better. Break even if we're lucky. That's a lot of money, Farrell. A lot of money riding on the inadequate shoulders of a man like Lyman who quite clearly is out of his depth. A fact," he said more gently now, "of which I'm sure you're aware."

Angry at himself for silently agreeing, Farrell tried to think quickly. "What about me?" he asked, a possible new evasion suddenly occurring to him. "My column is syndicated. Forty papers buy it. That's money too. I'd have to give that up."

Haig went to the big desk and glanced down at a scrap of paper. "Your column is syndicated to thirty-eight papers. You average less than four hundred dollars a week from syndication." He looked up. "One of your columns was sold to Hollywood. The film was never made. The option lapsed."

Farrell gave a brief laugh. "You do your homework, don't you?"

"I'd pay you seventy-five thousand. You make fifty now, salary and syndication."

"What sort of control would I have? Whose word would be final on story selection, on hiring and firing, on the tenor of our editorials?"

"Mine," the publisher said. "I own the paper."

Farrell threw up his hands. "I don't know why you ever bothered to offer the job."

Haig let the remark slide. "Of course the final authority has to be mine. The responsibility is. But you're posing a theoretical objection. You're a professional. So am I. During these little trips of ours around the city I've gotten to know how your mind works. Sometimes I disagree with you on details. But basically, I think we both know what we want from the *Mail* and generally how to go about achieving it. I don't want a weak editor here in New York. I want a man who's going to make tough decisions and to stand behind them. On a major difference of opinion between us I'll listen to your side. Listen and, often enough if you're as good as I think you can be, end up by agreeing with you. In those rare cases when I don't, well, I've been blunt in telling you my decision will be the one that obtains."

He sensed movement on Farrell's part and, throwing himself into a chair, he now took on a friendlier tone. "Look, I've got twenty papers to run. I've neglected them for months now. They need me. I want a strong anchor here in New York." He paused. "I need you, Farrell."

Farrell was silent for a moment. "Can you give me time to think about it? A couple of weeks?"

Haig smiled. His smile did not make Farrell happy. It was the smile of a man who had just won something of value. "No hurry," he said. "Take a week."

Alexandra Noyes flew into LaGuardia in midafternoon. She phoned Sean Farrell from the terminal.

"There's this new Bob Fosse thing tonight. Some benefit. I had to buy tickets. Will you go with me?"

No apologies, no explanation, no reference to their disastrous evening. He said, "Yes." He did not consider saying no. He wondered why her sudden about-face.

He had been at his desk in the city room, typing a few overdue letters, his column long since composed for the next day's edition. Now he gave himself over to thinking about Alex. Her voice had been indistinct, airport phones being what they were, but her words had been clear enough. When he hung up he looked over at Brophy, at the next desk, furiously tapping out a splendid story about two hoodlums, *two*, found wrapped in plastic in the trunk of a late-model Chevy in Jackson Heights. Brophy was never happier than when violence had been done. Farrell was tempted to say something to Brophy about Alex. He did not.

He went home early to his apartment in Turtle Bay to shower and change shirts. Maybe, he thought as he washed, maybe Alex Noyes is a nut case. On again, off again, a toggle switch of emotions, teasing him, drawing him on, shutting him off. Was this aristocracy's way of twitting the peasants? As sensitive as Farrell was, as suffused with *amour propre*, he recognized there was no chance at all he would have rejected her invitation.

Still in preview, Fosse's new musical work was clearly going to be a smash. During the intermission they stood in the back, smoking, chatting about nothing, saying hello and being helloed by the sort of people who show up at Broadway benefits. He knew quite a lot of them, and Alex seemed to know everyone. She was wearing something black and short, velvet, he thought it was, cunningly cut under the bosom to display her magnificent breasts. He caught himself trying to see more of her legs. They looked fine but he had the suspicion she might be a bit heavy in the thigh. Hell, he thought, there's got to be *something* wrong with her. Nobody possessed physical perfection.

Dinner, her suggestion, was at The Palm, *his* idea. The Italian waiter brought them the good, big bloody Marys. While they waited for their food he said, "I was surprised when you called. The last time we didn't seem to get on all that well."

"That was me," she declared flatly. "I can be an awful bitch. I'd phoned you on impulse and then regretted it and there was no way that evening could have worked."

"Well," he said, "I'm glad you're not sorry or anything. I hate to see a lovely woman sorry."

"I'm glad you're glad."

"Do you think a beautiful celebrity can really be friends with an ugly reporter?"

Her smile was truly dazzling; the heavy hacked-off hair moved nicely as she shook her head. "Only with a handsome one."

"D'you know one?"

"Some of my best friends."

"Name one."

"Sissy Valentine. I am *too* sorry," she said.

"Sissy *is* a handsome reporter—the only one I know." Of course she and Sissy would know each other.

"I said I was sorry."

"Okay. Can I interview you?"

"Only if you promise to misquote me. Ask me some question that gets to the real me."

"Right," said Farrell happily. "Why do you cut your hair like that?"

"I had this long hair," she said without considering. "Blond, of course. And I just got tired of seeing pictures of myself in magazines and papers and being called 'Golden Girl.' I don't always *feel* like a Golden Girl. I was tired of the constant brushing and the tangles in the morning, I was fed up with a look I'd had for a long, long time. So I had it chopped off. Why," she asked, her gold-flecked eyes serious now, "does it bother you?"

"I think it's the damnedest haircut I've ever seen," he said. "And I like it very much."

"Good."

She ate everything. She drank with him, keeping abreast through the bloodys, the wine, and the brandy. They went over to Tudor

City to a little bar with a piano and got a corner table and drank more brandy.

He told her about Haig's offer. She was the first person he'd told. The pianist, an old black man, was playing to Alex now. She was the best-looking thing in the place.

"Will you take it?" she asked.

He still didn't know.

"Why?" she asked, in that way she had of pinning equivocation.

He shrugged. "Listen, I've been around long enough. I've even had protégés. No, don't laugh, I have. Young kids who thought I was the Second Coming and they wanted to be there to say hello." There was a thoughtful instant. "And all I ever wanted from a protégé was that he had a spare couch in his living room if I got stewed, and the same shirt size."

"Then it's Haig," she said. "Dislike of Haig. Or you just don't want responsibility. Is that it? I thought all reporters wanted to grow up and become editors."

"Look, I'm a good writer," he said. "I've published some pretty good short stories. I wrote a novel that was terrible but I learned how not to do it. The next one could be good. My columns are fine. I'm a natural writer. I doubt I'm a natural editor."

"What's natural about writing? I thought it was sweat and hard labor."

"It is, I suppose. But it pours out of me. I'm never happier than when I'm writing. I'm lazy as hell in many ways but when it comes to writing I have these terrific work habits. Discipline. I work six, seven hours at the typewriter and get up feeling better than before. Fulfilled, happy. Squared with myself."

Farrell liked the way she listened. He risked revealing more of himself than he usually did. "Michelangelo said the statue is already there, in the stone. And all the sculptor has to do is chip away what he called 'the negative stone.' Get rid of what you don't need and you have your statue. In writing, you throw out everything redundant and what's left is pure and it works. I don't get it right every time, of course. But often enough to know this is my craft. This is what I do best."

"I like that Michelangelo bit," she said. "Did you steal it?"

They talked and drank several more brandies each until he heard the beginning of a slur in his own speech. But none in hers. She was clear as a bell and she was drawing him out, asking the questions. All about the job—bright questions, to the point. A good interviewer, she would be.

He knew he was being led but he was happy and he talked, talked.

"I want to stick to my art. Not ride herd on other people doing what I like to do."

"And you don't like Haig," she said. "You don't want to be taken over."

"Hell, I don't know," he answered.

Toward the end, while they walked uptown to her apartment in the cold, clear night along the river, he got the impression she was daring him, testing him against this challenge of Haig's.

"I don't think you ought to take it," she'd said. "I don't know Haig but he and you don't sound the same sort of people at all."

He was still young enough and tough enough and Brooklyn enough that Alex Noyes's opposition could swing the scales. He would resign from the fraternity of madmen and become their keeper.

A few days later he went upstairs to Haig's office and said he would take the editor's job.

Haig had barely looked up.

"Well, then," he said, "see what you can do about page one tomorrow. Today's looks like it was laid out by a drunken barber."

That evening Haig took Lyman to dinner at Christ Cella and gave him the word. He had the impression the old editor was relieved. On the next morning Sean Farrell's appointment was announced. Among the notes that fluttered in over the course of the day was a wire. "Now who'll cut the negative stone?" It wasn't signed. But he knew who had sent it.

15

The unnaturally brief winter had come to a premature but welcome end and three generations of the Valentine family greeted the equinox in individual ways.

Old Meg, weaker now, the ravages of terminal illness working their way through her spare body remorselessly, overcame her dislike of doctors and medical facilities to fly to Switzerland for a week at one of the famous spas. She would drink the waters, permit herself to be probed and cozened, and bite back cutting retorts to what she considered decidedly personal questions about her bowels. One final, desperate toss in the game of life and death. It was a pity, she thought, as the Swiss Air jumbo jet climbed over Kennedy and banked gracefully toward the sea: The political year was heating up, Campbell Haig was as much an enigma and a figure of controversy as ever, and Sean Farrell was demonstrating energy, if not always sound judgment, as the new editor of the *Mail*. She hated to be away, to be out of touch, while all this was going on. New York *needed* her at a time like this. So did the *Mail*. A stewardess arrived to plump up her pillow only to be informed briskly that she needed no such coddling. "And would you be good enough, young woman, to bring me a Manhattan, straight up."

120

Junior Valentine was traveling as well. Some new genius had mounted a seminal play in Texas, Audrey Wood had touted Junior on it as worthy of investment, and Meg's only child had flown south "for a day or two" to have a look. He had now been there two weeks. There was a girl in the cast doing a walk-on and understudying the ingenue, but Junior discerned great potential.

Sissy Valentine, pale from a New York winter and grieving over the loss of Farrell to her best friend, had taken a week's vacation and had gone out to East Hampton to open up her father's house for the season. Recruiting a sturdy Polish girl from the village, she bustled through the great rooms, dusting, polishing, moving wicker furniture onto the lawn, dickering with a local painter to redo the exterior of the house, riding along the empty beaches on a livery hack, tanning in the first slim sun of spring. At night she drove the bright yellow Jeep into Bridgehampton or up to Sag Harbor to dine alone at the Long Wharf or Bobby Van's or Melons. One evening, at a corner table in Bobby's, she had a third vodka and told herself, primly, how unfair she was being about Alex and Sean. After all, what business had she being annoyed? She had no hold on Farrell. Perhaps, if she had to do it over again, she would have taken Alex's advice, been more aggressive.

Her reverie was interrupted by the waitress. A man at the bar wanted to buy her a drink. Half annoyed, half pleased, she looked up. It was a tough-looking Bonacker who was staring at her with a moody, blatant lust. "No. Please tell the gentleman I'm leaving."

As she paid her bill Sissy thought she remembered his face from somewhere. Perhaps he had done some work on the property. As she drove away, the man was watching her through the front window of Bobby's, watching as she tooled the Jeep into Main Street and nimbly made a U-turn toward the east.

Alone in a big, empty bed in the big, empty house, she lay for a long time listening to the distant surf, to the creaks and groans and faint rappings common to great houses, to the wind coming off the ocean, until she had nearly dozed off. Then, as crude and obtrusive as his approach at Bobby's, the image of the Bonacker came to her and shattered sleep.

Sissy was not a virgin, though laughingly confessing her naiveté she would joke, "I was a junior in college before I understood why boys danced so close." But it was a joke. There had been two boys in college, two or three since then. No more. Not religious, not frigid, Sissy Valentine was a continent woman in a profligate society. She had the hungers of a healthy twenty-four-year-old. She also had standards. The Bonacker would not meet her standards. Yet now, alone in the big bed, she could see him as plainly as if he were there. His image tormented her. Her breath came faster now. Her buttocks moved slightly against the mattress. "No!" she cried aloud. She rallied her mind to concentrate on other things and finally, her body stilled, she fell into a restless sleep peopled by strange figures thrusting and tearing and biting at her. But she slept.

Sissy's brother, Willie, was also on Long Island, but only for the weekend. The star space salesman of the *Mail*, as he liked to think of himself, was, as usual, broke. It was two o'clock in the morning and Willie Valentine was standing in the corridor of a sprawling motel in Southampton, a bunch of keys held carefully, silently, in his lean hand. He moved along the carpeted corridor, trying to combine the casual stroll of a motel guest returning late with the stealthy tread of an intruder. At the first door with a plastic Do Not Disturb sign dangling from the doorknob, he paused, shifted the keys deftly from one hand to the other, chose one, and cautiously inserted it in the lock. It turned and he felt no resistance from an inside chain. The door opened and he stepped quickly inside, his excellent night vision permitting him immediately to focus on the bed. A man alone, bulky, snoring loudly. On sneakered feet Willie moved straight to the chest of drawers. There, atop a copy of *Penthouse*, the man's wallet, keys, a watch. He scooped up the watch and wallet, glanced again at the sleeper, and, as silently and as quickly as he had entered, left the room. Outside in the hall he could feel the familiar wet rivulet of sweat running from his back along the spine.

Forty minutes later he was in the parking lot inserting another key, this time into the ignition of a nondescript rented Plymouth. Seven rooms had yielded results, eight had been double-locked and prudently passed by. In one a man had spoken in his sleep and frightened him badly.

He drove the car slowly from the lot without turning on his headlights until he was on the street and headed for Route 27 and beyond it the Long Island Expressway and sanctuary in Manhattan. Now he permitted himself to think as he drove west in the night.

That last room. There was always one like that, one that would stay with him long after the money was spent, the jewelry pawned. Always one room that he would see again and again in his dreams, in drowsy moments of the day.

In this room the man was a vague, bulky figure wrapped in a blanket, the pillow half over his head. In the other bed the sleeping face of a young madonna was turned toward the bureau where Willie did his chores, her long black hair graceful and fine as lace on the pillow. She had kicked off the covers and he stood, transfixed, for a full minute, breaking his own rules, staring at her body. She wore a nightgown, one of those men bought from catalogues or in airport gift shops: transparent, strategically perforated. The filmy netting cupped the girl's exquisite breasts, the gown rode high up on her ripe belly; her legs, long and curving, bare and straddled, captured him, held him motionless. Perhaps she was fifteen. Sixteen, certainly no older. Had the man paid her for their night together? Why was she there? What had he done to her, into what postures had he forced her body, what had those legs contributed, where had that lovely mouth probed and what had it tasted? Willie Valentine's legs began to tremble, his groin to tense. He forced himself to turn away.

The car raced west on the expressway. The windows were opened against drowsiness. But there was no reason to fear. Willie would not fall asleep easily this night. In Manhattan at dawn he would find a girl. Perhaps the *Cosmo* cover girl. If not, maybe someone else. There were always girls available for Willie Valentine when he was flush with money, self-confident, triumphant. He had done it again! He had conquered fear and conscience and convention. Let old Meg keep her money. Let her die rich. He would always find a way. And as for the girl he would make love to at the ragged end of this night, whoever she was would be the dark young madonna of that last motel room.

16

Just as spring had drawn certain Valentines out to Long Island, the same warming breeze, revolving damply around the vortex of a stationary Bermuda high, drew Dick Osborn back to New York.

Osborn was an ex-mayor of New York who had left the city in disarray. His last march up Fifth Avenue on St. Patrick's Day had been unpleasant. The boos from the crowd had drowned out the pipe band ahead. It was unusual for so crass a political hack to be so unpopular with the rank and file. But Osborn had consoled himself with a new career.

An acknowledged charmer, whatever his executive shortcomings, he had gone into real estate sales and rode the boom to relative wealth. He'd moved from one ocean to another, from Gracie Mansion to a beach house in Malibu, balked at buying or selling any house and lot under a million, and made himself available to any number of attractive young women. California, he decided, was where he had always belonged. But now, like the true politician that he was, Dick Osborn began to yearn again for office. He decided that the voters had forgotten their loathing for him and that it was Dick Osborn time again.

Serious about a political comeback, he made arrangements to

sublet his house in Malibu, broke the bad news to his girls, wondered whether to sell the Alfa Romeo or ship it East. He even gave up volleyball. He had eighteen months before the next mayoral election. It was none too early to begin putting in the fix. The several fixes. He flew East.

Osborn had met Haig once before and had done none too well with him. It was when Haig had first taken over the *Mail*. On that occasion Osborn had struck in Haig an unsympathetic vacuum, and his vaunted charm had chilled, dissolved. But Osborn was not the sort of man to resent a slight. He needed the city's newspapers. Haig, he guessed shrewdly, needed an election winner. Dick set down his Vuitton luggage on the wide board floors of a splendid duplex apartment (lent him) on Park Avenue and before unpacking had Haig on the telephone.

Haig had Farrell meet him for breakfast before the session with Osborn.

Farrell hated Osborn as only New York Irishmen can hate Protestant politicians. It puzzled Haig, the westerner, who had none of the race memory of Tammany Hall that still resided deep inside Farrell's political subconscious. Now Farrell trotted out for his publisher a mixed bag of negatives about Osborn, some of it documented chapter-and-verse, some credible hearsay, some rumors too wild for checking and clearly skirting the edges of libel.

"But can he win?" Haig asked pragmatically.

Farrell laughed. "This town elected Jimmy Walker. Of course he can."

"You see what I'm driving at."

"No," Farrell said.

They were in the St. Regis, the old King Cole Bar now parsonstable white and artsy crafty. Farrell was devouring eggs. Haig pushed a bit of toast around the edge of his coffee cup.

"Let me explain."

"I never thought there was a chance you wouldn't," Farrell said sourly.

"The *Mail* is, we can admit privately, the weakest of the four dailies in town. For us to back a political favorite is nothing. If he wins, the *Times* or the *News* or Murdoch gets the credit. If he loses in an upset, we share the blame."

"Fair enough," Farrell said, waving for more coffee.

"But if the *Mail* backs a longshot, and by some fluke he wins, all honor and glory the *Mail*! Correct?"

"What if your longshot is a Goddamn incompetent like Dick Osborn?"

Now Haig laughed. "You've just described half the elected officials in the country. Anyway, I'll see Osborn. Let's see what he has on his mind, who his backers might be, how he assesses the rest of the field."

If Osborn had oozed charm six months earlier, now it was straight talk, blunt pragmatism, one pro to another. "It's me this time or a Jew," he announced as he flopped into a chair in Haig's office.

"Oh?" Haig said. "And who else do you see in the race?"

Osborn waved a suntanned hand and showed numerous white teeth. "A dozen or more at the outset. Reformers, nut cases, a Puerto Rican, a couple of blacks—they'll kill one another off. The governor will have a stooge. Some dame, maybe Bella. But they'll run out of money and commit gaffes and alienate the leadership and it'll come down to me and two, maybe three others in the primary. You want another Jew in City Hall? After these last two? Do you, Mr. Haig?"

Rather stiffly, Haig said that he really didn't care what the man's religion was.

"After Koch and Beame?" Osborn demanded incredulously. "After how they nearly wrecked us? Drove us near bankruptcy?"

Haig said mildly that Wagner and Lindsay and Osborn himself had not been Jews. Hadn't they a share of the blame?

Osborn nodded. "That's a valid point." He was in his sincere posture now. Very sincere. "I was hurt when I left office. Badly hurt. I can admit that now. I can see so clearly now what was veiled back then. I know part of the fault was mine. I've grown, Mr. Haig, and I want to be mayor again."

"And if not you, then a Jew," Haig remarked.

Osborn nodded his craggy, handsome head so that some of the graying hair fell gracefully over his forehead. "This isn't anti-Semitism talking, I don't have to tell you. My record is clean on that score. You ought to see the Anti-Defamation League scrolls I've got, the B'nai B'rith awards. No, it's just there are seasons for everything. As for vintage wines. Koch may have been absolutely right for his season. Four years from now, eight years, another little Jew boy might be perfect, say Jay Goldin. But this year? No. A WASP. A Catholic maybe. But this isn't a vintage year for Jews."

"I'm happy you cleared up my doubts about anti-Semitism," Haig said.

Osborn let the irony slide. "Listen, you run a newspaper. Newspapers back candidates. You back a winner, you sell more papers. Back a loser, tough titty. I could win this thing, Mr. Haig. I need you and I think you may need me."

A paraphrase of Haig's remarks to Farrell. Perhaps this fellow wasn't as stupid as Haig thought. Perhaps there was more to Dick Osborn than the bluster and the vulgar charm and the leonine head.

Haig stood up. "I'll think hard on what you said, Mr. Osborn. We'll meet again, I'm sure."

" 'Dick,' Mr. Haig, please."

They shook hands. Haig did not ask to be addressed as Campbell.

Dick Osborn was not the only politician wooing *The New York Mail.* In the beginning Haig met with them alone, listened, picked their brains, asked questions, and held his counsel. But as his respect for Farrell's judgment increased he was asked to sit in with Haig in these off-the-record sessions.

After a two-hour session with a real estate millionaire who had lived down his profession, made something of a reputation as a do-gooder, and now wanted to run New York, Haig shook his head.

"Listen," Farrell said in exasperation. "This town doesn't need a mayor. It needs a messiah." He got up and made himself a drink at Haig's bar. He looked at the publisher.

Haig shook his head. "Some soda water and ice," he said.

Farrell drained off half his Scotch. "A messiah," he said in disgust. "We need a messiah. All we get is hacks like Osborn and slumlords who've found religion."

Then, suddenly, there *was* a messiah. A Jew.

Haig first heard about him from, of all people, the cardinal. At a quasi-political dinner at the Waldorf, Haig was seated next to the cardinal on the dais and listened, intrigued, as the prelate told him about the work being done by parochial school nuns with black and Puerto Rican kids regardless of their religion.

"Their parents, and it's usually a mother alone, scrape the barrel to pay tuition. Not much, four hundred dollars a year, but to these women an extraordinary burden. But they shoulder it. Anything to get their children out of the public schools and into an environment of learning. A remarkable program and one I hope your newspaper will consider publicizing. Why, there's nothing like this sort of constructive energy being expended in New York schools with the possible exception of what Judah Wine is doing over in Brooklyn."

Haig set Farrell to digging up the story on Judah Wine. It turned out that Wine was an educator. Brooklyn College, graduate work at Columbia, a dozen years teaching, then the president of a local school board in one of the racial hotbeds, Crown Heights. There the gangs roamed, black and Jew, stoning one another, vandalizing the schools, terrorizing teachers. The local precinct captain joked grimly that morning fall-in took place in the high school gym because, inevitably, the school would be where the police tour would largely be spent, breaking heads, making arrests, infiltrating the drug rings, comforting hysterical teachers who had just been raped.

In four years Judah Wine had cleaned up the local schools, negotiated a rickety sort of armistice, and become a neighborhood legend whose name was becoming known around the city and beyond the precincts in which he worked. Pale, bony, wry, he spoke well, did not declaim, and apparently kept his word when pledged.

Haig had a tactic. He would say the opposite of what he believed to draw the other man out. Now, when Farrell came back raving about Wine, about his presence, his hypnotic abilities as a speaker, even before a hostile audience, his Lincolnesque looks, Haig snarled, "I suppose he'll be baptizing in the Jordan next. Feeding the multitudes. I'm wary of Elmer Gantrys."

Farrell's face fell. "I know we're supposed to be skeptical in this business, Haig, but this is a good man. A *good man*. So maybe he's not an old pro. I tell you, there's a potential here. Can't you suspend your Goddamn New Mexico cynicism for once and at least take a look at this guy?"

Haig was secretly pleased at Farrell's passion. "I'll listen," he said. "I won't promise more. But if he wants to talk I'll listen."

Campbell Haig had learned about politics in New Mexico. There they had it honed to a fine art. He had watched, fascinated, as deals were made, as weaker candidates gave way to stronger when their price was met, as judges were named and Mexican wards delivered. Haig did not consider New Mexico politics as much dirty as admirable, imaginative. Perhaps he drew the line at bribes, at ballot stuffing, at outright election theft, but when it came to patronage, to horse trading, to back scratching, to the creation of balanced tickets acceptable to every biased minority in the political spectrum, Haig had become a master. He was at home with politicos of the old school, men with white hair curling at the neck, men with great bellies and barbered faces, men who could tell you to within a dozen votes what any precinct could be counted upon to deliver when the voting machines were unsealed and the ballots tabulated. He knew he would have liked Mayor Daley, Curley of Boston, Talmadge of Georgia, the Kennedys. He'd known Lyndon Johnson as a boy and would forever wonder why the old master had let his presidency run down the drain with the filthy bathwater of Vietnam.

The well-intentioned amateurs left Haig cold. He could be comfortable even with a monster like Osborn. Dick Osborn was familiar clay. How many Osborns had he known in McAllen, men who reviled the Mexican over bourbon and wooed his vote the next election? His distaste for the noble amateur left him wary of this Judah Wine.

But Judah Wine remained in Crown Heights and made no pilgrimage to Campbell Haig's office on the river. Which might have been just as well. Haig had begun to concentrate his energies on a problem closer to home.

Haig was convinced the *Mail* must reduce its workforce by three hundred people. It would mean trouble with the unions, perhaps even a strike. But it had to be done if the paper was to survive and to make money.

"We're carrying passengers," Haig told Farrell, and his new editor agreed. Reluctantly.

It was not yet time to tell Farrell more. That time would come. Farrell was now part of management. Essential to Haig's plans to make the paper profitable. The employees respected Farrell, liked him, would take from him what they might not take from Haig.

But Haig did not tell Farrell this. Not yet.

Up on the sixth floor, where Haig reigned, where global strategy was determined and publishing philosophies argued, where mayors and governors and White House emissaries came and went, where department store presidents and ad agencies were wooed, the newspaper functioned at one level. Down on the fourth floor, in the city room, Farrell ran things and an entirely different range of concerns held sway.

His best photographer issued a passionate complaint.

"Look, Sean, they're wasting my time. I'm going uptown to Grand Central. Some asshole fell on the tracks and got decapitated. If I get a really good shot, they'll say it's too gory. They won't run the damn thing. Who the hell wants to waste time shooting pictures of a stiff's feet sticking out from under a tarp? You call that a news shot?"

A water rat, large as the proverbial cat ("Has there ever been a rat that wasn't big as a cat?" Farrell growled), was seen strolling along the food shelves of one of the waterfront bars where reporters ate. "Well, Jesus, don't eat there anymore," Farrell said in exasperation.

"But they've got the best egg sandwiches around," he was told.

Press agents cajoled the gossip columnist into mentioning nightclubs they represented and the basketball writer, a white man, accused an NBA owner of racism and was sued, and the ski reporter, who was nearly eighty, broke an ankle at Stowe, and someone riffled the cash drawer of the room where they sold stamps, and a Mafia hood slugged a *Mail* reporter covering an arraignment in Nassau County, and a copygirl got pregnant, and a reporter who thought he was the second coming of Winchell started wearing his hat in the office, and two of the editorial writers got into a brawl over U.S. policy in a banana republic, and reporters got drunk, and Farrell rejoiced over scoops and brooded over inaccuracies and wondered what strange, mesmerizing, and indefinable forces tied him to Campbell Haig's destinies and why he wasn't out in California writing screenplays and making love to young actresses with endless legs and smoky eyes.

17

Haig had nearly forgotten his off-the-record conversation with Peter Burke during which the FBI director had voiced his fear that the European malaise, political kidnapping, would inevitably reach these shores, quite probably in the great entry port of New York.

Now, months after their talk, it was about to happen.

At Miss Pruitt's School the girls still wore uniforms. Navy skirts and knee socks and Brooks Brothers shirts under, if the weather was cool, Shetland sweaters cut on the boys' model. To Petey Rossiter, coming and going along Madison in such a costume was unthinkable. She lived on Park Avenue, wintered in Lyford Cay and Aspen, knew how to drive all of the family's six cars and two trucks, smoked cigarettes (and occasionally something more), had been to Europe four times and to Brazil once, knew all the dirty words, and would soon be fifteen years old. She had long black hair, Delft blue eyes, a mouth unfashionably cupid's bow, and one of those boy-girl bodies.

As Petey and three other girls left the row of matching town houses Miss Pruitt had cleverly broken through to create her very exclusive school, they ducked into the local pizza parlor's ladies' room to roll their skirts four inches higher above the knee, to open their button-down shirts one button lower, to remove knee socks from summer-tanned and hairless legs (shaving was very much "in"), and to light their first Benson & Hedges of the afternoon. Across the street, in a rented car, Benedetto and Clarissa smoked and watched.

Pio had been left sulking at the rented house in Queens. He and Clarissa had botched an earlier kidnap attempt on the son of a banker. Shots had been fired. No one had been injured, and fortunately the police and the press had mistaken the incident for a holdup *manqué.* The fiasco had to be reported to Benedetto, who had returned to Milan leaving Pio in charge. It was then that Benedetto flew back to New York.

Months earlier they had dropped from their list of potential targets young adults like Sissy Valentine and Alexandra Noyes. Too old—adults, in fact—unlikely to win sympathy, to stir outrage from the juvenile public opinion of this child-worshiping country. Petra Rossiter was just right: old enough to understand her plight and to be cowed into obeying their instructions, young enough to evoke pity, pretty enough to titillate. And rich enough to earn the ransom.

The Rossiters owned hotels. They were not the Hiltons or the Sheratons, but when one considered the company was completely family-owned, their third or fourth place in sheer size warranted not only respect but something approaching financial awe. Nicholas Rossiter's wife was dead. The girl had no siblings. The abduction would occur in Manhattan in broad daylight. Guaranteed to rivet the attention of the sensation-hungry media, to draw the screaming headlines, to attract the sob sisters of the tabloids. To shock and to frighten. And to shake America's haughty disregard for the militant radical movement.

Petey Rossiter came out of the pizza parlor. There was a final conversation with the other girls, a bit of arm waving and laughter and swinging of knapsacks and small duffels full of books, a last girlish poke, a cigarette tossed into the gutter. Then Petra Rossiter was alone, window shopping north on Madison toward her house in the upper seventies. Benedetto touched Clarissa's arm. She nodded and slid out of the car.

Clarissa walked north, striding briskly, the Nikons and the lens cases swaying heavily as she moved, slim-hipped, jeaned, looking like the *Harper's Bazaar* photographer she had once been. The Florentine chic of knee-high, tooled boots and silk shirt blended rather than clashed with the lithe, boyish figure. Benedetto drove slowly north on the avenue. In front of the Saint Laurent boutique Clarissa overtook the girl, who was staring into the window.

Clarissa and Petey Rossiter were talking now. Benedetto couldn't hear them, of course, but he knew the script. "But aren't you Nicholas Rossiter's daughter? I thought so! Didn't I meet you at a party at so-and-so's? Are you at school now? How's your father? The cameras? Oh, I'm doing a photo reportage for *Paris-Match.* Pictures of American girls. You know, the sort of thing they do so well. *Mon dieu,* of course, why don't I get a few shots of you? Not that there's any guarantee they'll run, but still . . ."

Now they were walking together, these two children of privilege. Benedetto was himself a university graduate, *bourgeois,* "of good family." He understood class. He was a radical, a militant, a terrorist. But he recognized the commonality that existed between Clarissa and her victim. Clarissa: wealthy, educated, intelligent. And a killer.

They turned west onto one of the side streets. He drove carefully, watching through the rearview mirror and craning to see directly through the rear window. Small mistakes befouled operations. Stupid men, men like Pio, would get stopped for running a traffic light, draw attention by double parking.

They were headed for the park.

"A few trees in the background, a bit of grass, it makes everything so much more *simpatico,* no?" Clarissa asked, and the girl laughed.

They walked together.

"Ecco, there's my driver. *Minuto."*

Petey Rossiter, curious, drew closer to the car on the quiet side street with its shuttered town houses.

It was all over in a few seconds. The chloroformed cloth, the opened rear door, the shove. Benedetto had the car rolling before Clarissa had completely slammed her door.

They turned into Fifth Avenue and drove south. At Sixtieth Street they would turn east toward Queens.

18

Sean Farrell fell into the habit of saving things up to tell Alex Noyes, even though she was too often not available. He would dial her number and get the tape. "Hi, this is Sean. When you can," he would say in a light tone. He steeled himself against phoning again until she got back to him a day or two or three later. He trained himself not to wonder where she was or with whom.

She was fun to share things with, especially with Brophy on a short leash. "Got to get home to the wife, Sean," Brophy said, shaking his wattles. "She's heard about these groupies. Sean, I haven't laid a glove on a girl in years. Does she believe me? Is there any mutual trust? Like hell she does. Like hell there is."

One three-day period when she might have been in Newport or Pago Pago or who knew where, Sean saved up Coyle and Ms. Hopkins to tell Alex about.

Coyle was always there for a drink but was dangerous to drink with. On Sean's desk was a letter from the chief of production of a movie company. Coyle had shown up at a screening, fallen into the free Beefeater, talked filth in front of the leading actress, and exposed himself at a post-screening party at Regine's. When famous women ignored his advances Coyle was sure they were being coy. He would flash at them to get his message across. So far as Farrell knew the technique had never worked. What was Sean going to do about Coyle? the movie executive demanded.

It was a puzzler. Coyle was a hell of a reporter. Sean put the letter aside. He had more pressing problems.

Ms. Hopkins was a copygirl, a curvy little thing out of Radcliffe. She was sleeping with a reporter, a desk man, and the assistant feature editor. It was causing friction. Farrell called the girl in.

"Miss Hopkins," he began.

"Ms.," she said. "Ms. Hopkins."

He threw up his hands. "Okay, Ms. Now, I'm not going to start trying to regulate morals around here. None of my business, really. Until it begins to affect professional performance, relationships between employees. A city room has to function like the crew of a submerged submarine. Tight quarters, tension, heavy workload, people always brushing against one another. There's no privacy, it's noisy, people have to be considerate of one another. There's a normal give-and-take in the city room if it's any good. You see what I mean?"

"No."

She was wearing tight jeans and a T-shirt. Nothing under the T-shirt but Ms. Hopkins. Certain he was making a fool of himself, Farrell tried again. "Now, you're a very attractive person. A bright girl. I've seen your transcript and—"

"Woman," she said, "not girl."

"Yeah. And you obviously have a future in this business. Next opening that comes along as a reporter, you'll have your shot."

"Hey, great."

"But all that bright promise is going right out the window if management gets the idea you're a disruptive influence. I mean, I don't care about your personal relationships. Not a bit of it. But when there are several men in the city room who aren't talking to one another anymore, who can't work together, who—"

Her eyes widened. "Oh, you mean the guys I'm balling."

He got her out of his office. He had a hunch she was contemplating adding his own scalp to her collection. He would talk to the three men. Maybe he could get sense out of them. Otherwise the girl would have to go. Which meant a Guild grievance hearing where the whole sordid business would have to be trotted out in public.

Ten minutes after Ms. Hopkins left him Alex returned his call. They arranged to meet for dinner that night. Farrell's heart leaped; he took note of it. Did hers? he wondered.

"Jesus," he moaned later to Alex. "A Radcliffe girl. What do they teach them nowadays?"

"Why don't you ask Miss Hopkins?" Alex asked innocently.

"Ms. Hopkins," he said. "Ms."

Alex Noyes knew how to sustain him in his hour of need, if only at times she chose among her comings and goings. But as yet only with conversation and companionship. He wondered why it was going no further. She had stopped teasing. There were no sudden shifts of mood. She was no longer slumming. Still they did not make love. Why?

Where there was confusion in Sean Farrell there was unease in Alex Noyes. She was beginning to like him very much. He was intelligent. He laughed honestly and when he became enraged it was for the right reasons. He was unmarried, physically attractive, and he was quite clearly a goner for her. So what was wrong? Lying naked in her bed, half out of the bed clothes, thinking of getting up on this rainy April morning, Alex gave herself over to the problem of Farrell.

When you are the daughter of a President, when your mother is one of the great beauties of the age and still playing First Lady twenty years later, it is not easy making or retaining friendships based on foundations more solid than one's own celebrity. And love? True love? Sometimes Alex believed love was a state from which she had been permanently exiled.

Oh, there were plenty of men. Scads. But were they wooing you or a famous name, a specter, a social passport? Men on their first dates would begin by telling her how they admired her late father, the brief golden age he'd brought, his grace, his courage, his style. Worse, the encomiums to her mother, to the gallant and fabulous dignity that was Nora Noyes.

There was none of this with Sean. Like most young liberals he still venerated the dead President. But he concentrated on her. He had asked about Nora only once, had been informed fliply "My mother and I don't get along." He had dropped the subject.

Sean Farrell was like none of the men she was used to. He was tough, aggressive, eager. There was no fencing with Farrell. He didn't pretend. He knew precisely who he was and pride in his own abilities bubbled up very close to the surface. Refreshingly candid.

No, Farrell was all right. Which was the root of this annoyance with herself. She knew that for all his amiable companionship, his rough charm, his integrity, the fun they were having together, she would never love him. While he was falling quite openly in love with her.

Alex enjoyed leading men a certain distance down the garden path and then, the novelty evaporated, the game won, dropping them with a kiss, a smile. And the wispy consolation that for a time they had possessed a part of the famous Alex Noyes. Farrell, Alex concluded, was too serious to tease. But how was she to continue this pleasant and convenient relationship without hurting a man she had grown to like?

God knows, she was drawn to Farrell physically. He was the sort of man she turned to when the drive was on her. Even now, fretting about him, wondering how to drop him before he was hurt, she could visualize his face, the reddish hair, the big shoulders, the strength of his wrists and hands, the solid, impervious solidity, the sexual drive she knew was there.

Alex shook her head, the short hair barely moving. She needed help on this, on how to handle Farrell. Before she had thought the notion through her telephone was in her hand and Sissy Valentine was on the line.

They met at Jim McMullen's for lunch.

"Alex," Sissy said soberly, "I believe you and Sean are as close to perfect for one another as any people I know."

Alex nodded and sipped her bloody. What had it cost Sissy to say that? How could Sissy sit there and tear strips off her own hide this way? My God, Alex thought, it's not as if she were a cripple or had a harelip. She wasn't the little match girl. This was Sissy Valentine, tall, beautiful, rich, decent, bright.

"And Sean just may be one of the finest writers we have in this country today," Sissy continued. "His instinct for words and for—"

"I know," Alex said, "I know about the negative stone."

Sissy looked blank.

Instantly Alex regretted the remark. Farrell had never told Sissy about the negative stone or anything like that.

So Sissy's contribution was to encourage Alex to become more involved with Farrell. As if Alex needed that. She watched herself getting in deeper each time they met, fighting it, helpless against it. For example, the thing with Campbell Haig.

"What a dreadful man. What a rude, singleminded boor!" Alex exclaimed to Farrell one evening after they had stopped by Haig's suite for cocktails with the governor and other powerful men who were now part of Haig's set.

Farrell laughed.

"He spent the whole time we were there on the phone in the other room," Alex said indignantly. "We never even saw him. If you invite people in for drinks you talk with them. You don't disappear to conduct your business."

Loyally, Farrell pointed out that Haig had twenty other papers. He worked eighteen hours a day. It was natural that at seven in the evening there might be calls from the Coast that . . . Besides, Alex had insisted they flounce out before Haig had a chance to greet them.

"An awful man!" Alex reiterated, and Farrell changed the subject.

That night, in bed alone, Alex resolved not to air her dislike of Haig again with Sean. She was getting to sound like a wife, railing at her husband's boss. And she did not want to foster any sort of husband-wife relationship. She must break it off. She really must.

But Haig! Even his living arrangements smacked of the sort of *nouveau riche* behavior she associated with men like Hugh Hefner and Bob Guccione. Hotel suites and now, Farrell had let drop, a turreted Victorian mansion on the Hudson. Someplace he could "get away to" and spend hours on the telephone away from his guests. He had probably not even bought the house himself but had sent that Gideon Benaud. She could visualize the scene: "Gideon, go buy me a house somewhere. Make it large, vulgar, showy, impressive. Have lots of phones. Get someone to decorate it and have a lawn put in where people can sit while I ignore them."

There! She was doing it again—wifely resentment of Farrell's dreadful boss. That was it; the limit. She had to break it off with Sean.

A week later she was in Farrell's bed, staring at the ceiling at four in the morning, listening to him snoring gently beside her and wondering how the hell it had happened.

Well, she thought, and where fled *snobbisme*? Here was the daughter of a President of the United States falling into bed with an Irish newspaper reporter who had not only not gone to Harvard but hadn't gone to any college. Not even a Catholic one. She could see him dimly as he slept, the solid, blocky body pink, the reddish-blond hair mussed, the attractive, vaguely little-boy face relaxed in repose.

He had been the one to do the running.

"Look," he said one evening as they ate spaghetti and drank carafe wine in Little Italy, in one of the obscure and wonderful restaurants he knew. "You can trust me. I haven't got an axe to grind. I'm not out to make an impression on anyone. I'm interested in you. I don't really give a damn about making points by being seen with you. It's you I want. Not your image."

"You know," she said, "I'm leaving myself wide open to say so, but I think I believe you."

Farrell put down his fork and spoon. "You *think* you believe me? That's a hell of a thing to say to the most truthful, the frankest, the most intellectually honest degenerate you know! There's only one thing I want from you."

She laughed, encouraging him to go on.

"Sure," he said, "I'm damn near as famous as you are already. If they ever make a movie out of one of those columns, I'll be *more* famous. Richer, too, if the studios don't screw me with that two-tiered bookkeeping system they all use out there. What do I need you for?"

"You want to seduce a President's daughter."

"Why, hell, there must be *dozens* of Presidents' daughters hanging around. I could be wasting my time with one of the Nixon girls or Margaret Truman or Amy Carter. But no. I waste my time with you. I think that speaks very well of my evil intentions. Lechery! That's one of the few really pure motivations left. Nothing complicated about it.

I wouldn't care if your old man were a toilet seat manufacturer from Scranton and your name was Annette Funicello."

"You want to improve your social standing."

"Why, ever since I started to hang out with you it's played hell with my reputation around town. In the places that really count. The Garden, for example. And the Lion's Head. And P. J. Clarke's. You think I need you on my arm to get a seat to the Knicks or to get into Steinbrenner's box up at the stadium? Or get a drink at Bradley's? Some of my best friends, some of the really outstanding drunks in this town, refuse to associate with me anymore. I've been accused of social climbing and sobriety."

"It's awful," she said, "what evil companions like me will do to a person."

"Dreadful," he agreed. "Have some more wine."

She held up her glass to be refilled. "So I'm bad for you."

"Terrible," he said. Then he dropped the mocking tone. "And I wouldn't have it any other way."

She looked into the open, cheerful face. "Good," she said.

They went uptown in a cab to SoHo. A discotheque called Flamingo.

"They've got better lights at Xenon," Farrell told her, shouting over the din, "but this is the best sound system in town."

A plump faggot with orange hair came over to them. He clapped his hands and then kissed Alex on both cheeks.

"Oh, Alex, and I thought you'd abandoned us."

She made the introductions. "This is Sean Farrell, Richard. He's been explaining about your sound system."

"And I thought I was taking you someplace you'd never been," Farrell told her after Richard left. "I thought you'd get a kick out of slumming in a joint like this."

They danced.

The music was loud and pounding, the lights mesmerizing, the dance floor crowded. And it was hot. Steaming.

Finally Farrell, sweat streaming down his flushed face, called a halt. "Hey, I need a drink. A break."

"Can't take it, Farrell? Too much for you?"

He stared at her. He was not aware of it but his look was one of sheer hunger. Alex was wearing navy-blue velvet jeans and a silk shirt. The short blond hair was damp, her face slick with perspira-

restive, Petey decided that she could do something to help herself.

She had read all that stuff about Patty Hearst and she was sure that at some point either torture or sex would enter the picture. She was quite certain she would prefer sex.

There was a small bathroom off the bedroom. A sink, a toilet, some soap, a towel. Again, no window. But they had replaced the light bulbs. The first two days she had not taken off her clothes. On the third she'd washed her underwear and knee socks. On the fourth, her shirt and her underwear again. On the fifth, at the time Pio was due to bring her meal, she decided to force the issue a bit. When he came into her room, smiling pleasantly as always, she was seated crosslegged on the narrow bed, barelegged, wearing her school sweater and, apparently, nothing else.

"Good morning," he said, and then immediately regretted it. "Keep her disoriented; don't let her know the day or the time," Benedetto had warned. Since they ate pasta at every meal, this would not be difficult if only Pio would remember to be more circumspect.

"Hi," Petey said, her shoulders squared to push out her small breasts against the sweater. She took the tray and smiled her thanks. Pio started to leave and then, undecided, stood near the door, smiling and looking at her.

"You okay?" he asked in accented English that Petey found cute.

She put the tray next to her on the bed, moving just slightly so that he could see she was wearing panties.

"Sit down for a minute?" she asked, patting the bed.

"Sure," he said uncertainly. He sat down. Petey Rossiter looked into his face, at the straight white teeth, the wavy black hair, the good nose. Under other circumstances she could really dig this guy. Wouldn't the other girls at school just die! Pio sat there grinning, crossing his legs and recrossing them.

Well, Petey thought, if he isn't going to make a move . . .

She leaned over then and posed her face just in front of him, her lips pursed, her eyes half closed. His kiss was tentative, unsatisfactory.

"Hey," he said, "why you do that?"

She pouted. "Why, didn't you like it?"

"Sure," he said, "but . . ."

She lay back against the headboard of the bed, one leg flexed, the other straight out, long, tanned, slender. She did not say anything more but fixed her Delft eyes on him.

Pio was not very bright but he was not retarded. After a little while he stood up. *"Cara mia,"* he said, "you are too clever for me. I am supposed to be your captor, you know. You are a prisoner, not, I regret, a guest."

"Does it make a difference?"

He nodded. "I am afraid it does," he said, his regret genuine.

Three days later Benedetto, frustrated by Nicholas Rossiter's adamancy and the failure of the New York police to leak the kidnap story to the press, bored with this dreadful neighborhood and Clarissa's uninspired cooking, fretful over the idiot Pio, who was clearly infatuated with their captive, wrote his letter to Gerry Brophy of *The New York Mail.*

tion, the thin shirt plastered to her torso, snug across her breasts.

He leaned down so his mouth was close to her ear.

"I have a better idea," he said.

She hesitated for a moment. The music, the lights, the drinks, the sweat drying on her body, still trickling down the middle of her back toward her beltline, all combined to arouse desire. All right, she thought, he wants to. More important, so do I.

They went to his apartment. She preferred it that way; less likelihood of running into someone she knew. Wherever Farrell lived she knew it would be anonymous, featureless, private.

It was.

He scuttled ahead of her, tossing magazines off a couch and onto a table, picking up a newspaper from the floor.

"Well," he said defensively, "I never claimed to be much of a housekeeper."

There were whorls of dust and feathers under his bed. She noticed them as she undressed. He was in the bathroom, water running. Should she turn off the light? Let him do it. It was his bedroom. A small radio, battered and dusty, perched on the windowsill in front of venetian blinds that might have last been dusted last summer. She pulled back a comforter and the top sheet and slipped into bed, cradling the pillows behind her head. The bathroom door opened but Farrell passed the bedroom and went down the hall somewhere. She could hear his movements, the sound of glasses. Then he came into the room again, a half grin on his pleasant face, holding a brandy bottle and two glasses.

"Only one balloon, I'm afraid," he said, handing her the brandy glass. "The other's a jelly glass."

She took the balloon and as he poured she said, "Do you always spoil your guests?"

"Always. Except when they spoil me."

They made love the first time and then he filled the glasses again. Alex felt slightly drunk. But good. Then he took her glass and put it on the floor.

"I know what," he said.

"What?" she asked dreamily. Presently she said, "Oh, yes. Don't stop," her voice thick and excited.

When she woke, Farrell was asleep, curled like a small boy in a corner of the bed.

Alex pulled herself up, wedging a pillow behind her back, and reached for a cigarette on the night table.

Funny, she thought, how good she felt. No postcoital guilt, no muted blues. This shabby, dusty, old-fashioned apartment, perhaps that was what made the difference. A man lived here: slippers under the bed, books on the wall, snapshots, dog-eared magazines, a battered typewriter, clothes in a closet, a tennis racket stranded atop a bookcase.

She turned to watch the sleeping Farrell, the big, pink body, the reddish face, and the matching hair. She remembered Dartmouth, that first time. He'd been a redhead too.

Farrell moved in his sleep, curling toward her.

Alex Noyes stubbed out the cigarette and shoved down the covers to look at her own body. Her nipples stiffened in the predawn chill. Below them, foreshortened by the angle, her waist, her belly, the sticky wetness of her thighs.

She turned again and whispered, "Farrell . . ."

He stirred, and when she put her hand on him, he woke.

She slouched back against the headboard, breathing hard and waiting. Perhaps the difference was Farrell himself.

Word of Sean Farrell reached Nora in Newport. Nora reacted without the usual consultations with resident clergy.

"But, Alex," she said into the telephone, "a *journalist!*"

"Oh? What journalist?"

"Don't fence, Alex. This Mr. Flanagan you're spending so much time with."

"Farrell. Sean Farrell. And who said I'm spending time with him?"

"Oh, Alex," her mother groaned. "It's so . . . so *squalid.*"

That evening Alex Noyes called Farrell and told him she was getting a cab and would be at his apartment within the hour. She enjoyed these nights in bed. Now her mother's opposition added to their appeal.

She was no longer feeling even vaguely guilty. Or fretting about Sissy.

As for Farrell, he didn't really care why Alex was coming. It was enough that she was.

19

Petey Rossiter awoke. It was dark. There was the initial panic, then the memory of the Italian woman, of going toward the park. After a while she remembered the car and the man. She sat up. She was on a bed. She could move around, sit up. She felt the floor tentatively with her feet and then stood. A bit woozy. She moved slowly away from the bed; a few shuffling steps and she met the resistance of the wall. Well, that was something. She moved laterally then, searching for a door, trying to plumb the dimensions of the room. On the second wall after the right angle turn she found the knob. It turned, but the door did not open. She continued her way around the room. Small, very small.

She was totally clear as to what had happened. The thing the parents of girls like Petey always feared. Oddly, she was not frightened. The thought of Clarissa was comforting. The woman was civilized, educated. The thing had been cleverly planned, intelligently. These were obviously professionals, not weirdos like the people who took Patty Hearst. There would be a ransom demand, her father would pay it. She would be home, perhaps within the day.

The trouble was, Nicholas Rossiter did not pay. Not at once, not the way Benedetto had counted on. When Clarissa had called there

143

had been none of the hysteria they expected. Rossiter, informed that his only child had been kidnapped, had fumed for a few moments, then, quite coolly, had asked the demands. None, as yet, he was informed. Those would come later. In the meantime, he was to maintain his own counsel and not, repeat not, inform the authorities.

Benedetto knew that the police would be notified. The FBI as well. He was not concerned that this was so. In fact, he was relying on it. Much of the effectiveness of a terrorist *apparat* depends on the broadest possible public notice. How better to inform a broad public than to insist on secrecy? The police were reliable. One could have confidence in them to leak the information.

Three days later, when Clarissa called a second time, Rossiter said that he would not pay.

"Someone, somewhere, has to hold the line against people like you," he said somewhat stagily. Clarissa, under orders, had not argued or issued threats. She'd simply accepted his response and hung up, her demand for a million dollars hanging in the stuffy air of a subway telephone booth.

Petey had no idea her father had decided, singlehandedly and with his own child at hazard, to bring a worldwide terrorist organization to ruin by the simple tactic of saying no. She was still cheerfully confident the ransom would be paid, the radicals would count the unmarked bills, and she would be set free on some isolated stretch of the Jersey Turnpike any midnight now. Benedetto, calculating heatedly, decided that for the moment the girl was not to know her father had refused. If Rossiter continued adamant, of course, they would tell her and get the subsequent hysterics on a tape to mail to him.

Meanwhile Petey's strange existence in the inner room of the house in Queens took on routine.

Clarissa did the cooking. Except that there was an awful lot of pasta and no milk, it wasn't bad. Pio played waiter when Clarissa didn't. Petey preferred Pio. Much cuter and more talkative. Dante, he told her his name was. At first she was afraid of his solemn, handsome face, the black hair slick over his ears. By the third or fourth meal he served she was not frightened at all. He had begun to grin, his English pleasantly accented, his face softening into a boyish desire to please. By the fourth day, when she began to be restive, Petey decided that she could do something to help herself.

She had read all that stuff about Patty Hearst and she was sure that at some point either torture or sex would enter the picture. She was quite certain she would prefer sex.

There was a small bathroom off the bedroom. A sink, a toilet, some soap, a towel. Again, no window. But they had replaced the light bulbs. The first two days she had not taken off her clothes. On the third she'd washed her underwear and knee socks. On the fourth, her shirt and her underwear again. On the fifth, at the time Pio was due to bring her meal, she decided to force the issue a bit. When he came into her room, smiling pleasantly as always, she was seated crosslegged on the narrow bed, barelegged, wearing her school sweater and, apparently, nothing else.

"Good morning," he said, and then immediately regretted it. "Keep her disoriented; don't let her know the day or the time," Benedetto had warned. Since they ate pasta at every meal, this would not be difficult if only Pio would remember to be more circumspect.

"Hi," Petey said, her shoulders squared to push out her small breasts against the sweater. She took the tray and smiled her thanks. Pio started to leave and then, undecided, stood near the door, smiling and looking at her.

"You okay?" he asked in accented English that Petey found cute.

She put the tray next to her on the bed, moving just slightly so that he could see she was wearing panties.

"Sit down for a minute?" she asked, patting the bed.

"Sure," he said uncertainly. He sat down. Petey Rossiter looked into his face, at the straight white teeth, the wavy black hair, the good nose. Under other circumstances she could really dig this guy. Wouldn't the other girls at school just die! Pio sat there grinning, crossing his legs and recrossing them.

Well, Petey thought, if he isn't going to make a move . . .

She leaned over then and posed her face just in front of him, her lips pursed, her eyes half closed. His kiss was tentative, unsatisfactory.

"Hey," he said, "why you do that?"

She pouted. "Why, didn't you like it?"

"Sure," he said, "but . . ."

She lay back against the headboard of the bed, one leg flexed, the other straight out, long, tanned, slender. She did not say anything more but fixed her Delft eyes on him.

Pio was not very bright but he was not retarded. After a little while he stood up. *"Cara mia,"* he said, "you are too clever for me. I am supposed to be your captor, you know. You are a prisoner, not, I regret, a guest."

"Does it make a difference?"

He nodded. "I am afraid it does," he said, his regret genuine.

Three days later Benedetto, frustrated by Nicholas Rossiter's adamancy and the failure of the New York police to leak the kidnap story to the press, bored with this dreadful neighborhood and Clarissa's uninspired cooking, fretful over the idiot Pio, who was clearly infatuated with their captive, wrote his letter to Gerry Brophy of *The New York Mail.*

20

It was not, Gerry Brophy concluded, a vintage season for crime. For obscure reasons known only to men who conversed in various Sicilian dialects, the Five Families were, temporarily, at peace. Not a single victim, trussed and the back of his head shot away, had surfaced in the trunk of a parked car in Queens in weeks. The East Side Cover Girl Murder was only a memory. And it was with acute embarrassment that Brophy had handed in his only bylined story of the week, the murder of an elderly dog fancier on Central Park West, bludgeoned to death by parties unknown while he knelt to scoop up a turd deposited by his Pekingese.

One night on the way home Brophy promised himself things would get better the next day. But in the morning he found himself suffering from a severe hangover. He couldn't recall a worse one. He couldn't recall anything.

"I hope it's a brain tumor," he had told his wife that morning in bed, "because they can cure them with surgery."

It was what came, he reflected sadly, of drinking with cops. It was essential in his trade to do so. But hard. He much preferred to drink with gangsters. Cops drank cheap booze, never picked up a tab, and became mean when addled. The gangsters ordered the best, paid for

147

everything, and when they were drunk either whistled up a couple of girls or wept for their dead mothers. Last night it had been a cop.

They were at the bar of the "21" Club, not one of Gerry's usual haunts. The cop, a detective lieutenant, was assigned to spend the night with a Teamsters Union official. "You know, just go drinking with him so he don't get hassled." A more civic-minded reporter might have seen a good yarn in this, the misuse of city funds and city personnel on behalf of a private citizen from St. Louis. It never occurred to Brophy to write it. When you covered a police beat you did not rat on the cops. Otherwise you found yourself missing stories, refused access to prisoners, and barred from cruising around in prowl cars. This lieutenant had two hours to kill before picking up the teamster. After a while he began showing his revolver at the bar. He had a problem; he was a piece flasher. Brophy had drunk a lot to make up for the lousy company.

Most of Brophy's mail he threw away. He threw away press releases unopened and pleas from aggrieved litigants unanswered. He threw away letters written in pencil except those from prisons. Those he read; sometimes they produced leads he could follow. If they were just the usual whine about bad raps and prison mistreatment he threw them away. Clarissa had typed Benedetto's letter. Brophy read it, threw it down on the desk, put his feet up, and smoked another cigarette. Then he pulled the telephone toward him and asked information for the number of the Rossiter Hotel chain.

"I don't know what you're talking about," Nicholas Rossiter told him when he'd finally reached the executive more than an hour and eight phone calls later. "My daughter is fine."

"Good," Brophy said jovially, "I'm happy to hear it. Kidnapping is a terrible thing. And where is she now, your daughter?"

Brophy was a bulldog, each vague reply drawing another incisive question. After ten minutes of fencing Rossiter agreed to meet him.

Brophy waddled through the city room to Farrell's office. He went in without knocking, tossed the letter on Farrell's desk, and then turned to close the door behind him. A door always open. Farrell looked up at him, saw the excitement in the reporter's face, and picked up the letter.

"Well?"

"I think it's a true bill," Brophy said. "I got a date to see old man Rossiter in an hour."

"And the girl's missing?"

Brophy shrugged. "He keeps saying no, I keep hearing yes."

Farrell glanced at his wristwatch and then checked it against the Western Union clock on the opposite wall of the city room. "Nearly noon," he said. "The third edition's gone. You think we might have something for the final?"

Brophy shrugged.

"If I get it, you can have it. But I wouldn't start replating on the basis of it. I've got a hunch there's something here. Maybe it *is* a snatch. Maybe the kid ran off with some stud and she's trying the extortion caper on the old man. Maybe she's on drugs. There's something, though. I feel it in my Goddamn toes."

Farrell knew about Brophy's toes. "Okay," he said, "phone me from up there. Don't use a Rossiter phone, find a booth."

"Do bears shit in the woods?" Brophy inquired pleasantly. Thank God his headache was fading.

Nicholas Rossiter was fifty years old, silver-haired, glacial. Brophy didn't like him. Nor the office, a platinum-and-blond wood oval in the middle of the sixty-seventh floor of the General Motors building on Fifth Avenue. He had been passed on from one receptionist to a second, from one cool secretary to a second and then a third. Now Rossiter sat across a broad desk making a temple of his fingers and masking himself behind blank croupier's eyes.

"I'll be frank with you, Mr. Brophy," the hotel owner said.

"Good, Mr. Rossiter." Brophy knew he was about to be lied to.

"I don't like your newspaper. I don't like Mr. Haig's brand of journalism. I agreed to see you simply to assure myself you're not going off half-cocked with some incredible yarn that might embarrass my family or me or this company."

"We don't want that," Brophy said, pulling out a cigarette.

"Do you mind not smoking in here?" Rossiter said. It was not a question.

"Yes," Brophy said mildly, and lighted up.

Nicholas Rossiter's hands tensed, whitening the knuckles. This is a man with a very bad temper, Brophy thought, or a man who is very nervous.

"Now, your daughter . . ." He looked down at his notebook. "Her name is Petra?"

Rossiter nodded. "Petey, for short."

"Well, whoever wrote the letter got that right, at least," Brophy said. He handed over a piece of paper.

Rossiter looked at it. "This is nothing but a Xeroxed copy," he said.

"Sure," Brophy nodded. "The original's in the safe at the office."

"Aren't you supposed to go to the police or the FBI with a note like this? Isn't that the standard procedure?"

"Oh, hell, on a cheap rag like the *Mail* we can't afford them standard procedures. We just go out and ask people questions, you know, pester hell out of them until they tell us something."

"As you're doing now."

Brophy nodded. "Like now," he agreed.

It was pulling teeth. Three times Rossiter stood and ordered Brophy from the room. Twice Brophy threatened to leave. Rossiter mentioned two senators, one cabinet member, and several governors. Brophy said they could all fuck themselves.

"I'll call Campbell Haig!" Rossiter shouted.

"Fine," Brophy said. "It'll get me a raise."

Rossiter threatened to pull all his chain's advertising from every Haig paper in the country. Brophy threw up his hands.

"The Goddamn Mafia hit men I deal with every day don't pull that shit," he said.

That was when Rossiter ordered him from the office and meant it. Brophy phoned from the lobby of the building.

"Don't tell me," Farrell said wearily, "he's already called Haig. Come on back."

They let the final edition go. Brophy didn't want to tip the other papers to what was clearly, at least for the moment, *his* exclusive. "Let it simmer awhile," he said, "until I develop it a bit."

Farrell agreed. They didn't want to go off half-cocked. Haig nodded. He didn't want to lose the advertising by publishing half a story when they might get the whole loaf.

When Benedetto saw there was nothing in the final edition that evening and still nothing in the first edition the next morning, he was furious. "These Americans," he raged. "All these advertising agencies and television networks and public relations experts, and nothing! *Nothing!*"

Shooting off the kneecaps of Turin bank presidents was more profitable. He jerked his head toward the inner room, including

Petey Rossiter in his denunciation. What did she do all day but lie around half naked (a furious glare at Pio) and eat? Always she ate! Did the girl think the Brigades were made of money?

"Perhaps," Clarissa said, when Benedetto had stopped shouting, "perhaps a stronger letter this time. Perhaps with an ear lobe or a finger inside."

Pio's stomach did a little jump. Jesu Maria! Were they to start cutting pieces off that lovely child in there before he had her even once?

Benedetto nodded solemnly. No fingers, not yet. But another letter, yes. Again to this Brophy. And maybe a phone call. The inefficiency of postal systems in every country was a well-known scandal. Perhaps the first letter had never arrived.

Brophy had not been idle. A check of the school indicated the girl was absent. Had been for more than a week. Some family matter, he was told. Rossiter refused to take his calls. His sources at police headquarters were curiously mute. Then the second letter.

"Dear Mr. Brophy," it read. "Our patience is limited. We do not understand why our humanitarian plea for justice has gone unheard. We had been told you were a crusading journalist and that *The New York Mail* was a great and independent newspaper. Does Mr. Nicholas Rossiter control you as he controls his business empire? To repeat our earlier message: We want one million dollars in cash from Mr. Rossiter and certain political statements printed in full in your newspaper. We will wait another forty-eight hours. After that time has elapsed we are not responsible for the safety of Mr. Rossiter's daughter."

Farrell looked at the pudgy crime reporter. "So you're a 'crusading journalist,'" he said.

". . . 'on a great and independent newspaper,'" Brophy responded, "don't forget that."

"Haig can use it in a house ad," Farrell said.

Haig was closeted with the advertising director. He looked up impatiently when Farrell was shown in. "Tell Macy's no," he said. "Make any excuse you want and tell them we owe them one. But they can't have that position." The ad man went off pouting. "What is it?" Haig asked.

Farrell slid the letter across the big desk. Haig picked it up and read it. "We have to run it," he said quietly.

Farrell nodded.

"Page one?" Haig asked.

"I'd think so. Reproduce the damn thing. Let it all hang out. Have Brophy write an open letter in reply, pleading for the girl, that sort of thing."

Haig screwed up his face. "Oh, come on," he said, "that's Jimmy Breslin stuff. 'Son of Sam Rides Again.' "

"It'll sell papers," Farrell said doggedly.

Haig shook his head. "Just the letter, page one. You can make the last two editions. Run some inside stuff, pictures of the girl, of the old man, of the mother."

"The mother's dead."

Haig slammed a palm on the desk. "Presumably there are pictures of her when she was alive," he said.

Farrell knew he deserved that.

"And a listing of Rossiter's holdings, the hotels, the other stuff," Haig went on. "An estimate of his wealth. Then some speculation on who's behind this. Are they blacks? Europeans? Or just a couple of hoods out for the ransom?"

"What about famous kidnappings of the past?"

"Save it for the second day follow. And make damn sure Brophy calls Rossiter and—"

"He won't talk to Gerry."

". . . and leaves the message we're going with the story regardless. If he wants to make a statement, we'd be delighted to run it in full. And get a line from the FBI and the local police."

"Don't do my job for me, Haig," Farrell said.

Haig looked at him for a moment. Then, coldly, he said, "Fine, just be sure you do it."

While Haig lunched at his desk Nicholas Rossiter phoned. "All right," he said without preamble, "I'll give you your statement." He was angry.

"Then she *has* been kidnapped?" Haig asked.

"Ten days ago, no, nine. I had a ransom demand, with some political demands attached to it. The FBI have it."

"Then you were playing ball with the kidnappers when you wouldn't talk to us?"

The answer brought Haig's swivel chair smartly upright.

"No," Rossiter said quietly, "I'm not playing ball. Not playing ball at all."

"I don't understand," Haig said.

"I'm simply going to refuse to pay. I refuse to purchase advertising time on television or run newspaper ads to promote their perverted philosophy. I'm telling them to go to hell."

"But your kid?"

"I won't be held hostage to this sort of radical filth. Someone has to stand up to these people. It might as well be right now. Else there'll never be an end to it."

Haig exhaled slowly.

"Rossiter," he said, trying to maintain control, "your daughter is fourteen years old. These characters threatened to kill her. Isn't *she* the one being held hostage?"

That afternoon the Petey Rossiter kidnap story broke in the *Mail* and Alex Noyes's stomach did a little flop.

"Oh, Sean," she began as he walked in the door of her apartment that evening, "how you can print such awful stuff? That poor little girl . . ."

There was nothing feigned about his confusion. "What awful stuff, Alex? I don't understand."

"The Rossiter girl. The one who was kidnapped. All those big headlines. Maybe it sells newspapers but . . ."

Farrell tossed his copy of the paper on a hall table and pulled off his raincoat. Icily, trying not to say anything he would regret, he walked past her and into her living room. "Now, tell me what we've done wrong," he said, "and I'll try to supply the rationale. That is, if you care."

"Of course I care! And I'd just *love* to hear your rationale." She had gone as cold as he had.

Speaking slowly, precisely, he said, "I suppose you think the *Mail*'s story put this kid in peril. That we went ahead anyway because it would guarantee a big sale today. Is that what you think?"

"Well, yes, that's what I think. Yes." But she sounded less certain.

He nodded and began pacing the room.

"Cactus Haig strikes again! Yellow journalism! Sensationalism!

Criminal irresponsibility! Right? Isn't that what your mother would say?"

"My mother and I are very different people," Alex said quietly, "but, yes, on this, perhaps we might agree."

"I'm sorry, Alex. That was uncalled for."

"Yes," she said, "yes, it was."

He threw himself into a chair.

"Do you want a drink?" she asked.

Her voice was calm now, her antagonism flown or suppressed.

He shook his head. "No, nothing. You go ahead."

She went into the kitchen to mix a drink. Then he was standing behind her, his hands at his side, instead of around her waist as they would have been normally.

She had no appetite for battle. She felt drained, her anger at the headlines, the heartbreaking photo of the girl, oozing out of her.

"Sean, I don't want to fight with you."

"Okay," he said, his voice throaty and stifled.

Now his arms snaked around her and she sagged back against him, the drink forgotten, the argument, and there was only his body and hers, only the two of them alone standing in the kitchen.

He turned her slowly and leaned down to kiss her lips. Just the once, and gently. Then, as gently, he turned her and, his arm still around her waist, he led her back into the living room.

"I don't want to fight with you," she repeated, dropping onto the long couch and holding up her arms to him, drawing his big, tough body hard and close to hers.

Now that her anger was still he told her about Petey's father, of his megalomania, his refusal to negotiate, his cold sacrifice of his only child.

"But why didn't you put that in the paper? Show the world what a bastard he is."

"I wanted to. Haig wouldn't let me. He wants to save the girl but he wants the advertising too."

"I hate that man," she said.

Two days later, Petra (Petey) Rossiter walked into a precinct house in Woodside, Queens, leading a young terrorist named Pio (or Dante, there was still some confusion on that point) by the hand,

and would, over the next several days and exclusively, relate the story of her miraculous escape from the clutches of the Red Brigades to fat Gerry Brophy and *The New York Mail.*

Petey found herself overwhelmingly drawn to the *Mail* and its star reporter in a way that maddened the rest of the media. And to a large part of the news-eating public, which nonetheless bought up each new edition.

At the time every other paper, every newscaster, was castigating the *Mail* for risking her innocent young life to sell extra copies, Petey was refusing to talk to anyone else. It seemed the height of youthful perversity, equal to Patty Hearst's turning bank robber. Anger at the Haig paper reached an all-time high until it seemed the *Mail*'s "kidnapping" of Petey was more heinous than the action of the terrorists.

The simple secret was that to Petey it seemed that her moment of glory was given to her by the paper that broke her story. And Brophy's fat Irish charm made her love for his paper complete. "Uncle Gerry was the only one who cared," she told the world. Up to that point her father, fearful of giving his hotels a bad image by putting a lid on a story so big, had let Petey have her affair with the *Mail.* But the "Uncle Gerry" quote put an end, for the time, to Petey's public life. She was kidnapped again, this time by her father, and shipped to a place in the West Indies in care of an aunt who proved a more effective captor than the terrorists.

Charges against Pio were discreetly dropped. It seemed unwise to discourage his kind of defection to the ranks of capitalism. Pio disappeared, some said to a bellman's post in an overseas Rossiter hotel. Benedetto and Clarissa eluded the law for a season or two, only to be massacred in a hideout near Florence by a company of carabinieri.

21

The bad trouble with the unions began in June, earlier than Haig expected. As was customary, a minor incident was to blame. "Some damnfool thing in the Balkans" had ignited the First World War just as Bismarck had lugubriously predicted. Not even Haig could have foreseen how it would start.

There were two bars within a block of the *Mail*. Leo's was the hangout of the men who wore shirts and sometimes ties to work: writers, editors, reporters, some salesmen. The other was the Print Shop. Leo's was considered slightly more elegant in its cuisine, cleanliness of its toilets, the frequency with which a bar cloth mopped up the spills from the dark, polished wood. The Print Shop was celebrated for a pack of dogs that hung about scrounging scraps, for the filth of its glasses (most patrons prudently drank their beer from the bottle), and the surliness of its barmen. These things endeared the Print Shop to the hard-handed men who drank there; they invested it with a certain cachet. Legend held that an outsider, drinking sullen and alone there one day, was accosted by a typesetter who demanded to know his business. The typesetter was rudely rebuffed, and in righteous anger he and two companions carried the stranger across the road and dumped him into the river. Just then a squad car cruised by. The three men, thinking quickly, dived into the water and rescued their victim, and were later cited by a grateful city for gallantry.

On a June day one of the paper handlers, a man called Brasky, had been ticked off in the morning by his foreman. The paper handlers were great beefy fellows with huge forearms and lumbar problems deriving from manhandling 2,000-pound rolls of newsprint from the freight dock, where the Canadian tractor-trailers unloaded them, to the bowels of the press room itself. There was a little cog railway that ran from the dock to the press room and then spurs of tracks leading to each unit of the mammoth Goss press. The paper handlers rolled the paper onto the cog railway and then, at the other end, rolled it into position to be threaded onto the press. Brasky had arrived at six that morning in less than top form. He had not gone home the night before but had drunk beer until midnight, picked up a whore, risen from her lumpy bed in a dingy room in the East Village, and without shave or shower reported for duty. When the Print Shop opened at nine Brasky had nipped out through the loading shed for a bracer. At ten the foreman had cursed him for permitting a roll of newsprint to slip carelessly off the cog railway and for the remainder of his shift Brasky, red-eyed and hung over, had alternately sulked silently and muttered dire threats under his whiskey breath. At two in the afternoon when his shift ended Brasky had informed a pal that he was "going to see about this shit."

An hour later, very much out of his element, he was drinking in Leo's. When his foreman came in Brasky had thrown down his glass and punched the man, breaking his nose and knocking out two teeth. It would have ended harmlessly enough had the foreman been permitted to square accounts. Instead a couple of space salesmen who should have been out making calls pinioned the foreman until Brasky stalked out. The next morning the foreman had Brasky suspended. The shop steward promptly called for a grievance procedure. The mechanical superintendent backed the foreman and refused to reinstate Brasky.

To the foreman, whose nose had already begun to heal, the site of the assault was the issue. "What the hell was he doing in Leo's?" the foreman demanded righteously. "If he'd of punched me in the Print Shop I would of taken the matter no further."

Although wags in the city room delivered mock orations on the sanctity of Leo's as a watering spot for "the better classes," the shop steward and his superiors at the paper handlers' local were not amused. There had long been whispers about Haig. "He's a union buster," officers of the various locals muttered darkly. It was his history in the West, it was the pattern they thought they saw developing now in the Brasky affair. Brasky was a troublemaker, no more important to them than he was to Haig, but trade union officials deal in paranoia. They always assume the worst of management, and they are rarely disappointed. The foreman had dug in his heels, declared he would not handle another shift at the *Mail*, ever, if Brasky were reinstated, and in his own small way contributed to the hardening of opposing positions. It would never do for a union to accept mildly the dismissal of a dues-paying member. Neither was it tactically sound for management to fail to back up its executive, even one as low in the hierarchy as a paper-handling foreman. It had been a quiet season in New York labor-management relations and over at *The Village Voice* a columnist seized on what he gleefully termed "*l'affaire* Brasky."

"Campbell Haig," he wrote, "is a boss in the finest tradition of New Mexico union busting. He is accustomed to dealing with poorly organized wetbacks. It would be prudent for Mr. Haig, whose college nickname we are told was 'Cactus,' to realize that this is New York City, the strongest bastion of organized labor in this country, and not a dusty hamlet on the Rio Grande."

The *Voice* columnist, while underestimating Haig's sophistication and totally wrong on his supposed abuse of wetback labor, had touched on a weakness in the publisher's makeup; Haig still did not understand New York and New Yorkers.

Before he took over the *Mail* Haig had gone to Washington. His own senator as well as Speaker Tip O'Neill and the Secretary of Labor had met with him. He asked who was the best labor lawyer in New York. It was the chairman of the Senate Labor Committee who nominated Zachary Feinberg.

"He's worked both sides of the street, Campbell. Counsel for the ILGWU, assistant Secretary of Labor, associate General Counsel for Chrysler. Knows everything about labor. And labor law. But he won't come cheap."

He hadn't.

"I need you," Haig had told Feinberg, sensing from the first that to fence with this man would have been pointless.

Feinberg listened. He set his fee. Without hesitation Haig had pulled out a checkbook to scribble a check for a year's retainer.

"But when do you want me?" Feinberg had asked.

Haig gave him a thin smile. "You'll know," he said.

A few days before *l'affaire* Brasky, Sulzberger of the *Times*, as the senior publisher in New York, had summoned his fellow press lords to a private room in the University Club. Before the elevator took Haig to his floor it descended to the bath level. He smelled steam and heard the snorts of naked, paunchy men in the old pool. Perhaps it would be better, he fantasized, if he spent his evening here. But he remained in the elevator as the doors slid shut and it began to rise.

Feinberg was there before him. With Gideon Benaud. When serious negotiations began it would be men like those two who did the running. The principals, Haig and Murdoch and Sulzberger, would make the substantive decisions but they would stay away from the bargaining table. In that way a Feinberg of the *Mail* or a John Mortimer of the *Times*, when the unions proposed something unexpected or tried to force an issue, could say, "I have no instructions on that. I must consult with my principals." The principals never entered the room until the negotiation was completed and it was time for the handshakes, the signatures, and the smiles.

Sulzberger, Hunt of the *News*, Murdoch, Haig. They were the principals. Yet really, Haig thought, only Murdoch and I can speak without consultations. He has a board, one assumes it never meets. I have a board. It meets to ratify what I have decided.

The labor lawyer for the *Times* was introduced. "We have some nine months before the contracts expire at the end of next March. We have suggested this as simply the first in a series of informal meetings to prepare what we hope will be a unified front. We at the *Times* feel that . . ."

As the lawyer's dry voice droned on Haig leaned back in his chair, his legs out before him, relaxed, youthful, lithe. He watched his fellow publishers. Murdoch was listening carefully, his high forehead creased in thought, his strong fingers playing with a sharpened pencil. Sulzberger, who undoubtedly knew precisely what his own lawyer would say, listened nonetheless. Hunt of the *News* whispered comments out of the corner of his mouth to Kracke, the labor specialist.

Feinberg was up now. "Newspaper contracts differ widely even in contiguous communities," he said. "The decline of big-city dailies has been matched inversely by the rise of the suburban papers. Right here in New York *Newsday* on Long Island, the *Bergen Record* in New Jersey, Gannett up in Westchester, are murdering us, not because of the excellence of their product or the brilliance of their editors but because their union contracts permit them to put out large-circulation newspapers with a fraction of the work force we are contractually obligated to retain. The press room is perhaps the most outrageous example."

Haig had written this speech for Feinberg the night before. Now, as the lawyer spoke, Haig watched the faces of his rivals, the other publishers, trying to see in them some hint of how they would behave nine months from now when papers were struck and employees walked and machinery was sabotaged and bricks hurled through windows and trucks burned and people beaten up and millions in advertising were lost and still more readers had abandoned the daily paper for television.

"At the *Mail* we have two hundred men in the press room. *Newsday*, with approximately the same circulation, has eighty. We think we could do very nicely with fifty or sixty. The men work an average of four hours a day and are paid an average of nearly thirty thousand dollars a year. We have documented instances of pressmen who work two hours at the *Mail*, and are paid for a full shift, then hop into a cab and go over to the *Post* or up to the *News* to work another two hours and be paid for yet another full shift. Mr. Haig thinks it's time to face up to the issue of press-room manning."

Feinberg sat down. Haig said nothing. There was some chat.

Someone, perhaps it was Mortimer, was concerned about the appearance of things as opposed to their substance. Someone else took it up. Mightn't they, he asked, consider retaining competent public relations counsel for the climactic moment when management and unions had to fish or cut bait?

"I mean," he said, "Carl Byoir or Rogers and Cowan or someone like that to help get across to the public in general that we are reasonable men with a reasonable argument? That the unions have no monopoly on virtue, that we too have a valid case?"

Haig had snorted derisively, his only outburst of the meeting. Gideon had beamed upon him, delighted at Haig's control, his refusal to behave as expected, as the wild man from the West.

After two hours Sulzberger smiled graciously and thanked everyone for coming. He went out of his way to shake Haig's hand a second time. Unity among the management of all four papers was essential, he reiterated, sounding sincere. Haig nodded noncommittally and turned to hurry Zachary Feinberg and Benaud out.

"All very cordial and charming, Campbell," Gideon Benaud remarked as they went out into Fifth Avenue to look for cabs.

Haig nodded. "Too damned cordial and charming. No one even mentioned the drivers. We can send executives down to Oklahoma to learn to type on VDT's and run the presses. But it's all an exercise in futility if the drivers won't deliver the damn papers."

Feinberg said that, surely, that was given. It hadn't been mentioned simply because it was so obvious.

Haig looked dark. "It's the obvious things people fail to account for."

Several cabs came along and the others took them, but Haig wanted to walk uptown to the Carlyle. He wondered, as he walked, whether he was right joining with the other New York papers. Maybe he ought to go it alone, the way he usually did.

He was eager to challenge the unions, to get a real contract that promised real improvements, and yet with a new editor in Farrell and himself so new to the city, perhaps it was better if the test were not faced until next spring.

It was a pleasant June evening and Haig at last succeeded in quieting his doubts about the other publishers. He went to bed feeling reasonably confident. Feinberg had handled himself well and Gideon was, well, he was Gideon.

Four days later Brasky punched his foreman and the nine-month grace period before the union crisis had evaporated.

22

Sissy's birthday fell on a Saturday. Meg Valentine, back from Switzerland, showing a better color but with death eating its way through her, insisted she would give her granddaughter a party.

"I'll throw open the house. Have your friends all come. Insist on pretty dresses, black tie. I'll have some of my own pals in to provide the proper note of decadence."

Sissy laughed and ran to kiss the old woman.

On Friday her friends at the *Mail* took Sissy to dinner at a dingy place in the Village after work. The music critic, an aging homosexual who cultivated apples on his Connecticut farm and wept openly during concerts he found sympathetic, arrived in a cluster of helium-filled balloons. There were presents. Silly, wonderful gadgets and junk in tissue paper and pink ribbons filled the table. The waiter came and swept half of it away to make room for drinks.

"Careful there," someone cautioned him, "it's a party."

The waiter was Italian. He gave Sissy a kiss and sat down with them. "One drink," he said, "only one and then I go back to work."

Alice Jobert, who weighed two hundred pounds, kept cats, and banged out a home-decorating column, felt they were slighting Sissy.

"I wanted them to take over Studio Fifty-four for the evening. But they're so *cheap.*"

Dworkin, the financial writer, pounded the table. In his high-pitched voice he recounted his visit to Plato's Retreat with another man who was doing a piece about it for a magazine. Dworkin customarily restrained his enthusiasm for ten-point jumps in the Dow, but now he wanted to tell everyone about Plato's. "Naked women, naked men! Everywhere. A woman wanted us to join a threesome! Unbelievable!"

Dworkin had been married for fifteen years and his friends believed he had never yet seen his wife naked.

Alice shook her head. "I don't like dirty talk like that, Dworkin, you little orgiast."

Dworkin's smile was blissful.

Sean Farrell came in. He went straight to Sissy and kissed her on the mouth. "Sorry I'm late," he said breezily, snatching a chair from the next table and shoving in between Sissy and Alice, "but Haig called a meeting of department heads. I'm lucky to be here at all." He had brought no gift but to Sissy it didn't matter. She was feeling terribly grown up, terribly happy. To have Sean there at all, to have been kissed on the mouth, to have her friends see it, well, that was sufficient.

"Haig," the music critic said. "Ugh!"

Farrell grabbed the waiter's arm. "Black Label and soda," he ordered. Turning back to the table he said, "I dunno. He's impressive. Damned impressive. He knows more about circulation than the circulation director, more about classified than the classified guy . . ."

". . . and more about news than the editor?" the music critic inquired sarcastically.

Farrell laughed. "Sometimes he does. Sometimes he does."

Dworkin started to tell Farrell about Plato's.

Alice Jobert would have none of it. "Shut up, you poisoned dwarf," she said pleasantly. "I want to hear about our peerless leader."

"Well," Farrell said seriously, "Haig can be, like any of us, a pain in the ass. Meetings at five o'clock after a long day. Inspection tours at dawn. But he's a newspaperman down to his toes, a businessman as well. And you don't usually get the two in combination. And don't let that drawl fool you. He's tough, he's smart, and he listens. I'd say your grandma could have done worse than Campbell Haig, Sissy. A lot worse."

Sissy smiled at him. "And Haig could have done worse naming an editor," she said.

"Naked women, naked men. Everywhere!"

Dworkin was drunk. Alice Jobert threw a fat arm around his thin shoulders. "As I see it," she said, "Brasky did nothing wrong in knocking down that foreman. But entering Leo's? Well, now, that was an outrage. Don't you think, Dworkin, you little scoundrel?" Her arm was constricting his skinny neck and although his mouth, in the middle of his red face, was open, no sound came forth.

"Brasky," the music critic declared stentorially, "is the Battleship Potemkin of our society."

Alice liked that. "I hear he's hired himself an agent, affects pince-nez, and is holding a weekly salon, like Madame Recamier. He'll be all the rage in society in another month."

Sissy laughed. "Nora Noyes will be taking him up next," she said, and then, remembering that Sean was there, suddenly fell silent. No one noticed but Farrell.

"*Vive* Brasky," the music critic cried. "*Aux barricades avec* Brasky!"

Dworkin finally freed his balding head from Alice's clasp.

"Profligate!" he shouted drunkenly. "I'm profligate! Throwing over fifteen years of marriage for one night! Naked women, naked men. Unspeakable lewdness!"

Alice embraced him again.

"I love you, you profligate gnome."

The party degenerated before anyone ate. Sean took Sissy to dinner in the "21" Club's bar. They were both hungry.

The red-jacketed waiter brought drinks and menus and Sean said, "You know, it's damn good to see you again. I mean, outside the office."

She smiled. "I know. I feel that way too."

"Not only seeing you but being able to have a few drinks with the guys again. Since Haig made me editor I've been cut off from all of that. Brophy won't drink with me. Goes home to his wife."

"Ah, he must be really desperate."

Farrell laughed. "And not a mass murder in weeks. Poor Brophy. He's liable to go into decline."

"All three hundred pounds of him."

"Two eighty," Sean said firmly, "not an ounce more. I won't have a snippy little cub reporter slandering our great men of letters."

The meal was like that, pleasant office gossip. The way it was before Sean had become editor, before Haig, before Alex. Farrell insisted on wine. "It's your Goddamn birthday, kid. You have absolutely no say in the matter." He ordered knowledgeably. He had, indeed, come a long way from Gerritsen Beach. She was tipsy now, nicely so, and more in love with him than ever. But still they talked not of themselves but of the wonderfully skewed people they worked with and knew so well.

"Blackman is at it again," Farrell said. "How can he do it at his age?" Blackman was the paper's former Moscow correspondent, up in his sixties. Married to a young Mohawk Indian woman and drinking a pint of rye every night on the four to midnight shift.

"He sends copy kids out for it," Farrell said. "Usually it's their money."

"Don't I know it." Sissy laughed. "I used to be the copy kid."
That started Farrell on Langhorne, the old police reporter.

"Coyle told me Langhorne used to scare hell out of him. Langhorne used to go up to Sing Sing to cover all the executions, out of state on the big ones. Langhorne would do an imitation of how they jerked about on the end of the rope. And he'd tell just how the flesh smelled when they got it in the chair."

"Thank God I've finished eating," Sissy said. Over coffee she asked, "How's Alex?"

"Oh, well, you know Alex. Here today, gone tomorrow. Always flying off somewhere. Love-hate relationship with her mother. Won't see her for months, then off to Palm Beach or Newport for a week. I dunno. Maybe I'll never understand Alex."

"No?"

"Look, you know Alex as well as I do. And you know me. I'm gone on the girl. Totally. I have this awful suspicion I'm making a complete ass of myself and I go right ahead. I dunno. I'm not twenty. I've been around. There *have* been others. Still . . ."

Sissy didn't say anything. She left his words hanging in the air, in the pleasant hum of conversation, the ring of glass, laughter, waiters rattling crockery. Did Sean want her to play big sister? Didn't he even suspect how she felt about him?

"At first," he said after a moment, "at first I thought it was just the novelty. I mean, she's a hell of a good-looking girl, but I know a lot of pretty girls. But the President's daughter! I've never before gotten excited about a big name. They're my stock-in-trade. I've always had a healthy skepticism about the bullshit. Now, with Alex, suddenly I'm a green kid again."

There was more of this.

Finally, depressed by what he was saying and feeling rocky from the drinks, she reminded him her grandmother was giving a party for her the next night and she'd better get some sleep.

When he dropped her at her apartment he kissed her again.

"Well, happy birthday, Sissy. You deserve all the happiness you get."

She smiled. It was mind numbing that he could really not know what she was feeling.

Sissy. Little sister. For the first time she disliked her nickname.

Brasky's union was proving stubborn and so was the man himself. Haig had Zachary Feinberg and then Feinberg and Gideon Benaud sit with him. No, Brasky had declared with a flourish, he would not accept simple reinstatement. He wanted a public apology. The foreman was equally mulish.

"Mr. Benaud," he'd said, "if we let this bastard get away with punching me no foreman will ever chew out a man for wasting time again. You think you've got problems now with productivity? Just wait if this Brasky gets away with it. Just wait. They'll be demanding beer breaks every hour and paperback novels in the crappers to wile away the hours."

"I hate to get into it myself, Gideon," Haig told Benaud. "Better to keep top management above the fight until there's a really big issue. Something fundamental. Not this goon Brasky."

"The thing's a cancer, Campbell," Benaud said.

Haig gave in and summoned the paper handler to his office. Brasky arrived wearing what must have been a new suit, a starched white shirt, and a necktie very nearly knotted around his thick neck.

"Sit down, Brasky," Haig said.

The big man sat, sullen, uneasy, kneading one huge hand with the other.

"Now look, you don't want to be responsible for a work stoppage, do you? Not when the whole business can be settled with a simple apology? A handshake?"

Brasky stared at the carpet. And when he finally spoke his words had a dogged, persistent quality as if they'd been rehearsed.

Haig threw up his hands.

"Damn it, Gideon," he said after Brasky had been ushered out, "I'd rather referee a scrap between a drunken wetback and a redneck cotton farmer."

Gideon regarded the ceiling and urged his employer to remember the biblical account of Job's patience.

Haig was patient for a day. Then a roll of newsprint broke loose somehow in the press room, smashed some machinery, and put two units of the press down for two days.

"Damn it, Gideon, if that wasn't deliberate sabotage I've never seen any. We haven't lost a roll off the cog railway since we bought the *Mail*. It's their way of backing this thug Brasky!"

Benaud shook his head. "Finesse, finesse, Campbell. How many times have you told me that?"

"I'll finesse them," Haig muttered angrily.

He let Benaud fret for half a day and then, his anger spent, urged Benaud and Feinberg to meet informally with leaders of the nine other printing trade unions to see whether they might talk sense into the thick heads of the paper handlers.

"One mean drunk," Haig said, "could shut down the *Mail*. Throw twelve hundred people out of work. Deprive a million readers of their daily paper. It could spill over to the *Times* and the other papers as well. Is that what they want? Put it to them. Is Brasky an issue worth striking for?"

He paused.

"Tell them one other thing. This is—what?—late June. And July and August are low-revenue months. If I have to take a strike on this idiot Brasky business, I'd sure as hell rather take it now than in the fall, when we'll have fat papers again. Tell them that. Use my name."

Gideon repeated the message back to Haig.

"Good, you've got it," Haig said, "I want their answer by Monday. Let them have the weekend to stew about it. I'll be in the country. I don't want any calls from them. If they're unclear on anything they can phone you or Feinberg and you can get me. I'm not going to be dragged into this mess if I can help it."

He took the eight o'clock train Friday evening from Grand Central to Mayfair, the retreat Benaud had found him at Rhinecliff up the Hudson.

23

"Looks like more sabotage," said Gideon on the phone. "I hate to say so but that's how it looks."

And it did. Saturday morning was the easiest day of the week for an evening paper. You set type once, run off a couple of hundred thousand fewer copies than during the week, and unless City Hall is dynamited, you put out but one edition and you never, never replate.

Yet on this Saturday morning there had been web break after web break, each break in the long, seemingly endless roll of newsprint forcing the huge presses to stop their roaring rush of papers. After the third break the foreman had called the mechanical superintendent at home, the man had come in, inspected the roll, and ordered an undamaged roll installed in its place. Two hours and fifteen minutes lost, fifty thousand copies unprinted. Someone had been at the offending roll.

Haig listened, not giving in to the luxury of rage. Benaud knew this mood well, even over a long-distance phone. Haig's unnatural, icy control, his terse questions, his refusal to explode, sent shivers coursing along the older man's spine, reminding him, so many years later, of Beaverbrook in his chill ferocity.

"Okay, Gideon," Haig said, "I'll take a train in this evening. Meet me at the Carlyle. We'll have dinner, work out our strategy. Better get Feinberg. Farrell as well."

"Farrell?"

"Farrell. It's time Mr. Farrell learned what these bastards are doing to his paper and get on to Pinkerton or Wackenhut or whoever is the best security agency these days. I'll want men stationed in the paper dock, in the press room, at the front and back doors by the time the lobster shift arrives midnight tomorrow."

"Pinkertons, Campbell?"

Haig ignored the question. "And call Phillips in California and LaPlante in Texas and maybe Koenig in Chicago. Tell them I want a dozen of their best men, trustworthy people, company men, who can set type and run presses and engrave pictures and who might like the chance of a few weeks in the big city. I don't want them sent out yet. But they're on standby. Tell them to pack some clean shirts and draw some money. If the unions pull anything Monday morning I'm not going to let them shut the *Mail* down. I'll run it with *fifty* people if I have to. And put out a better paper than we're getting now."

Benaud was sitting in the lobby of the Carlyle when Haig got there. His red beard, his hulking frame, the wise old eyes were tonic to the publisher. Haig rubbed his hands together.

"Well, Gideon, like old times, eh? A fight on our hands. Pity the Beaver couldn't be around to see it."

They went upstairs to Haig's suite. He got on the phone.

"I want four steaks, salads, lots of black coffee in a hour. Send up some beer, some Perrier water. What? How the hell do I know how the steaks should be done? Do half of them rare and half well done." He slammed down the phone.

"Do you have a cigar, Gid? I feel the occasion warrants having one over the quota."

Now that the waiting seemed to be over, the time for action arrived, Haig was no longer brooding over Brasky. He wasn't even angry. There was a job to do now, a job whose parameters he understood as well as any man in the country. He'd had newspapers struck before and he'd gotten out editions, late and full of typos, slim papers with ads fouled up or left out, full of wire-service copy and canned features, terrible papers, but he'd gotten them out. Through

chanting picket lines and bottle-throwing thugs, through police lines
and through fire bombing.

"By God, Gideon, this is an awful cigar," he said. But there was
a grin on his face as he exhaled the foul smoke.

Farrell and Feinberg arrived, and Haig insisted they eat before
getting into why they were there. Farrell noted, with amusement,
that Haig addressed him as "Farrell" or "Sean" while with Feinberg
it was always "Mr. Feinberg." There was an old-world courtliness
about Haig. Especially with an outsider like Feinberg who was on
retainer but was not an employee. Dinner was pleasant, no one
seemed concerned over Haig's vague approach to how steaks should
be broiled, and the talk was relaxed. Haig talked a good deal about
the country surrounding Rhinecliff. Amazing, he said, that so near
to Manhattan there were still small towns where people rode horses
and drove old pickup trucks, where there was space, real space,
where the back roads were as appealing as back roads anywhere.

"I'd always imagined New York, not the city but the whole state,"
Haig said, "to be one great urban sprawl. Each city's suburban slum
backing up against that of the next. Yet here you can travel for miles
between the towns. Staying away from the main roads, of course.
There's no escaping the shopping centers and the fast-food outlets
and the rest of that depressing blight."

Feinberg said, "Your advertisers, you mean."

Haig laughed. "I take their money, Mr. Feinberg, but that doesn't
mean I have to endorse their existence."

Benaud told stories of old Beaverbrook. Farrell was entranced.
The stories were good and he was seeing yet another side of Camp-
bell Haig. This unexpected passion for open country, for example.
The man could have been Thoreau at his first sight of Walden Pond.

The waiter cleared away the dishes and Haig said, "Gideon, you
tell Farrell and Mr. Feinberg what happened this morning. I'll fill
them in then on what I think our response should be."

Benaud told them. He was careful not to go beyond the morning's
events. He understood Haig, knew the publisher would outline his
plans in his own time, his own style.

"The bastards!" Farrell said. "And you're sure it was sabotage?"

Benaud nodded. "Demanding a bit much of coincidence for it not
to be this time," he said.

"Jesus!" Farrell said. He had friends in all the unions: teamsters, bartenders, the lot. He had been a member of the Guild. But this struck at the heart of his passion. Farrell lived for getting out the paper.

Feinberg asked a couple of technical questions and then Haig stood up.

"I've heard it said that I'm a union buster. Not true. I accept the necessity for unions. I may not like them very much but they're a fact of newspaper life. At the same time"—and he was pacing now —"we have got to win some concessions, reduction in the work force, some streamlining of the work rules, attrition perhaps, or in ten years we'll be out of business. So I was prepared for confrontation in some form next March."

He looked around the room at the three men. "It looks very much as if we are to have our confrontation now."

He sat down now and asked Benaud if the paper handlers struck over Brasky, which, if any, of the other unions would cross the picket lines, and which would stay out.

The pressmen, Benaud thought, might stay on the job. Creegan, their chief, was something of a statesman and the pressmen had a long-term contract. He was unsure about the Guild.

Haig snorted. "I can hire fifty reporters tomorrow and Farrell can turn out a paper without the Guild."

Farrell started to say something and then checked himself. Better to hear this thing all the way through. This is, he told himself, the legendary Campbell Haig. Haig was tough "but fair." They always added that. "A son of a bitch but direct. Never says one thing to your face and another when you've left the room. His word is good. But the bastard will fight. He'll fight like hell."

Once, when a negotiation had dragged on endlessly and become mired in stalemate, Haig, exasperated, had asked the union committee: "Then every damn thing is nonnegotiable. Is that what you're telling me?" And when the labor men had nodded yes, Haig had smiled, a terrible smile none of them would ever forget.

"All right," he said, reaching into a vest pocket and producing a ring of keys, "here are the keys to the place. *You* buy the paper. *You* run it. *You* pay the bills. *You* meet the payroll. *You* run the bloody show! From now on it's *your* newspaper!"

He'd tossed the keys on the bargaining table and walked out. It was six hours before they could find him and get him back, six hours in which the unions had decided that perhaps not all of their positions were all that nonnegotiable.

That was Campbell Haig.

Benaud completed his assessment.

"Okay," Haig said, "half of them may walk. Maybe all of them. But the only really crucial union is the drivers. We can write and edit a paper with nonunion people, we can set type, we can engrave pictures, we can print the damned thing. But if we can't get the paper to the newsdealers, we're shut down. Gideon, have you had any sense of what *they* think?"

Benaud shook his big head. "Cozy, Campbell, they're playing very cozy. Upchurch has an election coming up. He's got tough competition. He can't afford to appear too chummy with management or the militants in his local would draw and quarter him."

"What about the Teamsters?"

Feinberg said, "Mr. Haig, you get Teamsters in here and you'll never get them out. They'll have everyone in the place organized before you know it. The payoffs alone would break you. Better to make a deal with your own drivers or even take a shutdown."

Haig looked thoughtful. "All right," he said, "so we can't predict what the unions will do. Here's what I've done: I've got some good men on our other papers ready to fly in to New York if we're struck. Gideon's contacted the big syndicates. We can buy all the canned material we want. AP and UPI will both sell us full service for the duration."

He paused now, knowing that what he would next say would surely bring reaction. "And I'm going to insure we have no more sabotage. I'm bringing in Pinkerton guards at midnight tomorrow." He was looking at Farrell.

Farrell exploded. "Now wait a minute. I've been with you up to just now. I may not like it all but it makes sense from management's point of view. But Pinkertons? Armed guards in the *Mail*?"

Haig continued to look directly at Farrell. "Would you rather have someone wreck the presses the way they did to Kay Graham down at the *Washington Post*? Then where's your precious newspaper, your million loyal readers?"

Farrell got up. "It's only prudent to keep an eye open, I grant you.

Keep your foremen on their toes. I have friends down there, I can pass the word. We can eliminate sabotage ourselves if we're alert. But armed Pinkertons?"

"You prefer to be shut down?"

"No, and you know damn well I don't. But this is old-fashioned strike breaking. Guns! Pinkertons! If you want to set up that asshole Brasky for beatification, if you want to make another Walter Reuther of that clown, with blood streaming down his face like outside the Ford plant when the goons came in, well, you just get your Pinkertons. I guarantee you a bloodbath down at the *Mail.*"

"Can you guarantee me the paper will be published if I don't?" Haig asked, angry now too but trying to rein it in.

Farrell swore under his breath.

"This isn't dialectics, Farrell," Haig said, "this isn't theory. This is real life. Either we publish or we go out of business. Grow up, Farrell, stop the debating society postures."

Farrell wheeled on him. "This is class warfare, pure and simple. You're turning this Brasky episode into an us-versus-them situation. You've let it all escalate out of all proportion. One day a drunk slugs his foreman. The next day you're sending Cossacks into the street."

"Riding down women and children," Haig said sarcastically. "A very noble speech. Eugene Debs would be proud of you. And now that you've said it, are you still the editor of the *Mail* or do I look around for your successor?"

Benaud looked from one man to the other. Haig, cool and cutting, gauging his man; Farrell, explosive, red-faced, fists clenched. Sean took a step toward his publisher, his heavy shoulders sloping, his hands held low and menacing, his eyes on Haig's.

"Now wait a minute," Gideon said, jumping up with startling bounce to step between them. "Look, now, Sean, what is it that pinches? Is it the Pinkertons themselves? I don't think Campbell ever had it in mind to have them armed. Guards, certainly, only 'prudent,' to use your word. But guns? No one ever said guns, did you, Campbell?"

Haig understood what Benaud was doing. He did not want to lose Farrell now. Farrell was good. More important, he was popular.

"Of course not," Haig said. "No guns. Guards. Watchmen. We *do* employ watchmen, you know, Farrell."

Sean Farrell stood there in the middle of the room, feeling stupid, tricked. He knew his tendency suddenly to madden into violence. The moment passed. But they had just thought that up, about not arming the guards. He was sure of it. He felt the blood in his face. He felt it deepen. Could he trust them?

Did he want to give up the *Mail*?

The moment was really past now. They had him, they had tricked him. He cursed a few times and said, "Okay, if I have your word on the guns."

Campbell Haig smiled thinly. Farrell's face remained dark and solemn.

24

Sean Farrell had his own equivalent of Haig's Rhinecliff retreat. A refuge, a lair in which to lie up and sulk or lick his wounds or simply to think. Farrell's did not overlook a broad river set in green hills; it was on the scabrous coast of Brooklyn where he had been reared. Sunday morning he rose early. Despite the scene with Haig he had slept soundly. He usually did. Farrell's self-doubts and agonies intruded only on his waking hours. Now, in the morning, they were working at him again, and he got out the car and drove through the Battery Tunnel and down the Belt Parkway to Gerritsen Beach. It was only June but already the place had a baked and summered look; the fishing boats were out with parties and the wooden docks were quiet, empty; the pasteboard cottages looked as they always did, another season drabber and duller; on the sandlot some kids were playing baseball, the same lot on which he once played, where he had been playing that day his mother had come toward him, running...

Thanksgiving Day. Twenty-one years earlier. The sleet bounced off his helmet, off the tattered jersey stretched thin over his broad shoulders and the monstrous pads, bounced off and danced across the hardscrabble, whitening it, obscuring the already vague yard markers. Sean Farrell did not feel the sleet or the swollen lip or the trickle of blood from his right nostril. Not while he was playing football. Not as he reckoned whether there was still enough purchase in the ground to swing wide the next time he got the ball or if they should concentrate on going straight up the field. To his right he could see Mountain and Red the Jew and Hanley lining up. Then they were calling signals and the ball was coming to Farrell and he was moving smoothly despite the sleet and then not so smoothly as the two men hit him and after another yard or two he went down. How fine the ground felt, how good to hit and be hit. Farrell lay there for a moment enjoying the sheer physical pleasure of the game.

"Sean, you okay?"

Farrell nodded. He was more than okay. He got to his feet, feeling wonderful.

He was sixteen years old and a junior at James Madison High. At Madison he was the starting tailback on the varsity football team, and according to the rules he should not be playing now at Gerritsen Beach with the local sandlot team. But a game was a game and Sean Farrell did not like to miss one. He was six feet tall and would grow no taller, but at one hundred fifty pounds his broad frame would fill, mature, thicken. Trotting back to the huddle Farrell noticed the crowd of perhaps seventy-five people still there along the sidelines. Sleet didn't bother a crowd like this one and surely someone had a bottle. As they started for the line again from the huddle, he saw movement way off to the left, coming across the fields toward the gridiron. A woman, skirts flapping. His mother. He knew the gait.

"Ralphie, time out for God's sake."

He nodded toward the approaching figure.

"Time," Ralph said, and on both teams boys threw themselves to the whitened ground and took off helmets to breathe. Sean Farrell moved toward the sideline to intercept his mother before she could come onto the field itself.

Behind him a voice said, "Hey, lookit this."

It was someone on the other team, not knowing it was anyone's mother but seeing the sturdy legs flashing below the apron and the breasts bouncing under the housedress. Jesus, Sean thought, why can't she wear a bra like the other Goddamn Irish mothers? He hated the guineas to see her like this, or the niggers.

Then he saw his mother's face and knew that something had happened. Something awful. He ran to her. "Dad?" he said.

She nodded and ran to him and they collided, both of them big-boned and solid, and she held him without saying anything but panting heavily, her eyes wet. He could feel her big breasts cushioned against his lean, hard chest. But he had stopped thinking about his mother's breasts. He was thinking only of his father.

Jack Farrell was a fisherman. Not the sort of half guide, half bartender who worked the party boats out of Sheepshead Bay, but a blue-water trawler fisherman out there a week at a time, pulling and lifting when they were not searching and bouncing. Hard work, hard men. They fished for the market, nothing sporting about it, hauling in big cod and blues and tuna plump and sleek as footballs. Heavy rods, big hooks without barbs so the fish came off quickly, smoothly, twine like clothesline. Men like Jack Farrell didn't sportingly play a fish. They derricked it out of the ocean and aboard the boat. Their work was as glamorous as farm labor. They stood in water up to their waists on the taffrail, dipping the lines, pulling up the fish. After an hour of it a man without experience would be sobbing uncontrollably, his back and arm and shoulder muscles torn, his hands bloody, his feet and legs frozen. Jack Farrell had been working at his trade fifty weeks a year for more than twenty years. His hair was bleached, his body hard, his face mottled by skin cancer that he disregarded as he might a sunpeeled nose.

Later it was said the *Valiant* should not have been approved by the Coast Guard and there was talk of a lawsuit. But it never came to anything. Mae Farrell and the other widows received a few months' pay and vacation time and that was it. That and Jack Farrell's ten-thousand-dollar policy from the war. It wasn't much. Sean did not worry about the money. Mae did. That and not even having a body to mourn over and to bury.

The *Valiant* had simply vanished. No radio signal, no smoking flare on the horizon. There had been a storm; there were always storms in the Atlantic in November. They no more halted the fishing boats than they did the great liners. Perhaps the engine had failed and, unable to keep her head to the wind, the *Valiant* had swamped and sunk. Perhaps there had been an explosion. Weighted

have been unfair to the newspaper, to the staff, to, let's admit it, Haig. It would have confirmed the unions in their righteousness. Fourth, it would have looked as if he were siding with that cretin Brasky. My God! Finally, there were a lot of wise boys out there, some of them pals, others less so, a few enemies, who would have chuckled over Sean's discomfiture and would have nodded "I told you so."

He was at the end of the line of piers now, where a bit of grainy shingle began. Local kids called it "the beach." How many times had he swum there, launched leaky rowboats, dug piss clams, later, when he was a teenager, necked with girls there in the lee of the marsh grass and the dunes, bitten by sand flies, stung by mosquitoes, with some tough little Irish girl's mouth against his with her body moving and his hands and . . .

A good current was running through the narrow cut now, an outgoing tide. He was still drawn to the sea that had killed his father and, in the end, driven him away to the army and eventually to this trade he now practiced. He could stand here for hours watching the infinite permutations of wind and water and reflected sunlight. What if his father had not drowned? Would he have stayed in Gerritsen Beach? What would he then have become?

Boys who grew up in Gerritsen Beach had few options. They became cops, they became stickup men, they went to work on the docks, they went to sea, they became bartenders or bag boys in the A&P. A few broke out, became lawyers. Some were priests. . . .

A gull flew close to his face, causing him to duck instinctively and break the thought.

A stickup man, he told himself. *That* was as likely as any of the options he might have taken.

He walked back toward the car. On the lot the ball game was still in progress, or perhaps another game. All the kids looked alike. They shouted a lot. Mostly four-letter words. Did we swear that much, that loudly? One boy, fifteen, no more, torn T-shirt, ragged sneakers, red-haired, freckled, pugnacious, playing third base. It could have been Sean Farrell. He looked down at himself, as if to check. The neat blazer, the polished loafers, dusty now from his walk, came as a shock.

It was early afternoon but there was a stream of customers, mostly men, into the corner bar. First stop after the last mass. It was in this bar his mother used to meet her men. Oh, hell, he'd exorcised that ghost years ago, hadn't he? He crossed from the edge of the ball field and went into the cool darkness of the bar.

"Heineken," he said without thinking.

"Sorry, pal. Rheingold, Schlitz, Shaefer?"

There were six or eight men at the bar, a few women. Half the booths were taken. He recognized the barman, not his name but the face, that banana nose and the build, short, squat, powerful, nearly dwarfish. He finished the beer and the man refilled the glass without asking. He stood there with his bar rag and jerked his head down to the end of the bar where a man in a suit and two women were drinking.

"From Flatbush," the barman said caustically, "slumming. They come in and order mixed drinks and want to know where are the peanuts. I'll peanut them."

Farrell looked at the trio. They did seem out of place, the women wearing rather silly hats and one of them using a cigarette holder. There was a clatter of falling boxes from somewhere in the back of the bar and heads turned instinctively.

"Mother Riley," the bartender said, "dropped her pants. First time in twenty years."

Farrell laughed. He remembered Mrs. Riley, the widow who owned the place. So she was still alive. The barman came back to him, leaned his thick, short arms on the bar.

"I know youse, don't I? Sean Farrell. Right?"

Farrell nodded. "You've got a good memory."

The man waved a hand. "Oh, I knew youse right away. When youse first come in. Not the name right away. But I knew youse. Youse work on the newspapers now."

"Yeah. The *Mail.*"

"Shit," the barman said. "Glad somebody got out of this Goddamn hole. Here, have another. On Old Lady Riley."

Farrell took the beer. The jukebox was playing. The people at the end of the bar rapped for service. The bartender ignored them. "Bay Ridge, that's where I should of gone. Years ago. Gotten a place of my own. But y'know . . ."

"Yeah, I know," Farrell said.

The man at the end of the bar called, "Hey, do we get a drink down here?"

The bartender shrugged. "Whaddya gonna do?" He ambled in their general direction and they told him what they wanted.

Farrell looked around. A couple of young girls, blond, sunburned, pretty in a Gerritsen Beach sort of way, saw him looking at them and they giggled. They were wearing summer dresses. More church goers.

So the barman in the Beach still thought of Bay Ridge in terms of escape, of a break with dreary reality, the way farm boys thought of big cities, maybe the way Haig thought of New York. Haig! The man had begun to dominate his thoughts. Even now, drinking a friendly beer in a bar on the Brooklyn waterfront, there was no evading him. What would Haig have done last night had their roles been reversed? Farrell suspected that if Haig had bothered to feel strongly about an issue, the Pinkertons or whatever, he would have gone through with his threat, that if he really objected, he would have quit. On the spot.

Farrell sipped at his beer, contrasting his equivocation with Haig's sure confidence and, he admitted quite honestly, not coming off at all well in the comparison.

One of the girls was eyeing him now without being subtle about it. What, he wondered, would the girl say if he went over and told them who he was, the job he held, the girl he dated? The President's daughter. My God. And what would Alex think if she could see him now? What would Alex think of a place like this?

She would enjoy it, would soon be in deep conversation with the stunted bartender, would agree with him that, yes, those bastards at the end of the bar with their mixed drinks were decidedly slumming, most definitely in the wrong place. There were no wrong places for Alex Noyes. She fit in everywhere. Beautifully. The barman here would adore her, would buy drinks, would ignore the rest of the bar to tell her his stories, to tell her of his dreams of Bay Ridge. Alex had the ability to draw people, every sort of people. Farrell, who was born here, who was drinking beers in joints like this when he was fifteen, sixteen, could appreciate the gift. Places like Riley's recognized the phonies, recognized and rejected them. Alex would not have been rejected. She would have been welcomed, cheered, and admired. Even without being the President's daughter. She had the gift.

A big sailor came in now. He was drunk. He took a space at the bar just down from Farrell and ordered a rye and a beer chaser. He wore a dark red T-shirt and his arms were ropy, sinewy. A hard case. Vaguely familiar. Maybe he had sailed with Farrell's father. He looked as if he might. Talking to himself, he muttered something about Farrell, inclining his head in that direction.

"Hey," the bartender said, "knock it off. That's Sean Farrell. Jack Farrell's boy. You remember."

Farrell was not sure if the man did or not. But at least he confined his muttering to the glasses in front of him and his reflection in the mirror. It was only three in the afternoon and he was drunk. Well, Sean thought, in the Beach they start early.

The people at the end of the bar called for their check. They had had their outing, their little thrill. They had had enough. Maybe the sailor with the big arms had frightened them. The barman tossed a bit of damp paper in front of them. The man peeled off some bills.

"Don't leave him a tip, Harold," one of the women hissed.

The barman stared at her. "Tip, hell, I can buy youse and sell youse, Harold."

"Well," the other woman said, but Harold, who seemed to know when he was outgunned and on a distant shore, said:

"Forget it," and they got up and left.

The barman watched them go. "Mixed drinks," he said. He made it sound profane.

One of the two girls came over to Farrell now. "I don't mean to butt in," she said, "but didn't I see you on the television?"

Farrell laughed. "Must have been some guy looked like me," he said.

"I was sure I seen you on the television," she said, screwing up her face so she could think.

After that he bought the two girls a drink and left. He got into the car and turned it west, toward Manhattan. It would have been pleasant to hang around, to get drunk on beer, something he had not done in a long time, maybe to go to bed with one of them.

But he had been thinking of Alex and that sort of thing was out. He had also begun thinking about his mother. Places like this were where she went after his father's death, drinking with men like the sailor, with Old Man Riley, with cops and longshoremen and, it was possible, stickup men. She drank with them and slept with them, and he had found out but had not understood and had turned against her. He had not understood hunger in those days. Not the way he did now, with Alex.

He drove west. There was a dinner that night and the mayor would be there and young Sean Farrell, from Gerritsen Beach, was to sit on the dais with other great men and feel superior.

"Oh, Jesus," he prayed aloud in the car, "how did it start with Alex and where can it end?"

Then he remembered that in another few hours the Pinkertons would take up their posts at the *Mail* and that tomorrow morning would be one hell of a thing.

Well, he was a big boy. He was management now. Not just another anarchic writer paying dues to the Newspaper Guild. He was Haig's man now. His friends, some of them, would be on the other side if it all expoded into confrontation and strike. He was still paying dues but of another sort.

He tried to stop thinking about any of it, Alex or the damned newspaper or Campbell Haig, and to concentrate on the Sunday traffic and the road.

25

"I am the *editor* of the fucking newspaper," Sean Farrell said coldly, staring into the eyes of the uniformed black man.

"Yes, sir," the Pinkerton man said, "and may I see your identification?"

Farrell pulled out his wallet and showed his police department press card with its Polaroid color snapshot. The guard looked at the photo and then at Farrell.

"Thank you, Mr. Farrell," he said without warmth.

Farrell snatched back the press card and turned toward the elevators. Behind him three or four other *Mail* employees had begun to queue up.

"What the hell is this, Sean?" a white-haired salesman asked, bewildered.

"Ask Haig," Farrell snapped, and got into the elevator.

Campbell Haig, who owned the paper, had himself been halted that morning as he entered the building. It was only three o'clock and another guard had asked for identification. Haig did not have a press card but then the guard's superior, scanning a hastily prepared list of employees at the front desk, looked up.

"It's okay, Ben. That's Mr. Haig."

Haig turned to him. "How did you know?"

"The accent, Mr. Haig. Don't get too many of those in New York."

Delighted, Haig sprang into the elevator and went upstairs. At three thirty he was in the stereo room, a cardboard container of coffee in his hand, chatting with the crew.

"Had some damage the other day downstairs. Roll of paper was cut. Second time in a week. Mr. Benaud thinks it could be sabotage. We're just being careful. Can't have the paper shut down, all of us thrown out of work because some nut case may be loose."

A few men nodded coolly. The rest merely stared.

Perhaps some of them accepted his explanation. He didn't have any qualms about blaming Gideon. That's what general managers were for, weren't they? Later he went to the press room, had another coffee and tossed off a similar explanation.

"Shit," someone said quietly. Haig didn't challenge him on it. He didn't expect them to applaud. Better to have them let off a little steam.

Even before Farrell had gotten to his office one of the financial writers, a big man with muttonchops, grabbed his arm. "Hey, Sean, I hear the moat and drawbridge go in next week."

Farrell scowled. Gaudy chance he had of getting much inspired work out of the staff today. The damned Pinkertons would be the only thing anyone would be thinking about.

At ten o'clock there was a call from Channel 5. "We had an anonymous call Haig's got your place ringed with armed guards. Anything to it? We'd like to send down a crew and get some footage for the evening news."

Farrell told the man to bugger off and hung up.

At eleven Mabel Hermann, the Guild shop steward, an ample woman with rimless glasses who looked like a librarian, came into his room. "I'm calling a chapel meeting, Sean. My membership resents this business of having to—"

"Mabel," he said, "go call your meeting. Just let's not miss any deadlines."

At two that afternoon the paper handlers called a press conference. Benaud refused to let them do it on the premises. A dozen men, all after their shift was completed, moved across the street to the riverbank. Channel 5 was there. So was Brasky. Someone had found a wooden box. Brasky mounted it. "Fellow workers," he began. Then, seeming to run out of ideas, he abruptly stepped down. The handlers' shop steward got up.

"Thank you, brother Brasky. Men, ladies [there were no women present], citizens of this great city. I . . ." He went on for ten minutes. The camera crew had long since stopped filming and were packing up their gear.

That night they ran the footage on television and an official of the Allied Printing Trades Council made a speech. Even Farrell thought the man drew a rather long bow. After all, Haig hadn't had anyone deported to Siberia or shot. Not yet, anyway.

There was a scare on Tuesday. Ketchel, one of the desk men and a solid, serious sort, asked to see Farrell.

"Sean," he said, speaking in a low tone, "I didn't want to tackle you on this out on the floor but these Pinkertons, are they carrying guns?"

Farrell started to snarl a quick denial. But Ketchel's face halted him.

"Why?" he asked instead.

"I came up in the elevator after lunch with one of them and I swear the guy was carrying a rod in his belt."

"A *rod?*" Ketchel had been editing crime stories for too many years. "Look, Ketch, I don't know. I haven't seen any. They aren't supposed to. But let me find out. Don't repeat this to anyone. I'll go see Haig and get back to you."

"Sure, Sean. Just thought the editor ought to know."

Haig had scoffed. "They've got two-way radios in their belts. Walkie-talkies. Can't anyone around here tell a radio from a gun?"

But by four the rumor was all over the building.

Late that afternoon five of the nine unions declared in an announcement that the *Mail*'s hiring of guards "who may be armed, though this has not been ascertained" was insulting, degrading, and frightening to the staff of the newspaper. They called for a protest rally the next afternoon, at four o'clock (shrewdly *after* the last edition had gone to press, Haig noted), and invited all trade unionists in New York to join in a "protest of trade union solidarity and in strenuous opposition to union-busting by management."

That evening Haig and his executives met in his office. Everyone but Haig looked gloomy.

"Oh, come on now," the publisher said, "they're setting up a straw man. The guards have no guns. They know that perfectly well. Every major newspaper in the country has uniformed watchmen, guards. We didn't have enough of them, we suffered some sabotage, and we've done the prudent thing in calling in qualified professional security. The paper handlers have gotten nowhere on this Brasky farce so now they're stirring up the employees with another diversion. Let them have their damned rally. Let off a bit of steam. Might make them all feel better the next morning."

On Wednesday when Farrell came to work there were three strangers in the elevator. They wore western boots. Jesus, Haig is bringing in strike breakers even before we have a strike . . .

The "protest" was a fizzle. The unions tried. They really did. But although Wednesday afternoon was sunny and cool, no summer heat to bake away militancy, the small square at the corner of the *Mail* building failed to teem with the angry multitudes that had been urged to show their strength. Haig had been right.

Mabel Hermann, the shop steward of the editorial floor, had purchased a new dress on Fourteenth Street at lunchtime and was happily haranguing a TV crew in the square. People from the paper clustered around her trying to get themselves on television. There were a lot of signs, hastily scrawled cardboards hoisted on sticks. As many signs, it seemed, as there were protestors. Variations on Haig's western origins were popular: REMEMBER THE ALAMO FORGET HAIG! urged the Paper Straighteners and Handlers International Local 246. GO HOME ON THE RANGE HAIG . . . NEW YORK IS A UNION TOWN . . . SHOOT WETBACKS NOT REPORTERS . . . WHERE ARE YOU MEG VALENTINE NOW THAT WE NEED YOU . . . DON'T SHOOT "CACTUS" COPYBOYS DON'T CARRY GUNS . . .

Haig had called another briefing just before four.

"Let 'em go out," he told his department heads. "Don't try to stop anyone. The edition will be out of the way. We won't lose much time. It'll all be over by five. The Printing Council gave me its word on that. Don't give them an excuse for new grievances by taking names or docking people or getting into slanging matches. Let them have their fun. I'll sit it out. They'll want me to come out but I won't. They'll shout themselves hoarse and then someone will realize it's five o'clock and supper's on the table and they'll head for the subways."

Farrell had left the meeting silent and depressed. He might be Haig's man but he hated to see the union sell out. Now, as Haig had predicted, the small crowd put up a mechanical chant: "Come out *Haig* . . . Come out *Haig* . . ."

Good to his word, Haig made no appearance. Farrell knew it wasn't because Haig was afraid.

26

The protest had been a noisy, chaotic, ineffective sham. Farrell had gone out to stroll through the line of marchers, been good-naturedly booed, had offered to buy one of the copy desk men a drink he'd owed him for some time, and had gone back upstairs to his office, duty done. A little after five, as Haig had confidently predicted, the crowd began to disperse. By six o'clock the film crews had gone and only the littered street, the torn posters, the broken sticks from picket signs indicated anyone had been there, anything had happened. In one way Farrell was relieved. There had been no serious trouble. But there was something frightening in Haig's secret contacts with the top union leadership before the protest.

Haig and the union leaders had worked out the scenario in advance. In a suite at the Metropolitan Club.

"I can't hold my people forever, Haig," the stereotypers union president said quietly. "They want blood."

"Don't they always?" the Guild's man murmured. There was little love lost between the two unions.

"Shit," the chief paper handler said, "it's my man we're talking about here. Brasky belongs to me."

"Thank God," said the head of the electricians, a small, precise man who kept rolling a bit of tape between his fingers.

Haig said nothing. Let them all talk, get it out on the table. Benaud sat like some occidental Buddha, mute and patient. Feinberg, the labor expert, chain-smoked. The site of their deliberations had been carefully chosen by Haig. The room's high ceiling, the ornate moldings, the huge, gilt-framed portraits of eighteenth-century men, the marble staircase they had ascended, the liveried doorman, all these spoke of authority, power, wealth. The turf of publishers, not of trade unionists.

When they had had their say, when the bickering was done, Haig rapped a knuckle against the leather-topped conference table. "I suggest you call your people out," he said quietly.

The room tensed. The man who ran the typesetters stared at Haig. "Am I hearing right? You're suggesting we walk?"

"Yes, I am. Take them out for a few hours, organize a demonstration, picket the *Mail*, permit them to let off a bit of steam."

"I never thought I'd hear a publisher suggest a strike," the Guild man said.

"Why not?" Haig asked. "You're having trouble holding your people in line. Okay, so let them raise a little hell and shout for my head. Once you've defused the situation, you and Mr. Benaud and Mr. Feinberg can sit down quietly, without pressure, and try to work out something. Otherwise we're heading for an explosion. I don't want that. I don't think you do."

"Shit," someone said in an impressed voice.

Haig stood up. "Just tell Mr. Benaud what day will be most convenient to all of you. I'll go along with whatever you and he work out."

He strode from the room.

"Jesus," the chief paper handler whispered.

Poor, impassioned jerks like Mabel Hermann thought they were igniting a revolution. Haig had known all the while that the matches were damp, the tinder wouldn't burn. The rest of that week after the demonstration passed calmly.

Sissy Valentine was feeling much better about things. Alex Noyes was back in town and had called her and, as they used to do before

Farrell, they had driven out on Saturday to Sissy's father's house in East Hampton. The old boy, as Sissy called him, was there. Unaccountably. Maybe he was running short of money. And he was not alone. With him, as Alex put it, was "the ingenue of all ingenues."

The girl, a frizzy blonde with legs and huge eyes, was clearly embarrassed. At the same time she seemed pleased and excited to meet the daughter of a President. She alternately gushed and broke into sobs, insisting on addressing them as "Miss Noyes" and "Miss Valentine," and carried on in what Sissy thought of as the best ruined shop girl tradition.

When he had Sissy alone in the hallway her father hissed: "What a lack of tact! Couldn't you even have called ahead? After all, it *is* my house!"

Sissy giggled. "Really, Daddy, you let years go by without coming here. If I'd had the slightest idea you were entertaining . . . Look, I'll explain that Alex and I were just passing by and dropped in to pick up some swimsuits."

When they drove off the ingenue was standing on the lawn overlooking the golf course, staring dramatically into the middle distance.

"Curtain!" said Alex. "That's the best final scene she's ever played."

They stopped in Bridgehampton for dinner and a drink and then drove back to town. It was a long drive, out and back the same day, but as Alex dropped her friend at the apartment she said, "I haven't laughed so much in years."

"I know," Sissy said. "It's my father and I shouldn't. But that girl!"

Best of all during the drive Alex had confided to her that she had decided to break with Farrell.

"He's in love—infatuated is more like it—and I'm not. And he's just too good a guy for me to amuse myself with, play my usual bitchy tricks on. But I have this awful premonition he's about to pop the question or some other mad gesture. I won't hurt him. I won't."

Sissy was driving now, her turn, and she was glad of it. She could stare at the night road ahead of them and not show Alex her face. "But it *will* hurt him, won't it?" she asked in a small voice.

Alex sighed. "I guess so. I *know* it will. But just for a while. Then he'll read about me in his lousy tabloid, some stunt I've pulled, and he'll be thankful he's clear of me."

That night, in bed, despite the fatigue of the long drive, Sissy Valentine could not sleep. To think that Sean Farrell would once again be available to her . . .

This time, this time, she vowed, she would go out and get him. And keep him! It did not occur to her to think of Farrell as discarded by Alex Noyes. And if it had she would not have cared. She was too happy.

The following Tuesday Sissy had interviewed a newly arrived ambassador and his wife in the delegates lounge at the UN, grabbed a sandwich at Louis East, and taken the subway back to the office. It was real summer now. She walked down the hill through Chinatown. How beautiful the children were, honey-skinned, lean, agile. She loved the sounds of the district, the sing-song voices of the women, the smells of the produce shops, baskets of greens blocking the sidewalks, the shouts of the kids in half Chinese, half New York–accented slang. The garish neon signs, the business notices beckoned: the True Light Lutheran Church; the Golden Valley Cocktail Lounge; Charles Mah, Attorney; the Wah Sing Wang Funeral Corporation; the Szechuan Taste restaurant on the corner of Chatham Square.

Sissy's long legs carried her down the hill toward the waterfront and the *Mail*, her tanned arms swinging as she loped past the housing project, cheerfully ignoring the invitations of Puerto Rican loafers lounging on a pipe-rail fence. Before her were the bridges—the Brooklyn, last-century stone; the Manhattan, this-century steel—arching majestically. Beyond them the bay with a freighter making way.

"Howdy," the Pinkerton said as she flashed her I.D. card at the back door and nipped inside the building on her usual shortcut. It was cool inside, out of the June sun, cool and familiar with the heavy roar of the presses. She glanced at her wristwatch. Two o'clock. The late market edition. The next to last.

The freight elevator was, as usual, out of order and she pushed through the swinging doors and strode into the roar of the press room. One of the crew waved a grimy hand and mouthed "Hello,

Sissy." She waved back. As she stepped over the moving cog railroad she noticed three or four men standing close together by the middle unit of the great Goss press. They seemed to be arguing. They argued a lot down here. With this noise, who could blame them? Then one of the men broke away from the others. He was shouting. She could not hear the words but she knew they were harsh, angry. She could see it in the man's face when he turned.

Brasky! This was the famous Brasky. Now, what was *he* doing here? Wasn't he still suspended? Well, this would be something for the gossip mill in the city room. She started to skirt the retreating Brasky when another man, it was the foreman he had punched, lunged at him.

"Hey!" Sissy yelled. No one heard her. It was all she said. Brasky wheeled and dove toward the foreman. One of them spun into Sissy, and as the heavy body collided with hers her legs went out from under her. Instinctively she threw out an arm, grabbing at the safety rail to break her fall.

The last thing she felt was a powerful tug on her arm, yanking her toward the madly spinning press. She may have screamed. No one heard it.

They heard only the crunch and the unfamiliar *bump-bump-bump* as the roller of the press encountered something thicker, more resistant, than the endless ribbon of newsprint and, groaning under pressure, spun chaotically on for just an instant and then, as the safety mechanisms tumbled into action, began to slow. Not quickly enough.

On the sixth floor Campbell Haig was signing checks as the press noise altered in timbre and then ceased. He pushed his glasses atop his head, looked around, and asked, "Now what the hell . . ."

On the fourth floor Sean Farrell was chairing the afternoon news conference. The Washington bureau chief, Spengler, was holding forth. Some new nastiness from the White House press secretary that he felt demonstrated yet again that . . . Farrell, his feet flat on the concrete floor, felt the slowing and the stoppage, held up a big hand to Spengler and said, "Wait a minute, Bill, we seem to have a problem here."

Throughout the building men and women heard, or felt, or sensed the interruption in the newspaper's circulatory system. More sabotage? A routine web break? Some breaking news that might demand a replate?

In the wire room just off the city room they knew it could not be a news bulletin; no bell had rung on the AP or the UPI wire, alerting news rooms across the country that something big was about to be transmitted. Those bells rang when Presidents were assassinated, when wars began.

There were no bells. No bells for Sissy Valentine who now lay unconscious, maimed and bleeding, on the bare concrete of the press room.

Ironically, it was Brasky who got to her first.

Brasky started to turn her over. The foreman pushed him aside. "Don't touch her, for Chrissakes," he shouted. Then he saw blood spurting out, ejaculating as her heart pumped, and the foreman knew they had to move her and find the wound.

He nodded okay and he and Brasky carefully, gently, turned her on her back, her slim body moving easily. She lay there, her eyes closed, her face pale, her dress shredded. How awkward she looked. So much blood . . .

Then they saw why she looked so odd, so unbalanced.

She no longer had a left arm.

Brasky stared for a few seconds and then wheeled to vomit on the concrete floor, spattering himself and the shoes of the foreman and the long, unmoving legs of Sissy Valentine. The foreman stood up, shaking his head as if demented, his fists raised helplessly in the air. He reached instinctively for his middle, realized he was wearing suspenders, and cried, "Brasky, your belt!"

The paper handler stood motionless, uncomprehending. Then, as the foreman cursed him, his big hands went to his belt and he pulled it rapidly through the trouser loops. The foreman knelt and, averting his face from the spurts of blood, slipped the heavy leather around what was left of her left arm, tugging it down hard. Almost immediately the flow of blood ceased. Behind him the foreman could hear the sound of running feet on the concrete floor of the press room.

"Oh, Jesus," he said, focusing for the first time on her face. "It's Sissy Valentine."

It took the ambulance only a few minutes to get there. It seemed an hour. Haig paced up and down the floor of the press room, not saying anything. Farrell cursed steadily, urged haste, and got in everyone's way. Finally they had the girl on a wheeled stretcher, an attendant walking alongside holding a bottle of whole blood that was already flowing back into her body. They rolled her through the door into the hallway that led to the lobby and then into the street. Farrell ran along with them, shouting for a company car. Left behind were the press-room crew, somber, silent, big men shuffling their feet and not knowing what to do, what to say, where to put their ink-stained hands.

Haig glared around him angrily. Brasky was seated on the floor, dazed, mute, spattered with blood and vomit. The foreman, even bloodier, wiped his face with a grimy handkerchief. Haig noticed how the man's hands trembled. He looked down at his own hand. It was still.

The mechanical superintendent, a white-haired, meticulous man, stood by his side.

"Hell of a thing, Campbell," he said.

Haig nodded. What was there to say?

Then, knowing one of them had to do it, he made an effort to restore some vestige of normality to the room, to the crew. "Is that unit out for long, Chief?" he asked, his head inclined toward the press.

"Dunno, Campbell. I'll have a look."

The superintendent climbed awkwardly over the safety railing and disappeared down between two big rolls of newsprint, held in place by the tension of flexible steel strap. Haig shoved his hands into his pockets and watched. Behind him the press gang hung back in a rude semicircle, watching, not saying much. A maintenance man appeared with a bucket and mop.

"Don't do that," Haig ordered. "They'll want to know where she was, where she fell."

It did not occur to him just who "they" might be. He supposed someone—the police, perhaps, or the insurance company—would want to see where she lay. The man went away.

Now the mechanical superintendent, his gabardine business suit smudged with black ink and with something crimson, climbed back out from under the overhead element of the press unit. His face was sweat-covered, pale.

"I think it should work, Campbell," he said, his voice nervy, cracking.

"No damage?"

"None I can see. Can't really tell until it rolls. If we get any vibration, then it's off center. But it looks okay: A lot of blood, of course."

Haig looked into his face. "Did you see it?"

"No," the superintendent said, "it's in there somewhere but I couldn't see it."

"Where would it be?" Haig asked, his voice flat.

The superintendent shrugged.

"As fast as it was running, anywhere along there." He motioned vaguely toward the other end of the press room. The press-room gang clustered more closely around the two executives.

"Any chance of getting it out?" Haig asked in a low voice.

The superintendent shook his head. "What would it be, Campbell, after running through a couple of those babies? You know what they weigh, the sort of tensions . . ."

Haig walked away from his superintendent for a moment, the crowd of men parting to let him through. He did not seem to see them, but he knew they were there, waiting. It was his decision. His alone.

He glanced at his watch. This edition scrubbed, of course, one more to go, the Wall Street final. A couple of hundred thousand readers out there, newsboys waiting, newsstand dealers, the drivers snoozing in their trucks out past the loading platforms. And these men in the press room. All of them waiting.

He returned to the superintendent.

"Chief," he said, "what will happen if we start up?"

"Run blank for a few minutes. It'll clean itself out. Then, when we start getting a clean sheet, hook up and start to print newspapers."

Haig nodded. "All right," he said, his voice raised for the first time so the gang could hear him, so they would know it was his decision, "we run the press. Start up whenever the make-ready is set." He turned and walked a few yards away but did not leave the press room. The men, chivvied by their foreman, straggled back to their usual positions.

After a minute or two a warning bell rang and then a foreman pushed a button. The great presses began to roll, ponderously at first, then spinning rapidly, smoothly, filling the big room now once more with the accustomed roar. Haig stood motionless, staring at the press that possibly had killed Sissy Valentine. He watched the endless ribbon of paper race by, the red stain streaking out against the stark white of the paper.

At last, the mechanical superintendent nodded and another button was pushed. The great press engaged and freshly inked newsprint began to roll off at the far end of the room. Campbell Haig turned and walked from the press room.

Here and there on the filthy concrete floor under the press a spray of red soaked into the ink and the dust. But above, the ribbons of newsprint raced white and unstained toward the freshly inked rollers.

Whatever remained of Sissy's arm had been rolled into nothingness.

27

Haig wasn't the same, people said, after that. When the police had come and he and Benaud and the mechanical superintendent and the chief of the Pinkertons had huddled, after he had perhaps irrationally given his orders, Haig had returned to the press room alone. Someone from the insurance company had been there already and chalked on the floor the rough outline of a body, presumably the place where she had fallen. Someone had put down newspapers to cover the blood but here and there it had seeped through, dried rusty brown. He had stood there looking at the chalked outline, at the stained newsprint, and then, systematically, painfully, he had scuffed away the chalk with his shoe, as if he could also erase reality.

Haig had seen strike violence before. You didn't run newspapers and not. Smashed truck windshields and bloody noses and slashed tires and fire bombs and viciously wielded baseball bats. But through it all no one had been killed, no one maimed. This time the legendary Haig luck had not held. Had this whole business of *The New York Mail* been ill-conceived? Had New York itself been a mistake? Was he out of his depth, a country boy dazed among strange people with strange ways?

He had walked across the Brooklyn Bridge. Already in his mind was the notion that he had to see Sissy Valentine. Simply to see the girl. It was a need, fierce, instinctive, pointless. He had not yet had his first drink, but disorientation had taken him in its grip. It was as if he stood outside himself, watching through a lens that seemed just slightly out of focus. This was not the time for him to appear at the hospital. Not that he feared confronting Meg Valentine or the girl's father or emotional people like Farrell from the paper. It was just that when he saw her they should be alone: the crippled girl and the man who was to blame. He had to be alone with what he had caused to happen. As he always had to be.

Forget Brasky and the foreman and the damned guards. Haig himself had brought on the crisis, only he carried the burden of responsibility. In the past he had always taken the cheers when a labor negotiation had worked out well. Why shouldn't he now take the brunt of this?

The Manhattan end of the Brooklyn Bridge was a few blocks south of the newspaper. It was evening now, but still bright under the late June sun, and the approaches to the bridge were jammed with truck traffic, with commuters in their cars, a choleric cop with a red face waving them on, on toward Brooklyn. He dodged through traffic, once nearly being hit and drawing the rage of a truck driver, before finding in the maze of the bridge approach the narrow pedestrian walkway. He mounted the old steps and walked upward and to the east. Beneath him were the rotten wharves of an unused waterfront, to his right the Statue of Liberty, behind him the World Trade Center. He saw none of it, barely felt the cool breeze coming off the upper bay.

And in his confusion, as he mounted the old stone bridge, what Meg Valentine had told him so long ago about Roebling and his telescope, somewhere over there in Brooklyn, crept back into his consciousness.

That memory of Roebling and the wind, the river, the height, the sea so close to hand, all the symbolic elements of cleansing, purging, should have had their salutary effect on the stricken Haig. He should have arrived on the Brooklyn shore with hair tousled, a bit footsore perhaps, but with a clear head. He did not. Out on the bridge there was once again the sense of disorientation he had experienced earlier. He was alone, the thousands of cars passing in both directions only a backdrop, not really imposed on his consciousness. At midspan he paused, and a nervous observer might have seen in him a potential suicide. But Haig entertained no such thoughts. It was just that he had become confused and was not sure, after having gotten that far, just why he was there and whether he should continue. He did. At nine that night he was in Brooklyn, hiking south on the Heights, passing pleasant-looking brownstones lighted now against the darkness, houses in which lived people he knew or who knew him. It never occurred to him to pause and to knock.

Beyond Brooklyn Heights lay Red Hook, Fort Greene, Bushwick, Bay Ridge. This was Farrell's ground. Haig had been over it, in one of their demented dawn patrols, but then swiftly and by day. Now, at night and afoot, he recognized nothing. But it would have been the same had his strange walk taken him through the streets of McAllen, New Mexico. He was not seeing, not registering, not reacting. If he passed men that night whose motives were less than pure and in whose pockets were knives or worse, none bothered Campbell Haig. Perhaps it was the instinct of wild things on the hunt, perhaps the tension in his very posture, perhaps the hotly staring eyes; whatever it was, no one approached him.

At Fort Hamilton he hailed a cab. It was after midnight. The big Veterans' Hospital reared up starkly above the seawall, beyond the little comic-strip military base with its anachronistic coast artillery. He told the driver where he wanted to go and sat back. The driver was Puerto Rican and did not talk. Haig would not have answered him with any intelligence if he had. He kept seeing the chalked outline on the press-room floor and seeing himself standing there looking down at it, trying to scuff away its horrible reality.

The emergency room was doing its usual brisk midnight trade but the rest of the hospital was quiet. He asked at the front desk for Sissy, was given the floor and the room number, after having lied that he was her father. The floor nurse was not so simply fooled.

Haig handed her some money. He didn't do it furtively or use any of the ritual code words. This was no "contribution to the nurses' lounge"; this was an outright bribe. The woman stood there looking down at the bills in her hand. She had expected him to produce some impressive business card or something when his hand went into his pocket. Instead, this. She could see twenties and a fifty. Impressed and frightened, she pointed down the hall toward Sissy's room. He nodded and turned.

The room was lighted. The girl was still being checked on a thirty-minute schedule. There were a lot of tubes, an electronic scanner of some sort by the bed. Haig did not look at them. He went to the foot of the bed and looked into her face. Except for the tube in a nostril and being pale, her face still looked the way he remembered her from the city room, from the time old Meg had introduced them. The covers were pulled up high and there was no way of knowing she had no left arm, though its slender, tanned mate lay outside the covers with its snaking tube and mottled puncture bruises. Had she felt pain? Immediate unconsciousness? Had she realized her arm was being torn off? Or had it all happened so fast there was awareness one instant and the next . . . nothing? Had, Haig wondered, his father felt anything when the bomb under the pedals turned him from a sensate intelligent human being into a scarlet gruel?

Always the bomb, always Sam Haig, always the main street of McAllen, always the car, and always Campbell Haig, the only son, half a continent away, drunk and in bed with a girl called Sharon. Would he, twenty years from now, still see himself in his sixth-floor office, remember precisely what he was doing and every detail of the room, his desk, the river beyond the window, at that instant the press-room alarm sounded?

He moved to the side of the bed, reached out a hand. Her forehead was cool. His fingers, so lightly they could barely sense the skin, rested there for a moment or two. Then, without looking at her again, he turned and left the room.

The rest of that night was less clear. He walked again after having left the hospital. He knew that. Somewhere there was another cab, hailed and instructed to drive him to the Carlyle. At the hotel he did not get out. Instead he explained to the driver how to get to Rhinecliff. There was some dickering about money. Haig handed the man some bills. They drove to the river and onto the highway at Ninety-sixth Street. He may have slept, or perhaps that too was only part of his state of mind, imagining sleep, not really experiencing it. It was still dark when the cab rolled onto the gravel of Mayfair. He remembered watching dawn break over the hills. He did not remember unlocking the door of his retreat, his wooden castle, so like old houses in his native Southwest. He did not remember when he started drinking. He did remember giving the caretaker money to go down to the village to buy the bourbon.

He had called Benaud at some point, told him to handle things, that he was not to be called, all mail was to be held. He had no recollection of this but it was what Gideon told him later.

That night he got some sleep. The bourbon did it. Why had he told the caretaker bourbon? Some subconscious link to New Orleans? He disliked the taste of bourbon. The next day he drank and dozed in one of the big chairs in the den. The caretaker knocked, but he growled that he was working and he could hear the man's footsteps receding on the path. He had been awake Friday night at midnight when the girl had come. Awake and so drunk he had become rather good at it. The retching and the headache had vanished, just the bleary recognition that he was drunk, that nothing was quite real except the drunkenness.

know," she insisted. "I don't give a damn about the eight hundred other patients in this bloody butcher shop. I care about Sissy Valentine, and you *ought* to know." The doctor backed away, warily.

Tears were now rolling down Meg's old face. She looks awful, Farrell thought, really old. It was the first time that had occurred to him.

Meg wiped away the tears with a handkerchief she had fished out of her sleeve.

"Strong girl, Sissy. Young, too. She'll be all right. They're doing marvelous things with prosthetic devices, I'm told. Incredible things."

Farrell turned away. He did not want to think of Sissy and "prosthetic devices."

Meg and Alex went out to dinner, and Farrell said he would join them later back at the hospital. Now he went back to the paper, up to the sixth floor. Miss Mayhew was putting on the hat she always wore.

No, she said, Mr. Haig was not there. He'd left. After the . . . accident. She did not know where he might be. No idea. Farrell went along the hall to Benaud's office.

"He's not here, Sean," Benaud said, even before Farrell asked.

"Well, you know where, then?"

"I don't."

"I want to see him. I expect you'll be talking with him later. Let him know I want to see him. I'll go uptown to his hotel. Wherever."

"Important, is it?" Benaud asked, his lively eyes peeking out over the red beard.

"No," Farrell said. "Not important. A girl had her arm torn out. A spot of union trouble, as they might say in Fleet Street. Nothing significant, of course."

Benaud's eyes flashed. "Listen, you, Mr. High and Mighty Farrell, I know about that girl and Campbell knows about that girl. What the blazes do you think we are up here?"

Farrell's voice rose. "I think you're a couple of Goddamn cold fish, that's what I think. You've pushed this pitiful Brasky farce to a point where there wasn't a laugh left in it. You'd squeezed them all. You and your damned Pinkertons. You have Pinkertons hiding in the

Goddamn toilets behind the stools and yet Brasky strolls in off the street like it was Labor Day and he's leading the AFL parade. Where were your Pinkertons *then*, Gideon?"

Benaud made the effort to control himself and then, softly, he asked, "But where are they now, Sean?"

Farrell went back to the hospital. In the cab he realized there hadn't been a guard on the front door when he went back to challenge Haig, nor at the desk outside the executive offices on the sixth floor, only the ordinary *Mail* watchmen.

Haig had called off his dogs. Put them on their leads and locked the kennel. Called off his cowboy heroes after they'd roused a fury that had to end in this or something like it.

Alex looked worse after dinner. Meg looked better, almost cheery. "Press rooms have always been dangerous places," the old woman said. "I remember in the 1940s we had a foreman lost his arm; no union trouble then, just an accident. I must send Mr. Haig a note about raising the safety fences."

Alex signaled to Sean. They got the old woman seated in the waiting room and went down the hall a few yards. Alex took out a cigarette. Her hands were shaking.

"Deliver me from another meal like that," she said.

"The old lady flip out?"

"That's the odd thing. She sounds perfectly sane, rational. But it's this abnormal 'silver lining' stuff that's crazy. She mentioned that business about the safety railing . . . is there such a thing? I suppose there must be. Anyway, she made notes about it during dinner. Haig ought to raise the rails at least six inches, she said."

He snorted. "Haig's disappeared," he said.

"That bastard."

Meg came out into the hall. "Why all the whispering?" she demanded. "What do you know that I don't?"

It took another thirty minutes to get her to go home. Farrell went down with her to the car and he and the chauffeur helped her to climb in. He had never seen her so feeble.

At midnight they wheeled Sissy out of intensive care. She was very pale and unconscious. Alex tried to walk alongside the trolley to her room but the attendants shook their heads.

"Well?" she said, turning to Farrell.

"Come on," he said. They got a cab.

It was Friday midday before Alex learned about Haig's Rhinecliff retreat. Farrell was no help to her. If she had told him she planned to confront Haig at his country hideaway Farrell would have taken over, insisted on going along, would probably end up by half killing Haig and getting blackballed in the newspaper business. So she could not ask Sean. But Alex's father had had friends who were still in high places, and after a dozen phone calls she had Haig's address in Rhinecliff and his unlisted phone number. In a phone booth she dialed and when a man answered she hung up.

Now it was night, and as she drove the small silver car north on the highway there were flashes of heat lightning and rumbling thunder off the Catskills to her left. The top was down and the breeze cooled her face. It was a mad expedition she had mounted, impulsive, angry, emotional. She did not know what she would do or say when she had the man in front of her. Slap him? Curse him? Paint a pitiful picture of the maimed Sissy? But there was no doubt about his guilt. Haig had forced the union confrontation, had brought in the guards, had caused the fight in the press room. And he had ordered the press started up. . . .

Alex could not remember when she had begun to hate Haig. The roots of it were there when Farrell first began to speak about him. Haig owned a chain of sleazy papers, exploited ignorance and misfortune not just for gain, she was sure of that, but for the cruel pleasure of doing it. And she would go into his unspeakable lair and let him have the heat of her outrage. For what he had done to Sissy he was not to have the protection of his telephones in other rooms, of his monstrous insolence. He was to know what it was to be hated by Alexandra Noyes.

The highway sign read "Rhinecliff" and the little car began to slow as her foot eased off the accelerator. It was eleven o'clock at night, and she hoped she would remember the very precise directions her source had given. She drove through the main street of the town and made the turning uphill abeam the railroad station.

Her heart jumped. It would be all right. She would find the house. Haig would be there. She would, well, she would do the right thing, say what was right, at the moment. She had good instincts. They would not fail her. She would have her confrontation with Campbell Haig and then drive home to New York, a small duty done in Sissy's name.

She knew one other thing: It was finished with Sean. He had belonged to Sissy and Alex, playfully, had taken him away. It was finished now. She had told Sissy so and she must keep her word.

29

The man who opened the door of the big old house stood there for a moment, blinking into the darkness and then asking politely, "Yes, may I help you?"

Alex's resolve failed her for an instant.

"Mr. Haig?" she asked.

"Yes."

"I'm Alexandra Noyes," she said.

He shook his head. "It's late," he said. "I don't think I—"

"I was . . . I'm a friend of Sissy Valentine's."

He stepped back a few inches as if hit. "Oh," he said, "come in. I guess I expected you. Someone."

He stepped to the side and she passed into the hallway. There was only one light and beyond its range the house loomed enormous, silent, empty. With a courtly half inclination of the head he led her through a series of the rooms. How polite we are, she thought, how circumscribed by convention. This man has destroyed my friend. I hate him. I have come here to tell him that. For now she knew precisely what she would say, and in what cold, condemning tone. And yet we are performing the ritual minuet of callers to a great English country house.

They were in a big room, a den, she supposed, lined with books. Haig switched on the table lamp. Now he turned and faced her.

How young he is, she thought, how slight and young. A slender man of medium height, youngish, with brown hair pushed to the side, wearing a crumpled business suit. Only the tie, slightly loosened at the throat, gave any hint of informality.

"Yes," he said again, his voice a bit vague and unsure.

She stared at him, unaware of a rudeness she would ordinarily never commit. His eyes were rimmed in red but within the redness pale green, not the piercing eyes she had expected. He was unshaved, but only that and the loosened tie hinted at anything but the soberly dressed businessman.

She swallowed, her throat constricted. All the way here she had been sure the words would come, the right words. She felt embarrassed, then angry.

"I wanted you to know that I went to see Sissy," she began. Her voice was quavering. But *why?*

"Yes," he said, again vaguely, "so did I."

Her cold anger returned. "Oh, yes," she said cuttingly, "I heard about your little midnight visit. Trying to bribe people. Well, I'm glad they didn't let you in. I'm glad that someone could tell you no."

He moved slightly and put down a hand on the heavy table beside him. "Oh, but they didn't," he said. "They let me in."

"You saw Sissy?" she asked, her eyes widening.

He nodded. "I gave them some money."

"You just paid someone money and they broke the rules."

"Yes, I'm afraid that's how it was."

"How much money?" she asked, realizing as she asked that the question was silly, superficial.

"I don't know. I gave them what I had. A few hundred dollars, I suppose."

"You can buy anything, can't you?" she said bitterly.

He moved again slightly, as if hurt, and then half raised a slim brown hand.

"Miss Noyes, do you mind if we sit down? I'm a bit dizzy. I've been drinking and I'm afraid I'm not very used to it. . . ."

His voice trailed off on the half apology, half plea.

"No. Yes, of course. Sit down. I didn't . . ."

He moved slowly and unsteadily to a couch, and as old men do put down his hand behind him to be sure the couch was there before he sank into it.

She continued to stand where she was. She didn't want to sit down. Could she continue at all? The man was drunk. That was the strange note in his voice, the stilted movements. Well, if he thought he could evade her fury simply by drinking himself into . . .

"I'm sorry," he said from the couch, "but I interrupted you."

Her shoulders sagged. "No," she said, "I wasn't saying anything. Nothing you'd understand. Nothing that would be significant to you."

She was defeated.

To drive all this way, storing up the anger, the hatred, the hurt, the horror of two whole days, to have before her the image of the pale Sissy on the hospital trolley, to seek out and finally to find this man, to stand before him alone and without witness, prepared to do and to say awful things, to lash him with his guilt and his burden, only to discover not a monster but a shaken drunk. What was the use of going on?

"Oh!" she said aloud, angry at being cheated of her vengeance, all the energy of hate oozing from her.

"Yes." His voice came oddly from deep in the couch.

She looked around the room. It was just a room, not the lair she'd first seen. It spun, slightly. She was badly shaken by the sudden lessening of tension. The room spun. This must be how it looked and felt to the drunken Haig. And she'd not had a drink at all.

Haig stared at her from the couch, barely focusing. Perhaps he had to watch some fixed object to keep the room from turning.

It had been stupid to come. What good did it do Sissy? And now why was she still there? She could not reach Haig if she wanted. He was beyond insult, sunk deep in his own web of torment or guilt or fear.

"Mr. Haig," she said, raising her voice slightly as one does with children or drunks, enunciating carefully, "I'll be leaving now."

She turned but from behind her she heard:

"Wait."

She ran from the room and through other rooms toward what she remembered was the entry. Behind her she heard his pursuit, clumsy, once knocking solidly into something, then more lightly, shambling drunkenly after her. Oh, God, she thought, if the door's locked and I have to face him again . . .

She was at the door. The knob turned. Outside, the country night was still and warm. She breathed deeply.

"Miss Noyes."

Not wanting to, she turned. He stood there, silhouetted in the light of the doorway, swaying slightly. How harmless he looked.

"Miss Noyes," he whispered.

"Yes." Her voice was strained, her throat muscles tense.

"I wanted to show you out."

"Oh." The night calm around them, ordinary summer night, reducing things. "Thank you." But why was she thanking him?

He lifted his right hand in a sort of salute and then, very slowly, quite gracefully in fact, he fell sideways, struck the frame of the door with his shoulder, and collapsed on the step, half in, half out of the house.

Her car gleamed pale in the starlight.

Go home, every instinct shouted, get in your car and drive back to the city, leave this pitiful wreck to sleep off his guilt. Forget him, label him not worth your hatred, not worth . . . what had happened to Sissy. She turned toward the car.

The night was not all that silent now. Crickets, the horn of a distant auto, what might have been a train whistle, far off. Beyond the great lawn gleamed the river. Her hand was on the door handle, her car keys were out.

Behind her Campbell Haig lay still in the open door.

Irritated, angry, impatient, her body rigid, she hesitated and then, her shoulders sagging, her head down, the fight gone out of her, Alex turned back to kneel by Haig's unconscious body.

30

Alex Noyes was dreaming. She knew it was a dream. All very muddled. She was in a big house, glimpsed vaguely, darkly, briefly; not Sissy's house in East Hampton; certainly not one of her mother's great houses. Within this uncertain imagery of structure, all else in the dream was crisp, recognizable. Sissy was there, unmaimed, cheerfully nagging Alex for not doing something with her life. *You really must,* the girl kept saying, *you have a duty.* To do what was left unsaid. Farrell was there, silent, grinning, familiarly posed behind one of the old office typewriters, a cigarette dangling from his lower lip as if, as with Jean Gabin, it had grown there, a friendly appendage trailing smoke. Sean watched but did not speak. Nora was there, with one of her resident monks, all bustle and purpose, arranging furniture, or so it seemed, tidying up, chattering to the monk, ignoring Alex and Sissy and Sean, the monk murmuring in response a sort of Gregorian chant of platitudes. She could hear his voice, hear the soft *slip-slop* of his sandals as he minced across the hardwood floors in Nora's wake. These were all people among whom she spent her life. Not so the last figure in the tableau: costumed (it was clearly a costume and nothing more) as a doctor all in white, the salesman with whom she had sweated and moaned in West Palm Beach. She remembered his body, his face, but not his name. Yet he was there in the dream, solemn, chiding. Had Alex completely abdicated all responsibility, he demanded to know, had she forgotten who she was and what position she held? His assumption of authority was complete. It angered Alex. Who was he to chide her, even in a dream? Alex moaned now, not in ecstasy but in fear and resentment.

She woke. For the inevitable, brief moment she was confused, then she knew. A long, dark-leather Chesterfield couch in one of the ground-floor rooms of Haig's house. She had gotten a rumpled raincoat from the trunk of the car, kicked off her shoes, and slept. There were bedrooms upstairs, she assumed, dozens of them, but the idea of sleeping in one of Haig's beds was repugnant.

She sat up, stretched, swung her feet to the floor, and looked at her watch.

Seven thirty. Daylight. With day's noises: birds, distant traffic, trees rustling in a breeze that must come off the river. A glorious day, or so it looked through huge windows. She went to the front door and opened it. Glorious indeed. The smell of honeysuckle from her dream! Vines of it snaked up the Victorian Gothic walls and around the wide door, framing the doorway where Haig had fallen. She went back inside to fetch her shoes. Should she slip in to look at him once more, to be certain it was just a drunk and nothing more? Then, over the scent of the honeysuckle and the other smells of country mornings, came the unmistakable odor of cooking, coffee certainly, bacon perhaps. For an instant she panicked. Was there someone else in the house? A woman? Or . . . worse . . . had Haig slept it off and now, unaware of her presence, was he going about his little domestic chores? And what was she to say if he walked in here as he might any moment do?

"You awake yet?" a voice called from the depths of the house. "Miss Noyes?" His voice was closer now.

"Yes," she said.

He entered the room carrying two mugs of coffee.

"Good morning. I owe you breakfast. And an apology. I don't know what else besides."

His eyes were reddened but other than that he seemed to have recovered nicely, wearing slacks and an old tweed jacket.

She took the mug he held out. "Thank you," she said.

He raised his mug in salute and sat down in an easy chair well over on the far side of the room, as if, in establishing distance, he was insuring safety.

"Well," he said mildly, "I take it you witnessed my shame and played samaritan."

She shrugged. "You collapsed. I couldn't just leave you there."

"Collapsed? Where?"

"The front door," she said. "I couldn't close it with you lying there. I dragged you inside."

He nodded solemnly, impressed. "All the way back to the den."

"When did you realize I was still here?"

"This morning. I was wandering through the house telling myself what a damn fool I'd been and there you were. On that couch. I took that as my cue to stop mumbling and cook breakfast."

"Do you do that very often?"

He looked puzzled. "Breakfast?"

"No, drinking too much and collapsing."

He paused for a moment and then he said, very quietly, "No, not often."

This had gone on long enough. "Look," she said, "thanks for the coffee. I stayed over because I was too tired and upset to face the drive back. I'll be going now."

She slipped her feet into the shoes.

He got up. "No, no, you mustn't run. There's bacon and—"

"Mr. Haig," she said, standing now, "this *wasn't* a social call. I'm a friend of Sissy Valentine's. It was probably stupid of me, certainly not very constructive, but I drove up here last not to tell you that, to tell you a number of other things as well. Well, I didn't. You were, well, you were in no condition to listen and by then I realized how foolish the whole idea had been. All I want to do now is get home to New York."

"But it wasn't a foolish idea at all," he said. "You mustn't think that." He sounded irritated as if someone else had been critical of her actions and he were defending them.

"I won't argue the point. I was very angry. I'm not anymore. So I'll be going."

"I won't argue either," he said, "but it's so rare that anyone tells me off, I mean literally, and to my face . . ."

She could not resist.

"Perhaps you'd be better off if someone did from time to time. Maybe even Sis—maybe we'd all be better off."

She was about to say "Sissy" and did not. He caught this and appreciated her tact.

"Haig the monster," he said, half to himself.

She shook her head. "But it was that more than anything that shut me up last night. More than just that you were stoned. You weren't what I'd expected." She held out a hand. "Good-bye, Mr. Haig."

He took it, looking into her eyes. "And you don't hate me," he said.

"I don't know," she said. "There isn't much point, is there?"

"If hating me would bring back that girl's arm . . ."

She turned and opened the door. Twelve hours ago she could not wait to look into this man's face and to cut him to pieces with talk of Sissy. Of Sissy's arm. Now . . .

He was watching from the door of the house as she drove away in the small silver car.

From the moment he had first seen her standing in the doorway Haig had known. He had been too drunk to recognize Alexandra Noyes, the famous face in all the papers and magazines including Haig's own, but he had known. Before they had their aimless truncated dialogue, before he passed out, he knew that the immediate nightmare had ended and that something quite fundamental in his life had changed and that he would never again be the same man. He was drunk when he first knew this but he was still sure of it the next day when he was not.

Haig knew that he had been waiting for her not for a few drunken hours but for twenty empty years.

31

Neither knew about the other, but two men were now in love with the same woman, though she was one Alex to Farrell and another to Haig. Farrell's Alex brought him periods of joy and then longer ones of fought-down fear and jealousy. She would drop out of his life for days, then reappear, calling up, responding to his messages as briskly as she had the first time. But now, after Sissy's accident, she had not called at all. Sean reasoned that she might be grieving in seclusion, but it was painful to him to be allowed no share.

Haig's Alex, so newly and briefly known, had brought an unquestioned serenity to his secret life. After one meeting he had no doubt of the outcome.

Both men had the great blessing of an occupation, and they went on in this no matter how anguished or elated in their private natures. But Farrell's rage at Haig over Sissy Valentine came close to ending their working together.

Farrell had braced Haig bluntly when he came back from his binge at Mayfair. He had stalked into the office and launched his attack without preamble.

"You knew damn well once those uniformed thugs came into the building there was going to be violence. You went looking for it. You just couldn't wait to prove just how Goddamn macho you were, how you were going to teach the unions a lesson."

Haig had anticipated this. He was still suffering shock over Sissy but he was not going to be bullied. Neither would he be forced to fire Farrell, not even by the hot-tempered editor himself. He needed Farrell now more than ever.

"You made that point before," Haig said. "A point well taken. You're entitled to say 'I told you so.' "

Farrell paced the room while Haig watched from behind the big desk. "Doesn't help that poor kid much to know I was right, to have you confess you were wrong. That doesn't bring back her arm." Farrell was reddening, the demarcation of skin and hair disappearing in a now-familiar way.

"Shouting about it won't do it either," Haig said coldly. "If I'm man enough to admit how bad I feel, to accept responsibility, to agree that the Pinkertons were a mistake, why can't you be man enough to accept that and stop this blustering?"

Farrell stopped and stared at his employer. "I hate your Goddamn guts."

"I've hated a lot of people in my time," Haig said, smiling thinly. "I was able to work with them despite it. Intelligent people usually can."

"Intelligent!" Farrell roared. "Where's the intelligence in letting a petty feud between a couple of press-room goons escalate into a full-blown tragedy?"

"Farrell," Haig said patiently, "the thing is done. Your hating me won't change that. Do you think it's easy for me to wake up each morning thinking about that girl lying in the hospital without an arm?"

Farrell was pacing again.

"Isn't it time to look ahead now?" Haig asked. "Instead of backward?"

Farrell went mulish, Irish. "If you hadn't been so arrogant. Goddamn it!" Then he was shouting. "So there was an accident. What kind of man would turn on that press again and run a woman's arm through it? What the fuck are you, Haig? That's the question that stays unanswered."

Haig sat quite still, paper white, green eyes glittering. "I think the question now is, whatever our differences, your opinion of me, do you stay on as editor of the *Mail*?"

Farrell's head, doggedly hung a moment before, lifted quickly. "Are you firing me?"

Haig found that encouraging. "No, I want you to stay. Regardless. The paper is settling down. You're learning the job. You understand the city. We're all expendable—"

"Even you?"

Haig ignored the interruption. ". . . and there are other competent editors around I could find. The *Mail* is an attractive editorship. But I don't want to lose more time looking, don't want to waste more time training and meshing with a new man. I'd rather you stayed. It would be better for the paper, better, I think, for you professionally."

"I was a pretty good columnist," Farrell said.

"And could be again. Granted. And the *Mail* would probably continue to run your stuff if it came to that. But I think you're more than a columnist. There are plenty of bright boys with typewriters. There are damn few good executives. I think you are one. Or will be."

Haig knew that Farrell had been bitten by the bug of authority, responsibility, management. Though he wouldn't admit it, Farrell liked running things. Liked it that each day the whole newspaper was, in a very real sense, his. Haig watched the Irishman turn his head away furiously, watched him fight down his rage, consider, staring out at the bridge. The blood faded under the clear skin, Farrell's face and hair became different countries again.

Farrell exhaled. "As long as you understand my feelings toward you. Personal feelings."

Haig nodded. "You've made them quite clear. Now what about Lenny Sparg?"

Lenny Sparg and his ever-present wife wanted to talk about Lenny's running for mayor. Haig wanted Farrell in the room with him when Lenny presented himself. "He gives me the creeps," Haig said. "I don't like being alone with him."

Farrell gave a short laugh. "He's the petitioner. Think how nervous he is."

"Is Big Mama coming?"

Farrell shrugged. "Of course. Who would there be to tell Lenny when to talk?"

"That bad?"

Farrell flopped into a chair and stared at the piers of the bridge. "I've seen them all in politics in this town. Crooks, thugs, liars, hysterics, egomanics, cowards, a few likely men. But Lenny beats them all. We've had effective politicians who were stupid, some very intelligent people who were mean as hell. Lenny is both: stupid *and* mean. Nasty combination."

"Then why do we give him an audience? Why do we even consider having the *Mail* back him in the race?"

Farrell turned to look at Haig. "Two reasons: No one else is a natural choice and there's Big Mama's money. She bought the kid his first local election twelve years ago, bought him a seat in Congress four years ago, she might just be able to buy him City Hall. It's been done before."

From a distance, as when he first entered the publisher's big office with his wife, Lenny Sparg looked fine. Very Robert Kennedy with the shock of unruly hair dripping boyishly over one eye. Up close, when they had seated themselves around the table Haig used for conferences, was something else again. Haig had met Sparg before, but on this occasion, in the cruel morning sunlight coming off the river, he was struck by how weird-looking the young man really was. The teeth were abnormally fine, tribute to the orthodontist's skill, but the eyes darted wildly and the face in which they were set, which seemed to shine with youth and vigor, had an unhealthy aspect, as if it had been cosmetically scraped or rebuilt by plastic surgery. And Haig found his gaze straying to Lenny's feet, trying to discern what the whisperers insisted were elevated shoes.

Directly opposite sat Mavis Sparg, the wife, the earth mother, the bankroll, her famous smile in place. As Mavis Ratchett she had been for nearly two decades the most enduring female talent in American television, host of her own talk show, the star of a hundred television specials, the woman the network sent to royal weddings and presidential inaugurations and rocket launchings. And for all those twenty years she had been investing, pyramiding her money in a series of ever more profitable real estate schemes. Mavis Ratchett, plump, jolly, wisecracking, shrewd, tough, and insatiably ambitious for her younger husband, who seemed on the threshold of the great political career from which she herself was seemingly shut out by reason of her sex. She had married Lenny twelve years ago, when he was barely twenty-five. She claimed to be five years older. In reality it was more like eleven. She smiled now at Haig.

Farrell preferred Mavis to Lenny. With her you were dealing with power, with recognizable craft, with an intelligence. It was corrupt, he felt sure, but it was predictable. With Lenny, bright eyes glaring madly, there were only impulse and ambition, unleavened by thought, unreined by caution. If it were Mavis running, Sean thought, I could buy it.

"Mr. Haig, Mr. Farrell," Lenny began, "many New Yorkers have been encouraging me to declare my candidacy for mayor. I hold a safe seat in the House, I think I've made substantial contributions to the city in Congress. If I decide to seek the nomination I'd obviously want the support of the *Mail.* I have enemies and I know they're spreading stories about me, all of which, I might say, are baseless. I thought it might be useful for me to come here and talk frankly about myself, answer any questions you might have."

He sat back, pleased with himself. From across the table Mavis beamed. Lenny had gotten through his preamble without a single lapse.

Haig asked the usual questions: What were Congressman Sparg's attitudes on crime, on the schools, on taxes, on debt management, on reversing the flight of middle-income families, on welfare? Young Sparg answered as if someone had prepared file cards and he were reading from them. Whatever else he is, Haig thought, he has a good memory.

"Lenny," Farrell said when the congressman had finished, stressing his informality, "you've heard these stories that are around, and I guess we have to ask . . ."

"You mean about girls?" Lenny said quickly.

Mavis tensed.

"Let me be absolutely candid on that," said Lenny. "Those stories were fabricated four years ago when I first ran for Congress. By an unscrupulous opponent. And I can assure you if there were anything to them, anything at all, it would long since have come out. Why," he said expansively, "there was even a rumor Mavis gets the girls for me." He smiled beatifically at his wife.

The older woman shrugged. "Ridiculous, isn't it, Mr. Haig?"

"Yes, yes," Haig said quickly. Something was ridiculous, for certain.

Lenny was aglow with warmth now. "And there are even worse stories," he said, beaming. He proceeded to tell a few.

Haig was appalled. The man was sick, glorying in the repetition of the foulest sort of canard about himself. Across the table Mavis fidgeted as Lenny ran off his catalogue of slander and smiled expansively.

"That's the sort of men who oppose me," he said righteously. "Evil men. Men who fear me. Who know I represent a powerful independent voice. That the party doesn't own, that the bosses can't harness me. They fear my wife. They fear me. They know I can't be controlled."

To which Farrell added dryly, "I'm sure they're right on that."

Haig recalled reading somewhere that when Lenny was seventeen years old he had declared he would one day be elected President—and that old Mavis had said the same thing on their wedding day. They would buy the White House as they bought a safe seat in Congress. As they now proposed to buy the mayoralty. Farrell dove in with more questions, and after an hour Haig stood up. They would carefully consider the congressman's candidacy, they appreciated his candor. Mavis Ratchett Sparg came around to the other side of the table to shake Haig's hand.

"You see," she said shrewdly, "they claim Lenny is my puppet. That I pull the strings. And here for an hour I said hardly a word. Not one."

Farrell was also standing. "One," he said, "you used the word 'ridiculous.'"

Mavis did not smile but Lenny did. The boy obviously felt he had been a hit. Haig walked them to the elevator, leaving Farrell behind to gather up his notes. And to wonder.

32

Meg Valentine was being firm. Her behavior the night of the accident had frightened her badly. In it she had seen the onset of senility, of the transformation from crisp sanity to foolish old woman. Now, a month later, she had thrown off that fear. She had only suffered an aberration, a natural reaction to shock; she had convinced herself of that. She was with Sissy now, in a large and sunny hospital room crowded with flowers.

"This place smells like a funeral home." Meg Valentine snorted.

"I know," Sissy said blankly. "I tell them no and they just keep coming."

The old woman tugged her chair closer to her granddaughter. "Now, look, Sissy. It's not too early to start making plans. I've spoken with the best men in the field and they want to have you go down to Baltimore. Johns Hopkins. They feel confident there's enough there for you to handle an artificial arm." Meg could not bring herself to say "stump."

"Grandma," Sissy said, "you promised not to. I don't want to talk about it."

"We *have* to talk about it," Meg declared.

Sissy shook her head. The old woman talked on. The girl stopped listening. She was up for several hours a day now, she would be released in another week. Then all she wanted was to disappear. She and this thing that used to be an arm, with its horrid tubes and its pain and the awful smell of what oozed from it. Sissy stared ahead of her and wished the nurse would come in and give her a shot or take her temperature or something. Anything.

Meg talked on.

When they let Sissy leave a week later she stayed in Meg's house for a few days, then, upon promising to make her scheduled visits to the specialist, she was permitted to regain her own apartment on Central Park West. For the first time she felt free of the hospital. She roamed through the high-ceilinged rooms, drank in the aerial view of the park in summer, rejoiced in freedom from the hospital, from the hated tubes, from dear, wonderful, cloying Meg. Then, on the second night she was home, the reaction. A nightmare, ripped bodily from her memory of the accident, the two big men brawling, her loss of balance, the tug at her arm, the scream cut off even before it reached her mouth. She awoke drenched with sweat. The air conditioner was on and to avoid chill she got up and changed the bedclothes, awkwardly tugging the wet sheets from the bed, even more awkwardly wrestling to get the fresh linen in place. When she was finished she looked down at herself. The nightgown was soaked, stuck to her body, and she pulled it off. She went to the bathroom then for a drink of water, leaving the light off, working by touch, not wanting to see herself.

Three days later Meg Valentine died. Peacefully, at home, following dinner with an old friend and watching the evening news on television from her bed.

Alex went to the funeral. She found herself comparing Meg to her own mother. Like Nora, Meg had lost a young husband. But she had gallantly rebuilt a life, not of best-dressed lists and sycophantic priests, not of gauzy poses and meaningless gestures, but of substance, of work, of reality.

Haig came, somber in his dark clothes, eyes startling green. Alex had to admire him for coming. He must have heard the whispers— that Sissy's accident had killed the old woman.

Sissy came, pale, black-clad, more slender than ever, her missing arm masked as she huddled close to her brother.

Willie mourned his grandmother. Deeply, sincerely. He had not yet realized she had neglected to sign over to him any share of the proceeds of the sale. Mercifully ignorant, he held his sister close and wept.

As did Junior Valentine, plump, pale-faced, and mourning. For Junior knew his last opportunity for reconciliation had passed, that Meg had written no last codicil. Desperate and frightened, Junior barely listened to the eulogy, intent instead on his hatred for Campbell Haig and his indignation that his mother had sold his newspaper —*his!*—to this cold-eyed man who had maimed his daughter.

Farrell came. How could he not? In some ways Meg had been the mother he abandoned twenty years before in Gerritsen Beach. Imperious, arch, meddling, and erratic, Meg had been all these things. But that was not as he remembered her. He had not prayed for a long time yet he prayed now for Meg, for his mother. And for himself.

And the press lords came. Great newspaper publishers miss neither editions nor the funerals of one of their own.

So passed Meg Valentine. And the glory of her.

Sissy went back to her great empty apartment. There she stayed secluded except to visit the doctor. When people called she fended them off with one transparent excuse or another, Alex Noyes along with the rest. Sissy heard the hurt in Alex's voice but could not care.

Her grandmother's death seemed a distant event, something represented by still photos in a motion picture, something read about on microfilm. Sissy saw everything that way now. As far as she comprehended the fact of Meg's death, she was relieved by it. Meg had become her chief tormentor, the chief disturber of her seclusion, and Sissy was glad she had gone away.

33

When Campbell Haig's letter arrived Alex Noyes read it, put it aside, read it a second time, and then crumpled it and threw it into a wicker wastebasket. Her anger had melted away at Mayfair, but she did not want to see Haig again.

He did want to see her, he had written. Not only because it was important to him, but because he thought it was important to her. The arrogance of it! He suggested that her visit to Mayfair had been so brief, under such unusual conditions, that a more conventional meeting in New York, a dinner, perhaps, was in order. He would not call, would not pester her. It would be Alex's move. And there were his phone numbers.

"I'll be *damned* if I call him!" Alex cried aloud.

The next morning before her maid had come she retrieved the letter, smoothed it, and stuffed it in her purse.

Sean Farrell was on her mind these days. She had to phone him, to answer the calls he left on her tape, to tell him their times together were over. Could she tell him why? The reason would seem futile to him. He had never wanted Sissy, never made a move her way. Alex knew that. But Alex could never again be with the man Sissy had wanted. It was cowardice to avoid telling Farrell how all this was, she knew, but she continued to put it off.

So now Alex was again alone. Her friend was incommunicado, her lover was out of bounds. She wondered if her old night forays would begin again. They seemed part of another lifetime, but there she was, beached and restless.

In this mood she went off to the affair with Philip Levitan. Diana Ross had opened at Radio City Music Hall, a big, splashy musical extravaganza complete with laser beams, male dancers in white tails, a quartet of shirtless, oiled Nubians to carry Miss Ross on and off stage, and a glittering charity audience that had paid a hundred dollars a ticket. There was even a warm-up act, a man who did bird calls and imitations of the common housefly. Which drove Philip Levitan to distraction.

He leaned over and grabbed Alex's arm.

"Alex," he groaned, "I can't take this anymore. I'll be in the lobby, at the bar."

Levitan was one of the bankers who floated the loans that saved New York, a smooth, fortyish mittel-European with good manners, a chauffeured car, and a passion for Alexandra Noyes tempered only by the fact that he already had a wife who lived in Greenwich and, conveniently, refused to come to New York for evenings like this. A complaisant escort, who posed none of the emotional problems of a Sean Farrell, a man whose sophistication and dry wit consoled him when Alex, as she inevitably did, turned down his occasional invitation to join him in bed.

Alex nodded. The warm-up was inane. But she didn't feel like making that long walk back from the second row with all those curious eyes picking her out, hearing the whispered "Isn't that Alex Noyes?" as women elbowed their men to attention.

Ross finally came on, Philip returned, and the rest of the performance was fine, if you liked that sort of thing. Afterward they made their way through a lobby full of people they knew, who said hello and stuck out hands, or kissed cheeks, then the sidewalk with the paparazzi and the celebrity groupies, then the calm and security of his limousine and finally the party at Diane's place on Fifth Avenue.

Philip had fetched her a drink and was deep in conversation with one of the editors of the *Times*. Alex had said the usual things to the usual people and now stood by one of the oriels looking out over the park, watching the moving lights of the cars on the winding drives, the moon reflecting off the reservoir. It was a good party,

Diane gave no other sort, and Alex amused herself by watching the ebb and flow around Liv Ullmann and Warren Beatty and Diane Keaton and Capote. This really *was* what New York was all about: power, glamour, money, talent, recognition. I belong here, she told herself. I'm one of them. And yet . . .

She found herself thinking about Campbell Haig. It was strange they had never met before the accident. Perhaps he didn't go to parties like this one, which was also strange. In her experience newspaper publishers were expected to make appearances, to show the flag, to smile and shake hands and indulge in whispered confidences with men like Levitan and department store presidents and movie producers and the chairwomen of important charities. Perhaps that wasn't the way they did it in New Mexico. Perhaps he was simply uninterested. Or shy. That was it, shy. That was an odd attribute in such a driven, ambitious man. Yet when she thought of Haig at Mayfair, slender, almost boyish, the soft brown hair slightly mussed, the half embarrassed and rather courtly manner . . . So different from the Haig of reputation. Different yet again from the tone of his letter to her.

They were serving a buffet and Philip Levitan fetched her a plate. No, she said, thinking of her legs and the fact that she was once again nearly one hundred thirty pounds, and instead took another drink. Levitan, always sensitive to her mood, promised to keep her supplied with drinks and found a place on the floor next to Barry Diller and Helen Gurley Brown. Alex wandered through the apartment, outwardly serene, chatting, responding, smiling. Inwardly it was something else, a yearning, an impatience, a vague sense of being unfulfilled. After the fourth drink it was no longer vague. Instead, an acute sense of need, physical desire, one of those recurrent drives of pounding, tangible sexual hunger. She was wearing a long dress, the skirt velvet, the top crepe de chine, and she was suddenly conscious of tactile sensations: the unlined velvet rustling against her stockinged legs, the filmy top moving lightly but perceptibly over her breasts as she walked, gestured, bent to kiss a cheek. As she raised her glass even the movement of her arm, drawing the crepe de chine lightly across her nipple, excited her. Hey, she thought, struggling to regain control, this is crazy or I'm drunk.

Philip Levitan came up to her. "Alex, everything all right?"

She made an effort to smile. "Fine, just tired, I guess."

"It must have been the bird calls."

"The common housefly."

He grimaced. "Well, just give me the word and we'll go."

"No, you stay. No point in ruining your evening. When I'm ready I'll just slip out. The doorman will get a cab."

He said nonsense but she prevailed.

"I will have another drink, though," and he signaled a waiter before returning to the others.

She was drinking hundred-proof Stolichnaya and it was having its effect, an effect that dovetailed nicely with her growing sensuality, reinforced the sense of reckless abandon, papered over the faint voice of caution. Her eyes swept the room. No one here, certainly that was the first rule. Never with anyone who knew her, never, snobbishly, with a man of her set, her class, her station. When she was like this, no matter how driven, how drunk, that one rule never varied, was never broken. No, no one at this party, no one in this wonderful room. But out there, somewhere beyond the park, somewhere across the city, a bar, a stranger, a moist tongue, a body, eventually a bed.

The cab drove south to Washington Square and turned west. She was still sufficiently under control to avoid the East Village. She wanted a man to make love to, not a motorcycle gang. On Eighth Street she tapped on the Plexiglas shield and the driver pulled over. She handed him some money. Inside the bar was dark, cozy, the jukebox not too loud, the music not too raucous. Good, she thought, a lucky choice. The barmaid was busy but there was a vacant stool. Behind her people were dancing. There was conversation and the sound of glassware. She ordered another vodka, and before it came a woman on her left touched her arm and said something flattering about her dress. She looked down. A long dress in a Village joint. Well, it wasn't the first time she'd looked out of place on one of her wild hunts.

Her eyes had grown accustomed to the gloom and as she drank she looked around the room. There seemed to be more women than men. A few of the men she could see were patently homosexual. Well, she thought, it *is* the Village. She looked down the bar. None of the traveling salesmen or cheating-husband types that were her usual prey. Which was damn rotten luck. She was quite drunk now and sexually primed. She put her glass down on the bar and was surprised to realize it was empty, only a half-melted ice cube at the bottom. She looked for the barmaid.

"I'll get her. Let me buy the next."

It was the woman on her left. Alex half turned on the bar stool.

"That's okay," she said. But when the barmaid came the woman got her way and fresh drinks were made for both of them.

"Well, thanks," Alex said.

The woman had a nice, plain, early thirties, what Alex thought of as a midwestern face. No makeup, good bones. She was tall and lean in a tank top and white duck pants. Her feet were tan in sandals.

"I was at a party," Alex said, knowing that apology was unnecessary. Drunk talk.

"I figured," the woman said. "I'm Sarah Deschler."

Alex shook her hand and gave a name. Amy something.

Sarah had a nice dry wit. She pointed out various characters in the place, who was a writer, who an artist, whose love affair had just broken up, who was drinking on tick and running up a tab that made the barmaid nervous.

"But there are hardly any men," Alex said.

Sarah put a hand on her arm. "Amy," she said, genuinely surprised, "but this place is gay. I thought you knew."

Alex was drunk but not too drunk to feel embarrassed. "God," she said, "you must think I'm an awful turkey."

"Then you didn't know?"

"No. Really."

Sarah paused. "Do you mind?" she asked.

Alex laughed. "No, I don't mind. If you all"—she gestured toward the rest of the bar—"don't. Besides, I'm so wrecked I guess it doesn't matter anyway."

She knew she'd made a mistake with that.

"What are you stoned on?" Sarah asked, her voice lower now, more intimate. Had she moved her stool closer to Alex's?

"Just vodka. I didn't mean drugs." The barmaid had brought another glass and she found herself drinking it. Sarah *had* inched her stool closer.

"Do you do drugs?" she asked.

Alex shook her head. "No, I mean grass sometimes. And I tried coke. But it isn't really my thing." The room spun.

"Good," Sarah said. "Anyone who really needs it usually turns out pretty dull anyway."

Alex was wondering what that meant when she felt something hard nudging her right thigh. A pretty blonde in an aluminum jumpsuit was grinning at her. It was her knee. "Hi," the blonde said, "how ya doin'?"

"I'm okay, thanks," Alex said, unable to resist grinning back into the open, freckled face. The odd thing was that the pressure of the knee excited her. Behind her Sarah was now standing even taller than she had seemed.

"Listen," Sarah said, speaking across Alex to the blonde, "why don't you just butt out, sister. My friend and I are having a talk and a drink."

The blonde shrugged. "So let's all be friends," she said pleasantly.

Sarah took Alex's arm. "Come on," she said, "this music is great. And you said you wanted to dance, didn't you?"

Alex had not danced with another female since dancing school, when she was twelve years old and they were short of boys. Sarah led. She danced very well. She held Alex close but not unnaturally so.

"Listen," she said into her ear, "stay away from that sort of trash. I've seen her before. She's a cheap pickup. Just wants the one thing."

Alex nodded, her head spinning. And what do I want but the one thing? she asked herself. And aren't *I* a cheap pickup?

When they went back to the bar the blonde was still there. Somehow their stools had been taken and Alex found herself wedged between the two women. Behind her the blonde was openly pressing herself against Alex's back. In front Sarah, annoyed but not wanting to lose Alex by playing the bitch or seeming overly hostile, let her hand drop to Alex's hip, which she stroked slowly, possessively, as she stared into her golden eyes.

And Alex did nothing. Every instinct told her this was insane, that she should put a few dollars on the bar, issue a brief farewell address, and get the hell out of there. But she could not. She had gone too far, she was too drunk, the two bodies so close, so insistent, had aroused her just as if she were with a man. My God, she thought, half frightened, half amazed at the realization, maybe there *isn't* any difference.

Alex had never experienced a lesbian urge. Yet here she was, reacting, softening, moistening in response to the touch of strange women! Was she some sort of freak? Was this the logical culmination of her bizarre midnight bar crawls, her reckless motel adventures?

Now there was another drink in her hand. Sarah had seemingly accepted the blonde, and now her hand, the palm flat, slid down Alex's belly, gently, and then with increased pressure, moving against the mound beneath the velvet. The other girl now moved so that she could cup Alex's breasts from behind. Alex moaned, her hips squirmed. No one seemed to notice the three of them. Had the lights dimmed even more? Was the music playing or was it in her head? How many drinks had she had and why was she asking for another?

She had to go to the bathroom. The blonde wanted to go with her but Alex smiled and said no. As she crossed the room she was conscious that she was weaving. She had never been so drunk. In the tiny lavatory she dampened a paper towel and, while she sat on the seat, wiped her face. It felt cool, wonderful. Then she saw there was no toilet paper. She reached into her purse for Kleenex. A bit of crumpled stationery fell out. She leaned over, dizzying as the room went round, and picked it up. Haig's letter. Hadn't she thrown it away? She seemed to recall that she had. She stood up, stupidly staring at the letter.

"If you should ever need to reach me . . ." That was the phrase that had set her off, the arrogance of it, the vanity.

She looked at herself in the mirror. A blurred image. Did she really look that bad or was it the dirty glass? She dampened another towel and rinsed her face again. Her hair, chopped short, looked all right. She was grateful for that. Someone was rattling the doorknob. Then she remembered the two women outside. Sarah and the other one. Waiting for her, their hands, their mouths, waiting.

Alex shuddered and began to cry. Then, without reasoning it through, she unbolted the door and stumbled out into the little corridor to the phone. It took forever to get the first dime out of her handbag and then she dialed a wrong number, but she persisted. After two wrong numbers she got the Carlyle.

Haig had been asleep but he said he would be there in twenty minutes.

34

It took longer than twenty minutes. She had been vague about the bar's location. When at last he found it the cab driver peered at him dubiously over his shoulder.

"You sure you want this place, mister?"

"Yes," Haig said, pushing a ten-dollar bill into the man's hand. "Take this and wait. I'll be right out."

He went down the three steps into the bar and pulled the door open. A blast of music, a few flashing strobe lights, the whiff of marijuana flowed toward him. He shoved past two women talking in the doorway. One had her arm around the other's shoulder. There were perhaps a dozen women along the bar itself, perched on stools, lounging, glasses in hand. It all looked very ordinary. But on a small, raised platform he saw a small, slender girl shuffling to the slow beat of a record while four or five women stared intently up at her. The girl was naked. Then he saw Alex.

"Hello," he said quietly, careful not to say her name. The two women who flanked her in the dark corner booth looked up. There were a lot of glasses on the table in front of them, the ashtray spiraled smoke. Alex's face split into a sappy grin.

"You came," she said.

"I said I would."

Behind him the music played an old recording of "American Pie."

Her blouse was unbuttoned, her lipstick smudged, her skin shone with sweat, her hair hung damp and lank. Her gold and blue eyes were wide and blank. Haig thought he had never seen anything quite so beautiful.

"Come on," he said, "we're going home."

He reached out a hand past the blond woman.

"Hey, what is this shit? Who the hell are you?" the blonde demanded.

Haig ignored her and took Alex's hand, drawing her to her feet.

The blonde had a filthy mouth. She used it now. The other woman was more polite but just as stubborn.

"Look, isn't this Alexandra Noyes?"

Haig shook his head, continuing to pull Alex out of the booth past the blonde who sat rigidly, her knees inhibiting Alex's passage.

"It's not. I'm her physician. She goes off like this every so often."

More filth spewed from the blonde's mouth. Haig gave Alex one final tug and she was standing now, free of the booth, free of the pressure of the blonde's legs.

He wondered if he were going to have to hit the blonde.

With his free hand he pulled out some bills and dropped them on the table.

"This ought to pay for her drinks," he said.

The blonde told him what he could do with his Goddamn money. Sarah was standing now too. More reasonably, she had accepted the inevitability of loss, and she moved to Alex's other side to help support her.

"Come on," she told Haig, "I'll give you a hand. She doesn't belong in this place."

As she went through the door into the cool night air the blonde continued to curse all three of them from inside the bar. Haig thought he could still hear her screeches as the cab pulled away.

Alex was sick once in the cab and the driver was furious, but Haig kept pushing crumpled bills at him with one hand and trying to keep her head up and to clean off her face as best he could with a handkerchief.

He put her in his own bedroom and he took the spare. He did not want to undress her but the dress was soiled and he had to. He wet down a large towel and cleaned her up as best he could and then rubbed her dry so she wouldn't chill and got her into a terry bathrobe and into bed. She was out some of the time, conscious but very drunk at other times, not making much sense, not calling him by name, but mumbling apologies and, when she could focus, smiling up at him in what he guessed must be gratitude.

That was when he said, aloud, not really to her, more to himself, "Miss American Pie . . ."

During the night he heard her stagger to the bathroom to vomit repeatedly and at length. After she'd gone back to bed he waited a decent interval and then tiptoed into the room. In sleep she was tranquil and very lovely, more a beautiful child than the formidable young woman he knew her to be. Having her asleep under his protection filled him with certainty and satisfaction. *Whatever* had propelled her off on her binge, had drawn her to a lesbian joint, he had no doubts of her. And he took supreme pleasure in a certain thing: In all New York, when she was in trouble, she had called him. He turned quickly and left her, shaken by emotion stronger than he had ever felt for any woman.

He lay in bed, a few yards from where she slept, propped on an elbow, ready to go to her if she again were ill. It did not occur to him that she might call out to have him come to her for other reasons.

Which was strange. For ever since he had first seen her framed in the doorway at Mayfair he had felt a powerful attraction, over-whelmingly but not solely physical. He had been the one who was drunk then, who would collapse, she the ministering samaritan. How strange it was they should now meet for the second time in roles so startlingly reversed.

Why was she so special? Why? What made her different and more than different, unique? He had known some of the most alluring women in the world. And now, Alexandra Noyes, daughter of a President, sleeping off what must be a historic drunk in a bed in his hotel room, wearing his robe, washed and dried by his hands. Not just another beautiful woman. Distinctly herself. The mystique of the White House, was that it? The tragic, truncated presidency? The rivalry with her fabulous mother?

It was all part of the mix, he suspected. With her chopped-off hair and her solid legs she was not physically the stuff of magazine covers. Not perfection. And yet she was often there. His own papers must have run hundreds of photos of her, from childhood, through adolescence, into the era of what his tabloids had labeled the playgirl from the White House, the madcap heiress, the Golden Girl, Alex the Great. At last he fell asleep, a montage of his own newspaper headlines and captions framing photographs of Alexandra Noyes.

In the morning he went into the bathroom and tried to shower quietly, which was difficult. But when he came out she was still asleep and he dressed quickly and called down for a big breakfast, everything doubled. At ten she was still asleep and he had had room service return twice with a fresh cart and wheel away the other, untouched. He did not eat, took no coffee, and made only one call to the office to tell Miss Mayhew he was taking the day off. When she began to read to him from his daily calendar he said, "I know," and hung up. The papers had been sent up and he went through them, started to jot down a few notes but found them silly, inconsequential, and gave it up as a bad job. He could not concentrate. Except on her.

At a quarter to eleven Alex Noyes woke up.

She came to the door of the bedroom and looked out at him, sitting on a couch with newspapers strewn all around.

"I suppose you'll fill me in on last night," she said, smiling bravely. "I'd sort of like to know before I die."

Haig leaped up. "Oh, you won't die," he said cheerfully. "If you got through last night you'll live to be a hundred at least. Like those Russians who eat yogurt."

She made a face. "Please, no mention of food. Do you have Bufferin or anything?"

"The medicine chest," he said, "that way."

She nodded and moved, very slowly, in the direction of the bathroom. Haig phoned room service and had them send up breakfast for a fourth time.

Her hair was still wet, very straight, and her face was less pale now, but not made up, as they sat across from one another at the table. She was still wearing the big terry robe. He ate voraciously and she picked at some toast.

"I remember calling you," she said, "and then you were washing my face and talking to me. But nothing in between. What happened, or is it better I don't know?"

"Oh, but I think you *should* know. You remember the bar?" She nodded. "And the two women, Sarah and one other?" She nodded again, this time unhappily. "Well, when I arrived there were legions of women slavering over you, vying for your favors. Very impressive."

She watched him drink off half a cup of black coffee before she spoke. "That bad?" she said.

"Uh-huh."

She licked her lips. "Well, I mean, nothing happened. With the women, I mean. At least I don't think so. I'm pretty sure."

He said nothing and then, like a little girl, she blurted out: "I *didn't* do anything. I didn't. I didn't!"

He reached across the table and took her hand. "I know you didn't," he said quietly.

She was crying now. "How do you know?" she said. "How can you be sure?"

He waited for only an instant and then he said, his voice even lower, "Because you're you."

She dabbed at her face with the big linen napkin and looked miserable. "But the awful thing was," she said, "for a while there I thought I wanted to. To try it."

"Alex . . ." He stopped himself and grinned. "You know, I'm not sure if that's what I'm to call you. Or should it be 'Miss Noyes'?"

"Alex," she said.

"Alex, we all do things we later regret. And if we're drunk or upset or . . . lonely . . . we experience yens and urges and drives that in normal circumstances would be unthinkable. You were very drunk last night. So much so that . . ."

"Diminished responsibility," she said, "is that my excuse?"

"If you need an excuse, yes. But I don't think you need one. I don't think your life is made up of patched-over excuses and plea coppings or evasions or 'diminished responsibility.' I think you're a woman who is honest with herself and honest with people who count. You don't lie and you don't shirk and you don't cheat."

She dabbed again with the napkin.

"And you don't soil," he said, deadly serious.

Her weeping continued, increased until there was nothing to do but give in to it. It was what he had said that made it so awful. If she could have believed him. That she was not soiled, Daddy's girl . . .

"Alex, you're tired. You feel rotten. You should get some more sleep."

She looked up. He looked so concerned, she had to smile. "Campbell, would you mind if I went home now and let you get some work done?"

He stood up, alarmed. "But you can't go," he said. "You . . . you could take another nap or something. I wouldn't bother you. I could just sit out here and . . ."

". . . and watch over me?"

"Sure," he said. "Why not?"

"You're afraid I'll do something foolish."

In the end she had her way. She borrowed a raincoat of his and bundled her evening dress in a shopping bag and he called his chauffeur and had him drive her home. He wanted to go with her but she wouldn't have it.

"You do have to work, remember?" she said. "I'd heard that was all you ever do, work."

He held her hand at the door, not wanting her to go. "Call me up," he said. "Let me know you're all right. I . . ." He trailed off, gazing at her intently.

"I know," she said, and leaning toward him, kissed him lightly on the cheek. Then she was gone.

35

A long, elliptical driveway led up to the great white house at East
Hampton. Sissy had learned to drive on it when she was thirteen.
And she had relearned there, using the one arm to maneuver the
yellow Jeep. She was in the driveway now, sitting in the driver's seat,
holding the wheel so tightly her knuckles were white against her
suntan. This was the real thing.

She had come to East Hampton alone, the week after Labor Day.
This had always been her favorite time, the summer crowd gone, the
children in school, the sun still hot but the air cool, the blue water's
warmth lingering. For nearly two weeks she had practiced in the
driveway with the Jeep, done her exercises, sunned by the pool. At
first she could not look at herself in the mirror; now she could, and
with a grim satisfaction she watched the stump brown and firm and
lose that crosshatched pallor. There was no longer any pain. Nor had
she ever had the sensation of hurt in a limb no longer there.

The nights had been bad. At first the pain, then the trauma of
loss, finally the lopsided feeling that she experienced more acutely
when she was horizontal. She had always been a sound sleeper but
an active one, rolling this way and that through the night. But now
the arm was not there to push against the mattress, to provide

leverage and balance, and she woke often, first not knowing why, then realizing she must have moved and done it awkwardly. It was at these times, awake, restless, alone in the big bed in the empty house, hearing the waves booming up on the beach, watching the stars, or clouds racing across the moon, that she began thinking about sex.

She lay there remembering the times she had slept with men—not many times, and those times when love was imminent if not in full flower. There had been no sex for its own sake. Now she wondered. Would that other road be open to her? Now that the highway was closed to her, was there the detour she had always shunned? If men could no longer love her—she was sure they could not—could they desire her still, as some once had?

Months ago she had lain in this bed and fought back the temptation of that mythic male, darkly lustful, who had appeared unbidden in a fantasy so vivid that Sissy had almost succumbed to it. Now, if he came, would she succumb?

To her wonder she could not visualize that man. He hung back beyond the reach of memory. She tried to conjure him up to use his image as the real man had wanted to use her. The image would not come to her.

Was she past willful pretending of this kind?

Would the real man come to her aid now, if his phantom held back from her as she now was? That idea took root in her succeeding nights and days until Sissy was determined to find out, to force the issue.

She turned the ignition key and the motor kicked over. It was about nine, a weekday night. She put on the headlights and drove down the driveway and onto Dunemere and then east toward Montauk, where *nobody* went, nobody who knew Sissy. Montauk of the fishermen and the Bonackers and the oceanfront motels and waterbeds and mirrored ceilings.

She was surprised how easy it was.

The bar was called Pete's. There were more men than women. Sissy wore good jeans over soft, knee-high boots, a yellow cashmere sweater, long-sleeved. A tweed hacking jacket on her shoulders. Her long hair hung straight, she was tanned; except for a watch the only jewelry she wore could not be seen: a thin gold chain lightly girdling

her waist. She rarely wore a bra and tonight she was naked under
her jeans.

"Hi, what happened to your flipper?" the man said, glancing at
her limp sleeve.

"Oh, nothing. An accident," she said.

"Shit," he said in a sympathetic tone. "What are you drinking?"

At midnight they were both slightly drunk. His name was Larry,
he sold storm windows for a chain, he was halfway through a week's
vacation. "Our peak season starts about now. I was damn lucky to
get away at all."

He had his arm around her waist, under the tweed jacket, his hand
straying knowingly under the back of her sweater, slipping over her
smooth skin. She was on a stool, he stood next to her, her right thigh
solidly against his hip. He was stocky rather than large, not especially
good-looking. His repartee was predictable but he was pleasant,
seemingly gentle, and he wanted her. That was the miracle.

He made rather a show of looking at his watch.

"Hey," he said, "it's pretty late. The motel isn't far. Feel like
dropping by?"

"Oh, yes," she said.

It happened in the parking lot. She knew who it was the instant
she saw the hat, that painter's cap with the bill tilted crazily upward,
the dark man of her dream. He knew her too. His sullen face split
into a grin.

"Well, well," he said, "long time no see."

Larry had been digging into pockets for the car keys and now he
looked up expecting to be introduced to some acquaintance. Instead
the stunned expression on her face told him otherwise; instead of
smiling at the girl's "friend," he slid instinctively into a wary, less
open stance.

"Still early," the man in the cap said to Sissy.

She shook her head. "No," she said.

It was the sort of fight that happens in a thousand parking lots
outside a thousand gin mills any midnight. Larry said something, the
man in the cap said something. When the Bonacker reached out
toward Sissy, Larry went at him. It did not last long.

The winner was very brisk. Nursing a split knuckle in his mouth
he turned from Larry, slumped against the fender of his car. "Well,

now," he said, "about that drink? My name's Caz. Bar's still open."

She did not answer.

"Sulking?" he asked. "Baby, that's kid stuff. Now if you just . . ."

Her eyes had gone empty. He could see that now. Scared? he wondered. He went to her, reached out and took her hand, tugged it with surprising gentleness.

"Hey," he said, "you okay?"

She was not. The brief fight had opened doors of memory. She had again seen Brasky and the foreman flailing at one another in the press room, had felt herself knocked off balance, falling. The deep, narrow memory of that awful instant had been wrenched up out of her to the surface. She froze, shocked and rigid.

"Hey," he said, more quietly.

He looked around. Larry was up and with a disgusted wave of his hand, a handkerchief pressed against his face, he got into his car. The car started and rolled slowly out of the lot.

Caz and Sissy were alone. Behind them the lights of the bar illuminated little squares of sandy ground, the music of the jukebox floated out into the September night. He let her hand fall from his. It hung, loosely, by her side. It was then, for the first time, he noticed the empty sleeve.

Caz knew the girl well. Not by name or address but by type. This was the sort of girl a charter boat fisherman rubbed up against only on the water. Plenty of them there, fetched along, pouting or childishly eager, by fat-cat older men with two hundred dollars for a day's sport and the yen to have a girl or two along for the ride, to admire their skill with a rod, to *ooh* and *aah* when the big billfish and the tuna and the blue sharks hit. This was a girl like that.

He spoke to her again, and when she did not answer he took her good hand and led her to his pickup truck.

Drugged, that was it. Well, why not? He grabbed her tweed jacket, which had begun to slip from her shoulders, and stuffed it into the storage space behind the seat. He helped her into the cab and went around and got in the other side. Sissy sat looking straight ahead, her back square against the worn leather, the cashmere sweater gently curved against her small, high bosom. Caz turned the key and the motor coughed and caught.

His boat was moored at one of the more workaday wharves of the local fishing fleet. It was a good boat, sound, efficient. But because he lived aboard (his wife had taken the house in the divorce) it was a bit more than that: a clean, economical, very snug berth. He got Sissy out of the cab and led her across the brief gangplank to the boat's deck. He led her across the pleasantly moving deck and down the three steps of the ladder to the cabin. He switched on an overhead lamp.

"Okay, honey," he said, "I'm mixing myself a quick one but don't feel you got to join in. Maybe what you took already is enough, huh?"

No response. She stood there, that was all.

"Jesus," he said, this time aloud. It was creepy the way she didn't seem to hear, the way she stood. She *looked* okay, if the eyes didn't bother you. He led her to a bunk and very gently sat her down. He took a glass from the galley cabinet and poured himself a straight vodka.

Glass in hand he sat next to her on the bunk. He leaned over and kissed her on the mouth. She didn't pull back. Neither did she respond. He drained the glass.

"Hell," he said. He put the empty glass on the deck of the cabin, stood up, and with a practiced movement stripped her cashmere sweater off over her head. She neither resisted nor reacted.

He only glanced at the stump. His eyes were on her suntanned breasts with their firm little nipples. Then his hands were on them and he pushed her back onto the bunk and he was unsnapping her jeans.

She stared at the ceiling.

36

Alex Noyes was thinking guiltily about Sissy while she dressed for dinner with Campbell Haig. She phoned her every week but the conversations were unsatisfactory, as if Sissy had her mind on something else. Alex took care not to ask her about her physical condition. The girl sounded vigorous enough but not herself. Not the old laughing Sissy. She wished Sissy would come into the city, hoped she was not becoming a recluse. Each time Alex had suggested driving out to see her Sissy had invented a reason not to. Well, she'd just *go*, that was all. Show up at the door. Only when? Her own life had its distractions now. Thinking of Haig, she frowned and opened yet another drawer, trying to decide what top to wear with her calf-length cashmere skirt. She picked up a thin black wool sweater with a cowl neck, held it up against her bare upper body, stared at the full-length mirror, and then, impatient with herself, tugged it on over her cropped hair, pulled it snug and straight, and decided that she liked the way it complemented the chocolate skirt, the way it clung softly to her upraised breasts.

He'll like that, she thought.

It would be their first "date." That was the word Haig used on the phone the day after he rescued her. "I'd like very much to see you again. Take you out on a date." She could hardly believe that this powerful, assured man would ask her for a "date." But he had.

"You don't really have to, you know," she'd said, and he'd immediately blurted:

"But I want to. Really, I do."

He was tentative about where they'd go. "But I don't care," she said, "I really don't. Pick a place you like." Finally she said "21" sounded fine to her.

He was very shy. They got one of the good banquettes in the bar and neither of them wanted a cocktail. She recalled, all too painfully, how much she had had the night they last met and where it had led. Haig said simply, "I don't drink very much." The captain brought them the big menus and when they'd ordered Haig asked for the sommelier. The occasion called for something.

"What is the oldest Bordeaux you have?"

It was a Rothschild wine, pre-war.

"Is it still drinkable?"

Alex had thought he was fooling, making an elaborate joke. When the man went away to fetch the wine she said, quite seriously: "Listen, you don't have to do that. I barely know the whites from the reds."

He shook his head as if to say he knew *that* wasn't true and then he said, "But I want to. This is a very special night."

The wine was incredible but he barely sipped it. Conversation was awkward. He blurted out remarks intended to please, but although he was obviously sincere, she was immune to such talk. Still she liked him, the bashful sincerity, the intelligence masked by an almost boyish desire to win approval, but she found him tense, uneasy, as if his remarks had been prepared in advance. While liking his looks, the way he looked at her, she found herself glancing at her watch and wondering when she could decently thank him and say good night. They were waiting for dessert and coffee when she first realized all his conversation had been about her. Nothing about himself.

"Look, Campbell," she said, "we've met twice. Both times under what you'd have to call 'unusual' circumstances. It's natural that being together like this seems, well, a bit strained. I've seen you at what I imagine is your worst. You've seen me at what was definitely mine. Can't we just relax and enjoy what's left of dinner and this fantastic wine I seem to be monopolizing?"

For an instant he looked stricken. "Is it that bad?" he asked.

She nodded. "Pretty bad."

His shoulders slumped and then his mouth split into a wide grin.

" 'Cactus' Haig," he said. "I never was much for small talk. But then I should have known you didn't need it."

She reached out and touched his hand. "Look, we've had an hour of me. I want to know about you. What makes you tick, if you're the monster everyone claims, about this fetish you have for newspapers. About what brought you out of Arizona—"

"New Mexico."

"Okay, New Mexico, and just why you're in New York. How you got old Meg to sell you the *Mail* and what you're going to do with it."

Haig looked thoughtful. He did not answer immediately. Then he said, "I never knew a plain black sweater could look so good."

"Plain black sweater! Do you have any notion of what cashmere costs and—"

"Tell me," he said, "tell me everything."

Now it was two hours later and they were in her apartment. She had shucked off her shoes and was curled up in the corner of a couch, her legs under her, a coffee cup and saucer balanced on her lap. Haig was roaming about the room. Talking. As he had been talking since the bar at "21". About himself. About the newspaper. About his father. For the first time to anyone he was telling about his father.

She sat and listened. No longer bored, no longer surreptitiously looking at the time.

She was surprised. At herself, at him.

"They say awful things about you," she said.

"I know. A man who works for me was at a dinner party one night and the woman next to him asked what he did. Poor Gideon said, 'I work for Campbell Haig.' And the woman threw a glass of wine into his face. Completely respectable woman."

"Perhaps she had a reason. Something your papers had written."

He waved a hand. "People always think they have reasons."

"But it *is* an awful newspaper, you know."

"Oh?"

"And that isn't just Nora talking. Or even me. Everyone says so. The sensationalism, the violence, those terrible headlines . . ."

Haig would not have responded to such criticism from anyone else, would simply have shrugged and turned away. To Alex he made thoughtful reply.

"I'd like to own the *Times*," he said. "But they wouldn't sell it to me, and if they would I couldn't raise the money. I started with a very small paper in McAllen. I've never had much money. Always had to borrow to expand. Always had to buy what was available. The sick papers. The second paper in town. Never the first. So I had to turn them around. I couldn't get the advertising right away because the paper was so weak. So I went for the big circulation. I was always fighting for survival, and big headlines were the weapon. I don't expect you to like the *Mail*."

The man was off center, improbably, quaintly old-fashioned, the ravening press lord commingled with the bashful suitor. Like any college boy he lapsed into awkward silences punctuated by the outpourings of his most secret guilts and fears.

He must have catalogued to her every love affair he had ever had, from London society girls to Riviera playgirls to casual pickups in the Southwest or the great cities where he operated papers. Such litanies of conquest were not unprecedented in her experience. The difference was that Haig wasn't boasting. There seemed a genuine regret.

"You really should have been a Catholic," she said, smiling.

"Oh?"

"Yes, you could go to confession and not have to save up like this."

He looked shocked. "Is it that bad?"

"Worse," she said, smiling.

He laughed then, the smile his absolution. "It's one of the handicaps of being a Scot. Presbyterianism contains so few escape valves. We suffer privately what you expiate in that little closet."

"I'm not sure how helpful confession is for most of us," she said, "but I'm sure it helps the priests."

"What a consolation it is," he said, "to be in the presence of a true believer."

They talked nearly until dawn. About everything. Even about Nora.

"What is she like?"

Alex's face screwed up just slightly, wrinkling her nose in a way he loved. "Strange woman."

"How so?"

"Well. You know, or maybe you don't, but Catholics are always supposed to pray for the grace of a happy death."

"I didn't know. Is that what she does?"

"Oh, yes," Alex said. "Nora prays every day at mass for the grace of a happy death for everyone she knows. Even for me, I suspect."

"Well," he said uncertainly, not wanting to attack either her religion or her mother, both of which were mysteries to him.

"Yes, and I don't believe Nora ever once prayed for the grace of a happy *life* for anyone."

When she caught herself yawning it was not out of boredom. "You've got to go," she said.

"But I don't want to leave you. Ever."

Alex laughed. "Go away. You may not need any sleep, but I do."

At the door of her flat, which he thought was the most wonderful and welcoming place he had ever been, he took her hand and shook it, gave a little bow, and backed out into the hallway.

As she shut the door behind her she leaned against it.

My God, she thought, does it really happen this suddenly?

Farrell, who noticed everything, noticed yet another change in Haig. Something had distracted him, softened that singleminded intensity.

But it was not a harmful distraction. It was nothing like those days after Sissy's accident. From that weekend Haig had returned to the office stripped of confidence and surehandedness and instinct. Their interview with Lenny and Mavis Sparg, for example. Haig had been at sea, drifting, confused.

This new thing, whatever it was, was nothing like that. Haig had come back to work as steady and shrewdly competent as he had ever been. But more buoyant. And it was a damned good thing Haig was back in form. So much was happening, so much depended on his decisions, decisions crisply and correctly arrived at.

Farrell, without knowing it, was grateful that Haig had fallen in love. Alex had not told him. Farrell assumed she was traveling.

She was not. She was with Haig in the Carlyle.

They were in his bed. "I wanted to make love with you the first time I ever saw you. But it wasn't necessary. There was no rush. It was enough that you were there. That I was with you."

"You're easily satisfied," she said.

"No, Alex, that's where you're wrong. I'm very difficult to satisfy."

They'd gone to the preview of the new Redford movie in the screening room of the MGM building. There was dinner at Le Cirque, they talked, he touched her hand once in reflex and then, as he withdrew, she covered his hand with hers and gently pulled it back. He knew then it was time. They both did.

"Seventy-sixth and Madison," he told the cab driver.

"The Carlyle," she said softly, curled into his body, his arm lightly around her shoulder.

"Yes."

In the darkened living room of his suite he turned to face her. She came to him. They kissed, standing close, his arms holding her, his body feeling the entire length and strength of hers. Then he turned, taking her by one hand, and led her into the bedroom.

"I know this is right," she told herself, "I know this is different from anything else I have ever done."

She stripped off her dress as he tossed back the bed covers. Forgotten were the motel rooms and the bars and the faceless, rutting men.

Alex came to him then with an urgent, pulsing passion that surprised even her but to Haig, who expected nothing less, it seemed precisely, achingly, drainingly, wonderfully right.

There is a stage in the process of falling in love when a man suspends all critical judgment. Later, when the giddiness has passed, the excitement dulled, he may believe anything about his woman. Even the worst. But not at the start. Alex Noyes did not understand this.

"Look," she said, "you've got this all wrong. You're erecting pedestals for me to stand on. This isn't me you're seeing. It's some idealized, unreal, totally implausible creature you've conjured up."

"I know," Haig said happily, not really following her but simply being acquiescent.

They were in his bed. They had made love, twice, and Alex was making an effort to bring reality into the dream. She found it difficult to believe that a man who ran great newspapers, who wielded tremendous influence in New York and in the country, a wealthy man, willful and self-oriented, was behaving like some love-sick college boy, mooning over her virtues, virtues she knew she did not possess.

"Look," she said again, in her sternest tone, "I'm not evil or vindictive or for God's sake some sort of awful pervert. But there are things you don't know about me, things you ought to know."

"Sure," he said vaguely, tracing small concentric circles around her right nipple.

"Campbell, you say 'sure' and you don't know what the hell I'm talking about. Do you?"

"No," he agreed. Pleasantly.

"You see! Okay, I mean, let's not hold this against me or run it tomorrow in your damned newspaper, and I hope it doesn't shock you, but information had reached me recently that whatever you think, I am *not* Saint Teresa, the Little Flower. Nor have I been confused lately with Sister Kenny or Mother Cabrini."

"Who's she?" he asked.

"No sidetracking. We're discussing my true character."

"Okay."

She turned onto her side so that she could look at him in the dim light of the bedroom. The blinds were open and moonlight came in off Madison Avenue, bathing the bedroom in a soft, nocturnal glow. She could see his profile quite clearly. With the soft brown hair falling tousled over his forehead he looked boyish.

"I don't believe you're forty," she said.

"I'm not," he said. "I've lied to you from the very start. I'm really sixty-five. Living on Social Security. And I have this wonderful little rose-covered cottage in a senior citizens' community down on the Jersey shore. You'll like it. We play shuffleboard and Chinese checkers and—"

"Campbell, be serious."

"All right. Let's go to sleep."

She sat up abruptly. "Hey, not until I tell you what I started to tell you."

"Oh?"

"Yes, about me. About this ridiculous image you've built up of me. That's just as wrong and crazy and out of focus as the crap the gossip magazines write about me. Except they exaggerate the bad and you exaggerate the good. Neither one of you is right. You're both looking at me through cracked lenses."

"Okay," he said patiently, "tell me."

She let herself sink back slowly onto the pillow. Then, looking not at him but at the ceiling, she said, quietly, seriously, "All right. First of all, there have been a lot of men. I don't mean hundreds. But not just one or two. I fool around. Okay?"

He did not say anything but lay there, alert now, listening. She went on.

"Most times I didn't even know them. I just . . . well, I just went to bed with them. I picked them up, they picked me up. Motel rooms, really cheap stuff. I didn't mean anything to them but a quick lay. They meant nothing to me. I did what they wanted. I don't mean any really kinky stuff, but, you know. . . ." Her voice trailed off.

"You don't have to tell me any of this," Haig said stiffly. "None of it matters. Only you matter."

"It does matter," she said stubbornly. She talked some more. About men.

"Why do you think you went with them?" he asked quietly.

"Oh, damn, Campbell," she said, "don't start asking psychiatric-type questions, will you? I mean, that's one thing that really gets me, when someone I care about starts playing shrink."

"Withdrawn," he said.

"Good. And nothing with women. I mean, not until the other night."

"That was being drunk," he said firmly, "that's all it was. And you know it."

"Okay," she said, "and thanks for saying it." She waited a moment. "Really . . . thanks."

"Don't say that again."

"Okay. I won't. Now, besides sex—"

"Let's stay with sex," he said playfully.

"No, I'm serious. I drink too much, I smoke pot. I've tried some other stuff. You know, cocaine, poppers. But you don't have to worry about that," she added hurriedly, "because I don't do them much. I was never really into that."

He lay quietly for a moment, not really listening. "Alex," he said then, "I'll concede you one fault."

"Oh?" she said, trying not to sound disappointed.

"Did anyone ever inform you that you talk too much?"

She lay awake for a long time after he fell asleep. She was startled to realize how very happy she was with this man who was like nobody else she had ever known.

Perhaps it was his twenty years of working and waiting. But she had never felt so well, so thoroughly loved.

As for Haig, everything that had built up in him for all that time seemed to have been drained by her. She had never been so filled, he had never been so pleasantly empty. And best of all, for neither of them was there guilt.

They both knew guilt far too well to be mistaken. There was none of it here. Love had left no room.

37

Caz Krantzke was not drunk. But he had been drinking. No denying that. A good day on the water, the big blues coming in, even a big striper that should by all things natural have been asleep on the bottom at two in the afternoon. The party had been good, not the usual trash out from the city for a day but guys he knew from the Bays, from Bridgehampton, from Sag Harbor, guys he'd gone to school with, guys he drank with, farmers and workingmen like himself. They were drunk now even if he wasn't. Or at least well on their way.

"Hey," he said, glancing at the clock over the bar, "another round. On me, this one."

They joshed him for that. The day, the boat, the fish, that had been his treat. Where did he get off thinking he could buy the drinks as well?

He made little motions with his hands.

"A date," he said apologetically, he had this date.

It took him another fifteen minutes to get away. Jesus, he thought, he really didn't want to go. This chick, Sissy, she was too much. Her and her fucking hangups and the polite way she talked and all the time she was holding him, nailing him down, telling him how important he was to her, how he must never leave her, how she needed him. Needed him, shit. She needed one thing. And he gave her that. Plenty.

She was in the cabin when he got to the dock. Who the hell gave her squatters' rights? You'd think she'd wait until he got there. He stumbled slightly as he crossed the gangway. Sissy smiled when he entered the cabin.

"Hey," she said, "I was getting jealous. It's nearly nine o'clock."

"I know," he said, "I know what fucking time it is."

She knew his moods. In three weeks she had become very smooth at accommodating to them. As she did now.

"Caz . . ." she said slowly, drawing out the word, "shall I make you a drink? Or do you just want to . . . ?"

He looked at her. She was wearing that shirt he liked, unbuttoned one button too low, and the leather skirt. Her hair was down already, the braid undone.

"Yeah," he said, "make me a drink."

He threw himself into the one chair in the cabin to watch her back as she deftly tucked the vodka bottle under her maimed arm and uncapped it, then poured the drink, neat, as he liked it, and then one for herself, on the ice. She had a nice ass, he told himself for the hundredth time, and the way the leather moved over it . . .

"Here," she said, handing him the glass.

He took it, drank off half of it, while she sat on the edge of the bunk and sipped hers.

"Caz," she said, "you're staring. What's the matter?"

He shook his head. "Nothing," he said. "Nothing."

He was thinking of the boys back at the bar, getting drunk, picking up the waitresses and the local high school girls and the occasional cheating housewife who would be drifting into the joint by now. He should be there, instead of here with this Goddamn kook he was saddled with. He drained off the rest of the vodka. He felt better now. Sissy sat there, smiling her stupid smile. He knew what would come next: "Another drink, Caz?" in that sweet way of hers. Then, why then she'd begin reaching for him and dragging him into the Goddamn bunk. She couldn't get enough of it. Nympho. What the hell did he really know about her? About what she did all day while he was out on the boat? Women could do it all day long even if a normal man couldn't. Whore!

"Caz," Sissy said, "shall I make you another?"

She stood up.

"*Shall* you make me another," he shouted, mimicking her. "*Shall* I this and *shall* I that? I'll tell you what you fucking *shall* do. You come here and kneel down."

"Caz," she said, not knowing why he was angry.

He motioned her to him. "Down here," he said.

She put down her glass and knelt. He reached down and opened her shirt and then sat back in the chair, looking at her breasts.

"Now," he said, "let's cut all the bullshit and do what you're here for."

She looked up. His face was red, determined, brutal.

"Okay, Caz," she said.

Her right hand trembled as it reached up to the belt of his trousers.

Sissy was naked now. She lay in the bunk, not so much resentful as puzzled. She watched his strong back as he poured himself some vodka at the sink. When he turned, her eyes moved instinctively down.

"What the hell are you looking at?" he demanded.

"Nothing."

He came to the side of the bunk, reached down, and took one of her nipples between his thumb and forefinger. "You like that?" he said. "You want me to hurt you a little? You dig that?"

She shrugged. "Caz, you know ever since I first came here, it's whatever you say. You tell me, I do it."

"Anything?"

She nodded.

He snapped his fingers. She needed a lesson, she did, looking at him that way when he was limp, putting him down. Couldn't get enough of it, could she? Well, he knew how he could fix that.

He tugged a pullover over his head and slid a leg into his jeans. "Just stay right here, baby. Just like you are. I'm gonna invite a couple of friends to drop by. So we can party a little. You and me and them."

He went up the ladder and disappeared. She felt sick to her stomach, and when she tried to sit up her legs trembled and did not respond.

Would not.

Had he asked her to do it she would have, at first, been shocked. Then she might have considered it. One orgasm after another? One pounding, sweating, pulsing climax following another in series, the classic female sexual fantasy, always a man erect entering and exciting and fulfilling her? One man or many? Did it really matter? She knew that it did but suspected that if he had suggested it as a new threshold of pleasure they should cross together, another dimension of sensuality, she might well have swallowed her reticence. Why not?

But it was being forced on her. Rape. Gang rape. Not an invitation to experiment with the new and forbidden, but contempt, hatred, the need to debase. Had Caz wheedled and cajoled and teased her into it . . . Surely all around her young women her age were doing this sort of thing and more. All the orifices were there to be taken, all the pleasures there to be enjoyed. Only she had held back, primly, Victorian, slightly embarrassing in her reticence. Alex. Did she not sense a quiet, secret smile on Alex's mouth, hinting?

He came back into the cabin, his steps heavy on the ladder, drink wresting from his usual sailor's agility. "Only two of them, baby. The others left. But two plus me makes three. That going to be enough?"

His leer was not suggestive, carnal. It was stupid, brutish. He whipped back the blanket covering her and stood there looking down at her on the bunk, her long legs out straight in front of her, her knees maidenly together. She slowly spread her legs and her hand strayed down over her belly to her mound. She looked up at him, her mouth moist and open.

"Sure, Caz. I guess you need all the help you can get."

He hit her then, his big, competent hand open, the movement coming before she could dodge or set herself. Then he turned away to pour himself another vodka. She was still whimpering and her nose was bleeding when she heard the loud, drunken masculine voices and the footsteps on the wharf.

There were not two of them. There were three. The bartender had come with them. Since he had bought them a round Caz let him be the first.

38

Campbell Haig knew, as he usually knew, precisely what he wanted. "Damn it!" he raged. "We love each other. There's no one else in my life, no one else I want or ever would want. We're both free, we both have money. Is it being a Catholic that stops you? Is it that?"

"Of course not."

"I'll marry you before a priest if you want. The children will be Catholics. If they want me to sign a paper, I'll sign it. I'll—"

"Campbell," Alex said, "will you please shut up, darling? Just shut up and listen?"

She had not hesitated at all telling him about her urges that had sent her trembling into the night. She was more reticent about discussing her parents and her fear these were genetic problems. Not only her burden, but perhaps her children's.

"You mean 'our' children, don't you?" he said when finally she had blurted out an awkward, halting explanation.

"Yes," she said, uncharacteristically subdued.

Haig took her face between his lean hands. "Alex, you seem to overlook quite conveniently any imperfections but your own. Sure, I've read some of that stuff about your father. I realize from what I've heard, from what you tell me, that Nora is a handful. But, my God, Alex, are you forgetting who *I* am?

" 'Cactus' Haig? The wild man of American journalism? The smut artist, the sensationalist, the master of the smear campaign, the libel lawyer's delight? The yellow journalist, the new Hearst, and worse? You've read all that, you've heard it. You'll hear it again, you'll read it again. So will your children. *Our* children! It's the kind of man I am, it's the kind of newspapers I publish. D'you think it never bothers me, hearing that sort of filth hurled at me? I pretend to be impervious. But I'm not. No one is. I hear it, and it hurts.

"Okay, it's one thing for me to take that sort of crap. I'm a big boy, it's what I do for a living, it's how I make all this filthy money. But you? Alex Noyes, the President's daughter? Nora Noyes's little girl? Don't you think I agonize over the very real possibility someday someone will throw a drink in your face, will scrawl dirty words on the door of your house, will harass one of your kids—our kids—just because I am who I am and I run papers like the *Mail?*"

He was pacing the room now.

"I happen to like the *Mail.* I love my work. The paper is what I want it to be. So I'm insulated to an extent from all the static, the criticism, the sheer hatred. Because the *Mail* is me! But you, you don't have that kind of insulation. You don't even like the *Mail.* It isn't part of you the way it is of me.

"So please don't try to frighten me off with sad tales of your parents. I'm carrying a heavier handicap into your life than you could ever bring into mine."

But again she said no. She was not ready, she said, she was still nervy about lifelong commitments. Then, as he raged, impotently, and feared he had lost, she told him matter-of-factly, "Campbell, I think you and I should live together."

Part of the attraction was that Haig had never known a girl like this one before. Never! One day it had been decided they would live together, the next day she told him they had to move.

"My apartment's just too small and my neighbors are nosy as hell. But, Campbell, you can't live in a hotel. And I *won't!* It's just tacky. I know it's the Carlyle but still . . . Desk clerks and bellboys and room service. I feel like we should be slipping up the back stairs. And this furniture. Neo-bordello or early motel, I'm not sure which. Look, you like the East Side, so do I. I'll find us an apartment. The seventies okay with you?"

He said yes, not really having either the opportunity or the will to say no. Late the next afternoon she called him at the *Mail.*

"Listen, I found a place. Great! Well, not great, but really right. Farther south than I expected. Sixty-fifth. Just off Fifth, closer to Madison. Eighteen hundred a month. We can have it effective last Tuesday."

"Last Tuesday?"

"Yeah, that was the first and I didn't want to take a chance on losing it. You'll like it. Now, listen, do you know anything about furniture, about carpet, are there any colors you just can't stand? Are you modern or period? No, don't tell me. You wouldn't know anyway. Except for your pictures you don't really care what's in the place, do you?"

"Yes," he said, finally getting a word in, "I care that you're in the place."

There was a brief, uncharacteristic silence. Then she said, slowed down and soft, "Why, Campbell, that's nice. When you say things like that I understand why I love you."

He was never quite sure whether the operators monitored his phone calls and so he simply said, "Good, me too." And then she was off again.

"It's Thursday and Bloomies is open. I'm going to buy some stuff. Where are we having dinner? I'll be there right after nine."

He was examining the menu at the Veau d'Or when she blew in.

"Whew," she said, flopping into the chair opposite and extending her hand to touch his face, "you owe me"—she pulled out a batch of receipts and began to add up numbers in her head—"you owe me four thousand, two hundred and sixty bucks. Forget the sales tax. That's my treat."

She passed over the batch of sales slips. He glanced at them. She gave him a running commentary.

"Furniture, china, glassware, I've got the silver, some new Revere ware, a couple of rugs, we'll need a couple more, I have a good television. And your pictures. We're in business."

"Well," he said.

"We move in next week."

He shook his head. This was one thing he knew about.

"No one gets furniture delivered in a week," he said. "It all comes from North Carolina."

"Uh-uh, I bought floor samples. I know the buyer. Saved money and they have it right there in stock. It'll be there. I promise you."

And it was. She paid for things with her own money and he wrote checks to pay her back. She tipped the superintendent and the doormen and the handyman ("Listen, there's no money in the world better spent than a couple of dollars when you move into a new place!") and they addressed him as "Mr. Noyes" and held the door for him.

"Now, Alex," he said, "this 'Mr. Noyes' business . . ."

She slapped her forehead with the heel of her hand.

"Oh, damn," she said, "I ought to have made it clear. I'll straighten it out in the morning. And we'll have both names on the intercom and on the mailbox. That'll unconfuse everyone."

"Haig-Noyes or Noyes-Haig?" he asked.

She leaned over and kissed him.

"You come first on the intercom; I do on the mailbox."

He was accustomed to making decisions. Now she had taken over the chore and he found himself luxuriating in her decisiveness, enjoying a languid, almost sinful, and entirely unfamiliar passivity.

It was not all middle-class setting up house. He came home from the paper one night to find her curled up on the couch in jeans and a sweater, barefoot, and smoking pot.

"Alex!" he said, genuinely shocked.

"What?"

"Do you smoke that stuff very often?"

"Sure, whenever I feel like it. I told you I did. Why?" She looked up and saw his face. "Hey," she said, putting down the cigarette, getting up and going to him, "you mean you don't? Not ever?"

He said no. Not ever.

"Oh, come on, Campbell. I mean, *everyone* smokes a little."

"I don't," he said stiffly.

She stepped back.

"Look, Campbell, I don't want to make an issue of this. It's something I do. Most of the people I know do. If you don't want to . . ."

"And I *don't,*" he said stiffly.

She went back to the couch and sat down. It was nothing like the pleasantly relaxed pose of a few minutes earlier. She looks . . . wary, he thought.

"Well," she said, "are we going to have a fight about it?"

He did not answer. He did not want a fight. Neither did he want to back down.

She mistook his indecision for a sulk.

"Look," she said briskly, "half the people in this country take a break at the end of the day. They come home from work, they mix a martini, they open a can of beer. I've been working hard all day, with the painters and carpet men. If I'd been sitting here with a glass in my hand you probably wouldn't have said a word." She paused, remembering how he felt about alcohol. "Or maybe you would have."

He stiffened. "That's a cheap shot, Alex. I don't expect cheap shots from you."

She inhaled and then, abruptly, she stood up and walked to him, placing her hands on his arms, looking into his face.

"I'm sorry, Campbell. It *was* a cheap shot and you're right, you shouldn't expect them of me."

How odd it was, he thought. Here he was, the press lord, the power broker, sophisticated, ruthless, arrogant. And now he was facing, for the first time, the sort of minor domestic crisis suburban parents confronted every day. The young girl of the family has been caught smoking marijuana. Only, in this case, the young girl was not his daughter but his lover.

For twenty years he had lived in the great world, had been exposed, or so he thought, to the weaknesses, the vices, the ambitions, the secret cravings of powerful men, of seductive women. The rich and the famous, the influential and the infamous, the great and the mean, these had been his companions on the great journey, his intimates, his playmates, his familiars. Had he not, in all that time, been faced with greater, more complex challenges? The answer, he knew, was no. Because he had never cared about the others.

Now, and the regret mingled with joy, he was in love. Now the simplest problem became a tremendous chasm, yawning between him and his woman.

He threw himself into a chair. She stood there, not knowing if she were rejected.

"Campbell . . . ?" she said, not knowing.

He looked up. How beautiful she was. How young. How miraculous it was that she loved him.

"Alex," he said, "I don't know about such things. I just don't know. Be patient. Explain them to me. Tell me why and I'll understand. I'll try to understand. I really will. If I'm closed and short with you, well, that's how I am. Be open with me. You're better at such things than I am. It's one of the reasons why I love you."

She relaxed now, the tension draining from her arms and hands.

"Oh, Campbell, my love, of course. Of course I will."

They battled over other things.

"Look," she said, "there are gaps between us."

"There are always gaps. That's what love is about, it takes the place of bridges."

She shook her head angrily. "Now don't go lyrical on me, Haig. I'm not in the mood for figures of speech."

"Sorry."

"I've tried to understand about your work, the kind of papers you publish. I didn't like them but then, as you always say, they aren't edited for me. I accepted that. I love you for yourself, not for the Goddamn *Mail* or one of those other awful rags that printed all that stuff about my father and his girl friends."

"That story came out of Congress. That was a congressional leak. Were the newspapers supposed to ignore it? Engage in some gentlemanly conspiracy to—"

"Campbell, you loved your father. I loved mine. Yes! They should have hushed it up. Yes!"

Quietly, knowing she still felt the pain, he said, "Now, you know they couldn't have done that."

"Campbell, I was seventeen years old and just getting over an absolutely dramatic schoolgirl crush when all that stuff came out. You think that doesn't hurt, doesn't cripple? Do you know how gay and witless and irresponsible a teenage girl can be when she's in love and then to see those big black headlines and those smirking pictures and to listen to those Goddamn pious hypocrites sucking their teeth and sermonizing over what he'd done. My father had been dead for twelve years when they cast the first stone!"

Haig nodded, miserable and silent.

More calmly now, Alex said, "My childhood ended then. After that I never stood a chance of privacy. From then on it was Macy's window and it was always high noon. No wonder I took strangers out of low dives and went to bed with them in motels. In motels they never want your real name. It's easier for them not to know."

It was so easy, Haig thought, to counter this sort of criticism at a journalism school seminar, on a convention dais. Simply trot out the First Amendment and the "public's right to know" and that old saw about how sorry Jack Kennedy was that the *Times* hadn't run its scoop before the Bay of Pigs and made him cancel the whole damned fiasco. It was not so easy when the critic was the woman you loved and one of the offending stories was about her father's infidelities.

They solemnized their home without witnesses, alone, in bed and in a dozen other ways. And they celebrated it with a party. Alex curled up on the couch with a pad and listed the names Haig's Miss Mayhew would send invitations. His nominations came first. She wrote dutifully for a few minutes. Then she put down the pen.

"Campbell," she said, "don't you have *any* friends in New York?"

He looked puzzled. "Of course I do. I've just given you twenty names. More."

"Campbell," she said, disappointment in her voice.

"What?" He did not understand.

"Here," she said, "just listen to your list so far. "The governor, David Rockefeller, the mayor, Herman Badillo, Walter Wriston, Punch Sulzberger, Walter Cronkite, John Lindsay, Howard Squadron, Senator Javits." She looked up at him.

"Well?" he said. "I know them all. They know me. I want them to meet you."

She shook her head. "First of all, I know most of them already. Second, they aren't *friends*. They're people you know in business. The only woman you've listed so far is eighty years old."

He contradicted her on that. "Marion Javits."

"Campbell, you don't know anything. Jack and Marion *never* attend parties together. It's like parents who won't fly in the same plane."

"Oh," he said.

"I mean, you ought to ask some people you enjoy, you have fun with, whether they're in politics or the media or not."

He paused for a moment. "I guess you're right. I really *don't* know too many people outside of the paper."

"Well, *I* do. And we're going to ask them."

"All right," he said. "But take down my list first, okay?"

"Okay."

"Where was I? Yes. Sean Farrell—"

"Who?"

"S-E-A-N—"

"I know. He's your editor," she said. She wrote the name down. He won't come, of course, she told herself.

Ten days later the apartment, with Haig's precious pictures duly hung and everything else Alex's selection, reverberated to the sounds of a Manhattan cocktail party. Campbell Haig wandered through the crowded rooms, shaking hands, smiling, uncertain, confused. Waiters circulated with trays of canapés, pretty girls kissed cheeks, a pianist played Cole Porter on a piano that had arrived only that afternoon, two makeshift bars mass-produced drinks.

"Who *are* these people?" he asked.

"But you know, I told you. You saw the list."

He shook his head. "I don't," he said. "Who's that man?" he demanded.

Alex followed his glance.

"A gangster. He owns a club in the Village."

Campbell's brow creased. He never knew if she was being serious. A plump, orange-haired man with glasses minced past.

"I wish my sex life were as busy as her dress," Haig heard him say. He shook his head again.

Alex's friends were writers and fashion designers and actors and young lawyers and models and musicians and girls she had been with at various schools and interior decorators. There was one former priest who'd fallen out of favor with her mother, a black who played for the Knicks, a girl she knew from Newport who'd just been divorced. Several men who had been suitors, now were friends.

Willie Morris came with Barbara Howar and Bill Bradley with his wife and Vonnegut with Jill Krementz and Woody Allen with some lovely young girl and an actress quite clearly stoned on something.

Farrell did not come. And Sissy had begged off, as expected.

It was, as far as Alex was concerned, a successful party. Later, when everyone had left and only the smoke hung in the empty apartment, she and Campbell went to bed.

"Hey," she said, "I love you."

"Good," he said, "I'm glad."

"I mean, you put up with my friends. Not everyone would do that as gracefully as you did."

He turned on the pillow to look into her face. "You mean I'm really not as stuffy as you thought."

"Not at all," she said happily. "There's hope for you yet."

"I certainly hope so."

She was naked, as she often was in bed, and she twisted slightly so she could reach him. Her hand moved. He moved too.

"Oh," she said, "yes, yes."

Later he had said, somewhat smugly, "See, I'm not at all stuffy," and she had said, no, not one bit.

She lay awake, listening to him as he slept, glad she was living with him, glad her life had a focus at last.

39

Farrell had learned, of course, about Alex and Haig. He was furious. Furious that she had dumped him. Furious that it was for Haig of all people, after all her tirades against the monster, after what Haig had done to Sissy Valentine. Furious and hurt that she'd never told him, never even gotten around to saying good-bye. The usual resentments of Haig multiplied, deepened. It wasn't fair for one man to own both the *Mail* and Alexandra Noyes, the two things Farrell believed he really loved.

It had been impossible, of course, in a city like New York for their affair to go unnoticed. Items began to slip into gossip columns, blind items at first. "What well-known local publisher is spending all his waking hours with a 'golden girl' who once called Washington home?" Later, when the libel lawyers had muttered approval, their names were used. An enterprising photographer peddled pictures he'd taken as they emerged together from the Carlyle.

It was through a rival tabloid that Farrell would learn why Alex never called anymore, why she would never call again.

"Damn you, Haig," he cried during a turbulent, drunken night on the town. And no more. His proud disdain for admitting injury rendered his fury silent thereafter.

Farrell watched Haig now with a new attention, looking for signs, any hint, of Alex's influence on him. And there was a change, a softening, a warmth in the man. Farrell first noticed it the day he had stormed into Haig's office wanting to fire Strong. Strong was a lanky, potbellied young Texan who had once, for about fifteen minutes, been a magazine editor and could never after that adjust to the more formal disciplines of a daily newspaper.

"Well, just what has he done?" Haig asked.

"I won't have the man capering around the city room doing chimpanzee imitations and hopping up on desks."

"Oh, he does that?"

"That's just for warm-ups. He has this huge Miss Piggy doll he props up in his chair behind the typewriter. He ties gas balloons to his eyeglasses. Last week I sent him to cover a David Rockefeller press conference and he wore a Groucho Marx mustache. When I spoke to him about how he represents the *Mail* he said, 'Yes, I know. That's why I wear clown costumes.' "

"Not grand enough for him, are we?"

"Smartass," Farrell muttered.

Haig considered. Strong was one of the *Mail*'s more felicitous writers. Whatever his contempt for the newspaper it did not show in his copy. "So?" Haig asked.

"I want to can him."

Haig shook his head. "Tell him you won't put up with the vaudeville and put him on rewrite for a month."

"Not fire him?"

"What the hell, Farrell, what the hell."

Farrell slammed the door on his way out. "Haig's gone soft!" he raged to Brophy that night in Costello's. Brophy, owl-eyed, nodded and said that was fine with him.

"I might get a few of those balloons for myself," he observed.

"Jesus!" Farrell said, slamming a stein down on the bar.

A year earlier Haig would have sacked Strong without hesitation. Now he found amusement in the man's foolishness and even more in Farrell's impotent fury. Alex was the difference. For twenty years Haig had pursued the singleminded existence of a religious zealot, closing himself off from either pleasure or pain, from anything that might distract from avenging his father. He had become cold, hu-

morless, impatient, ruthless in the pursuit of journalistic power.
Without such power he knew, and Sam Haig's tragic fate served as
inarguable proof, that he was himself as vulnerable to the wicked and
the politically connected as any small-town newspaper editor who
crusaded for the right without reckoning the terrible costs.

Alex had not changed him completely. No one ever could. But he
was no longer the driven loner battling to survive in a hostile world.
Alex was more than his lover; she was the prize at the end of the
long race. Victory had softened him. The competition was over. He
had won.

"We're educating one another," Alex told him one evening as
they dined at a window table atop the World Trade Center, one of
those crystalline nights when New York seems all airy lights and
verticals, transcending reality. Airplanes flew past at window level
and bridges swayed above the black rivers.

"Oh," he said, "then it's a mutual thing?"

"Of course." She laughed. "You teach me about things. Newspapers and politics and money."

"And you teach me . . . what?"

"About people," she said, mock solemn.

In a way he knew she was right. She had the instincts. They must
have been her father's, those shrewd, instant judgments, snap ap-
praisals that were invariably accurate. He took her to Kissinger's flat
in River House for cocktails and watched, delighted, as she turned
Henry into The Frog Prince, performing his not inconsiderable
social acrobatics, cutting up rival diplomatists with a phrase, mocking himself with the line "I may occasionally have been mistaken;
I was always decisive. And never more than when I was wrong." She
took Haig to Mark Goodson's duplex in Beekman Place. A new
Picasso was being unveiled to the usual buffet crowd, pretty girls and
actors and art *mavens* and the constant *demi-monde* that will go
anywhere for a free meal. Kosinski and Warhol greeted her and,
gravely, as little girls do at tea parties, she introduced him to all of
them, much as she might have shown a treasured, faithful teddy
bear. Haig listened, rapt, as she talked hockey with Warhol, the
marketing of craft jewelry with a delicately lovely blond girl. Alex
told him precisely how many times a fat, sweating press agent with

a stutter and a middle-distance stare had slipped into the bathroom for a snort of cocaine.

"In Hollywood," she said, "the new houses will all have very tiny living rooms and huge bathrooms."

"How do you know these things?" he asked, marveling.

"I just do."

He believed her.

There was a weekend flight to London with a great, dark suite in the Connaught at the other end of it: vast bathtubs and creamy oatmeal for breakfast, theater tickets in the West End, lazy drinks in front of the fireplace of the small, inside bar; a dinner hosted by Murdoch and attended by the Prime Minister. She knew London, of course, but not as he did.

"In a way I grew up here. That year after my father died. Grubbing around Fleet Street, learning my trade. Beaverbrook was dying but he remembered my father and he knew what was wanted. A crash course in newspapering. Gideon was the brightest of his bright young men and he took me under his wing. A month fetching tea for the subs, a month taking classified ads over the phone, a couple of weeks in circulation. I wrote cricket and edited the gardening column and sat in the press gallery on the House and sold advertising and did rewrite on William Hickey. Did every damned thing but sweep up after the last edition."

"And loved every minute of it."

He grinned. "I developed a lifelong antipathy to cricket. But otherwise you're right. I had a bed-sitter in Lambeth. That side of the river was cheap then. Lived on pub sandwiches and whatever I could cook on a hot plate. Probably why I've always preferred eating out."

"And it's why you think I'm such a great cook," she said, "having nothing to compare it with."

"You *are* a great cook," he said, and meant it.

There was a memorable weekend at Hyannis Port. She liked Ted Kennedy, bearlike, tending to fat, alternately jolly and driven, a big, energetic man who talked constantly while Campbell pulled on cigars and listened.

"Well?" he said, as they flew back from Logan to New York, "what do you think?"

"I like him," she said, "I like him and yet somehow I don't trust him."

"Good," Campbell told her, "you should always have reservations about ambitious men."

Wherever they went the paparazzi followed them, but by now Alex was developing a callous, becoming more like Campbell, barely noticing when her picture with him appeared in a magazine or in one of the other newspapers. They had a private life together no camera could penetrate, no lens capture, a loving, passionate intimacy that was proof against the world.

Nora Noyes threw down her copy of *People* magazine. The brown-frocked monk looked up from his sherry.

"My dear," he said, in that smooth and practiced tone.

Nora struggled valiantly to restrain her temper. Only her eyebrows, her flaring nostrils betrayed her. "Oh, Father, I didn't mean to . . ."

Her legendary control, her icy calm, the famous Noyes sangfroid —all these were at hazard, and in front of this tame cleric. Yet how could any mother, even Nora Noyes, sit there calmly while a cheap gossip sheet like *People* ran photos of her daughter, smiling and arm in arm with that dreadful Haig?

Nora was in New York, the Gracie Square triplex, for the affair at the Metropolitan Museum that night. Dear Diana, so clever. Givenchy was in from Paris and in his luggage the most regal evening dress in crepe de chine, in model size. She had it in her closet now, on approval. Givenchy was clever too, knowing she never took anything without eventually buying it, paying for it even, though, if she caught him in a good mood, at something less than the asking price. Nora had been looking forward to the evening. But then to see that awful photo of Alex . . .

"Nora," the priest said soothingly, "perhaps if you told me what upset you . . ."

She flashed her loveliest smile.

"It's not easy being a parent, Father. Not easy at all."

His lips pursed and his head bobbed sympathetically, the little bare spot of his tonsure gleaming dully in the afternoon sunlight of the great living room.

"My dear," he said somberly, "more saints there are in the world than behind cloistered walls."

Nora smiled her smile of sweet suffering. The Franciscan sipped at his wine. He was easy to have around, a bland background to the cacophonous world, but how she wished her Jesuit from Farm Street were here. Or her Dominican, cutting, incisive, brilliant. This fellow was a dear, so gentle, but with his epigrams just slightly out of plumb, his tonsure histrionically overstated, not at all the sort to handle Alex.

She turned to him with a beautiful smile. "Father, my daughter will be here shortly. A . . . personal matter. You know, the sort of mother-daughter dialogue that—"

He rose. "My dear lady, of course. In any event, I've not yet read my office." He bowed again and left the room.

Alex was late and Nora, uncharacteristically nervy, was being dressed when she arrived.

The girl kissed her mother's cheek. "What a lovely dress. Where to tonight?"

"The Metropolitan. A summons from Madame Vreeland."

Nora's voice communicated fatigue, ennui, rather than the eagerness she actually felt.

Alex flopped into a chaise. "Well," she said, "what's up? You wanted to see me."

Nora's eyebrows raised, then genuflected toward the maid. "Kristin," she said, "a few minutes, please."

The girl left. Alex, who knew what was coming, let herself go limp, her mouth relax into a grin. She was *damned* if she'd sweat and tremble in anticipation.

Nora waited until the door had closed. Then, carefully arranging her dress behind her, she descended gracefully into a chair, primly, decorously, the antithesis of her daughter, slouched loosely on the chaise with one shoe kicked off.

"This man," Nora began, "this journalist."

Alex grinned. It was good of Nora to behave predictably. She herself would be obtuse. Nothing drove Nora to distraction so effectively. "Sean Farrell?" she asked sweetly.

Blessedly, Nora had forgotten about Farrell. Now he was imposed upon her once more, scabrous and irritating. "I simply don't understand this bizarre appeal these sordid little men hold for you. And you know I don't mean that Farrell person."

"Oh?"

Nora tossed the copy of *People* magazine away from her as if it had a bad odor. "This man Haig," she said.

"Yes?"

"I want you to stop seeing him."

Despite Alex's resolve, her grin did not simply fade, it evaporated. There wasn't going to be any diplomatic fencing, was there? And Nora still had the capacity to wound with a word, a glance, a measured beat.

"Oh?"

"I won't dwell on how unattractive he is as a publisher, the sort of trashy papers he puts out, the libelous attacks his publications have made on me, and, indeed, on you, for so long. That's his business, I suppose, and I won't dignify it by my comments."

"Then what do you have against him, if it isn't that?" Alex asked, genuinely puzzled.

"Your living with him in sin."

The phrasing was so old-fashioned, so Victorian, Alex could not suppress a giggle. Nora's face stiffened.

"I'm sure you find this amusing. I *don't.*"

"But, Mother . . ." Alex said, sitting up on the chaise, as if to indicate she was not being flippant.

"You have a certain position. A responsibility to me, to your family. To your church, if you don't find a reference to religion anachronistic. To your . . . father. His memory. His presidency."

Alex stood. She was damned if she were going to take this. "My father's been dead twenty years," she said coldly.

Nora winced. "I don't need any reminding," she said. "I've lived those twenty years. Alone."

She was very effective, Nora was. But Alex had seen this particular performance before. Often. "Oh, yes, *alone,*" she repeated, "and where is your current house chaplain?"

"I saw no reason to impose an unseemly family quarrel on Father Luke," Nora said. "Not that a little spiritual guidance might not be helpful."

Alex looked at the ceiling in exasperation.

Nora pressed on. "I'm not really cloistered, you know. I have some vague idea of what goes on. Virginity is out of style, I'm sure." Her voice hardened. "But when your flaunt your relationship with this man, when you commit public scandal, when you openly cohabit, when you—"

Alex interrupted, her face angry, her fists clenched. *"That's* what bothers you. That Campbell and I are seen 'publicly.' Not that we sleep together. But that we don't lie about it or hide or sneak away in the afternoon to cheap hotels under assumed names."

"Not at all. I—"

"Yes, that's *precisely* what you mean. It's the honesty that offends you, not the sin itself!"

Nora stared at her daughter. Then, quietly, she said, "I suppose it's hypocritical of me but, yes, your conduct offends me because it *is* so open, so blatant, so crude and vulgar. If you *must* see this man . . ."

"He *has* a name."

"If you must see Mr. Haig, good taste would seem to dictate circumspection. Not this cheap exhibitionism."

Alex shook her head. Why did she punish herself by submitting to this?

Nora mistook her silence for retreat. She drove in on her daughter. "What is it you see in him? What?"

"I love him," Alex said gravely.

"I suppose he hasn't had the decency to offer marriage. Or is there a wife *already,* some homespun, loyal little woman in gingham off in the prairie?"

"He's not married and we haven't discussed marriage. It's sufficient right now that we're together, that we love one another."

"Love," her mother repeated, turning the word into something distasteful.

"Damn you, Nora," Alex snapped, her voice hard and cold and barely under control, "do you have any idea what Campbell Haig means to me? Do you even suspect what my life was like before he came along? The public fishbowl, the President's daughter, the poor little rich girl, the madcap heiress with the nutty mother and her facelifts and her charities and her best-dressed lists and her priests?"

Nora held up a hand. "You're evil to say such things of me."

"And you're evil to think and say what you do of Campbell. You don't know a damn thing about love. Or even about sin, however many tame Jesuits you keep stabled around this place. Do you want to know what true evil is? Really is? Not what Campbell Haig and I do together, in public or not. It's the things I used to do *before* Campbell. Things you never knew about. Nights in Palm Beach that I slipped away from your dinner table and drove into West Palm and cruised the bars and hustled salesmen and—"

Nora paled under exquisitely applied makeup. But her daughter continued.

The President's position was so solid now it was hard to remember the shaky, uncertain time he had had in the primaries. But the President remembered. Campbell Haig's early decision to support the President had been viewed as a sort of talisman. Now, just before Christmas, Haig was asked to dinner. The President wanted his supporters all in place; another election year was coming soon. One of his men called Haig.

"Honored, Spencer, honored to come down. Only there's a small problem," Haig said into the phone. Spencer was a longtime political crony. "There's a young lady I think might really like to come along."

Spencer laughed. "I'll *bet* there's a young lady, Campbell. But I'm afraid you're down as a stag. Wives are invited, but that's it. You know how stuffy the First Lady can be."

Haig didn't hesitate. "Well, then, Spence, I'll just have to respectfully decline. I'll get off a formal note of regret to the President."

"Damn it all, Haig, he wants you here. Put your name on the list himself."

"Can't do it, Spence. Not going to leave her here in New York."

"Just who in hell is this paragon?" Spencer squealed. "Or is that a secret?"

"Alexandra Noyes," Haig said. "She used to live there."

In the end, of course, she was asked. Not even a "stuffy" First Lady thought it politic to prevent Alexandra Noyes from coming home. Alex and Haig flew down on the afternoon shuttle.

"Nervous?" he asked.

"No. More like curious. I haven't been there, you know, since my father died."

"Surely you were asked."

"I dunno. Probably. But Nora always made decisions like that. Nora has always been very good at saying no for me."

Alex Noyes and the President wandered through the warm, comfortable rooms of the family quarters. He had her gently by the arm and was conducting a sort of guided tour, his low, trained voice as effective in conversation as in oratory.

"Do you remember this room?" he asked. A bedroom, vaguely feminine.

"I think so," she said, "but I was only five. And the wallpaper, the curtains . . . it's all so different."

"It was your bedroom," the President said. His tone conveyed no doubt at all.

"It is. Of course it is," she said wonderingly. "But how did you know?" she asked. "Twenty years ago, twenty-one."

He smiled, the flat mouth pleased. "There are records, of course. The housekeeper's office. But my wife had someone phone your mother to be sure. This afternoon. She told us which room was your nursery."

Alex laughed, a bit nervously. "I didn't tell my mother I was coming here."

"Oh, I do hope we haven't inadvertently—"

"Oh, no, Mr. President, don't worry. It was very gracious of you. Nora and I don't see eye to eye on a number of things. Never have."

"On Campbell Haig, for example?"

"Campbell is a symptom. Nora and I were at war long before I ever met Campbell, even before he came to New York and bought the paper."

"He's a remarkable fellow."

"Well, yes, I think he is."

The President led Alex through other rooms, down other labyrinthine ways, away from the subject of Haig.

"I was an obscure Californian when your father was President," he said. "My wife was raising our children. I suppose there's some other obscure politician out there whose wife is raising their kids who'll be living in this house twenty years from now. And they'll grace it as well as any of us have."

They had reached the staircase that would lead them back to the others. The President paused. "I don't know why every family who lives here doesn't give a little dinner once a year for you and your mother and every other person for whom this house was once home. Massive egos, I suppose, fear of being co-opted, loss of immediate political advantage."

"It would be nice, Mr. President."

He nodded, and then he said, "There's a continuity in this house. A sense of those who lived here before me and those who are yet to come. And it comforts me."

Impulsively, she took his hand and held it.

"Why, thank you, Alex Noyes."

"No," she said, meaning it, "you're the one to be thanked."

She told Campbell of their conversation on the last plane to New York that night. And he listened thoughtfully but said nothing. Campbell knew the President would be wanting his support in battling Congress. Was the President being courtly and charming or was he using Alex to keep Haig in his corner? Campbell resolved to keep his options open in the months ahead.

40

Spring. A time to love. But this year, in New York, a political season that began with a riot.

It did not start, as so many feared, with poor blacks "coming downtown." This was not the "black revolution" the great cities feared they would again endure, the urban nightmare that roused big city mayors in midnight sweats. But this violence, the Byers Street riot, was like nothing any of them had ever seen.

They came down the street, the men in their black hats, their beards and long, curly hair moving in the warm breeze. A cop looked through the grimy window of the stationhouse.

"Jesus," he said, "there's a million of them."

They were chanting. Inside the stationhouse the cops could hear it but they did not understand what they were saying. There was a sergeant and three men. It was a quiet Saturday afternoon and the other officers on the precinct rolls were on their beats.

The sergeant moved his fat buttocks off his chair behind the desk and went to the window grumbling at the patrolman who had seen them first. "A million? Doyle, you're so full of shit—"

Then he saw Byers Street and the crowd coming, perhaps fifteen or twenty abreast, and behind them their ranks filled the entire street, their long black gabardine coats opened in the sunlight, showing white shirts without ties. The sergeant stared at them for a moment. Then he wheeled and glared at one of the men.

"Call headquarters," he said. "There's no way we're gonna handle that many."

The policeman called Doyle smirked self-satisfaction.

He was wrong, of course. There weren't a million Hasidim out there. There were three thousand. A Jew had been stabbed to death that morning on his way home from the synagogue. A black had done it, or a couple of blacks. News of the murder had spread through the Hasidic community, sped by its being the Sabbath and hearing about it in temple, or in the clustered groups outside temple on the sidewalk. The news was true, and it was bad enough, a man dead. The rumors were not true, and they were worse: that the cops had not even responded to an alarm, were not trying very hard to find the killers, that nothing would be done that might arouse the sullen black community.

Now the crowd was in front of the stationhouse, spreading out along the front of the old red brick building and stretching back down Byers Street as far as the cops could see. Eight or ten men mounted the steps to the door of the stationhouse, open in the pleasant weather. The sergeant went to the open door and stood there.

"Yes, folks, and what can we do for you?" he asked, nervously wondering just what the hell you *do* say to a mob.

There was a babel of voices mingling English and Yiddish. A few feet from his face men were shaking their fists. The sergeant did not understand what any of them were saying and he held his hands up in a calming gesture.

"Now if just one of yiz would tell me what—"

A tall, thin young man with curls shouted, "They killed Shlomo. Fucking niggers killed him. And you do nothing. *Nothing!*"

The sergeant waited while they shouted. He knew a homicide had been committed that morning. He had not yet come on duty but it had been entered on the blotter. "We're after them now, folks, you can be assured of that. And as soon as the alleged perpetrators are caught, we'll let you know. Until then—"

There was more shouting then and behind the leaders the crowd moved forward, not able to hear the dialogue, impatient with the delay. The leaders were pushed up the steps and through the doorway of the stationhouse. The sergeant backed inside in front of them, continuing to hold out his hands, continuing to talk soothingly. Nobody seemed to be listening to him, even if they could hear above the crowd noise. Jesus, he thought, I hope they get here soon.

The front room of the stationhouse was typically dank and drear, the institutional green paint peeling on the walls, a faint smell of mingled disinfectant, sweat, and urine. Behind him the sergeant could sense his three men moving backward as well. He did not turn to place them. He disliked the idea of giving his back to the mob. You never knew when someone might throw something. If he kept watching them perhaps he could duck it.

"Never again!" someone shouted. "Never again!"

The sergeant started to say something and from somewhere to his right a fist exploded against his cheek. The blow was only a tap, no real leverage behind it, but the violence began then, unleashed by the knowledge that someone in the mob had hit a policeman, that now they had to go ahead with it, and within a few seconds there were dozens of fists, scores of hands reaching out for the sergeant. He fell backward, losing his balance, and they came in over him and surged up against the desk, behind which the three patrolmen waited, bewildered. What did they know, in Brooklyn on a sunny afternoon, about the wild hatred born in a hundred Polish and Russian pogroms, a thousand Nazi roundups? The police, the hated police, Cossack or Gestapo, only the uniforms were different, and a Jew was dead. The mob swept through the room, battering the three remaining cops to the ground. Later, one of them, Doyle, would wonder aloud why he hadn't pulled his weapon.

"Because they would of fucking killed us," one of his companions said angrily, "because they would of torn our arms and legs off."

There were three thousand Hasidim in the street, and only a few hundred of them could fit into the old stationhouse. But a few hundred was enough. They turned over tables and chairs, pulled out file cabinet drawers and threw papers around, ripped the wires out of the switchboard and the communications computer,

ripped out wash basins and tore the seats off toilets. There was no
one in the four old cells in the basement. Which was fortunate. In
this precinct the prisoner was inevitably black.

The first squad cars began to arrive. The cops got out at the far
end of Byers Street. The cars couldn't go any farther. The police
station was perhaps a hundred yards away and they could see men
in black coats pushing into the building. There was no way they
could know what was happening inside the precinct house. They
started to move forward, slowly, pushing their way through the
jammed street, their clubs held low. Then a cop tripped and went
down and as he did his club cracked across the shin of one of the
demonstrators.

That was when it really started. Before it was over sixty cops had
been hurt and a dozen Hasidim. The local assemblyman, resplen-
dent in his shawl and yarmulka, cried "police brutality." A deputy
inspector called a rabbi a "lousy kike." The mayor wrung his hands
and promised a court of inquiry.

Two of the black kids who killed the Jew had been arrested several
hours before the riot began and were being grilled by homicide
detectives for the names of the others involved in the attack. Homicide had not announced the arrests to avoid scaring off the other
"perpetrators." The riot had been for nothing. But the mayor transferred forty foot patrolmen from other precincts to beef up security
in the neighborhood and to keep the district in the Democratic
column for the next elections.

It seemed to Campbell Haig only one man in Brooklyn was talking
sense in the wake of the Hasidic riot: Judah Wine.

Sean Farrell sat on the windowsill of Haig's office, holding the first
edition turned to an editorial Haig had ordered written. He was
disturbed. Months had passed since Farrell had urged Haig to see
Wine, and now their positions were reversed.

"Sure, it takes guts for a Brooklyn Jew to buck the Hasidim on
the law-and-order issues. They're emotional as hell. They don't want
to listen. The guy has chutzpah, I grant you that. But what is he?
A schoolteacher. The local assemblyman, if he made sense, would
have an impact. Wine has no power, no constituency. He's hollering
down a rainbarrel. No one's listening."

"I'm listening," Haig said.

Farrell made a throwaway gesture.

"Sure, and three dozen people and my Aunt Nellie read the editorial. Come on, Haig, we're both too old for idealism."

"Are we?" Haig asked. "Are we?"

That night Farrell, not for the first time, pondered the enigma that was his employer. A publisher of sensational trash, a cynic, the unremitting foe of organized labor, a man who, Farrell suspected, programmed his life by computer. Now Haig was personally directing the most quixotic sort of editorial campaign, a foolish, aimless crusade practically guaranteed to lose readers by putting them to sleep. So a newspaper's job was to print the news and raise hell. Well, Haig was raising hell now. Would it be worth it? Do you run editorials against Jews in New York when a newspaper lives or dies on the number of pages of advertising it sells to Macy's and Bloomingdale's and Gimbels and Alexander's?

Haig had gone out of his way to support a little-known Jew like Judah Wine against his own people. Farrell liked Wine. But it made no sense at all. The only consolation, Farrell told himself, was that no one paid much attention to editorials in the *Mail* anyway. It wasn't as if it were the *Times* thundering. Maybe no one was listening except Haig. He hoped that would be the case.

He was wrong on that. At least one man was listening. His name was Ben Cork.

Ben Cork had just come home. He had been in jail. Like Mayor Curley of Boston, Ben had been in jail before and the fact never seemed to dampen the enthusiasm of the voters for their duly elected representative in the Congress of the United States. Like old Curley, he kept being reelected, and by increasingly impressive majorities. The Boston Irish loved it that Curley was putting it over on the Protestant brahmins who made up that city's power Establishment. And the blacks loved it that Ben Cork ripped off the WASPs who ran New York and the country besides.

This latest incarceration had been so trivial as to be laughable. Indictment as a heroin trafficker. The only awkward part of it was that the narcs had picked him up on a Friday afternoon and he had been unable to raise bail until Monday morning. Men like Ben Cork are opposed to spending weekends on Rikers Island, and Ben was in an impressively sour mood. What the hell was happening to the bail bond business when they didn't even work weekends anymore? Rikers was a shithole and it was an embarrassment even to visit the place, as he had often done as a congressman. To be locked up there was an insult. Not that they hadn't tried to salve his annoyance. The wardens of prisons understand all about congressional appropriations, and this particular warden had permitted Ben to stay in his own spare bedroom rather than suffer the ignominy and the cockroaches of a cell. When he left, Ben thanked the warden for his courtesy and promised that his Washington office would be in touch. "Just let me know if you ever need anything, Warden," he had said when the limo came for him, and the warden had been deeply touched.

Now Ben needed something. A woman. She was on the way. Rather, *they* were on the way. Enforced celibacy over a Friday, Saturday, and Sunday was unusual for Ben, and he had issued very precise instructions to his staff. Now he ate a late breakfast on the terrace of his apartment on Riverside Drive, dressed in a Sulka robe, eating grapefruit and idling through the newspapers. That was when he saw Haig's editorial. It stopped him and he read it carefully. He was not accustomed to reading editorial attacks on Jews in New York papers, especially when the Jews had been demonstrating against blacks. He had missed the story of the riot itself. His district was upper Manhattan and the South Bronx. Ordinarily he wasted little sympathy on Brooklyn and its problems. Compared to Harlem and the South Bronx, Brooklyn was Vatican City.

He made a note of Judah Wine's name.

Then the buzzer sounded and as his valet hurried to the door, Ben Cork put his newspapers away and stood up. He strode into the living room, a big, handsome man. Under the robe he was naked, and already the excitement was rising. He heard voices and then the two girls were shown in.

"Well, hello," he said, extending a hand to each of them. The girls smiled and said hello. They seemed pleased to be there, honored. Ben gestured toward the master bedroom and gallantly let them go ahead of him. The office had done very well, he thought, his mood brightening. He was not sure whether he would start first with the black girl with the afro or the little blonde with the pony-tail. Perhaps he would have them make it together while he watched and then he could choose. It was pleasant to have little concerns like this to worry about. A hell of a lot better than sitting on his black ass up there in Rikers Island.

41

April. A quiet time in the Hamptons. Sissy lay alone in her bed in Junior Valentine's house, no longer awkward about her arm, no longer unbalanced.

It was early evening. But she was sleepy. She had taken a long ride on the beach that day. She had watched the sun, going down later now, sink over the pond. A mallard duck had strolled toward the house, wobbly, unsure.

It was six months since that first night with Caz. The first of those months had been more like a year, a decade, a life. A month that had reassured her, restored her, at a cost. . . . Oh, what a cost it had seemed in some of the guilt-stricken daylight hours of that first month.

Sometimes when she was first with Caz she felt herself spinning totally out of control, reason jettisoned, the animal in her rampant, dominant, triumphant. On his fish-smelling boat, in his narrow, tousled bed with its stale linen, under the overhead lamps of its cabin, a cultured, disciplined young woman who used to be Sissy Valentine had died. And a moaning, thrusting, slavering, insatiable whore had replaced her, had slipped into her very skin. That night when he hit her, when he had the men from the bar come aboard and take her in turn, that was the moment when she could have rebelled, cursed Caz, screamed unsubtle threats, walked out.

She had not. She had stayed. Not because he wanted it but because *she* did. *She,* Sissy Valentine, who used to be a nice young girl of good family with two slender, graceful, suntanned arms. That was what had surprised the men. Drunk as they were, as inflamed by her naked body, her palpable openness, her availability, as by his crude goading, as rough and insensitive as they were, there had still been a hesitation, a momentary pause as if they were asking themselves, was this some elaborate sort of practical joke? Does this chick really mean it? Are we being put on?

It was that moment of hesitation that had sent Sissy careening into total abandon. As she lay there, sulky, frightened, appalled, she had immediately, neurotically supposed it was the sight of her arm that was holding them back, disgusting them, chilling their drunken passion. It was the physical rejection she had feared since first waking in the hospital bed.

Then, one of the men had reached over and put his hand on her. She looked down, saw the big, grimy, black-haired paw sliding slowly down the white, gentle curve of her belly, and shuddered, not in disgust, but in gratitude.

She had looked up at the man, she could not recall now which it had been, and smiled, moving her legs slightly to provide the opening he sought.

And they had begun.

The next night Caz, sobered now, had greeted her with a nervous grin, aware he had gone too far the night before, recognizing in his dense, muddled fashion that this was a girl with money, with friends, with (always a sinister thought) *connections.* And he did something he rarely did, he essayed courtesy. "How about a drink? I'll make it."

Sissy half giggled. A nice turnaround, she thought.

"No," she said firmly, "just relax. I'll get it."

He continued to watch her as she stood with her back to him at the galley sink, deftly opening a bottle, cracking ice cubes from the tray. Sissy turned and carried the glass to him. When she had her own she raised it in his direction. "To you, Caz, for teaching me what I am."

He grinned, but again, uncertainly, and gulped the drink. He did not know what Sissy knew, the depth of her fall, how desperate she was, how pure, animal sex had come to dominate her life.

"Caz," she said, her voice lazy, her body relaxed, pliant, "could you get us some drugs? You know, stuff to take while we're in bed? Ludes, maybe? Huh?"

Still not understanding, he mumbled that of course he could scare something up, sure, absolutely. But why?

She stood in the middle of the tiny room, staring at him, her tongue moving slowly over her lips. "So we can try new things. So I can make it even better for you."

"Oh?" he said, knowing how it was going to be all right, better than all right.

"Yeah. And last night, Caz . . ."

He tensed again. "Yeah?"

She took a drink before she said it. "Caz, would your friends like to come back again tonight?"

Now she lay alone, remembering. Winter had ended, spring had come to the Hamptons and to a continent. And Sissy's nightmare, compounded in equal parts of pain and pleasure, guilt and defiance, shame and satisfaction, was coming to an end. She did not know this, she had no plan, no powerful spiritual or psychological renascence had occurred. She was still a cripple, with one arm and one stump. But no longer the same frightened, emotionally wrecked girl she had been six months earlier.

How she and Alex had laughed about her father's "ingenues." How they'd laughed. Only now it was at Sissy that decent people might laugh and point. Sissy the easy lay, Sissy the whore, Sissy the object of fun and laughter. How . . . just.

She had laughed at her father's girls, was amused by them, pitied them. Yet her father was, if a fool, at least civilized, educated, generous, rather touchingly vulnerable in his weakness. But what of the men Sissy Valentine screwed? Drunks and fishermen and bartenders and auto mechanics and layabouts and anyone who bothered to buy a cheap whiskey for Caz, anyone with a pair of pants to be taken off, a fly to be unzipped, a body to be satisfied.

Once, at school, there were rumors of a girl involved in a gang bang. Half the basketball team, and this single stupid, beer-drunk girl. Sissy recalled with ice-water clarity the mingled contempt and shock she had felt.

It all comes back to us, doesn't it? It all comes full circle.

She had considered suicide. First over the arm, later over what she had become. Poetic imagery, sea kelp strewn over her pale face, a slim, still form composed and decorous in her own bed, a slumped figure in the front seat of a running car in the closed garage. Those urges had passed, she could not say why. Perhaps she had toughened up. Perhaps the ordeals, first of the maiming, then of sordid shame, had done it. If she could survive such tests she could, and should, survive anything. The knowledge that she could still function sexually, even at this basest of levels, had helped her over the rocks and shoals. Now, although she did not yet know it, pride was creeping back, unexpected and unwelcomed. The pride of old Meg Valentine.

Sissy lay abed alone, having refused for the first time in months a summons from Montauk, and wondered about Alex Noyes, whether she was happy, whether this affair with Haig was going well. And she wondered about Sean Farrell, who had abandoned her first for Alex, and later, also understandably, because she was a grotesque cripple. Could she really blame him for either betrayal?

Sissy was not the only one asking questions of herself.

As cool as she had been with Nora, Alex knew she had been shaken by the bitterness of their last meeting. Mothers and daughters did not hate one another in books or in the women's magazines. They were supportive, they exchanged mutual confessions of love, they cemented combinations in restraint of everyone else. Mother love, daughter love. That was how it should be. But with Nora and Alex Noyes, how it wasn't. Shaken, too, in another way, by her visit to the White House. Memories of childhood, of her father, of a simpler, more innocent time tumbled before her. The President had spoken of a sacred continuity that bound families, that bound the very nation together. Yet Alex had lost a father, had broken with her mother, had betrayed Sean, and had found her own true love in Campbell, but even with him, was living a sort of restless half-life neither married nor single. If only there were someone to talk to about it all. If only she were a better Catholic. Surely there were real priests, not the sort who mixed cocktails for Nora, but truly wise and holy men with whom she could talk. If only Sissy were whole again and within reach . . .

Well, she thought, why not? She picked up a phone and dialed East Hampton.

It was one of those late April days of false summer, unseasonably warm, the low sun bouncing off the deceptively placid ocean, still frigid, still harboring in its depths the memories of ice and winter's fury. They had kicked off their sneakers on the dunes and walked now along the damp sand at the edge of the Atlantic, Alex Noyes and Sissy Valentine, two tall, slender young women who had once been friends and who had not seen each other for half a year.

"I'm glad you came," Sissy said, "so very glad."

"I should have come before. But each time I phoned . . ."

"Alex, I wasn't ready. I didn't really want to see you. Or anyone. It was a time when I had to be alone."

"And that's over now?"

Sissy was silent for an instant and then she said, "Yes, I think so."

A lone gull squawked overhead. How long it had been since the two of them had lain by Sissy's pool in the sun with that lovesick boy mooning over his infatuation. How much had happened. How much both of them had changed.

Alex watched Sissy out of the corner of her eye as they walked. Everything seemed the same. Everything was different. The long, slim legs in well-cut jeans, the smooth sweater, the long, lovely hair, the beautiful, well-bred face. There was the missing arm, of course, but Sissy seemed unaware of it. Which was strange. And there were other differences. There was a new . . . toughness, perhaps that was the word, a self-reliance, a sureness the "old" Sissy had never had. It was as if she had grown up. Then, as if in response to a question never asked, Sissy said, "There was a man. Out here."

"Oh?"

"His name was Caz."

"Yes?"

She told Alex then. Everything. At the end she deftly lighted a cigarette with one hand, shaking out the cigarette, flipping the lighter in a practiced way, cupping the flame against the wind.

"He dragged me down," she said, "not that I didn't want it. My arm never repelled or revolted him the way I was sure it would. It never stopped him from wanting me, wanting my body. It never stopped him from being cruel. He treated me as well and as badly as he would have treated a whole woman. And when I hit bottom, with his drinking buddies and the drugs and the rest of it, I'd had all of him I could use. All I needed. I was freed. I guess I'm cured. That bastard saved me."

Alex, listening to her story, felt a chill on her back. A trickle of sweat ran down between her shoulder blades under her sweater. Sissy's account of coming back to life had affected Alex physically: Alex's own troubled memories paled, seemed wholesome and girlish compared to this recitation of horrors. And was this Sissy who had come back from hell—was she the same Sissy, or someone else? She *was* different. The lovely, gentle, open girl who had held long, tanned arms to the sea, to life, that night so long ago . . .

That girl was gone. In her place, a different person, a woman, firm, resolute. Maimed and yet strengthened. Alex couldn't help admiring her, the childhood friend, on whom this ugly thing called life had played such an awful trick.

They were at the jetty now, the natural turning point, and as they reversed their course, picking up their own footsteps on the smooth sand of the vacant beach, meeting themselves coming, as it were, Sissy asked, "And you? Does it go well with you?"

"Yes."

"He's good to you?"

"More than I deserve, probably," Alex said, noticing how carefully Sissy had asked the question, without ever mentioning Campbell's name.

"And you live together."

"Yes, almost from the very first. I did something very stupid one night and here came Haig, galloping to the rescue. That was when it began, I suppose."

She was conscious of her own selectivity in talking about it. No mention of their first meeting, her mad, angry dash to Mayfair, her first view of the drunken, remorseful Haig. Recounting that to Sissy would be unfair, a cruel reminder of what had happened.

Instead she told her about her own drunken adventure in the lesbian bar.

When she had finished Sissy said, "Will you marry him?"

"I dunno. I don't think I'm yet ready. He wants it."

Sissy stopped then and turned toward her. Behind Sissy the surf rolled smoothly up the empty beach.

"Oh, Alex, for God's sake, if you love him then grab him. Nail him down. Get it done officially and forever. I wasn't strong enough to get the man I wanted. I backed away and curtsied and left Sean to you. I should have fought, should have cheated and schemed and done anything that had to be done. Instead . . ."

"What I did with Sean was unfair to both of you," Alex said somberly.

"No, no," Sissy said, shaking her head violently, her long hair dancing. "There's no fair or unfair in love. There's only . . . love or no love. The fault was mine. The weakness. The stupidity."

"But you're not weak," Alex interrupted. "You're not weak at all."

Sissy looked into her face.

"No," she said, "you're right. I'm not weak. Not anymore."

She wasn't, either. Alex knew this. The tone of her voice, the way her bare feet bit into the sand, the proud angle of her neck. There was a new strength in Sissy, in her body and in her character.

"We always got whatever we wanted, you and I," Sissy said, talking to herself as much as to Alex. "There was always money. Family. Looks. Connections. Even some brains. But I never had your singlemindedness."

"You mean ruthlessness."

Sissy resumed walking slowly, and remained silent for a moment. And then, "Yes, I guess that's exactly what I mean. Ruthlessness. Not in a critical sense. You always had the guts to go out and get what you wanted. While I . . ."

Alex responded angrily. "But you were the one who got a job. Built a career. Did something with your life. While I piddled around and played Nora's daughter."

Sissy laughed. "A job? On my grandma's paper."

"On merit," Alex insisted heatedly.

Sissy shrugged. "My family owned the paper. And that big, noisy, Irishman Farrell was there for the taking. And I did absolutely nothing about it."

"Will you now?"

For the first time Sissy glanced at the empty sleeve of her sweater tucked neatly into the waistband of her jeans.

"Too late," she said, "too late."

Alex thought of Haig, of their home, their love. The sort of love Sissy should have, that she deserved. The love that Haig, without meaning to, had taken from her.

"Oh, no, Sissy," she cried out, "it's never too late."

A gull, frightened by her cry, wheeled toward the Atlantic.

42

The Deputy Inspector of Police drummed his fingers on the dashboard of the command car at the corner of Washington Avenue and Pitkin.

"Jews and niggers," he muttered, "Ben Cork and Judah Wine." He shook his large head. Seven months away from retirement and a seventy-five percent pension and they had to come up with an explosive mixture like this one. God, how he hated Crown Heights. No matter how this evening culminated, peacefully or violently, the cops would be blamed; *he* would take the rap. If anyone was killed, even badly hurt, then the police had been lax, he himself had been ineffective. If by some miracle the thing came off without any serious damage, Gestapo tactics would be charged. Suppression of legitimate rights of assembly and protest.

He breathed deeply.

"All right, Mike, the Academy of Music. But slowly."

The red-headed driver nodded and the big car began to move forward. He didn't need the caution about moving slowly. There was no way they could roll faster than a crawl through the crowds headed from the bus stops and the subway stations toward the old music hall. Streams of black faces, of bearded Jewish faces, emptying from their respective ghettos, all with the one destination, an antique chamber more accustomed to *lieder* than to bitter confrontation.

Campbell Haig had arrived even before the first of the police, long before the first civilian, black *or* white. Farrell had arranged it.

"I want to see this fellow Wine in action, up close. A pressure situation like this one ought to tell me something."

Farrell was sardonic. "If someone doesn't take a shot at him." He paused. "Or at you," he added pleasantly.

"Just set it up, will you?" Haig said impatiently.

There would be working press in the Academy that evening, of course, including reporters from the *Mail*. Haig made it clear he didn't want to be part of that.

"Find me somewhere I can see and hear without sticking out like a sore thumb. I don't want it around that I'm in the room. Especially I don't want Wine to know. Or Ben Cork."

Cork was the most exotic aspect of the whole crazy business, the great gamble by Judah Wine. Being out on bail was not unprecedented. But Cork was not contrite, not in the least. He flaunted what the Hasidim hated, a black disdain for white law. But Wine had insisted.

"There is absolutely no point in my debating this issue with someone the community will brand an Uncle Tom," he'd declared. "Give me Ben Cork up there on the platform and there's a chance, a real chance, to make a breakthrough. Put any other black face up there and they'll hoot us both out of the hall."

The mayor, characteristically unpredictable, had said yes. "What the hell, I'm not running again," he cheerfully informed an angrily protesting police commissioner, "so if anything goes wrong they lynch Judah Wine, that smartass."

Sean Farrell had a pal inside the music hall. It seemed whatever the venue, whatever the situation, Farrell had a "pal." The "pal" led Haig through the big, empty, echoing hall.

"I thought about it, Mr. Haig," he said, "and I think anything out front is bad. The house lights will be up the whole time. Not like this was opera or a play, y'know. And backstage? There's just gonna be cops crawling around everywhere. No, I found a place. If you don't mind standing."

The prompter's box, just in front of the orchestra pit, shielded

from the audience, in view only to those onstage and then only if
he flipped on the hundred-watt bulb the prompter used to read the
score or the script.

"You leave that light off and your own mother wouldn't know you
was there," the man assured Haig.

Haig liked the plan. It appealed to the manipulator in him, the
offstage presence who had mounted the *divertissement*. And how
appropriate. The prompter! No one, not even Farrell, knew just *how*
appropriate. For Campbell Haig was stage managing this entire
production, on which the election of the next mayor, on which the
entire fabric of the city's racial relationships could hinge. He went
up a backstage staircase to the men's room and then, with a Thermos
of black coffee thoughtfully supplied by Farrell's "pal," slipped into
the prompter's box and prepared for the long wait. Unlike the
prompter, he had no score's bulky pages to turn. He knew the
scenario.

For Haig had written the script, in his and Alex's apartment in
the sixties with two, no, make that three, collaborators, during seven
hours of frenetic argument, pleading, rationalization, and emotion
the night before. His collaborators? None other than the unpredictable Jewish educator, Judah Wine, and the charismatic black leader,
now a furloughed convict, Ben Cork. The final collaborator had been
Alex Noyes, who stonewalled phone callers (even Sean Farrell, who
was *not* to be kept informed) with cryptic non sequiturs, pleas of
headache, and outright lies, and who once descended to the local deli
to have sandwiches made up. She kept shuttling cold drinks and
steaming pots of black coffee into the living room where the three
men hammered first at one another and, at the end of seven hours,
on an agreement.

When she was not serving, Alex curled up in a corner of the big
leather Chesterfield sofa, her legs under her, in a bulky sweater,
jeans, and bare feet, her short hair tousled as she ran a hand through
it absentmindedly, chain smoking, drinking coffee, and watching
Campbell cajole the two natural enemies into cementing an alliance
that might be as fragile as it was convenient, as short-lived as it was
pragmatic.

She had met Judah Wine before. A tall man, gaunt, Lincolnesque,
he had a large hooked nose, a narrow blade that worked with his face,

a shock of black hair. The broad shoulders, the lanky grace, the large hands, the frayed shirt collar, the necktie that had seen better days, the broken fingernails, the slightly yellow teeth gave him an air of careless self-confidence. The habit of scratching his head or whatever else gave him pleasure as he wrestled with the preposterous proposals being put to him by Campbell. Or as he reacted, or stonily refused to react, as he was doing now, to the smooth charm, the quickness, the occasional flashes of bitterness, from Ben Cork that intrigued them all. Wine had come to their apartment nearly a month ago. It had been Campbell's first private meeting with the man, a session that dragged on so long Alex had finally succumbed to yawns and drooping eyelids and had excused herself and gone to bed. Neither Campbell nor Wine had seemed even to notice her going. It was that evening, that long conversation, that had convinced Haig it was this man, and not the weirdly powerful Lenny Sparg or the handsome spellbinder Osborn, who held out at least some slim promise for the future of the tormented city.

Cork she had never seen. Not as tall as Wine, he was bulkier, but in the controlled, flat-backed, thick-thighed manner of a professional athlete, a Reggie Jackson lookalike, down to the mustache. Did black men of his generation consciously mold themselves on the Reggie Jacksons, with the rimless glasses, the purposeful "cool," the quiet conversational tone, the air of total control, of contempt for lesser men coupled with a superiority so immense they could afford graciousness, even to their foes?

He had addressed her first as "Mrs. Haig." Campbell, amused, had corrected him. "It's Miss Noyes," he said, "and in her more militant manifestations, *Ms.* Noyes."

Ben Cork apologized, with a great deal of charm. He knew precisely who she was, had committed the blunder as a tactic, wanting from the very first moment to establish if she were hostile, an ally, or an impartial observer. He had gotten there first, had come up from the basement on the freight elevator, direct from the chauffeured car.

It was good of him, Haig said, in that turn-of-the-century courtliness Alex so loved, to give of his very first evenings "back in town."

Cork had smiled.

"It *had* occurred to me to do one or two other things," he said, turning toward Alex as if to suggest that as a sophisticated woman she must of course know precisely what priorities a man just out of prison might have on his first free night.

She had smiled back, enigmatically, she hoped.

When Judah Wine came in he was less relaxed, openly nervy. You'd think he was the one just out of prison, Alex thought. Cork was expansive, as if this were his house, his party. Campbell, lacking small talk, smiled a lot and rubbed his hands together, impatient to get to the substance of the meeting. That was when Alex helped bridge gaps. She chatted, she reacted, properly, to Cork's flirtatious eyes, she was duly somber in response to Wine's ponderous gravity, she was girlish and voluble when Campbell lapsed most obviously into thoughtful, distracted silence.

For the first hour, Cork slouched in a deep armchair, Wine pacing the room, Campbell tensely on the edge of a sofa, they fenced. Then, the first confrontation.

Wine was impatient. The blacks wanted community control of the schools without any semblance of municipal leash. Fine in theory; unworkable, he said, in practice. The result was chaos, reading scores appallingly below national or even citywide averages, still another flight of middle class, mostly Jewish, teachers to the suburbs.

"The damn thing doesn't work. It just flat doesn't work."

Cork sneered at his impatience with the experiment.

"We've been waiting a hundred years for a piece of the action, and *you're* impatient?"

Wine wasn't having it. "Let's not bog down here in communal guilt," he said sharply. "What happened fifty or a hundred years ago is a damn shame. It's the root of today's problems. But wringing our hands over past history doesn't help the black kid trying to learn to write in today's sixth grade."

"The teachers are Jews," Cork said quietly. "Consciously or subconsciously they have no real interest in teaching blacks or Hispanics. They put in their five hours a day and hold their breath waiting for June and another summer in Europe."

"Nonsense," Wine said, waving his arms, "sure they're Jews, but who the hell goes to Europe on twenty thousand a year? You're setting up straw men. Teachers aren't the idle rich. They're working people who've invested a hell of a lot in their own professional education and then they spend their time keeping order in the classroom. They *have* to. No wonder their teaching suffers."

"They don't teach," Cork said stubbornly. "They consider the children their inferiors and they—"

Wine wheeled on the black man, fists clenched. "Jews have been persecuted for centuries. They *understand* bias. It's unruly, sometimes violent kids, parents who don't care, who—"

"Now who's wringing his hands over ancient history?" Cork asked mildly, almost amused.

Haig looked frustrated. If they were going to keep this up, to bog down in recrimination and swapping race insults . . .

Alex saw it in his face, in the tightness of his shoulders, the arch of his neck.

"Campbell," she said pleasantly, as if she had heard none of the anger in the room, sensed none of the narrow bitterness, "perhaps our guests would enjoy a drink."

"Oh, yes, yes," Haig said abstractedly.

She went into the kitchen. Cork came in after her.

"Ms. Noyes," he said, "which way is the bathroom?"

She told him. He left the kitchen after permitting his deep eyes to linger a half second longer than permissible.

"The man's a rascal," Haig had told her. "The guts of a jewel thief, the charm of a confidence man, a blend of supreme assurance and ghetto shrewdness."

Campbell, thought Alex as she finished making the drinks, had Mr. Cork down rather accurately.

Cork returned from the bathroom, from a trip he had not really had to make. A President's daughter, he thought admiringly. Haig did pretty well for himself. His opinion of the publisher rose.

Haig had switched on WQXR and Wine was deep in a conversation with him about Bach.

"His Weimar period," Wine was saying. "He'd just discovered Italian music and was trying to juxtapose the baroque with his own disciplined, Teutonic order. A fascinating collision of two styles, two substances."

Cork laughingly entered the conversation as if none of the bitterness of the past hour had ever happened.

"Like you and me, Mr. Wine. Wouldn't it be nice if we could make pretty music together like old Johann Sebastian?"

Wine's head went up. "You know Bach?"

Cork nodded. "Sorry I don't live up to your prototype," he said.

Wine laughed for the first time. "Sorry," he said. "Didn't mean to be so obvious."

They had their drinks, the music, heavy, serious, and quite beautiful, a pleasant backdrop; Alex's small talk, her tangible loveliness, even more pleasant.

Haig was more relaxed now. The first couple of hours in a confrontation like this one were always the worst. That was when men took personal, as opposed to professional, dislike to one another. That had not happened. These two men were the products of antithetic, even hostile cultures. Yet here they were needling one another over the music of Bach, both of them reacting to Alex's beauty, her earthy common sense, her humor. Well, he thought, I've seen head-knocking sessions that promised less.

"Gentlemen," he said, "suppose we get back to our problem."

Four hours later they had their solution. There was no euphoria; each of them, even Alex, for whom there had been yawning gaps of incomprehension or of physical absence during the long night, knew how flimsy a house of cards they had constructed.

"But it's *something,* damn it," Campbell had said in bed after the two men had left. "If two hardnosed mavericks like Cork and Judah Wine can accept risks like these, then we've gotten somewhere, we've moved off the bloody dime."

Yes, Alex had said lazily, lovingly, and she had moved to Haig, to tell him in more than words how well she thought he had handled his "mavericks."

After they had made love, Campbell Haig lay there beside the sleeping Alex, thinking about her, about his gamble that had brought the old enemies together, about himself. Through all of it was threaded the image of Alex, this healthy, loving, this *good* woman. How she had helped with her charm, her instinctive intelligence. When the Wine-Cork "summit" was seemingly headed irretrievably off the tracks, plunging down slopes into hate and stubborn implacability, she had said something, fetched sandwiches, or simply by moving through the room had broken the tension, lent a sense of warmth, of true welcome, to the apartment, to those who were there as her, as *their* guests. She was, Haig concluded, the sort of wife a diplomat should have, a politician, a President.

The Academy had filled. Haig could not see the audience from his prompter's box but he could visualize the sea of black and white faces, could imagine how they had (in fact) segregated themselves on different sides of the aisles, could not help but hear them, the low animal roar of the mob. No, be precise, he told himself, not a mob. Not yet it wasn't. Judah Wine and Ben Cork were on the stage. A number of community leaders and several lower-level city officials had spoken, had largely been ignored, except for catcalls, by an audience impatient with the warm-up acts, anxious for Cork and Wine, for what Alex had called over breakfast that morning Campbell's "Odd Couple."

Except that his legs were cramping, Haig found the prompter's box ideal for his purpose. Although he knew what they were to say, had orchestrated it to a large extent, he didn't want either of the two men to see him, had not told them he would be there. His presence might inhibit their spontaneity. And he did want to observe Wine under pressure. He was very nearly sure this was the man for the *Mail* to back. But he wanted to be certain. What would happen in the next hour on this stage, before this audience, in response to the formidable Ben Cork, would tell much about the enigmatic Judah Wine.

Cork was recognized first. That was how they had arranged it. The moderator, an energetic young Irish priest (chosen, presumably, as someone *both* sides could enthusiastically despise), made the introduction.

"And now," the priest said, "speaking on behalf of the black community, Congressman Benjamin . . ."

He didn't get the rest of it out. Or maybe he did. In the prompter's box Haig could not only hear the roar, he could feel it in the soles of his feet, the voices, the sound of several thousand people bounding to their feet, the clapping and the foot stamping. It went on for several minutes. The few boos had been drowned out.

He saw Ben raise his hands. Several times. Finally they stilled and Cork spoke, the pleasant bass controlled, slow, effective.

"Friends," he said, and then, with a slight pause that drew laughter, "and others . . . I yield the floor to Mr. Judah Wine."

That too had been arranged. But it shocked the crowd. Some of the blacks hooted but only for the few seconds it took for the Jews in the hall to react. Their cheers and applause and foot stamping were only slightly less enthusiastic than those of the blacks.

Wine did not raise his arms. He stood there, his long arms dangling at his sides, his head down, the black hair hanging loosely down over one eye, until the sound subsided and eventually stilled. Then, turning first to Cork, then to the hall, he said:

"Ben Cork is no friend of mine. He"—there were shouts of outrage, scattered boos, a few curses, including one shrill "Jew bastard!"—"and I stand at opposite poles on so many questions it is difficult to imagine where we have any common ground. Tonight, here in Crown Heights, we are going to try to discover whether there is, indeed, a common ground on which he and I, and you out there, might comfortably stand. Not as friends; it seems still too early for that"—A shout of "you kiddin'?" brought a laugh—"but as New Yorkers equally aware of just how bad our public school system is . . . and how great it just possibly could be. We are here to map the future. Not for ourselves, but for our children. And their children."

Judah Wine was wasting no time on historic prologues, on flowery introductions, not even on a courteous salute to a tension-strained audience.

"This school system," he began, "is a disgrace to education, a sinkhole for teachers, a danger, both physical and intellectual, to your children. It—"

The curses and the boos, the fist shaking and the foot stamping of an audience quickly to its feet, drowned out his next sentence. He halted, looking down at the plywood lectern, patient, waiting. But the demonstration did not stop. A dozen blacks in the audience and perhaps a half-dozen Jews tried to climb up on the stage but were pushed back by several husky marshals. It was amazing, Ben Cork thought, a half smile on his handsome face, that with his very first words Wine had succeeded in antagonizing both warring factions. It must be a gift, he concluded. He permitted the shouts and the throwing of papers to continue for another few moments and then he stood up, went to the lectern, and took the microphone. Wine backed away a few paces.

"Now," Cork said, speaking calmly, conversationally, "we can spend the evening yelling or we can hear out the man. Personally, I'm sort of interested in hearing what he says. I may not agree with it, probably won't, but I'm kind of curious. Course, if you don't want to listen, that's something else. I think we ought to. For our sakes, not for his."

He stepped away and the furor gradually stilled. People took their seats again. Wine resumed.

"This system has the worst reading and other scores in the state," he said, speaking without notes. "One senior school official doesn't live in the city. He doesn't even live in the state. He lives in Bergen County, over in New Jersey. Not only isn't his nonresidence against the spirit of community control, it's against the law.

"Community boards have granted tenure to principals without the slightest suggestion they are qualified. One of them, a man I know personally, is a functional illiterate. Another has recently been refused a temporary teaching license for failing to pass his professional examination. Yet such men are today principals of schools in this city. Truancy runs ten percentage points above the state average, which is already, itself, the highest in the country. There were four murders, one hundred eighty assaults with weapons, eight rapes in school buildings or on school property in the past year."

"It's the niggers!" shouted a man in Jewish black.

He was hooted down. Again Judah Wine waited for silence. Then he continued.

"Competent teachers are afraid to work in a number of districts, including this one. The few qualified teachers you had have transferred out or have transfers pending."

"Jew bastards!" someone shouted.

He went on, his report piling horror upon horror, and in the prompter's box Campbell Haig went impatiently from foot to foot. All right, he said to himself, we know all that, Judah. Get to the point. Don't just bury them in bad news. They know all that.

As if he had heard the publisher, Wine plunged both hands into his jacket pockets and said, "None of this is news to you. But what I want to tell you now may be. I think I know how we can turn this district around, this entire city, end the violence, bring in some capable teachers, and resume educating our children."

"Right on!" a black woman in one of the front rows cried out.

"That's what I want to hear." Wine paused. "Now, listen, this isn't going to be easy, it isn't going to happen just because I talk about it. It's only going to happen if all of you—blacks, whites, Hispanics—agree to give it a try."

For the first time except when Ben Cork had spoken there was a real silence in the big hall. It was expectant, hushed, ready. Only Haig and Cork, who had helped Judah create the scenario in Campbell's house, knew what he was to say. But even they waited, metaphorically leaning forward in their anxiety.

Wine spoke quietly, slowly, almost pedantically, lecturing rather than hectoring the assemblage. Well, Haig thought, one thing at a time, but I can't have a candidate using words like "microcosm."

Judah Wine's proposal was sweeping, radical, but it was basically simple. As a director of the Board of Education he would move to suspend a community school board if twenty-five percent of the parents so petitioned. The board suspended, Wine could name an interim committee to rule. He could suspend principals, order revisions in the curriculum. New board elections must be held, of course, and he proposed that they should be, within ninety days. In the meantime, and they must understand this, he planned to function as a dictator.

"I'll insist on qualification tests for teachers," he said. "You may consider this revolutionary, surely the teachers' union will call it criminal, but I will demand that teachers know how to read and write before they enter a classroom in this district. And as far as the children are concerned, I want to put an end to this pernicious practice of promoting a child simply to get rid of him, simply to please his parents. Children aren't furniture, to be moved about so that the house looks tidy. A child who hasn't achieved certain basic skills should not be promoted. Period!"

An angry murmur had begun to swell up out of the audience on his proposal to suspend the community board. It rose as he demanded qualified teachers and now exploded as he declared that failing children should be flunked. Men and women were on their feet again, on both sides of the segregated house. Ben Cork sat motionless in his chair, permitting the demonstration of protest to spend itself.

After that the assembly collapsed into wrangling. No one seemed to be convinced by Judah Wine's proposal. The white schoolteachers, the black parents, yelling, gesticulating, arguing. Haig pulled himself down from the prompter's box, flexed badly cramping legs, and went through the labyrinthine ways of the old music hall to the alley and his car. Cork phoned him that night.

"Well," Haig said, "what did you think?"

Ben laughed into the phone. "Hell, that district's so screwed up, he couldn't do much damage. Maybe something might even come out of it. People aren't used to hearing straight talk without all the bullshit. It sort of shocks them at first. You know?"

Haig said he did. Then Cork asked, "What did *you* think?"

Judah hadn't solved a single problem up there on the Academy stage. But he'd been cool, he'd thought on his feet, he'd coalesced with Ben Cork. And he hadn't panicked.

Haig didn't hesitate. "I think we might have ourselves a candidate," he said quietly.

"For what?" Ben Cork demanded. "You talking about school boards?"

"No," Campbell Haig said. "Mayor."

43

The primary lasted eight weeks. It seemed, to those who endured it, more like years. It was a typical New York political dogfight. Kill or be killed. Party labels signified nothing. Not a single substantive issue was debated rationally. Three men were running and the victor, whoever he was, would carry far less than fifty percent of the vote. It was like France—each candidate had his own newspaper backing him. The newspapers were not supposed to inform so much as to arouse, inflame, obfuscate, smear. The *Mail*, under Haig, was no better or no worse. Dick Osborn had his paper; Lenny Sparg had his; Judah Wine had the *Mail*. The *Mail* lied and slanted and smeared no more than did the others. It presented Judah in the best possible light and his opponents, if it mentioned them at all, in the worst. One day an innocent typo scrambled the name of Osborn's campaign manager, one Fisk. The error made it "Fink." When a copy editor brought it to Farrell's attention he growled, "Let it stand. Corrections cost money. Besides, the son of a bitch *is* a fink." If Haig had known of the incident he would have approved.

Farrell was smoking too much, drinking too much coffee at the office and too much Scotch after hours, he hadn't been to bed with a girl for weeks. His eyes were reddened, his mouth tasted sour, there was a slight but annoying tic in his right cheek. He was tired, short-tempered, intent. He knew the campaign was going well. Damn well. Lenny Sparg and Osborn had begun to attack Wine, even Mavis had needled him on TV. In the early weeks they'd virtually ignored Judah, laughing him off as Haig's plaything. They'd reserved their abuse for one another. That was over now. Judah Wine was becoming a threat.

One of the copy editors rapped at Farrell's door and stuck his head in. It was Webster, a pleasant, learned, garrulous man whom Farrell customarily enjoyed, a good man with whom to swap office gossip. But today Farrell snarled, "Listen, unless you've got an exclusive on the second coming, I don't want to talk to you."

Farrell turned back to the editorial he was editing, ignoring the dramatically slammed door. It was an editorial that would never be published.

Dill was a professional newspaperman. He'd covered City Hall since Bob Wagner's amiable stewardship. "Just don't shit me" was Dill's unvarying advice to politicians who sought his favor. A man who lied to Dill was unlikely to get much of a break in his stories. Of course, Dill was a practical man and did not count campaign promises as lies. It was assumed they were false and he never held them against a man. But a *personal* lie, that was something else. Now, when Lenny Sparg's man took him out for drinks and slipped the manila envelope across the table to him, Dill opened it, briefly examined its contents, and asked, "You shitting me?" The man shook his head.

"Okay," Dill said, "I'll show it to Farrell."

Farrell spent considerably more time staring at the papers. Jesus, he thought, and just when it looked like we had a good one.

"Okay, Dill, obviously we'll have to check it out. But don't start asking questions until I talk with Haig. Let's keep it quiet until then, huh?"

"Sure, Sean," Dill said. He was not a man who tilted at windmills. If the editor of the newspaper wanted to keep something quiet, who was he to play Woodward and Bernstein?

Farrell called Haig at home.

"You better come up," Haig said, a hollow feeling in his stomach.

"What is it?" Alex asked.

"Sean Farrell's coming up from the office. Something about Judah Wine. Sounds important."

"Oh," she said uneasily. It would be strange having Sean here.

Being driven uptown in a *Mail* car, Farrell was thinking the same thing. Bad enough this business about Wine. Haig would be in a foul mood. That alone was sufficient for Farrell to worry about without having to concern himself with Alex, with seeing for the first time where she lived with Haig, slept with him, did with Haig things she once did with him.

He wondered how much Haig knew about Farrell's brief affair with Alex. He need not have worried. The publisher grabbed the envelope from him at the door of the apartment.

"Come in, come in. Let's look at it."

Farrell followed him into the apartment. It was a small and lovely place, full of the touches he would have expected of Alex. Haig waved him impatiently to a seat in the living room and, spreading the papers on a cocktail table, began to read, crouched forward, only his tailbone resting on a couch.

Then Alex came into the room.

"Hello, Sean," she said. She was wearing a long quilted robe. She seemed unaware of what it did to Farrell, seeing her dressed for bed.

But he said, "Hello, Alex," and forced himself to focus on Haig and the papers Haig was scrutinizing.

Finally Haig looked up and shoved his glasses atop his head, mussing the soft brown hair. But his eyes looked clear, he seemed rested. Farrell knew the hours he was keeping at the office. He imagined the hours he was keeping with Alex, hated himself for the thought, and he wondered why Haig didn't look tired.

"Oh," Haig said absentmindedly, "Alex, you know Mr. Farrell?"

She smiled. "Oh, yes," she said, "we've met once or twice."

"Good." Haig grunted. "Now, Sean, you feel this is a true bill?"

Farrell shrugged. "I can't say. But if Sparg's people put it out it's going to hurt Judah whether it's true or not."

"Don't agree. If it's a phony there could be a hell of a backlash for Judah. It could be just what we need to put him over the top. People are pretty fed up with mud-slinging that turns out untrue."

"*If* it turns out untrue," Farrell said.

As the two men talked, Alex listened, watching them. How strange it was. A year ago Farrell had been an ardent suitor while Haig had been but a distant, spectral figure, the grotesque sensationalist of newspaper legend. Today Farrell was just an old acquaintance and Haig was her lover. Seeing them together, she understood why. Farrell was blunt, open, emotional; Haig, subtle, thoughtful, complex.

"Well," Haig said, nodding toward the papers on the cocktail table, "what next?"

Farrell wanted to go to Judah Wine. He was the only man who would know the truth of what Dill had brought in.

Haig looked dubious. "Go to Judah with filth like this and if it isn't true it's just going to upset him. And what will he think of us? His good friends, his loyal allies?"

"Well, what?"

"Sparg."

Lenny Sparg was still wearing black tie when they got to his apartment on Central Park South. There had been some sort of dinner. Farrell and Haig virtually ignored Lenny. Mavis was there, also in evening wear, a long, satin dress.

Mavis Sparg was gracious, expansive, handing around drinks, patting her husband soothingly on the head. "Don't sulk, Lenny, it's their job. They have to ask questions. How else would we have great newspapers like the *Mail* in this town?"

"Cut the shit, Mavis," Farrell said, "it's too late and I'm too tired and this is too Goddamn serious."

"Sean," Mavis said good-naturedly, "my role here is one of guidance, of counsel, of assistance."

Haig nodded. "Well, then, Mrs. Sparg, perhaps we could start by asking just where your husband acquired these papers about Mr. Wine."

Lenny Sparg had been pacing the room, his familiar grin on display now that he'd been informed this was not the occasion for a pout. "I'll tell you," he began.

"Lenny, shut up," Mavis ordered in her authoritative TV voice. Lenny's grin broadened.

Mavis Sparg sipped a tall goblet of champagne. She was enjoying this. "A gentleman—I suppose I should use another word—came to one of Lenny's people on this. He—"

"Which of Lenny's people?" Farrell demanded.

"Some two-bit little schmuck," Lenny said. "How do I know?"

"Shut up, Lenny," his wife said equably.

"So this 'gentleman' handed over this material to one of your husband's aides, some 'little schmuck'?" Haig said, irony in his voice.

"Yes," Mavis said, nodding crisply. "The 'gentleman' was, it goes without saying, a homosexual. And as soon as I saw the material, or as soon as Lenny saw it, he understood right away this was a very delicate matter which should be brought to the attention of those supporting Mr. Wine."

"Very honorable of him," Farrell snarled.

"We'll have to have the name of the 'gentleman,' " Haig said.

"Not on your—" Lenny began.

"Of course, Mr. Haig," Mavis put in smoothly. "We have his name, his address. And the results of a lie-detector test we felt it prudent to have him take."

"Jesus," Farrell erupted, "you are a piece of work, Mavis."

The woman smiled and lifted her glass in mock tribute. "It was important we satisfy ourselves this wasn't just a smear by some disaffected voter," she said.

The papers alleged that Judah Wine was a practicing homosexual with a male lover, that he frequented bars and clubs notorious for their homosexual clientele. There were names, there were addresses.

"There are no dates," Haig remarked.

Lenny jumped up from the couch so suddenly Farrell started. "Dates? What the hell do dates matter? We've got the fairy dead to rights!"

Haig ignored him. To Mavis Sparg he said, "There's such a thing as youthful indiscretion. This could be something that occurred years ago. When Wine was much younger. It could be a closed episode in his life."

"It could be," she agreed.

"But it's not," Lenny shouted. Farrell noticed little specks of foam at the corners of his mouth.

"Lenny," his wife said, sounding old, fatigued for the first time, "please be quiet."

The young man threw himself into an armchair and began scratching his groin with violent digging motions. Mavis watched,

smiling proudly. Farrell stared at him. New York's next mayor?
Jesus!

Haig continued to talk to the woman in his calm, controlled
manner. "If it were that, an aspect of his life that Judah had put
behind him, would you feel you had to go public with this?"

Mavis Sparg put down her champagne. Speaking seriously, she
said, "Mr. Haig, ever since Lenny and I first met I've been waiting
for him to win election to a great public office. People say I want
him to be President. Is anything wrong with that? Is that an ignoble
ambition for a woman to have for her husband? So he isn't running
for President. But mayor of New York? That's not chopped liver, as
we say. An important election. And here, a terribly damaging indictment against one of his principal rivals."

"Lousy fag," Lenny muttered. No one looked at him.

Since Mavis said nothing more, Haig prodded. "But you haven't
answered my question. Would you feel you had to go public?"

She nodded solemnly. "Oh, yes," she said, "I would have to."

Lenny Sparg flipped on his idiot grin. Farrell felt sick.

"Well, Judah," Haig asked, "is it true?"

Judah Wine smiled gently. Even now there was a nobility about
him, a calm dignity. Haig did not think he had ever admired him
as much as now.

"Yes," Wine said.

Farrell groaned.

Haig said nothing. Then, reversing the roles, Judah Wine tried
to cheer them, to ease the shock, the sadness laid over the room like
a shroud. "Remember what Stevenson said when he lost to Eisen-
hower? 'I'm too old to cry and it hurts too much to laugh.' That's
how I feel."

They were in his house in Brooklyn Heights. Sparg's papers lay
on a table.

"How much time does Mavis give us," Wine asked, "before she
blows the whistle?"

Farrell wasn't giving up yet. "Judah, just tell us this was something
that happened when you were a kid. Something in the past. We'll
fight it. We'll—"

Judah Wine smiled again. "I appreciate that, Sean, really I do.

But it's not the past. There have been, well, continuing relation-ships. . . ."

Farrell's shoulders slumped. He looks like a beaten fighter waiting for the bell in the tenth round, Haig thought. "Judah," he said, "Mavis says there's no hurry. I guess she figures the closer to election day that it comes out the less time there'll be for a sympathy back-wash. She told us they wouldn't say anything yet."

"I don't trust that crazy husband of hers," Farrell said doggedly. "He's probably on the phone to the *Times* right now."

Haig shook his head. "Mavis Sparg is calling the shots. We have a couple of days."

Wine stood up. "Campbell, more than any man you created this candidacy of mine. You and the *Mail* have kept me in the race. If you want to disavow me, I'll understand."

"We're not quitting," Farrell said.

"No one would say you were, Sean," Wine said. "To stay with me on this could hurt both of you, hurt your newspaper. Years from now whenever you endorsed a politician people would be asking them-selves, 'Is it another Judah Wine?' I don't think you want to take that risk."

Haig got up now. "Mr. Farrell won't be making that decision, Judah. I will. And I don't yet know what it will be. I want to sleep on this. I think we all should."

"Campbell," Farrell said angrily, "you're not going to shitcan Judah? Because if you do—"

Haig shook his head. "This has been a lot to digest for one evening. We all need some sleep. Time to think. We'll leave Judah now and talk again in the morning. Judah, can you come to the paper for lunch?"

Wine said he could.

As the *Mail* limousine drove them away from his front door, Farrell kept looking back toward the old brownstone.

"What is it?" Haig asked.

"What a shit I am," Farrell said unhappily. "I was just wondering if there'd be some fairy waiting until we left to slip back in there."

44

Alex was, as always, waiting for him.

"What will you do at the paper? About Judah."

"I don't know. He offered to release me from my pledge of support."

"He would," she said.

"It's so strange," he said. "Tonight. First Lenny Sparg, a nasty little boy who's almost certifiable. Then Judah. A decent, intelligent, sensitive man. Yet because he sleeps with men and Lenny sleeps with women—"

"Whom his wife finds for him," Alex interrupted angrily.

"Well, that's talk. But whether he does or not, Lenny looks like our next mayor. And Judah will be just another unemployed schoolteacher. To be laughed at."

"Sex can be so awful," Alex said seriously.

Haig had felt so tired when he got out of the car he had thought of nothing but sleep. Now, instead, he moved to Alex, slipping a hand under the bodice of her gown to cup her breast. The nipple was already waiting, alert.

"Yes," he said, "but right now, so wonderful."

Campbell Haig was at the office before eight. Miss Mayhew brought the coffee. He had already been through the *Times* in the chauffeured car. Now he read the *News* and *The Wall Street Journal.* He dictated a few notes. At eight forty they brought him the first edition of the *Mail*, still damp. He picked up a telephone and called the city room to complain about photo reproduction.

"Gideon Benaud says he has to see you," his secretary said.

Haig nodded. "Well, I don't want to see Gideon. Not this morning."

He knew it would be bad news. When things were going well Gideon did not seek audiences. Forgive me, Gideon, he said silently, but today I don't need a catalogue of disasters. Not today. Not this morning.

Haig was aware there were difficulties. The big New York department stores, Bloomingdale's and Macy's and Gimbels, were advertising in the *Mail*. A page or two at a time. They were still waiting for the paper to coalesce before they committed themselves to the sort of multipage daily contracts they bought from the *News*, the *Times*, the *Post.* Circulation was up, by more than a hundred thousand a day. But at what a cost! For the first time in years there were newsboys, newsgirls even, on the streets of Manhattan, "hustlers," Haig called them, peddling the paper, crying "Wuxtry! Wuxtry! Wuxtry!" It worked. But it cost. Oh, how it cost.

The unions were causing trouble again. The uneasy peace that followed Sissy Valentine's accident had been an armistice, not a true end to hostilities. Campbell had tried to launch a Sunday edition of the *Mail*, something the paper had never had, something that would draw big revenues from the department stores. The drivers' union, the men who deliver the papers to the newsstands, balked. They wanted double time to work Sundays. Haig had raged at them. "The *News* doesn't pay double. The *Times* doesn't. Why should the *Mail*?" The union men had looked at him blankly. To them it was quite obvious. They had the *Mail* over a barrel and were in a position to make demands. With the other papers they could not. Nothing personal.

A copyboy caught stealing a typewriter had been discharged. He complained of unfair treatment and a grievance committee was set up. That was six months ago. The committee had met twice a week for those six months. The case was still undecided. Farrell, who had attended several of the meetings and had been forced to assign two men to the committee, cursed. "The next time anyone sees someone carrying a typewriter out of the office, call him a fucking cab and help him load it aboard. Then maybe we can get some Goddamn work done around here."

There was talk, which Haig put down partially, though not entirely, to scare tactics, that when the three-year contract with all the ten craft unions ran out, the *Mail* would be shut down and the *Post,* the *News,* and the *Times* would be permitted to continue publishing. As the weakest paper of the four financially, the *Mail* might be forced to make uneconomic concessions to avoid the long strike that could silence it forever. Haig's independence, or what some termed "arrogance," had sufficiently alienated several of his fellow publishers in the city, so there was little hope they would do anything to help his cause if the unions were to select the *Mail* as their target.

Two New York papers were creating difficulties for Haig without even trying. The *News,* feuding with Murdoch's *Post,* had briefly and disastrously launched an afternoon edition to rival the *Post.* And Murdoch, rubbing his hands gleefully in anticipation of another newspaper war, immediately produced a morning edition full of sports and entertainment and huge headlines just to spite the *News* and cut into its massive morning readership. Newspaper wars raised salaries, increased overhead, spread the advertising dollars even thinner, and broke marginal papers. The *Mail,* at this juncture, was decidedly marginal. Quietly, Haig began to consult with his old enemies, the unions, to see what he could do to torpedo both *News* and *Post.*

And it was not only in New York that there were problems.

Out across the country Haig newspapers were having their difficulties. Part of it was the mini-recession they were going through. But that didn't explain it all away. In every city where he competed with Charlie Messenger's papers, Messenger was waging an expensive, damaging circulation war. It was as if Charlie were still holding a grudge about having lost the *Mail* to Haig. Silly, Haig thought, silly to pour money down the sump just to get even. But it was what Charlie was doing. Haig was still winning in some of the cities but they were Pyrrhic victories. A few more like them and he'd be broke.

And there was something else. The market told him someone was buying up Haig stock. Quite a bit of it. No big bulk purchases, but a thousand shares here, two thousand there. Using nominees, Haig assumed, since none of the names were known to him. He wondered which of his several crises Gideon wanted to talk about. Well, Gideon could wait.

Judah Wine couldn't.

The candidate was there precisely at noon, looking remarkably cheerful.

"Judah, for a man under sentence of death, you're taking this awfully well," Haig told him.

"I'm a philosopher," Wine said, "which means the score is forty to nothing but we still have two minutes left to play."

The two men took chairs in the office over the river.

"I never tire of it, Campbell," Wine said. "This view, the river, this city. I love the place. How nice it would have been to be permitted to return to New York some of what it's given me."

"Well, you said it yourself, there's still two minutes left in the game."

Wine smiled. Who else was coming?

"No one. Just Farrell. I wanted Ben Cork but—"

"You told him?"

"I had to. Ben's out on a pretty long limb for you. It wasn't fair to let him twist slowly out there. You agree?"

"Of course. What precisely did he say?"

"I told him. The bare outline, what Mavis Sparg said, what you said. Then he didn't say anything for a minute."

"And?"

"And then he said, 'Campbell, then I'm bailing out. It's like the Catholic priest in the little southern town asks the black boy why he isn't at church, isn't he a Catholic, and the boy says, 'Listen, I'm having enough trouble just bein' a nigger.' ' "

"He's right," Wine said, smiling briefly.

"And you, Campbell, what are you going to do?"

The publisher's mood changed as Wine's had. "Wait until Farrell gets here so I won't have to go through it twice."

When they had eaten and the waitress had cleared the dishes, the three men sat over their coffee. Farrell and Wine looked at Haig.

"All right," he said, "here are the options—"

Wine interrupted. "You've cheered me up already. I didn't know we had any."

Haig did not rise to the lighter tone. "One, the *Mail* can wash its hands of you. Either sit out the election or endorse one of your worthy opponents. Two, we can make one more stab at hushing the thing up. Three—"

It was Farrell who interrupted now. "Not a chance of that, Campbell. If the *Mail* doesn't run it, Mavis will see that the *News* does. Or the *Post*. And you think young Lenny is going to sit quietly on his potty seat all this time?"

"No," Haig said, "I don't think that. I'm merely listing options."

"Well, that isn't one as far as I'm concerned. And even if it were, don't we have a responsibility as newspaper publishers to report the news as it affects a major candidate? Even if he is our candidate?"

Haig looked at the editor coldly. "I don't think, Farrell, that I need lectures from you on newspaper ethics."

There was an awkward silence. Then Wine spoke. "He's running through the options, Sean. Let's hear him."

It was fascinating, Haig thought. Wine was the calmest, the most dispassionate of the three of them. Damn! He could have been an extraordinary mayor! But he did not say that. What he said was, "Or we can acknowledge Judah's homosexuality and continue to support him as the best man in the field."

Farrell snorted. "Sorry, Judah," he said, "but that may save you my vote and Campbell's. Along with your own, that makes three." He looked at Haig. "Campbell, it won't wash. Judah will lose worse than anyone since McGovern. Worse than Goldwater. And the *Mail* will come out of it hurting. Hurting bad."

"I agree," Haig said. Farrell stared in surprise.

Wine sat looking at Haig, at Farrell. "I can withdraw," he said quietly.

Farrell stared at Wine. He might well wonder at that kind of self-control, Haig thought. What was Farrell thinking? Whatever it was, the color crept over his face. Farrell would be shouting or weeping or smashing things presently—relieving his own feelings while Wine kept his agony to himself.

What was the source of Farrell's wild ocean of moods? What was it all to Farrell?

Wine's whole career was going down the drain.

As for me, Haig thought, I'm cornered. I know it. Gideon knows it. Someone who is buying all that stock knows it. Can I afford to back the best man now? Where's my dream of running a real New York newspaper?

Haig stood up. He picked up an ashtray and came around his desk and held it out to Farrell.

"What's this?" asked Farrell, eyes wide.

"Throw it before you blow a gasket," said Haig. "And then we can get on with it."

"With what, for Christ's sake?"

Even Wine was looking at Haig oddly now.

"With the rest of the Goddamnedest mayoral campaign the *Mail* ever ran," Haig said. "We're backing Wine. All the way. The rest of the options stink."

They stared at him. The heavy ashtray slipped from Farrell's fingers to hit the carpeted floor with a thud all three would remember while memory lasted.

45

These, ironically, were the golden days for Alex Noyes, the time between the shock of Judah Wine's exposure and his final, terrible defeat. Perhaps for Wine the weeks and the months, disaster piled atop disaster, were compressed into a single, awful monolithic catastrophe. For Haig and for Farrell, for Ben Cork and for the few who, openly or covertly, suffered along with Wine, the spring, the summer, the early autumn were an erratic series of tragic, embarrassing mishaps. Only Wine was the candidate. Only he was forced each day, each minute, to confront the mirror of his own destruction. For the others, as committed as they might be, there were interludes.

Day and night now, as the campaign wound its way through the summer, the apartment was filled with politicians and reporters and the pitiful handful of Judah's supporters. Alex served coffee and put out cigarettes and emptied ashtrays and ordered sandwiches and locked doors behind the last of them and covered Campbell with quilts on the couch where he sometimes fell into exhausted sleep.

The men adored her. There always was coffee and something to eat and to smoke, no matter what time of night or day. That was the miracle, that Alex always seemed able to cope, whether it was

Campbell alone with an increasingly Lincolnesque and tormented Judah Wine or an apartment flowing with aides and lackeys and hangers-on.

The apartment took on the character of a wardroom at sea, Haig the ship's captain, harassed, industrious, distracted, cool, demanding, driving, questioning, distracted, sure and certain. Wine had his own headquarters, of course, in a mediocre hotel in midtown. But the apartment was where decisions were made, crises met, defeats absorbed, rare triumphs celebrated. Haig presided, Judah Wine pondered, and Alex fetched fresh coffee and emptied ashtrays reeking with dead cigarette stubs.

"But, Campbell," she said one night as she undressed for bed and he slouched against the pillows reading the latest depressing poll, "Judah has a campaign manager, a staff. Why must you run *everything?*"

"Everything? That's an exaggeration, isn't it?"

"I don't think so. When we first began to live together it was the paper. You were always at the *Mail* or fretting about the other papers. Now it's the campaign. And Judah."

"The poor fellow needs me. Needs someone."

"I know he does." She paused. "Poor Judah."

Haig put down the survey to light a cigarette and to watch Alex. Now he patted the side of the bed next to him.

"I'm a damned fool, you know."

"Oh?"

"Yes. When all I really need is you."

She sat next to him, leaning against his shoulder. His arm slipped around her bare waist, pulling her close.

"Liar," she said, turning her face toward him. He would never tire of looking into those blue-gold eyes, at that strong chin, the wide, cheerful, generous mouth. They kissed, her mouth sweet and wet against his.

"Liar?" he repeated.

"Uh-huh. If you didn't have your damned newspaper . . ."

He dropped his lapful of papers to the floor. His hands moved to her breasts, her hair. She swung her legs up onto the bed and slid out of her half-slip. He moved toward her and their bodies came together.

Their lovemaking was still capable of variety. She could still surprise him with her youthful, uninhibited vigor, the sheer vibrant animality of that strong young body. Haig, who imbued his lover with qualities he believed no other woman possessed, also believed fiercely that no other forty-year-old man had ever been quite as fortunate.

Now, when they lay satisfied, smoking in the dark, her hand lightly on his leg, she asked, "Judah doesn't have a chance, does he, Campbell?"

"No. Not a chance."

"But you stay with him. The paper finds something good to say about him every day. Or something bad about Dick Osborn and Sparg."

"I thought you didn't read my newspaper."

She ignored the jibe. "But why? If you know he'll lose?"

He turned toward her, propping himself on one elbow, his face thoughtful, determined, solemn.

"Alex, there are a lot of people in this town, a lot of people right across the country, who share your opinion of my newspapers. And most of them do not share your more subjective view of me as a person. Many of them, in fact, think I am a prime son of a bitch. Well, maybe they're right on that. They also think I'm an opportunist and a front-runner without a strongly held conviction in my body. They think I back and fill, that I trim according to the prevailing wind."

He seemed not so much to be talking to her now but to someone, something beyond her.

"Well, I may be a son of a bitch. Maybe an opportunist. You can't come out of McAllen with nothing but a two-bit weekly paper and a daddy that's just been blown to hell and get where I've got without taking chances, grabbing opportunities. But in this election I'm going to prove to those pious bastards that I can also take a licking. Take it and smile. And resume the fight the next day and not shed a tear. Judah's going down, all right, and the *Mail* will go down with him. I hope they enjoy election day. Because the day after I'm coming back at the bastards."

She leaned over then to kiss him again.

The next morning she began house hunting. She had decided that they had outgrown the apartment. And she had begun to think again about her decision not to marry him.

As was usual with Alex, the right house was swiftly found, just east of Park, on one of those wonderful Manhattan side streets of carriage houses and mansard roofs and ten-foot-square front gardens, some of them with garages. It was a tall house, four stories, and perhaps twenty feet wide. Behind it, across a postage-stamp bricked patio green with moss, glistened a tinted glass tower forty floors high.

When she told Haig she wanted the place he stared at her distractedly and said, "Yes, of course, buy it." And went on thinking about something else. But the next day she dragged him to the house and into the bedroom facing the glass tower.

"We can lie in bed at night with the lights out," she said, "and focus telescopes on all those windows and we'll know everything, postively everything, about them! And they won't ever have to know anything about us unless we sunbathe on the patio."

It was, Haig supposed, her way of turning the tables on an inquisitive world that had never permitted her the right of privacy.

The market was tight in New York, but then it is always tight for good town houses. It helps, however, when half of the couple who wants to buy the house owns a newspaper and when the other half has several millions in trust and, potentially, a good bit more. The thing was arranged. Once again, there was the awkwardness over their not being married.

"I think it's sweet being considered a 'limited partnership' with you."

Haig grunted happily and signed where the lawyer pointed.

They moved in a week later, into a bare and echoing house where nothing worked. That was her idea. Suddenly their apartment, where she had been so happy, was unlivable. This was their house, their home, and not another day must pass before they took occupancy. Haig winced and agreed, holding out only for telephones.

"If there aren't working phones, you go alone," he warned.

Benaud knew someone at the phone company and the thing was done.

Alex had commissioned a decorator and the great house became a latticework of ladders twined around with rolls of wallpaper. Pails of paint weighted down spattered drop cloths gay as flowers, swarthy men who spoke in tongues filled empty, echoing rooms with shouted, indecipherable orders and defiant counterorders, whinnied foreign jokes and grunted laughter. Windows were flung open to the air, the stink of paint watered their eyes and drove Haig sneezing from his own house. Men laying carpets came next, crawling under and past carpenters installing bookshelves, and mincing little men taking measurements and flashing swatches of upholstery fabric seemed to be everywhere, waving their white hands and exhaling excited adjectives.

"Will it never be done?" Haig demanded.

Occasionally, not often, they would break the pattern of this long, hot, political summer to pass a weekend in the country, at Mayfair. It was her idea. He loved the place but it was her idea. She worried about him. He had always been lean but the days at the paper, the nights with Judah and Ben and the others were wearing him down. Or so she thought.

"I'm just skinny, is all," he would say, a crooked grin splitting his face. But she could see the lines around his eyes, could feel the fatigue in his legs and arms at night, in bed.

"I know," she would say, "and the house is there and empty and the weather is fine and even if you don't, I need to get the hell out of town for two days."

She did not really mean this. She was saying it for him. In many ways Alex considered herself stronger than he was, more resilient, and, of course, younger.

They would take the Friday afternoon train with all the commuters and watch the river slip by on the left and laugh at the inevitable drunks weaving out of the bar car and eat the awful sandwiches and wonder, mockingly, how New York would survive a weekend without them. Or she would pick him up at the office, in the little silver car she had driven that first night he had ever seen her. He would throw a briefcase and some books and a thick slab of newspapers into the cavity that passed for a backseat and she would tool the car smoothly into the traffic along the FDR Drive and head north, the top down unless there was rain, the wind blowing her short hair straight back like a boy's, and he would slouch down out of the wind and watch her strong young hands on the wheel, competent and relaxed. He was not the only one to watch her as she drove. In other cars men invariably turned their heads to glimpse her profile and, having seen her, and then him, would turn back studiously, laughably obvious, to the road ahead.

"I do think," he said, "that half the male population of this country is infatuated with you."

"Only half?"

Unlike most men, Campbell was equally content behind the wheel or being chauffeured, whether by the bodyguard Dennis or by Alex. She drove very well, and he spent the time observing her or poring over papers or simply watching the green countryside flash by.

On Saturday mornings the caretaking couple would have the refrigerator stuffed with good things, local berries, fresh rolls, farm milk. She would prepare a tray and go back upstairs and into bed next to him for breakfast. They had revived the tennis court. He played a wild, undisciplined game, savage smashes, perilous rushes to the net even behind a second serve, the optimism of a man who went always for winners, never for the percentage shot. Had Alex not been a carefully coached and steady player there would rarely have been a sustained rally.

In the afternoons they rode. Up into the green hills, down along the railroad tracks and the river, across neighborning farms. People waved to them or said howdy and thought how nice it was this attractive young couple was bringing Mayfair back to something approaching its former grace. Few people seemed to know who they were, just that nice young couple who rode so well.

They attended country auctions, buying up old pieces Alex thought would go well in the new house. Sometimes Haig had the sneaking notion she, and her decorator, were singlehandedly cornering the market on old furniture. When he taxed her with it she did one of her unexpected shifts.

"Campbell, why don't we have them ship up your father's old rolltop desk for the den? I think you'd really like to have it."

He grunted.

"Don't just grunt. It means a lot to you. You've told me about it a million times. It belongs in your home."

"I dunno," he said. "I've been sort of holding off on that."

She looked at him, her eyes serious, her tone level.

"Campbell, I think you've earned that desk. I think any fair-minded person would say so. I don't think you're still auditioning. You're there. You deserve your father's desk."

He grinned. "As they say down home, 'The opera ain't over till the fat lady sings.' "

She shook her head.

And so these rare and wonderful weekends passed in a haze of summer sun and early fall smoke and the *thunk* of tennis balls and the pounding of hooves, in country breakfasts and quiet dinners, and the frequent twining of healthy, loving bodies in a big bed in one of the echoing bedrooms that looked out from Mayfair across the long lawn toward the west and the river.

Back in town the work on the house went on. When gangs of political henchmen tracked plaster dust from the bathroom into the room where meetings were held, when Haig, dashing to take a phone call in another room in private, might find his way blocked by a painter on a ladder, he raised his cry again. "Will it never be done?"

And then, on a Friday in October, it was.

"Let's not go to Rhinecliff this weekend," she said. "Let's just stay home in our beautiful new house and make love to it and to one another."

And they did.

For the first time in months their bedroom was sweet with the smells of man and woman, of perfume and powder, of cigarette smoke and the lingering heady fumes of midnight brandies, instead of paint and freshly sawn lumber, the stench of blowtorches, the strange odor of wheat paste.

She remembered other beds, other rooms. Forgotten men, remembered nights. Bedrooms where she had lain with men, where she had lain alone. Schools, the cottage at Newport, Palm Beach, her own Manhattan flat. They all meant something, had their place in the catalogue of nights, some hostile, some soothing, gentle. The slender beds of childhood, the stark pallets of boarding schools, the frilly lacy beds of her first *House & Garden* apartment, the plastic, mechanical beds of motels, Campbell's bed at the Carlyle, their creaky fourposter at Mayfair.

Now, this bed, in this house.

That night, that first night in their new house, she surprised herself with the raw passion of her lovemaking and then, when even her agility and energy had gone dormant and they lay, limp and wet and spent, she said, "Campbell?"

"Yes?" His response was absent, sleepy.

She trailed a square-cut fingernail over his lean torso. "Campbell, do you ever feel furtive?"

"Huh?"

"About us? When it comes to signing papers or having two sets of names for the phones and for the mail? Not being married?"

"No. Sometimes it's awkward. But, no, never furtive. Why?"

"I just wondered."

He hesitated and then he said, "Is this a proposal?"

"No, I don't think so. But it's something I think about. Maybe it's having our own house."

"Well, think about it some more."

"I will," she promised, and promptly fell into the deep sleep of the well loved.

46

Election day neared. The disaster was writ plain for all to see: Lenny Sparg and Dick Osborn narrowly split eighty percent of a polled electorate, while even in the *Mail*'s blissfully biased straw poll Judah Wine was left with the dregs. This did not inhibit Haig, of course. While Sean alternately sulked and raged and Wine acted out his biblical impersonation of long-suffering Job, Campbell Haig cheerfully orchestrated new journalistic monstrosities of slanted coverage. His crack sob sister, Liz Patton, was dispatched to Hollywood to interview pals, rivals, professional colleagues, and, hopefully, lovers for a series of hilariously inaccurate but inarguably pungent anecdotes about Osborn's year as a real estate tycoon. Osborn fumed and issued furious denials and appealed to the fair elections practices committee.

But it was against Lenny Sparg that Haig's journalism achieved the full flavor of truly biased tabloid attention.

"All right," Haig would bark during the morning news conferences, "if he wears elevator shoes then someone had to make them for him. How many manufacturers are there in this country, anyway? I want a reporter sent to see every one of them. Find out who makes the damn things. There's an angle for you!"

When he tired of the subject of Lenny's feet there was always Lenny's reputation for picking up girls. "Oh, for God's sake, Campbell," Farrell growled, "we've gone at that one too many times before. No proof. Not one girl."

"You're the man about town, Farrell," Haig would say with a grin. "You know all the cops, you probably know half the girls. I just don't believe there's nothing to a rumor that's had as broad a circulation as this one. Somewhere there's got to be a girl, some poor kid Mavis bought for him. Especially if we make it worth her while."

"Subornation of perjury," Farrell muttered.

Haig roared with laughter. "I'm not asking her to testify in court. Just tell you or Liz Patton or Brophy the sordid details. She can always deny it later if they put her under oath."

Farrell waved his handful of notes irritatedly at Haig and turned to leave, but when his hand was on the doorknob he stopped and turned halfway back, indecisively, eyes boring into the carpet.

"All right, tell me what's burning you now," Haig said.

"Campbell," said Farrell, "I'd like you to tell me why what you're doing isn't insane. Certifiable."

"You want to know that *now*?"

Farrell came halfway back to Haig's desk. "All right," he said. "Judah Wine's the best man in the race. We're fighting the good fight for good government, to save the city and Up Gay Liberation. But you know Judah's going to lose. He's going to *lose*, Campbell."

The green eyes glinted. "Go on," Haig said.

"When all the fun is over and the polls close down on election day, will we be proud we've run this reckless smear campaign against Lenny and Dick?"

"Farrell, Farrell," said Haig. "When did you turn Christer on me?"

The pink in Farrell's face deepened. "Haig!" he said. "We'll have one or the other, Sparg or Osborn, in City Hall. To live under four long years. If they win without us, if they know they don't need us at all, how will we live here? They might overlook our roughing them up, but we're trying to murder them."

"Turning yellow, Farrell?"

"I've had my say," said Farrell.

"The hell you have, you have lots more left." Haig smiled. "Why don't you go to the Lion's Head and have a few and tell your pal Brophy all about it."

Farrell did that. There was no need for Brophy to agree or even to listen. He was there solely as a sounding board as the monologue went on angry and relentless until Farrell was hoarse with rage, drink, and smoke.

"Shocking," Brophy said mildly. He did not seem shocked. He was distracted by a tall girl in designer jeans. He turned back to Farrell. "Sean, those jeans; how do you suppose they get in and out of them?"

Nor was Gideon Benaud entirely in sympathy with his employer's relentless crusade against their political enemies.

He shambled into Haig's office with the familiar accordion-pleated printout of the computer's latest dreary report on advertising lineage. Circulation, as Haig had predicted, was achieving all-time highs, nearly a million now. Dirty political campaigns may do little to encourage the democratic process, but they sell newspapers. Advertising, now, well that was something else.

"National is holding up nicely, Campbell," Benaud began, plumping himself heavily onto his accustomed couch across the broad desk where Haig sat, "but local retail? Down eighteen percent and more than that the first two weeks of October. Entertainment is off. And God in heaven knows if we'll ever get that Cadillac dealership back. The man's a close friend of Sparg's."

Haig took the printouts.

"But circulation continues up?" he asked. "Not a sign of softness anywhere?"

"Only in Staten Island. They don't like queers out there."

"Staten Island never sold peanuts, anyway," Haig grunted. "Bunch of farmers. They'd love the *McAllen Advance* over in Staten Island. Church and wedding news once a week, along with the feed prices and the pork-belly futures."

Benaud knew this mood well. As long as the paper was selling more and more copies, as long as newsstand sales were up, Campbell Haig was not going to listen to bad news about advertising or unions or anything else. If the paper was selling then it must be the fault of the ad department or the negotiators or the economy. It was Haig's blind spot.

Then it was election day and nothing seemed to go right. The election itself was a rout. Haig had thrown open the executive suite on the sixth floor of the *Mail* building to a party of Judah Wine's few remaining supporters. Television sets had been strategically placed around the room so they could watch the returns, a bar had been set up, caterers had produced a cold buffet. Miss Mayhew and Alex had supervised the preparations. Haig left it to them except for one bit of advice: "I'd have plenty of hard liquor on hand," he told Alex. "And don't lay in too much champagne. Not unless the suppliers agree to take it back undrunk."

"That bad?" she asked.

He nodded. "I don't believe in miracles."

There were no miracles. The polls closed at nine. Farrell and some of the other senior editors and writers, several of the columnists, had come up from the city room. Ben Cork had come downtown. Wine had his own reception going on uptown, of course, in a hotel. But it would not do for Cork to be seen there. Publicly he had backed Osborn. "I'll witness the shambles from your place," he informed Haig cheerfully. The few politicians still backing Wine had also come to the newspaper. Better to express their fidelity to Judah at a prudent distance. It was rarely considered good form for an ambitious politician to associate too closely with disaster. Some of the wives, the girl friends had come along. Alex busied herself playing hostess.

By nine fifteen CBS was predicting a close race between Lenny Sparg and Dick Osborn, dismissing Judah Wine as a limping third.

At nine twenty NBC huffed and puffed and reached the same conclusion. Haig spent much of the time on the telephone, calling Judah, checking with *Mail* reporters at various headquarters. At nine thirty ABC went the other networks one better. Wine was a loser, of course, and Sparg would edge out Osborn. By ten o'clock the debacle was confirmed. Judah Wine, said Channel 13, was about to make his concession. There were groans in the *Mail*'s executive suite and Alex muttered, "Not yet, Judah, don't give up yet."

Judah did not hear her. His speech was brief, gracious, relaxed. Like the man himself. There were boisterous scenes around him, they could see that even on the tube. The gay activists had taken Wine's cause for their own and slim young men and mannish women were shouting, shaking their fists, calling for revolution and civil liberties, in that order.

By eleven o'clock most of the guests had drifted away and the working newspapermen had gone back to the fourth floor to work on election stories. At midnight Osborn conceded. Lenny Sparg would be the city's next mayor.

Farrell roamed through the office, muttering to himself, clenching and unclenching his large fists. He had been drinking but it didn't really show. Only the anger, the disappointment, showed. Haig was calm, almost philosophical. Alex was no longer watching television, no longer playing gracious hostess. She was watching these two men. There was really, she concluded, no comparison. Sean was all surface, Campbell all depth and subtle layers.

Now Farrell, his voice still a roar, not realizing the volume on the television sets had been muted, said, "What the hell. Could have been worse. That con artist Osborn could have gotten in for another four years." He looked around as if daring anyone to challenge him.

"No," Haig said quietly, not so much contradicting as stating a fact, "Osborn is a hack. You can reason with hacks, pressure and flatter, get them to appoint some decent men to run the departments. Lenny's crazy. You can't reason with men like Lenny."

Then someone shouted. "Look," he said. They turned. The television coverage had switched to Sparg's headquarters. Alex moved to the largest set and turned up the sound again. Only she and Farrell and Haig and Ben Cork and half a dozen people were still in the room. The smooth voice of the election night anchorman said the new Mayor of New York was about to enter the ballroom of the Roosevelt Hotel to make his victory speech. On the screen there was a turbulent crowd. Then, a wedge of bodyguards and aides preceding him, carefully chosen for their small stature, Lenny Sparg came through a curtained side entrance and was carried along up onto the podium. Behind him, very close as always, they could see Mavis Ratchett Sparg. Mavis, who had dreamed of this day since the very hour of her marriage.

"She's not smiling," Ben Cork remarked. "Mavis should be smiling. She's won."

Farrell cursed. "She's thinking who isn't there tonight. Composing her enemies list."

Lenny was at the dais now. It was a typical political victory scene, the faithful and the hacks and the sycophants and those hopeful of favors whooping and shouting and chanting "We want Lenny! We want Lenny!" over and over again, while he held his hands up to silence them, and they would not be silenced. If his wife was not smiling, Lenny was. His hair tumbled casually over his right eye, his button-down shirt collar was loose, his rep tie slightly askew, his Brooks Brothers suit rumpled, soft. It was all very contemporary, very carefully thought through.

Finally the chanting weakened and Lenny held up his hands one last time and then began to speak. "My friends," he said.

Farrell mumbled, "Now he's FDR," and Haig, usually courteous, snapped, "Shut up, I want to hear this."

"My friends," Lenny repeated, as if he had heard Farrell's interruption, "we are here tonight to celebrate a great victory, a victory not only for me, but for the forces of decency and of good government in this great city. To have routed the dangerous men arrayed against me"—chorused boos—"I will not forget who they are. I will never forget!" His voice rose in volume and pitch.

Sparg was something to see. His eyes bulged, his tongue worked too quickly for the words, flicking against his cheeks in the manner of William F. Buckley's. His forehead creased and uncreased, his mouth fell intermittently agape as if he had, suddenly, lost the train of whatever inchoate thought he was chewing. His face filled the small screen. Alex stared at him, fascinated. There were flecks of foam at the corners of his mouth. His hands moved up and down in jerky motions, his Adam's apple bobbed. The voice rose from its practiced bass to its natural tenor and then beyond, to a soprano pitch more scream than shout.

"We will destroy evil," he was yelling, "the perverts and the crooks and the slumlords and the radicals and the drug pushers and the usurers and . . ."

"When does he get around to us?" Haig asked rhetorically.

". . . and all the obstructionist forces that have blocked this great city's progress and have mortgaged its future to the banks and to Wall Street and to Washington and Albany and . . ."

He went on. And all the while the camera, moving in and out would pick up Mavis Sparg's tough, intelligent face, full of hate on a night when pride might have been excused. Finally Haig walked to the set and snapped it off.

"Well," said Farrell, "meet the new mayor." He went to the bar and poured something straight into a water glass. "He's crazy, you know. He's nuts."

"Oh, yes," Haig said mildly, "but having him mayor isn't what really bothers me."

"No?" Farrell said pugnaciously. "It sure as hell bothers me."

"Uh-uh," Haig said. "What I'm thinking is maybe that's our next President."

Alex Noyes shivered.

47

It was a Friday night late that November, or more precisely, early Saturday morning, when the telephone call came. Alex picked it up.

"Here," she said sleepily, "it's for you."

Haig reached across her in the big bed to take the instrument.

"This is Saltash on the night desk, Mr. Haig. Sorry to bother you this late—"

"Yes, yes?" Haig said impatiently, recognizing Saltash as a fairly junior man with a nervous tremor in his voice.

"Warren Messenger died tonight."

Warren Messenger. Older brother to Charlie, the newspaper tycoon who hated Haig's guts for "stealing" the *Mail*. Warren, once nearly a President; head of one of the five or six wealthiest families in the country; chairman of the Messenger Foundation, and a lot more.

Haig pushed awkwardly at a pillow so he could sit up. "What happened?"

"Heart, they think," Saltash said. "Around eleven o'clock. In town. The obit looks in pretty good shape. And we're planning the whole front page around it and we're thinking of four pages inside. Lots of pictures."

"Right," Haig repeated, "lots of pictures."

"Except, Mr. Haig—"

Damn it, Haig thought, get it out, man! "What?" he demanded in irritation.

"Except there's some confusion about where he died. Who was with him. You know."

"Turn on that light, Alex," Haig said, wide awake now. She was alert too and trying to make sense of the one-sided conversation.

"What the hell are you talking about, Saltash? What sort of confusion?"

"The man on the police beat got one line. Our man at the hospital got another. One says he died in his office. The other says he may have been taken there after the attack. They"—he paused—"they think maybe he was with a girl."

"All right, Saltash. Call Mr. Farrell at home. Tell him to meet me at the office. What time is it?" He glanced at their own bedside clock. "Okay, just after one. Tell Farrell two o'clock. Who else is on?"

As Saltash told him Haig was already hanging up.

Alex was curled against bunched pillows, her golden eyes looking at him past a bare shoulder. He was out of bed now, dropping his pajama pants, pulling out dresser drawers. She watched him dress. Or rather she watched his face as he dressed. The irritation of an interrupted sleep was no longer evident, his shortness with the man Saltash had given place to something far different, an unleashed tension, an eagerness, a sense of . . . of what? The hunt? She waited.

"Warren Messenger's dead," he said, not so much sharing information with her as reviewing the bidding in his own mind. "They think maybe he was with some woman. Stories don't add up. I'm going down there."

"I never doubted that," she said.

He sensed the recrimination in her tone.

"Alex," he said, not defensively, "I run a newspaper. This is an important story."

"Don't they usually call the editor first? Why you instead of Sean? Isn't calling the editor the usual drill?"

"My orders," he said curtly.

"Don't you trust Farrell's judgment? Must you do it all yourself?"

"I trust my own judgment."

She nodded. There was a pack of cigarettes on the night table and she reached out and took one, lighted it with the gold Dunhill he had given her. She was not wearing a nightdress and, aware of this, she pulled the sheet and the down comforter higher on her body. Not quickly enough; he had seen her breasts, had been reminded of their lovemaking, of falling asleep next to her.

"Look," he said, more gently now, "look, on anything big they're to call me. Probably it's silly of me. Farrell and the others, they're all competent. But this is how I am, how my father was. They just work there. I *own* the bloody newspaper."

He came around to her side of the bed and kissed her, his tie twisted, his collar button still undone. The warmth of bed, of love, was there again with them. But only for a moment. And then he was gone. She finished her cigarette and then, sleep destroyed, lighted another and used the remote control to turn on television to see what they might be saying about the late Warren Messenger and wondering if there *had* been a girl.

Farrell was in the newsroom there before Haig, tieless, sport-jacketed, knowing it annoyed the publisher. He handed over the wire-service copy and stories written by their own staff. Haig sat on a desk and read them through.

"Nothing here about a girl," he said brusquely.

"We're still mining that vein," Farrell said. "Nothing yet strong enough to go into print. Did you see that statement by Luther?"

Haig nodded. Luther was the Messenger Foundation's flack. A copyboy bustled up with more wire-service copy, long takes fresh from the machine. Saltash and another editor stood there in their shirtsleeves, men with the pallor of those who work nights. Haig glanced at the new stories.

"Nothing," he said contemptuously. "Tributes from great men, international reaction. Nothing about a girl." He held out the copy vaguely and Saltash, still nervous, took it from him.

Farrell shrugged. "We're not going to have it just handed to us. Luther's statement is full of holes. It stinks. There's a time discrepancy on that first nine-one-one call. And what the hell was he doing in his office at ten, eleven o'clock on a Goddamn Friday night?"

"If he *was* in his office," the other night man said quietly.

"I want to see the reporters," Haig said, "and where's Brophy? Out stewed somewhere?"

Saltash answered. "We didn't think this was a police beat story."

Haig snorted. "Get Brophy. If he's drunk, sober him up. Who else should we have in?"

Farrell mentioned a number of people.

"And let's have some of that foul coffee," Haig said. "This is going to be a long night."

He was wrong. It was a long two days. Luther's official statements to the press about the death of Warren Messenger did not begin to unravel until Brophy found the girl.

It was Monday evening. They were in the publisher's office on the sixth floor. Outside, the dark river flowed past, ebbing toward the sea, the ribbon of headlights wound north along the FDR Drive. Haig sat behind Meg Valentine's desk, Farrell on one of the couches, a layout pad in front of him on a low cocktail table. Other editors, a half dozen of them, Gerry Brophy, and Gideon Benaud lounged or sat erectly in various chairs depending on their familiarity with this room.

"Well?" Haig said.

No one responded. Men moved uneasily in their chairs. Then Brophy spoke. "Shit, we have to go with it, don't we?"

There was another interval and then Farrell said, "I think we emphasize the lies, this awful con job Luther tried to pull, this stonewalling by the family, the lawyers, everyone. Isn't that really more important than that old Warren was getting laid when he died?"

Haig looked at him. "You mean, doesn't that make the *Mail* look better? More responsible, less sensational?"

Farrell snorted. The shrugged shoulders spoke for him.

Gerry Brophy got up and began to pace.

"Look," he said, "all you big-time executives are so much more sophisticated than me. All I know is I found the girl he was shacked up with, I've got a statement from her. It's a hell of a story. Why do we have to play politics with the son of a bitch? I say print the bastard."

"Publish and be damned?" Gideon Benaud intoned.

"Sure," Brophy said, "why not?"

Haig picked up a photo of the girl. "Not the glamour girl I would have expected," he said.

"Perhaps she possessed other talents," an editor said.

"I think we can be confident of that," Farrell said.

Campbell Haig exhaled and stood up. "All right," he said, "we'll go with the girl's story as the lead and a very strong sidebar pointing up the lies in Luther's cover story. Plus an editorial on the public's right to know."

"And a statement from the family," Farrell said insistently.

Haig nodded. "Yes. Someone will have to phone Charlie Messenger. He's the head of the family now."

"I'd rather call Luther," someone said. "Charlie'll be tough."

"Forget Luther," Haig said coldly. "We'll call Charles Messenger. I'll call him myself if I have to. He has to have the girl's statement read to him. If he chooses to persist with the cover story, well, it just makes him look as bad as Luther."

"It was his *brother*," Gideon said gently. "Luther lied for a paycheck. Charlie would lie out of family."

When the others had left, Gideon Benaud hung back. Haig looked up at him.

"You don't like it, do you, Gideon?"

The big man shook his head. "The funeral's tomorrow, the cathedral. The President will be there. Not very felicitous timing, is it?"

"No, Gideon, I'll grant you that."

"The children are young."

Haig slammed a hand on the big desk. "Damn it, Gid, please spare me the grieving widow. Do you think I'm not aware of how unsavory all this is? Do you think I've suddenly gone dense?"

"I just wonder if you've thought it all the way through. Balanced the advantages of a good story—"

"A *great* story!" Haig interjected.

Benaud ignored him and continued. "—against the long-term consequences? You know how powerful the Messengers are. The department stores, the shipping lines, the mines, the land, the newspapers, the TV stations, the textile mills. Do you expect them just to sit back and take this?"

"No, Gideon," Haig said quietly.

"But you'll publish regardless."

"It's news," Haig said, and then, turning back to his desk, he told Benaud without actually saying another word that their conversation had ended.

But it was not to be the final argument.

Conscious of having slighted Alex during the long weekend of work, he phoned her from the office. "Meet me at Grenouille at nine," he said. "I need a decent meal."

As she sipped a Kir and he ate smoked salmon, he told her about Warren Messenger's girl.

"Oh, Campbell," she said, "can't you just leave it alone? The poor man's dead. What possible good can come of—"

"Someone else will get to the girl. Another paper. A television show. She'll talk. We got lucky, we had Brophy, he got there first. It's news. This is a competitive business."

She put down her glass. "Campbell, suppose it were you and me."

"I'm not married to another woman. I don't have kids."

She shook her head in irritation. "That isn't the point."

"Look, Alex," he said, trying to make her see, "I'm not a Warren Messenger. I'm not one of the richest men in the world. I've never held elective office. I'm not likely to play a major role in the next presidential election. The President, whoever he'll be, probably won't attend my funeral. There *is* a difference. A public man like Warren makes conscious choices. Like trading off privacy for fame, for celebrity, for votes. He should have thought of what pain it might cause before he started seeing this girl. . . ."

"Oh, Campbell," she said, "I love you and I think you're so wrong. So totally, absolutely, obscenely wrong."

He pushed the plate away.

Somberly he said, "Well, you're not alone. Gideon is against me. For other reasons. He practically drew portraits of tousled-haired children grieving."

"As they well may be," she said, angrier now at his tone.

"As they well may be," he repeated in agreement. "Only that isn't what has brother Benaud so exercised. He thinks Charlie Messenger and the whole clan will be out to get the *Mail*, out to get me. That's what worries Gideon, not the widow or the kids or common decency. He's worried about the *business*!"

She drained her glass.

"And I'm worried about you," she said, looking not at him but straight ahead across the room at the lovely flowers.

It was a sordid little tale. Haig had been correct. The girl, all sensible eyeglasses and pulled-back hair, spinsterish, bookish, was *not* very glamorous. Warren Messenger, brilliantly faceted, sleek, ambitious, colorful, a man whose only failures had been in that keenest of all competitions, that for the White House, deserved better. If a Titan like Messenger must die in some adulterous bed, it should have been with a worthy partner, some magical young girl, some older woman of tremendous achievement, some artful courtesan of extraordinary appetite. Instead, this strapping drudge who had, at first reluctantly, later with unseemly enthusiasm, spun out her tale to a sour Gerry Brophy. "Soap opera," he muttered to himself at the typewriter. "She watches soap operas while she waits for him to come."

Haig phoned a summary of her confidences to the dead man's brother.

"Haig," Charlie Messenger said, "we're burying Warren tomorrow. Eleven o'clock. Your first edition will be on the street."

"Yes. A bit earlier than that."

"You know how that's going to look."

"Yes."

"You won't delay a day or two?"

"It's coming out, Charlie. You know that. The girl's talking. She doesn't seem very bright. Brophy got to her first on luck. The other papers can't be far behind."

Messenger was silent, and Haig decided it was time for the positive tack. "Why not issue some sort of family statement, Charlie? Confirming there had been a . . . relationship. End all the rumors. In a week it'll be forgotten. Let it come out like this in dribs and drabs and Warren's death becomes the stuff of Carson monologues."

"Luther says that—"

Haig cut in coldly. "Luther's lied from start to finish, Charlie. You know it. Your brother was a famous public figure, a man of great power. The public deserves to know what—"

"The public, bullshit!" Messenger shouted. "You Goddamn hypocrite, Haig, you don't give a damn about the public, about the right to know. That's just a buzz word for your cheap tabloids. You're a Goddamn sensationalist! You make old man Hearst look good. You . . ."

There was more of this. When Messenger paused for breath, Haig said in a cold voice, "I assume you wish to make no comment on our story."

Messenger had brought himself under control as well. "We will make no comment."

Haig exhaled. "Then our story will appear in all editions tomorrow."

Messenger said nothing for half a beat. Then: "I never doubted that it would, Haig."

Haig had also been right about the other papers. Even the *Times,* reluctant on grounds of taste to probe too deeply into the obviously tasteless, was forced to do so by the *Mail's* sensational exclusive. And the *Times,* with its range and depth of editorial resource, had, by week's end, outstripped the efforts even of the remarkable Brophy. The *News,* dismayed not to have broken the scandal itself, mischievously ran a series of leading authorities on whether "sex after sixty is dangerous."

Yet it was on the *Mail* and its publisher that disapproval, ranging from raised eyebrows to revulsion, crashed. The *News* would always be forgiven for its juvenility; the *Post* for its breezy commentaries; the *Times* for its thundering editorials. Only the *Mail,* owned and operated by the outsider Haig, would draw the full impact of Messenger family rage and the substantial public and private outcry its influence could summon up.

"They do hang together, don't they?" Haig remarked to Farrell. "They really do hate my guts."

Farrell raised an eyebrow over what he saw as Haig's naiveté, his innocence. "Welcome to the NFL," he said.

48

It was during Christmas weekend that Willie Valentine made his mistake. The weekend had begun rather well, the motels and hotels of the Hamptons fully booked with holidayers, married couples, lovers, everyone suffused with Christmas spirit. The weather was crisp, cold, and with a spit of snow, and in the evenings people tended to drink. Drunks slept more soundly, they were careless about their doors, about secreting their valuables. On Friday night Willie had scavenged a motel in Montauk, a hotel in the village of East Hampton. Nine different rooms had produced. On Saturday he was in Southampton. He was moving west, back toward the city. It made sense, getting closer to New York as the weekend waned. It made sense but it also gave the police a predictable method of operation. On Sunday night, Christmas Eve, he was in Westhampton Beach. At two o'clock Christmas morning, in the bridal suite of a sprawling hotel on the Dune Road, the police were waiting. The detective who made the arrest remembered later that Willie was smiling. "It was as if he knew we'd be there, as if he was waiting for us to catch him."

There was something to that. Not that he wished to be caught, not consciously, of course. But he seemed to sense that the string

343

had been running out, that his desperate, driven carouse of theft was coming to its inevitable end.

For two days he sat in a cell of the county jail in Riverhead, cordial, talkative, superficially pleasant the way salesmen are expected to be, but refusing to provide any substantive information about himself. The car had been rented in a phony name; he had, as was his custom, left identification back home in his apartment. He had admitted only to the crime of illegal entry to the particular suite in which he had been arrested, refusing to incriminate himself in any of the other burglaries to which the police confidently expected to be able to link him. He chatted amiably enough with the warders and the occasional detective who came by once again to press him for detail, swapping yarns about Christmas and basketball and this unseasonably fine weather the Island was enjoying. About his career in crime he would say nothing.

Until the third morning. The gray-haired detective who had done most of the running sat across from him in one of the offices, pushed some cigarettes at him across the desk, and began to break him down.

"Look, fella, I've been thinking about you a lot since the other night. The way you talk, the way you dress, this isn't a place for you. You're not one of them"—jerking his head back toward the cells—"you don't belong in here. But I think I know what's bothering you. You got a wife or parents or something and you're scared as hell about publicity. Right?"

"No wife," Willie said, not stubbornly but wanting to clarify *that.*

"Okay," the cop said pleasantly, "but friends, family, people who'll recognize your name. Right?" Willie nodded. "Sure, I knew it. I knew it that first night when you wouldn't tell us who you were. I said to myself, 'Sure, this young fella's in over his head and he's got himself in trouble but he doesn't want to hurt anyone else by having it come out that he's been arrested.' Right?" Willie Valentine nodded again.

"I admire you for that," the old detective said. "I really do. You're ready to take your medicine but you don't want innocent people dragged into it. You don't want anyone else to suffer."

He was rewarded by another nod.

"Sure, you could care less about yourself. It was them had you worried. Well, look, sooner or later we'll find your name. There are ways. Someone will report you missing. We'll get a call. It'll all leak out. Now, what I wanta propose is this. You level with me, name, rank, and serial number, and after the arraignment they'll set bail, maybe a thousand, maybe a little more, and you'll get out of here. You can go home, wait for a court date. This isn't the city, man, we don't call the papers or send out press releases. There's a chance no one will even notice. Come on, what d'ya say: Play ball and you can be out of here in a coupla hours. Otherwise"—he looked around—"you're going to be back there cooling for a long time."

Willie Valentine stood up. "Okay," he said, "you've got it. Give me a break on the newspapers and I'll give you a statement."

"Sure," the cop said, extending a hand, "you've got a deal."

There was no previous record and by noon of the next day bail had been posted and Willie was back in Manhattan, in his apartment.

That night he called one of his girl friends, a model, and went over to her apartment to borrow some Valium. He'd been tense, he said, the holidays and all. He was going away for a week. Sure, she said sympathetically, Christmas was hell, wasn't it?

He took her to dinner at Mortimer's, dropped her off before midnight and, having declined her invitation to come up, went home. He plugged in the Sony cassette recorder on which he taped his call reports and spoke into it for a long time and in some detail. People had always said Willie had a fantastic memory. He enumerated his various crimes, issued certain instructions, and, almost as a casual afterthought, blamed Campbell Haig for having bought his family's newspaper and never having given him the responsible chance at the executive suite he felt both name and achievement had earned for him.

The relief he had experienced when they swung open the cell door at Riverhead, the surge of sensual pleasure as he walked into his own apartment, had not endured. It was naive to imagine that the story would not leak out, that some thug of a police reporter, poring over the log, would not come across the report of his arrest, would not recognize his name. That was the way they were, journalists, like feral dogs tearing at the throats of their victims, never resting until their teeth found the jugular.

"What a rotten, stinking trade," Willie Valentine groaned. "What a cheap, lousy business!"

He was a salesman, not a reporter. He was always careful to make that distinction. He made it now, proudly.

Willie Valentine walked into his bedroom. Beyond the windows he could just glimpse the East River and the antique arches of the steel bridge to Queens, the tail lights of the stream of cars leaving Manhattan reflecting blood red in the dark stream. Nearly 3 A.M. The perfect time for motel rooms. He remembered, of all those nights and all those rooms, the young madonna asleep behind that balding old man.

Even now he could see her lovely face, could feel the reaction in his own body. For a moment, he thought of her, where she was now, what had become of her.

Then he turned to go into the bathroom. To swallow the Valium.

The report of Willie Valentine's suicide reached the copy desk of *The New York Mail* in routine fashion through one of the police reporters. A copy editor read the brief story and got up and went across the room to Farrell's office.

"Here, Sean, thought you'd better read this."

Farrell picked up the two sheets of copy paper. "Oh, shit," he said softly.

"Yeah," the copy editor said. "I thought you'd better see it. Since he worked here and was old Meg's grandson . . ."

"Thanks," Farrell said. "Leave it with me for the time being. I want to think about it."

"Sure."

Farrell swiveled his chair so he could put his feet up on the windowsill and look out at the East River. He held the story in one hand, dangling by the side of the chair. It would be simple if Meg were still alive, still running the paper. The story would be killed. Not that it would be right to kill it, not that being it was one of her Goddamn relatives made it right. But it would be an open-and-shut case of *force majeure*. She owned the bloody newspaper and it was her bloody family.

He got up. Well, he was damned if he was going to agonize about it. Let Haig decide. That was what they had publishers for, to hand down decisions from Olympus. He had just started for the door when his phone rang. His secretary said it was Sissy Valentine, calling from East Hampton.

"Sissy!" he said, not sure if she knew.

"Oh, Sean, it's Willie! He—"

Her voice broke. She knew.

"Listen, babe, I'm sorry. I really am. A hell of a thing."

There was a silence at the other end of the phone.

"I'm driving in," she said finally. "My father called me. Someone has to identify the . . . someone has to see him."

"Where is he? The morgue?"

"Yes," she said. It was a muffled sound. Then, louder: "Yes, the morgue. First Avenue and Twenty-ninth Street."

"I'll go with you."

"Thanks," she said, "I don't think I could do it alone."

They talked about timing. Then Sissy said, "Sean, there's one other thing. I don't want to see this story in the *Mail*. Not so much for Willie or my father or me. For Meg. It's hard to explain but—"

"Sissy," Farrell said, "it'll be in the other papers. There's no way they won't—"

Her voice was firmer now. "Sean, I don't care about the other papers. I care about not having the *Mail* write about my brother."

He said he would talk to Haig. It didn't seem to satisfy her, but he reminded her again where they should meet and hung up.

He was right. It hadn't satisfied Sissy. She telephoned Alex Noyes. She was very much in control now and it was Alex, who had not heard about Willie, who was shaken. "Now listen, Alex," Sissy said. "I called Sean Farrell and he's going to the morgue with me."

"Oh, darling, I'm . . . glad," Alex said awkwardly. Thank God I don't have to go there.

"Yes, but Alex, he was no help about the paper."

"I don't understand, Sissy," Alex said stupidly. What paper? She pictured a sheet of paper, a document . . .

"The *Mail*, the newspaper." Sissy sounded angry. "Sean was very antsy when I asked him to keep anything about Willie out of the *Mail*. He said he'd have to talk to Haig, I mean to Campbell. He sounded as if Campbell wouldn't agree. Alex, Grandma wouldn't have let anything like this get into the *Mail*. I couldn't bear to see this in the *Mail*."

Alex was relieved. "Leave that to me," she said. "Why, Campbell wouldn't do anything like that to a Valentine. I'm meeting him at six thirty downtown. They won't start making up tomorrow's paper for hours. I'll talk to him. Don't you worry. Campbell will understand." Campbell, Sissy had called him. When Alex had last seen Sissy she couldn't even utter his name.

The New York Morgue is a vulgar building near the river with a cheap modern facade. Sissy parked illegally on First Avenue. Sean was standing just inside the door as she approached it; he pushed it open for her, leaned toward her, and kissed her. "Ah, Sissy, Sissy," he said, eyes blinking with sympathy. "I'm sorry for your trouble."

My God, the Irish really say that. "What do we do, do you know?" she asked.

"I had them phone someone here who has some pull. They'll make it as easy as they can."

"Good," she said. They went up in an elevator to a hospital waiting room, or one that looked that way. A Puerto Rican woman sat on one of the cheap plastic couches sobbing. A tall black man dressed like a minister stood leaning against a wall, somber, silent. Farrell gave their names to an attendant. He disappeared inside and then reemerged. He beckoned them into a small room painted flat white with a harsh overhead light. There was no furniture. One wall of the room was glass. There was nothing behind the glass. Sissy was confused. She expected steel filing cabinets with huge drawers.

"They keep them in the basement," Farrell said. "They come up on a little elevator."

Then Willie Valentine lay covered by a sheet, only his head showing, on the elevator behind the glass. Sissy looked at him. It was not as bad as she had feared.

"He still looks like a boy," she said, to herself as much as to Farrell or the attendant, "the handsome little boy who's always in trouble."

The attendant looked at her.

"Yes," she said. He pushed a clipboard at her to sign.

He nodded, satisfied. The elevator had begun to descend even before they left the room. The Puerto Rican woman and the black man were talking now. They went through the waiting room down in the elevator. Farrell took her across the street to an Irish bar where, without asking, he ordered whiskies for both of them.

It was the first time he had seen her since Meg's funeral, and he had expected to be painfully aware of the missing arm. He was not. Nor did she seem to be. He was glad to see her again. Except for the tragedy that had brought them together, it was pleasant sitting there in the dark bar, drinking, chatting. She looked well, ruddy, wind-browned. She was thin but then she had never been heavy. Her eyes looked tired. From crying . . .

There was something else. Something on which he could not focus very precisely. A physical self-awareness in the way she moved; sexiness. The way she sat, the way her breasts hung, the way she moved her upper body. Was there a man out there in East Hampton? he wondered. He hoped so. It would be good for her. Then, unaccountably, he hoped there wasn't.

"Ah, Sissy," he said.

Her eyes answered him, smiling. What they said amazed him.

Alex Noyes was wrong. Campbell did *not* understand.

"I can't do that, Alex," Campbell said. "We've got to run it. Small, inside, discreet. God knows I don't want to make it a federal case. But it happened, it's a fact, his family is well known, he admitted a series of criminal acts, there was a formal arrest and arraignment. And a confession."

"And you can't just ignore it?"

He looked at her. "I *won't,* " he said.

He sensed her coldness, reached out a hand. "Alex, the man was no good. A thief. *He* disgraced himself and his family. The *Mail* didn't. Why are you and I arguing over a stupid thing like this?"

"Because he was Sissy's brother. Because I knew him. Because he's dead."

There was distant restraint in his voice now. "I can't believe he's important enough to come between us."

"Oh, Campbell," she burst out emotionally, "you can't just isolate you and me from what happens at the paper. What you do down there every day affects us. Us and everyone we know. We can't just shut it out."

"Why can't we?" he asked.

She dropped it then, not with the sense that anything had been settled, but with the awful feeling she, and both of them, were being drawn inexorably into something larger than their love, something infinitely powerful and menacing, and against which even love stood no chance.

Haig did not attend the funeral. Alex did. Sissy, standing close to Farrell but erect and steady, kissed her warmly. "I know you tried your best, Alex."

Alex took her hand, trying to smile, and said nothing. She believed Campbell had been wrong. But she was not about to admit that to the increasingly imposing list of people who seemed intent on driving a wedge between them.

49

At precisely noon on New Year's Day, Lenny Sparg was sworn in as the one hundred and eighth mayor of New York. He stood bareheaded on the steps of City Hall as a nor'easter swept sleet across the worn grass of the old park, twisting candy wrappers and trash around the chilled ankles of the few hundred people who stood watching. Up on the porch of the ancient, weather-stained edifice, among the honored guests, were members of the city's congressional delegation, including Congressman Ben Cork. After Lenny had spoken, briefly, and with none of the demonic hatred of election night, Cork sidled over to Campbell Haig, bundled into a navy melton overcoat.

"Well, Campbell, we've survived the first fifteen minutes of his reign."

Haig nodded glumly. He was cold, shivering, glad he had convinced Alex not to come. "Judah ought to be up there, Ben," he said.

"Oh, hell, Campbell. And if I were white I'd be running the Klan. You can't waste energy on what might have been. And he sounded a little more pulled together just now. Maybe the kid's growing up."

Haig shook his head vigorously. "Mavis stage-managed this little

351

farce. She had Lenny under reins, for television. Wait until he gets behind a desk. Feels his oats. Just wait."

Ben Cork did not have to wait long. Two days later, in his office on 125th Street, he was arrested.

CONGRESSMAN BUSTED FOR DRUGS shouted a headline in the *Post.*

Cork issued a statement alleging political dirty tricks. In Washington several of his congressional colleagues orated in support. Others sat on their hands. "Cork's a Goddamn wise nigger," declared one southern congressman in the cloak room. "I wouldn't be surprised at anything they caught him doin'."

There were the usual complications about setting, and then raising, bail, and Cork was dispatched, once again, to Rikers Island. That same night a "vice raid" in Brooklyn swooped up Judah Wine. Sodomy, public indecency, and impairing the morals of a fifteen-year-old boy were alleged. Farrell exploded.

"It's got to be a frame!" he screamed as Haig chaired the morning editorial meeting. "Why, it's in Brooklyn. In Brooklyn they can't even spell sodomy!"

"All right," Haig said. "First of all, the bail. The *Mail* will put up the money."

Gideon Benaud grumbled. "We're not all that flush these days, Campbell."

Haig withered him with a glance. "I'll put up my own money, then. Just get it done. Send our lawyers down there. I don't want Judah Wine spending another night in jail."

He looked at the faces around the table. Haig wished he could enjoy the luxury of Farrell's rage, wished he could permit himself to thunder and swear and smash ashtrays, pound desks with his fists, work off his frustration. He could not. Someone had to remain calm, retain control, continue to think. To think faster than Mavis and Lenny Sparg. He knew what the Spargs wanted: mindless, instinctive, blind, berserk reaction. He would not take the lure. Let Farrell roar and curse. Haig would contact his connections, would speak softly and search for a big stick.

The trouble was, this was a season in which Haig's vaunted connections seemed to have gone missing. An obscure presidential executive order had inspired a rather frenzied editorial in the *Mail* that Haig had not seen and that Farrell, thoughtlessly, had let slip by.

The Haig papers had supported the President's election, but now, when Haig wanted to call in his markers at the White House, not only the President but Spencer, Haig's normal contact, was inexplicably "unavailable."

Alex's dislike of the newspaper continued to fester. The Willie Valentine business still rankled.

"It's a violent city," Haig said. "A violent country. A violent world. A violent age."

"Is it?" Alex said.

He stared at her. "You, of all people, should know that it is. Violence, unthinking, erratic, thoughtless. But none the less cruel. None the less deadly."

She said nothing.

He looked at the girl he loved. "Your father: a plane crash. My father: a car wired to a bomb. Farrell: his father drowned in a leaking fishing boat. Sissy Valentine: an arm torn out. Her damned brother . . . Every day, in every way, we grow more and more—"

"Uncivilized?"

He nodded. "Barbaric. Savage. Cruel." He walked to the window. "Do you know how many death threats a daily newspaper receives? How many obscene phone calls? How many tires on delivery trucks are punctured in the night?" He paused. "Every day, any day, Monday through Friday, a paper like the *Mail* . . . oh, Jesus."

"What?" she asked, not arguing now but wanting to know.

He shook his head. "Crazies. Just crazies. They slash our tires, they send bombs through the mail, they ambush reporters on the lobster shift when they go out for a drink, a hamburger. They mug the printers. Rape the secretaries. Beat up the clerks."

She looked at him. "You're exaggerating. Those things don't happen."

"Don't they?"

Her shoulders slumped. He went to the window.

"Random violence," he said, half to himself. "People kill people they don't even know, they've never even seen. Without reason."

"Campbell," she said, confused now, "but then why do they?"

He shook his head again. "I dunno, Alex. If I knew . . ."

"Damn it, Campbell. I can't accept that. My father died because a plane ran into a mountain. Someone killed your father. There was a reason. Sean's father drowned. Sissy . . . well, that was something else. Don't blame everything on chance, on kismet. There's a reason. There must be. There's *always* a reason."

He knew she was wrong.

Stubbornly, Alex was just as sure she was right.

A winter's morning. Alex Noyes awoke, glanced at the clock radio to orient herself, and jumped from the bed, grabbing a short terry robe that she pulled on over her nude body before striding into the kitchen. Saturday, no maid. She had slept alone. Campbell had worked late, slept in the office, some crisis conjured up over Judah, she supposed. She had watched a late movie before sliding into the big, empty bed. Across the way in the glass tower other women too had been undressing, getting into bed, opening themselves to their men. God, but she loved him. With all his faults. With all *hers*. She had not wanted to see the lights of anyone else's bedroom, to imagine anyone else's sensual pleasure. Not without him, not without Campbell. At last she had drifted off to sleep. In the morning she did not need a mirror to tell her that she looked wonderful. Haig would be with her tonight. Tonight they would do all the things of last night's fantasies.

Alone, last night, she had thought about their life together. How much simpler it would have been to have fallen in love with someone less complex. Sean Farrell, for example. The physical attraction was there, the humor, the irreverence. But she would have ended by dominating Sean, and once he realized it had happened his predictable rebellion would have destroyed their relationship. There was no dominating Haig. Far from it. He adored her, he was awed by the sheer physical attraction she held for him, but he continued to be, well, Haig. It was a sign of her own maturity, she thought, that they could differ as fundamentally and severely as they did about his newspaper, over Warren Messenger, over Willie Valentine, and remain not only as close but perhaps even closer.

She supposed this was what the wise called love. Accepting, embracing, holding tight despite the faults, the arguments, the differences. She perched on a high stool in the huge kitchen, chewing on an English muffin and staring out at the tinted tower, musing pleasantly about making love tonight after last night's abstinence, and then, without intending it, laughing aloud at the thought of what dear mother would say if she could read her only daughter's mind.

Alex had lunch that day with Sissy Valentine at a new Brazilian place Sissy had discovered. And Alex discovered an extraordinary new Sissy, the Sissy Alex had first glimpsed on that empty beach in April. She spoke of her brother calmly, with regret but in control. She expressed happiness that Alex was content, doing so once more without ever mentioning Campbell. She intended to see more of Sean Farrell, she said, smiling.

50

Nora Noyes heard things.

Her priests, her philanthropies, her old political contacts, her society chums, comprised an intelligence network that in its limited way was as competent as the CIA and considerably more subtle. Her network now informed her that Campbell Haig was in trouble. The President had turned his back on him, someone down in the Street was quietly and efficiently raiding his stock. Mayor Sparg had clapped two of his more unsavory allies in jail, the formidable Messengers had declared war, even the Valentines had turned against him, with Junior Valentine openly blaming Haig for the death of his boy. There were vague rumors of growing disagreements with Alex. It was this last snippet of information that most intrigued Nora Noyes, as she sat in her vast bed, reading the mail and paging through newly delivered magazines.

Months ago Alex had rejected her protests about Haig with cruel disdain. Now once more the girl was flaunting her lover, delivering another slap across Nora's placid, lovely face. And once again it was the "cheap, rotten, yellow press" that was to blame.

Nora threw down *Newsweek* magazine and sat, nearly rigid, her back pressed flat against pillows, her arms tightly crossed over her breast, her mouth set and angry. A photo of her daughter and the owner of *The New York Mail* was featured prominently, in color, in the "newsmaker" department of the magazine.

Not even Nora could have explained with total accuracy why she was so furious. If she were being analytic at the moment, which decidedly she was not, she might say that what really angered her was her daughter's impudent disregard for her wishes, this blatant insistence on continuing a relationship Alex knew her mother found demeaning. It was as if Alex were flaunting this association with Haig simply out of spite, simply to anger her mother.

The truth was something else.

Across the room, opposite Nora Noyes's bed, stood a mirrored armoire. It was morning. As was her habit, Nora had picked up a magazine to glance through while she drank her tea, ate her half grapefruit. Morning was not Nora's best time. When a woman approaches fifty, it rarely is. Later, there are ablutions and the artifices of maquillage and coiffure to come to her aid. On first waking a woman is very much on her own. As Nora was now, staring unblinkingly into the objectivity of the mirror, seeing herself as she was, not as she would later appear. And it was the cruel verity of her mirrored image compared to the fresh and undeniably youthful beauty of her own daughter that at some level of consciousness had infuriated her. Now, unable to resist curiosity, she reached out a pale, graceful arm to retrieve the magazine. She turned the pages rapidly until she had found the offending photo once again.

My God, she thought, she really *has* become a beauty! The photo was in color, giving full play to Alex's extraordinary coloring, the blond hair, the eyes, the lightly suntanned, vibrant skin tones. Standing next to her, an arm casually around her waist, this dreadful man Haig. On his youngish, half-smiling face Nora thought she detected pleasant complacency. She groaned silently to see Alex like this, with a man Nora hated and warned she must discard, her loveliness irrefutable, Haig's very posture communicating possession.

They were sleeping together, of course. Even one of Nora's priests could have seen it. It was the source of Alex's blooming beauty, the reason for Haig's smirk. For twenty years Nora had survived without sex. Not since Matt. How unfair it was that her only child should . . .

Jealous, envious, frustrated, miserable, the most famous woman in America was too intelligent to waste more than a few moments fuming. Then, quite cold-bloodedly, she began to weave a plan to do something about a situation she found intolerable. Perhaps, she thought, it might be time, finally, for her to meet this Campbell Haig.

She telephoned *The New York Mail.* There was some difficulty in getting through to its publisher. Finally, using the leverage of her name, she reached Haig. "This is Mrs. Matthew Noyes," she announced.

There was the suggestion of a pause and the quiet, southwestern voice said, "Yes, Mrs. Noyes. What can I do for you?"

She was a blend of steely control and *grande dame.* It was a matter of some . . . delicacy. Concerning her daughter. She would be most grateful if Mr. Haig would call. Thursday evening would be most convenient. Mr. Haig worked late? No matter. Mrs. Noyes was attending an early dinner that evening, some charity or other. If he could drop by about ten they could have coffee and discuss . . . well, what they had to discuss. And she would appreciate his not mentioning the appointment to Alexandra. Not until they had had their little talk.

Of course Haig said yes. How could he not? Twice he was on the verge of telling Alex. But he had given his word. Besides, he was curious about Nora Noyes, intrigued. The journalist in him wanted to confront her. So did the man.

On Thursday evening he was at her house, greeted not by the powdered footman he half expected but by the lady herself. She was still in her dinner dress, black velvet, strapless, the white shoulders, the legendary swan neck glittering with a diamond necklace. She led the way through great rooms to a pleasant salon. It was a damp evening and there was a pleasant fire. When she suggested a brandy instead of coffee he accepted it, resolving to taste it, nothing more. They had worked late again on these damned charges against Judah and Ben Cork, with Farrell raging at him. He felt drained, frustrated, impotent. Nora fetched the brandy. Alex she was not—Alex who bounded through rooms, jumped in and out of bed, collapsed into chairs. Nora's every move was that of a ballerina. Her hand movements were as stylized as those in Egyptian paintings at the time of the pharaohs. Everything they had ever said about her, everything he had ever read, every photo that had ever come across his desk, they all failed to match the reality. Could she really be fifty? Was this Alex's mother? He loved the girl's body, her wonderful breasts, the vigorous movements, the strength, the musculature, the skin tone, the generous mouth and the lovely, strange, multicolored eyes, the thick, coarse hair. But much of that was youth. This woman, this Nora Noyes, who had loved and wed a President, who had been the First Lady not only of the United States but in another sense of the world, had left youth behind and still was beautiful. Glamorous. Dignified. And, yes, sexy.

They talked. It was not the sermon he expected.

"I was frankly curious about you, Mr. Haig. There are no secrets anymore, I suppose, which is rather a sad thing, and when I first heard about you and Alex I was, well, to put it bluntly, annoyed. I've not had the best of relationships with the media and now here was my daughter seeing a newspaperman. It gave me rather a turn. I spoke to Alex about it. She was very positive about you. Not just another journalist, she said." Nora paused. She did her pauses very well. "I'm prepared to accept that now that we've met."

Haig was accustomed to flattery, from people who wanted jobs, from politicians fawning to a purpose, from media groupies who wanted to be noticed, even if it meant going to bed with him. Such praise from a Nora Noyes, face to face, never overdone, was something else.

"Well, thank you," he said, recognizing the words as lame but unable to do better.

They had another brandy. What had happened to the first? This time she gestured that he should pour. He barely dampened his own glass.

Nora pressed some invisible switch and music, deep, rich, *important,* filled the room. Bach or Mozart, he imagined. Music was one of many things he knew nothing about. They talked. Perhaps it was the one brandy, perhaps it was simply that Nora was very, very good. He found himself talking, his hostility, his wariness subsiding. She wanted to know everything about him, *everything.*

He told her about his father's death, his mother's courage, about

Beaverbrook, and his early newspaper jobs. He talked about himself, which he rarely did except with Alex, and then only in the intimacy of bed, warmed and wet and twined together in the low murmurings of that total openness that follows intercourse. Yes, he supposed, he was driven; his father's violent death might explain it; and yes, he was ambitious; fascinated by power; fascinated by politics and politicians. If he were not so damned shy on a platform he might have run for office himself. Better this way, running the politicians who ran things. What else? Well, he supposed he could claim professionalism. She might have reservations about the sort of newspapers he ran but he could tell her this, he could set type and scale a picture and write a headline. He was rusty but in a pinch he could run "the bloody press if I had to."

"I like you," she said, once again disconcerting in her timing, her tone.

He grinned shyly, not knowing what to say.

She studied his face. Young, certainly he didn't look forty, and those eyelashes were almost girlish. But in person and up close there wasn't anything boyish about him as she had thought from photographs. No, this was a hard man, a confident man. She could understand why Alex . . .

Nora talked about herself. Haig was not a newspaperman for nothing. He got her talking. About Matthew Noyes, those terrible days and weeks following his death, about the nightmare of being forced from the White House literally over a weekend to find someplace new where she and her five-year-old daughter could live. About remaking her life, trying to retain some shred of privacy in the public fishbowl, coping with the press, the curious, the cranks. About trying to raise a fatherless child, "the incredibly difficult task, the awesome responsibility of molding another's life."

She said nothing about her priests, about Alex's disaffection.

It was nearly midnight. Haig could still feel that first brandy. He could feel something else: an aura of intimacy that had seeped into this room, emanating from this woman. He was not mistaken, he was certain of that. Pulses had gone back and forth. He shook his head to clear it, glanced showily at a watch. It was time to bring this thing to a conclusion.

"About Alex and me, Mrs. Noyes, I assume you're not pleased."

She turned slightly, giving him, and he was aware of it, the benefit of that celebrated Nora Noyes three-quarter profile so familiar from a thousand television screens, a hundred magazine covers.

"She's a child, Mr. Haig. My only child."

"She's twenty-six."

"Age is not counted only in years."

He was not to be bullied. "Alex is intelligent, sensible, quite tough-minded really. We have notable battles."

She smiled. Again, the famous Nora Noyes smile, as if in benediction. "So have I with her. Notable."

Not moving, she said, "Will you marry?"

He nodded. "I asked her at the very start. If she'll have me we will. I won't nag her. It was her decision not to, it will be hers if we do."

She stood then, the velvet dress, the bare shoulders, the lovely arching neck, the cameo face, and her eyes fixed upon his.

This was mad! He loved Alex. This was Alex's mother. And he knew—absolutely knew!—that if he moved toward her . . .

Recognizing that he was being suborned, that this legendary woman was offering herself, the unfamiliar brandy warm and curling within him, Haig did not hesitate. Alex was not there, she was not even aware of their meeting, but Alex was as much a part of him as his arm, his head, his heart. He got to his feet.

Nora mistook the gesture and moved another step toward him, her arms starting to lift.

He walked past her and left the room.

Nora stood frozen for an instant, tall and graceful, but with the luminous violet eyes gone to ice. Hatred was no stranger in her catalogue of emotions. But she had never known hate like this.

When the door had closed and control regained she made a mental note to call Father Hannon at Saint Ignatius in the morning. She really must go to confession. What she had done had been wicked. In the best of causes, surely, trying to save her daughter, laying down her own life for another. But she had, she knew, and with full awareness of the fact and the consequences, intended to commit a mortal sin.

In the very noblest of causes.

Haig never told Alex. And Nora did confess. The penance was not severe. Not nearly so severe as the cutting whiplash of rejection with which Haig had slashed her across the face.

It was obvious to Nora that Campbell was deeply, obsessively in love with her daughter. It would be interesting, she thought, cold and full of hate, to use that information, that intimation of vulnerability, against him. Eventually it occurred to her to discuss the matter with her old-friend Warren Messenger's brother Charles. She had heard it said that Charlie Messenger also hated Campbell Haig and had set out to destroy him.

Perhaps, thought Nora, she could be of some small assistance.

51

Gideon Benaud's "counting house," as he not altogether jokingly called his office, was a few yards down the hall from Campbell's suite on the sixth floor of *The New York Mail*. Like Haig's, Gideon's office had a view of the river. It was a view rarely enjoyed. Gideon's blinds were drawn against the daylight, all the better to read the desktop calculator's digital display window. As he was doing now.

"Disturbing, decidedly disturbing," he muttered to himself, after punching the calculator to zero and calculating all over again the data from which he had derived this unsatisfactory result. Now, convinced the arithmetic had been correct, he tugged in irritation at his red beard and concluded it was time to confront the publisher with some patently uncomfortable facts. Sprawled across his desk were the accordion folds of computer readouts, Xeroxed gibberish to the layman, but as readable and clear to Benaud as droppings in fresh snow to a deer hunter. He had read the computer printouts, he had punched up numbers on his calculator and he had not liked the result. Not one bit. Sighing deeply, he picked up the phone and dialed Miss Mayhew.

"I want to see Mr. Haig," he said.

Across town, in his office in one of the modernistic boxes on the Avenue of the Americas, Charlie Messenger and Ray Sloane had their own computer readouts, their own set of conclusions that, although they were virtually identical to those of Gideon Benaud, were not disturbing at all.

Sloane stopped worrying a fingernail long enough to break into a nervous, ticlike smile.

"We've got the son of a bitch, Charlie, got him by the short hairs."

Messenger chewed on the stem of his corncob pipe. "I'm not counting chickens until it happens, Ray. I've seen Haig slide under locked doors before. He's a mean boy and I don't take him lightly. I surely don't."

Sloane sobered. "I agree with you he's mean. Mean and slippery. But you've got him this time, Charlie. The figures don't lie. There isn't a bank in the country would advance him another dime, and where else is he going to raise cash? The paper mills are into him for millions and every paper he owns is in hock. On the *Mail* alone he still owes thirty million. Compared to Haig right now, Cleveland looks like a gilt-edged investment opportunity."

Messenger nodded. "I know, I know. You've done a hell of a job buying up his shares and pressuring his creditors. My hat's off to you, son. But I'm not ordering the champagne yet. He's still got old Gideon and that child knows bankers' tricks no one's pulled since Ponzi."

Emboldened by praise, Sloane pushed his point. "Sure, Gideon's smart. I grant you that. He's also practical. A pragmatist. Haig may be a romantic who doesn't know when to quit fighting. But Benaud's no dreamer. He lives by balance sheets, by P and L statements, by the bottom line. If Dun and Bradstreet ran a report on Haig right now they'd have to print it in red ink. Benaud could be the biggest ally we have in his camp. He'll talk sense. Hard, cold fact. And Haig'll listen to him. He'll know he's whipped. And then we'll just pluck him naked as a chicken, starting with *The New York Mail* and going right down the list. You want Haig's papers? You'll have 'em, Charlie, and within the year. I promise you."

Messenger continued to look dubious.

He did not like Ray Sloane. The man was a brilliant lawyer, no argument there, and he could find his way around a balance sheet. But clients did not retain lawyers like Sloane unless they expected the legal work might stray just ever so across the ethical line. There were attorneys and attorneys. You hired a Ray Sloane when you knew there was going to be kneeing and gouging and biting in the clinches.

Charlie Messenger had never been accused of being an altar boy. He owned more newspapers than anyone in America except the Gannett people and young Newhouse. Bigger papers, too, which put his company number one. Campbell Haig was a corporate midget compared to Messenger. A gnat. A pest. But he had crossed Messenger once too often.

Now Messenger was going to get the *Mail*. And a lot more besides. He was going to destroy Campbell Haig. Erase him from the blackboard. Run his ass out of town and back to New Mexico. Maybe he'd let Haig retain that family paper in McAllen. Then again, maybe he'd take that too. This was why he'd hired Ray Sloane.

"All right, Ray," he said. "Go to it. I want Haig's hide nailed to my wall within the year."

Sloane bit an already brief fingernail. "You'll have it, Charlie." He looked very pleased as he said it.

Both Sloane and Charlie Messenger knew there was another, unspoken reason for Messenger's vendetta. Warren Messenger had been his younger brother's idol. Charlie was more aware than any stranger could possibly be of Warren's flaws. But Warren had also possessed greatness, both of ambition and of spirit. Charlie would never forget his conversation with Campbell Haig, that fatal phone call. Haig's cold, measured reading of the girl's statement, purchased from her, Charlie was convinced, by Haig's bag men.

Charlie was, in his own phrase, "a big boy."

He was ready to compete with his rivals on whatever level. He could be a magnanimous victor, a gracious loser. But with Haig, the man who had smeared his brother, there would be no rules.

And as shrewdly competent as Ray Sloane might be, Charlie Messenger knew there was one route to vengeance of which the lawyer knew nothing. When Messenger had finally cornered Haig like the gutter rat that he was, there was one final weakness in Haig which Charlie fully expected to exploit. He could count on it.

Had not Nora Noyes supplied him with it?

Nora had told Charlie everything she knew about Haig, his pride, his ambition, the residual guilt he still felt at having failed his father. Most of these things Messenger had already known and in far greater detail. On only one subject had Nora really been of help to Messenger as he plotted Haig's destruction.

"I will say, Charles, that he worships the ground Alex walks on. It's beyond me what she sees in him but it's clear his passion for her borders on obsession."

"Oh?" Messenger said. Neither he nor Ray Sloane had plumbed this particular vulnerability.

"Yes," Nora said, chatting on gaily as if this were an exchange of gossip between old sorority sisters. "I think if Alex ever left him, if some attractive man came between them, it would ruin Haig. Insanely jealous, I'm told, totally possessive. His life revolves around Alex. And the girl is simply too young or too stubborn to realize they have no future together, that this is nothing more on her part but a girlish infatuation and a juvenile attempt to defy my wishes."

"She's a beautiful woman," Messenger said.

Nora resisted a retort. "Beautiful, yes," she said smoothly, "but wild. You don't know how difficult it's been. She's just a mad little fool who does everything on impulse. One of these days someone else will strike her fancy and she'll go off with him and that, believe me, will be the end of Mr. Campbell Haig. His vanity won't stand for it. She'll leave him and he'll just simply go to pieces. I've seen the way he looks at her. I wouldn't be surprised if he killed himself or had a breakdown. It isn't healthy, this hold she has on him. Even Alex isn't aware of the sheer power she has over him."

"But there's no one else?" Messenger asked, sensing he understood what Nora was telling him but cautiously not wanting to make a mistake.

Nora inhaled.

"There's no one," she said firmly. "Haig just scares them all away. But if some strong, attractive man, someone really suitable, were to appear . . . well, she's terribly susceptible."

"I think I understand."

"I'm sure you do, Charles," Nora had said sweetly.

There were other publishers who sensed that Haig was in trouble. Overextended. Strapped. They had no pipelines to Nora Noyes, they had not employed men like Ray Sloane to exacerbate his woes. But this did not mean Haig's other enemies were standing idle.

Perhaps it was his small-town upbringing, the casual and some-times violent laissez faire of the American frontier; perhaps it was that he had been a boy raised without a counseling, cautioning father in those formative, early years; or perhaps it was simply the necessity of salvaging his family's minuscule fortune from the exigencies brought on by brutal, callous murder. Or perhaps this was just the way Campbell was: stubborn, ego-oriented, insensitive, arrogant, too intelligent by half. The strength that attracted Alex to him was for others the cruelty that turned them against him. Whatever their reasons, none of the country's press lords was uninterested in Haig's difficulties.

In Los Angeles Otis Chandler instructed his people in New York to keep him informed. In Rochester Allen Neuharth huddled the Gannett board of directors. In Chicago the men who ran the *Trib*, and who owned a daily in New York called the *News*, studied confidential reports and considered whether the Justice Department would permit one New York paper to absorb another. Hearst and Tom Murphy of Capital Cities and the Charter petroleum money, and Si Newhouse and Jack Kluge and all of them watched, en-tranced, intrigued, tempted. As did Kay Graham and Time Inc. and Ambassador Annenberg. Only the three networks held aloof. Under the Federal Communications Commission rules they would not be permitted to buy a New York paper without at the same time surrendering their own New York flagship television stations. The concentration of American media was a continuing governmental concern. In Washington, where a now-hostile President prayed fer-vently for Haig's destruction, they wished it wasn't.

A brief in *Time*'s media section alluded to Haig's difficulties. Alex saw it. Was Haig really in trouble? she asked.

Haig shrugged off his difficulties.

The newspaper was selling. Circulation was up. Large type and loud stories were doing it. Campbell Haig was delighted. His lover was not.

"Campbell, really, this 'Killer Storm Panics Millions' headline. Isn't that a bit much?"

He laughed. "Type should have been bigger. Otherwise it seems all right. Why?"

"But I was listening to CBS a little while ago. They said everything in San Juan was completely calm. They had some man on who said he was trying to get a hurricane party started but everyone was too busy working to bother. I mean, that hardly sounds like millions panicking, does it?"

Haig put down a book and looked over at Alex, propped up in bed with her glasses atop her hair and a late edition of the *Mail* against her knees.

"If CBS says so, does that make it true?"

"Of course not. But why does the *Mail* always have to shout louder than anyone else? It's so damned . . . strident."

With a small irritation worming its way into his voice Haig said, "Look, that storm did a lot of damage to the out islands. It *is* a killer storm. And if they aren't panicking in Puerto Rico, they damn well should be."

Alex looked at him and in a level voice said, "Maybe if they read your headlines they will. Self-fulfilling prophecy."

"I thought we agreed not to argue about the *Mail.*"

She nodded. "I'm not arguing. I started out by asking about this rumor that you're in trouble."

"Alex," he said, with a certainty he may have felt, may not have felt, "everything is fine."

"Good," she said, unconvinced, her tough, strong face set in stone.

"Alex . . ." he said, playfully now, reaching for her.

"Yes?" she said. And then, later, her critical judgment suspended in passion: "Yes . . . oh, yes, my love."

At first they had been the swift, staccato jabs of an adroit boxer, punishing, penetrating, tiring but not lethal, these raids and counter-raids by the forces of Charlie Messenger. They hurt, they drew blood, they drained. But they did not kill. For a while it seemed as if Haig and the *Mail* would prove tough enough, sufficiently cagy, quick enough in the clinches, to avoid the knockdown, to stay off the ropes, to survive. Haig certainly thought so.

"By God, Gideon," he declared one evening in the sixth-floor office that had become their *führer-bunker,* "these figures aren't all that bad. Not bad at all. If we hold our losses at this level . . ."

Benaud had seen the figures. It was he who had handed Haig the computer readout.

"You've nothing there on newsprint. It's headed for six hundred dollars a ton. You calculate what that might do to our balance sheet over the next quarter?"

Haig grinned. "And why do you think I spent so much time on the phone with Helsinki these last couple of weeks? I've got a shipload and a half of four hundred forty-dollar paper. Enough for three months, maybe more. We'll pay the six-hundred-dollar price when we have to, and that won't be for a while yet. And I don't plan to absorb it."

"Pass it on, Campbell, are you daft? Your advertisers aren't going to accept a third rate increase inside a year. Why, they'll—"

"They'll pay, if they want their advertisements to run in *The New York Mail.*"

Benaud looked exceedingly bleak.

"Cheer up, Gideon, Messenger's taken his best shot and we're still here, still publishing, still alive."

They were still alive, but just barely. It was curious, Benaud realized, how downright sunny Haig's disposition had turned. Normally quick-tempered, even when things were going well, it was as if he welcomed Messenger's punitive campaign. His bed was full, his home, his heart. How could Charlie Messenger damage him?

Then, suddenly, they were no longer just grappling with Messenger, parrying blows, slipping punches, they were being hit solidly, hurt badly, battered by heavy blow after heavy blow. This was economic warfare of the fiercest sort, the mammoth resources of the Messenger clan arrayed against Campbell Haig. Something had to break. Someone had to capitulate or cry "Quarter." It was not likely to be Charlie Messenger.

The Finnish newsprint on which Haig was relying, still relatively cheap at $440 a ton, was mysteriously diverted to a publishing house in Hamburg. Three bank loans in England were recalled. They were demand notes, totaling $8 million. Haig had no choice but to pay. In sixteen of the twenty-one cities in which he operated newspapers, Messenger operated retail stores. The stores stopped advertising, stopped completely, and being in most markets the dominant retail operation, lesser stores took note of what

Messenger's was doing and did likewise. Four of the nine craft unions at the *Mail* grumbled about reopening wage negotiations, and when Haig angrily informed them they were in only the second year of a valid three-year contract, the unions replied equably that, yes, they knew that, but the cost of living had rather put a new complexion on things, hadn't it? There were strikes at Haig papers in five other cities, a fire in the computer center in Columbus, two armed robberies on payday, each clearly an inside operation. And in New York a consortium of banks inquired politely over lunch if Mr. Haig anticipated any . . . "difficulties" in meeting this quarter's payments on the millions he owed them.

"Jesus, Gideon," Haig exploded, "Messenger's doing everything but beat up newsboys!"

Messenger's hammer fell, over and over, again and again, each successive thudding impact worse than that before, each time Haig's thinly stretched resistance less able to tolerate punishment. A month went by, weeks, days, but they seemed hours, only hours, during which incident piled upon incident, disaster upon debacle, defeat upon loss, until, it seemed, there might be nothing left to surrender. Even if Campbell Haig were of the surrendering persuasion.

Always lean, small-boned, Haig was now wire-thin, pulled taut under pressure, the green eyes deeper than ever under the thick dark brows, a tic in one eyelid, another at the base of his left thumb. He slept poorly now, despite fatigue. His left leg was blotchy with something itchy he suspected might be shingles. He lacked the time, the interest, to consult a physician.

If there had not been Alex, he might have cracked. Now, sensing his fatigue, his desperation, the pressures that seemed relentless, remorseless, she stopped criticizing, she placed in limbo her contempt for Haig's journalism.

This was no time for tough-minded, objective, academic criticism, this was the time for Alex to go soft at the core, to love and not to ask, to prop up and not to beat down. Each night now, as he limped home, wounded, bloody, shocked, Alex was there, domesticated, tamed, loving. But there were some nights when he didn't seem to notice.

The battle was neither as deadly nor as long as the Wilderness Campaign. But for Haig this was no consolation.

When it was over a dazed Haig asked Gideon Benaud, "Gid, how did it happen? What did I do wrong? How could Charlie Messenger beat me?"

And Benaud, the red beard raffish despite his despair, answered heavily, "Campbell, he's been a bastard longer than you have. He's had more practice."

That night, when they lay quiet and alone in bed, Alex said, "Campbell?"

"Yes?"

"You remember, a long time ago, when you asked me to marry you? And I said no. And you sort of nodded your head and said, 'Well, the offer stands. I don't intend to be a pest about it.' "

"Sure," he said, "I remember. And I said when you were ready, you could damn well ask me."

She nodded. "Yes," she said, "I remember."

He did not say anything. He hoped he knew what she was about to say.

"Campbell?"

"Yes, darling."

"I want to marry you."

At that moment it did not seem important that his newspaper chain was bankrupt and that a man who hated him had won the war.

Alex phoned Sissy.

"It'll be small, private, not very glamorous. Otherwise I'd ask you to come in and play bridesmaid."

"I wouldn't, you know. As much as I love you . . ."

Alex understood. Her love for Campbell did not blind her to the way Sissy still felt about him. She did not argue but instead said: "You told me if I loved him to marry him."

"Oh, yes, Alex," Sissy said, and there was genuine satisfaction in her voice, "it doesn't *matter* what anyone else says. Or thinks. When you love a man, you must never let go. Never!"

There was an intensity in her words that would have been foreign to the Sissy of a few years before, a suggestion that she too had made a decision.

"Ah," said Alex, but only to herself, "if only she had someone like Campbell."

Three days later, in a nondenominational chapel in the West Village, Alex became Haig's wife. She would have preferred a Catholic service but the red tape and the specter of a dramatic last-minute appearance by her mother defeated her.

But that morning, the morning of her wedding day, Alex took a cab downtown to St. Francis Church, across the street from Gimbels, where she confessed for the first time since she was a schoolgirl. How wonderful she felt, shriven, and in love, and now to be a bride!

They flew that night to Bermuda for a week.

Sean Farrell did not attend the wedding. He did not send flowers. He had known for a long time that he had lost Alex but such knowledge provided small consolation.

"Damn you, Haig," he muttered.

The girl he had picked up in Elaine's and who now lay next to him in bed turned, curious.

"What?"

He shook his head. "Nothing," he said, "not a damn thing."

"Oh."

He had gone on a two-day bat. Not good. There had been a fight in the Lion's Head and Sean had hit a man he rather liked, a smaller man who had said something silly, something unimportant, but that Farrell, drunk, had resented. He felt ashamed as soon as he had done it and had apologized. But the other man, hurt and angry, had refused to take his hand. Red-faced, sore at himself, Farrell had brushed past men who stared at him, and went out into Christopher Street. There was a phone box on the corner and he called a girl he knew, a Ford model. She sounded sleepy but he talked her around and took a cab to her apartment. And all the time they made love he was seeing and touching and tasting Alex Noyes.

In the morning he went home and changed his clothes, ignoring the model's suggestion they spend Saturday in bed. He slept for a few hours and then started drinking again. At midnight he was in Elaine's. The girl he picked up worked for an ad agency. She knew who he was, she said the right things about how she used to read his columns. She was not the beauty the model was but she was very

excited and a bit drunk herself and the sex was fine. Except that once
again he was seeing Alex.

He was drinking again the next day. Alone now, in his flat, feeling
rotten.

Hating himself. Then his phone rang and it was Sissy.

That night, red-eyed but sober, he took her to dinner and then
back to his place. There she led him, without argument or cajoling
but with a firmness and a decision that surprised him, into his
bedroom and began to undress.

He stared at her. "I'm a bastard, you know."

She shook her head. "You're not," she said. "I know exactly what
you are."

"And you want me?"

"Yes," she said, "oh, yes."

He took her then. More accurately, perhaps, she took him. And
in the morning he realized he had not thought once about her arm.
Or about Alex Noyes.

Alex had had the idea of going to McAllen before returning to
New York. It was certainly the time. To delay longer would make
it less understandable. Now she sat at the table where Haig had
eaten every meal of his childhood and youth, with a woman who
shared some of her ideas.

"Mother accuses me of sensationalism," he said. "She sounds like
Katharine Graham."

"I realize times change, newspaper styles," his mother said.
"What Campbell does with *The New York Mail* may be perfectly
suitable for New York. I simply don't think it would be appropriate
for a small town like McAllen, for a weekly newspaper like the
Advance."

She was a tiny, fine-boned woman in a Nieman-Marcus suit. She
looked like a smaller, female version of her son; Campbell had none
of his father's looks, only his height. Behind her cautious reserve, so
much like Campbell's, she was warm and straightforward.

After dinner Mrs. Haig showed Alex through the house. The old
man's study, Samuel Scotland Haig's favorite room, had been main-
tained with museumlike care. Mrs. Haig ran a delicate hand over the
rolltop desk, polished, patinaed with age.

"This was Mr. Haig's," she said. "He did all his writing at this desk. He was writing at this desk that afternoon. Just before he died."

"It's a lovely piece," Alex said, noticing that the woman had very carefully avoided referring to her husband as having been "killed."

"I've wanted Campbell to take his father's desk. Put it in his office in New York. Write at it, use it, have it to remember his father by. But no, he smiles and says he hasn't earned it yet. And so here it sits, polished and waxed and dusted and fussed over like some valuable antique. Instead of just a mail-order desk his father had shipped in from Kansas City."

"Oh, but he should have it!" Alex said impetuously, "I told him so. He should."

The older woman looked at her. "Or if his office is too modern, he could keep it at home. Where he . . . where you live."

It was her first reference to their living arrangements. Rather sly at that, Alex thought.

"Yes," she said firmly, taking the bait, "it would look very well in our house."

Mrs. Haig pursed her lips. Then, instinctively, she reached out her small hand, so slender, so thin as to be almost translucent, and took one of Alex's large, capable hands in her dry, surprisingly strong grip.

"Alex . . ." she began.

"Yes?"

"All right, Alex, Campbell is a grown man. Forty. And I'm an old woman. This is hard country. Always has been. We're not so sheltered or provincial as a New Yorker might suppose. But, well, it was a shock, my son living with a woman and not married to her. I'm glad you're married now, and I'm glad you have come to visit me."

"I had to live with Campbell first to be sure. It's much harder being sure of things nowadays."

"I'm sure it is," the woman said. And then: "If Mr. Haig were still alive . . ." She left the thought incomplete.

"He'd probably consider me a brazen New Yorker. A fallen woman," Alex said.

Mrs. Haig smiled. "No, Alex. I think he'd take one look at you and another at Campbell, how happy he seems, and he'd give you a hug and a kiss."

Alex felt her whole body go slack. For the first time in McAllen she was relaxed. Unguarded. "That's nice," she said. "It's awfully nice to hear."

Mrs. Haig nodded, reminding Alex of a bird, perhaps a woodpecker, working at the bark of a tree. "And true. I knew Sam Haig," she said, "and that's exactly what he would have done." She paused. "And what I'm going to do. That is, if you'll let me."

"Oh, yes," Alex said, "oh, yes."

Delia Haig folded her into her arms, Alex a foot taller but feeling, for the first time in years, a small child.

52

A month later Alex and Campbell were again in a plane, headed west.

He had the window seat. "Funny, a short time ago I was flying out to San Francisco and we banked then, as we did just now, out over the Atlantic. Then, when we were landing, we banked over the Pacific. And I remember thinking what a good omen it was. For the first time I had papers right the way across the whole country, from one ocean to the other. I had just bought the *Mail.* I was alone then, I had no one to tell, but I kept thinking about it and thinking how fine it felt."

"You'll have them again, Campbell," she said, stubbing out a cigarette to squeeze her arm through his, leaning her head against his shoulder.

How lean he was. She'd noticed it again in Bermuda when they swam. He looked good, of course, the suntan setting off the green eyes, the brown hair slightly sunbleached. But he was very thin.

It eats him up. He doesn't say anything but it's just eating away at him.

Haig had lost.

"Messenger had the big battalions," he said, as if to shrug off defeat with a quip. "No one's fault, I guess. Maybe mine. Expanded

376

too far, too fast, picked up a few enemies along the way. The economy didn't help. Should have listened to Gideon. Gideon saw it coming but I wouldn't listen."

Alex had offered to put up her own money if it would help. Campbell started to darken, the old anger surfacing, the old pride, but then he laughed. "Alex, just how much do you have?"

"Well, I think about two million dollars in cash and C.D.s and negotiable securities. More later, but right now about two million."

He kissed her lightly on the forehead. "That would keep the *Mail* going for another six or seven weeks at my current rate of loss. But thanks anyway. You're grand to suggest it. Hang onto it. We may still need it for groceries."

"Campbell?"

"Yes?"

"You're a lousy comic. I'm not making jokes about the money. I mean it."

He took her arms in his hands and held her then. "I know you mean it. One of several reasons why I love you."

She thought about things his mother had said to her. Delia Haig and Haig's sisters had given a little dinner for them in New Mexico after the honeymoon.

"I'm sure I should be just brimming with maternal advice for you, my dear," Delia told Alex in a quiet moment after the dinner, "but I'm afraid I'm void. Campbell grew so fast and so far from all of us he's almost a stranger. I'm sure you know him far better than I do."

"He's not easy to know," Alex said. "He's so . . . complicated. But then, I suppose, that's part of why I fell in love with him. I'm pretty complicated myself, some might say pretty mixed up, but he seems to understand and to take everything into consideration. He's been very good to me. When I needed him he was there."

Mrs. Haig sat in an armchair in the living room of her house, a perky little woman in a floral dress that clashed with the print of the chair. She didn't notice that it clashed and if she had, she would not have cared. How different from Nora, Alex thought. Different too the dried skin of the southwesterner. Even Campbell's sisters seemed to have been touched, blanched by the sun. Alex's own rosy-blond sturdiness contrasted with their lean, weathered angularity.

"How beautiful you are," Mrs. Haig said, as if suddenly she had recognized revealed truth. "Your children should be . . . oh, dear, all the while I was waiting for you to get here I kept warning myself not to start planning your lives and here I am bearing children for you already."

"We will have children. I'm not going to be one of those 'modern' women who waits until she's thirty-five and then suddenly panics over not having any. I want lots of them, boys and girls. We have a big house to fill up."

"Your late father would have liked that, I'm sure. And Mr. Haig. Sam. I'm sure they would."

"I think so. I don't remember much about my father. But he seemed to enjoy me. He was very physical. I remember he was always picking me up and slinging me onto his shoulders. It's one of the few things I remember clearly about the White House, bumping my head on one of the door frames as he carried me into the Lincoln room. I cried for hours."

Delia's eyes misted. She was seeing another child, her son, in *his* father's arms.

"Campbell was a funny little boy," she said. "Not all that good at games but always a competitor. Sometimes he got into fights. Usually the other boys would win. They were bigger than he was. He was always skinny as rope and I can still see him charging at the bigger boy, arms and legs going like windmills, his head down, his hair in his eyes . . . and the next thing you knew the other boy would be sitting on top of him in the dust and Campbell would have lost again."

"He hasn't lost often as an adult."

Delia Haig smiled. "He hasn't lost with you, my dear, and that's the important thing."

Alex went to her then and held her tight, realizing she had received lesser compliments in her life.

"Oh, my dear, love him. Just love him and don't let him ever again be hurt as he was when his father died."

"I won't," Alex said, "I never would."

Now the great plane banked and, sure enough, there was the Pacific, that sea of infinite hope, stretching endlessly toward the far horizon.

Campbell tugged his seat belt tight and through clenched lips said, "Well, it's California. California and Charlie Messenger."

"It'll be all right," she said, knowing that he had lost this time and not at all sure that it would right.

"Of course it will. I have you, don't I?"

They were staying in the Beverly Hills Hotel.

"Why not?" he said, with the gallows humor he never quite was able to carry off very convincingly. "After this trip we may not be able to afford it."

One of what she thought of as Haig's "little men" had arranged everything. The bungalow was a winter garden of floral arrangements.

"Like a funeral," he remarked gloomily.

"I think it's nice," she said.

"Hummm."

"You're sure you want to be there?" Haig asked. "You could hang around Beverly Hills for a couple of days while I drive down there, spend some of your fortune with the robber barons who run the shops along Rodeo."

"I'm on an austerity binge," she said. "Besides, I'm not letting you walk into that lion's den all alone."

He still seemed dubious but he grunted something that sounded like a reluctant yes.

Oh, God, Alex prayed that night, let it be all right. Don't let them destroy him.

Charles Messenger was a bully, a type Alex recognized, remembered, despised. This insistence on turning a business negotiation into a social occasion was typical of the breed. A desire to rub it in, to preen and posture, especially in front of her, in the presence of Haig's woman. Even the magnificent setting played its role in his cruel yet somehow ridiculous strutting. Terms were to be dictated to Haig, at a site chosen by Messenger. How, like Hitler in 1940, to drag out the old *wagon-lit*, to have the French generals brought to Compiègne. Now, in the late afternoon, the magnificent house, the cliffs, the sonorously rolling Pacific itself, conspired to emphasize Messenger's triumph, Campbell Haig's defeat. The great red sun, growing larger as it sank, neared its rendezvous with the ocean as they sat with drinks on the western terrace.

Messenger had chosen a chaise opposite Alex's, his back to the sea. He could stare at her but she could not look back without blinking away the sunset. He wore linen trousers, pleated at the ample waist, a Lacoste shirt, Gucci loafers without socks. Pudgy, sleek, yet with sheaths, slabs of muscle under the fat, beneath the chi-chi. Strength, arrogance, cruelty. All there, Alex knew. Also there, she knew without the merest doubt, raw desire, not simply to have her, to couple with her, to enjoy her body, but to humiliate her and through her, Haig. Victory was not enough for this man. He wanted to abuse. Why didn't Campbell see it? Had defeat been so traumatic?

Haig finished reading the balance sheet Gideon and Messenger's man Sloane had put together jointly. The numbers were large but the arithmetic simple. Haig now owed amounts roughly equivalent to the total assets of his various properties. The moment for selective selling-off, a paper here, a paper there, the fending off of one creditor and the partial paying of another, that time was past. He stacked the sheets carefully and put them back on the low glass table between them. There was a breeze off the Pacific and Messenger leaned forward to slide a heavy ashtray atop the balance sheets.

Well? his eyes said while his full lips remained pursed and mute.

Campbell stood up to pace the few steps to the sea wall. Messenger's eyes, bright and watery, did not follow him. They remained on Alex.

Haig turned back.

"You want them all," he said. It was a statement rather than a question.

Charlie Messenger made a small movement with a surprisingly small hand.

"Why, no, I thought it might be appropriate for you to retain your father's old paper. In McAllen."

Haig stiffened but was silent. Alex could not stop the small groan of "Oh, Campbell."

Messenger smiled. He was rewarded by her pain. By the involuntary movement of her body as she said the words.

Haig clenched his fists, trying not to rise to the bait. If he didn't panic, didn't explode in anger, if he kept his head, maybe he could still win a point or two. Perhaps there was still some leverage neither he nor Gideon had explored.

"The *Mail*," he said, talking to the ocean, letting the words drift back to Messenger, "I'd want to keep the *Mail*."

Messenger shrugged. "Wanting something and being able to afford it are different things. Look at the figures again. The *Mail*'s your biggest asset, your biggest drain."

Haig nodded. "I know that. And I want it."

"So do I," said Messenger coldly.

Alex knew what he was thinking, that it was *The New York Mail* that broke the story of how his brother died.

Messenger intercepted her eyes and knew that she understood.

"I won't sell the *Mail*," Haig said stubbornly.

Charlie Messenger heaved himself heavily, powerfully, out of his chair.

"Well, I want to be reasonable," he said, still watching Alex. "Why don't you think about it this evening after dinner? We can talk again in the morning. Perhaps Benaud will have an idea. Maybe there's something else you can trade off for the *Mail*." He paused. "I'm a reasonable man."

She and Haig dressed for dinner in the lavish cottage assigned them on this bit of coast so remote from Los Angeles.

"This is grotesque," she said, "having to eat with him."

"He enjoys it."

He watched her dress. He never tired of her body. Neither did he ever tell her what to wear. She always knew and her taste was superior to his. But now, just this once, he started to say something.

"What?"

"Nothing," he said. She was buttoning a beige satin evening shirt and he had been on the verge of suggesting she wear a bra. She moved to the closet on long, solid legs and pulled out an Irish tweed skirt, heavy, nubby, and ankle length, and stepped into it.

"Hadn't you better dress?" she asked. "If we're late there'll be thumbscrews."

Against all odds the dinner worked. Neither man talked business directly. Instead there was the usual exchange of trade gossip. How many times had she heard it all before? From Campbell, from Sean Farrell, from old Gideon. By this time she must know as much about newspapering as any civilian who ever lived. Maybe she ought to have a paper of her own. She laughed, half to herself, at the thought, at what Nora would say.

Both men turned to her. There was the same bleak, watery look in Messenger's eyes.

"Say something funny?" he asked.

She shook her head. "No," she said, "just something inane I thought of."

Haig was never annoyed at the way in which men looked at her. Let them look, she was his. Indirectly it was flattering to him, he supposed. But now, with Messenger, he wished she had worn something else, that the top three buttons of her blouse were fastened.

They took coffee and went into a sort of den, paneled and with deep chairs and animal-skin rugs, horns and trophy heads mounted, and a big fire against the sea chill. A man brought brandy. Haig refused.

"I'm going to phone Gideon," he said. "He was working on some figures."

Messenger told him to use a phone in the next room but Haig said he would use the cottage phone.

"Back soon," he said. Alex thought he looked distracted. She wondered if Gideon really could come up with something. Anything.

Messenger stared at her, a small smile playing around his lips.

She drank the brandy. And Messenger got up to refill her glass from the decanter his man had left. He looked down at her as he poured. Alex was too old not to understand that look. She was accustomed to men looking at her breasts. But Messenger was different. She drank more of the brandy, glad of its warmth, of the distraction as it trickled down through her to curl inside her.

"This is a lovely house," she said finally, needing to break the silence, to shatter his concentration on her.

He glanced around briefly. "Nice setting," he said.

"More than nice. My mother has a place in Newport, on the ocean. But without the cliffs. That's something you get out here that we don't have, a perspective above the water."

"Sure," he said, "the cliff is fine. So's the house. So's just about everything." His eyes were fixed on her again, on her eyes this time, and then he said:

"I have nearly everything I want."

"But not everything."

"No," Charlie Messenger said, and she knew he did not mean Campbell's newspapers.

Their cottage had two bedrooms.

"Do you mind awfully if I sleep in there? I've got a stinking head. That damned brandy."

"Sure," he said, "I'm not much company as it is."

She undressed in front of him as she usually did, but there was no flicker of reaction. Benaud, he said, had come up bare. Nothing. Absolutely nothing.

"Do you think there's a chance he'll let you keep the *Mail?*"

Haig shook his head firmly. "Not a chance. He knows how much it hurts."

She stepped out of her satin tap pants and began to peel off her pantyhose.

"But even if he did, do you have the money to . . . ?"

Haig slammed a hand on one of the night tables.

"If he gave me a five-year note, even three years. If he held paper on the *Mail*, even at a few points over prime . . . with the other papers gone I could concentrate on the *Mail*, really run it. Work seven days a week, get it shaped up. Yes, damn it, if he'd leave me the *Mail*, just the *Mail*, I could pull it off. I know I could!"

For the first time since they landed in California there was animation in his voice, in the very way he stood, a coiled tension, an eagerness. Then, without saying more, his shoulders seemed to slump, his lean body to sag.

"A three-year note," she said vacantly. "That's the bottom line on what you'd need?"

He nodded.

"Three years. And let the son of a bitch name his rate of usury!"

Then, as if exhausted by the effort, Campbell sat heavily on the side of the bed to untie his shoes.

"But there isn't going to be any three years. Or any three months. Charlie's going to have his pound of flesh."

There was a boyishly hopeless sound to the words, and Alex got out of her chair to go to him, holding his head against her stomach, just under her breasts, her fingers gently twined in his soft brown hair.

"Oh, Campbell," she said, her voice as hopeless as his.

His hands held her, lightly cradling her strong buttocks, until finally she pulled away.

She knew what she was going to have to do and making love to her husband was not part of it.

She switched on the night light and looked at the face of her Cartier tank watch. One thirty.

The door to Campbell's bedroom was closed. There was no longer the band of light at carpet level as there had been when they retired an hour earlier. He might still be awake, he might decide to call Gideon in New York at any time, there were risks. As there were also possibilities. Unless she acted, and now, those possibilities would be foreclosed forever. She threw off the covers and swung her feet to the floor.

She was wearing one of those oversized football jersey T-shirts that were so comfortable and that made Campbell laugh. But now she reached down to the hem and with a single, fluid motion, drew it off over her head and tossed it on the bed. She went quickly to the closet, which stood open, as she had left it. At one end a white peignoir was suspended from a hook. She folded it over her arm and went into the bathroom where she brushed her hair and cleaned her teeth. She had not slept and her eyes were clear. She slipped her arms into the peignoir and belted it loosely.

There was a sea fog and the grass was wet and chill under her bare feet, tugging heavily, damply at the hem of the long dressing gown. At the door to Messenger's main house she hesitated. There were servants. If it was locked . . . ?

It wasn't. Either Messenger was very casual about such matters or very sure of her. She closed the door silently behind her and went up the carpeted stairs thinking, giddily, that her wet feet must be leaving a trail of clues. But she was not there to murder Charlie Messenger. There would be no detectives summoned next morning. Her footprints didn't matter.

It was a large house and again she hesitated. Then she saw the light under one of the bedroom doors.

Charlie Messenger put down his book. But he did not stand up. The time for *politesse* had passed. He had his own special incentives for hatred, for revenge. He had read Haig's woman accurately. Or else why was she there?

Alex stood in the middle of the room. She knew what she was going to do but awkwardly, she had no notion of how to begin. Crazily, she tried to read the title of the book he'd been reading. The Marquis de Sade? she wondered.

He remained motionless, a brocaded robe primly belted around his huge body, his eyes, redder-rimmed now, fixed on her face for an instant and then moved lower. Alex had a very precise idea of just what he could see and not see through the peignoir. She had chosen it carefully, cold-bloodedly, virginal yet provocative.

"Look," she said.

"Yes?"

"You must let him keep the *Mail.*"

"I must?" he echoed. "And why *must* I?"

"You know why."

"But he's broke. Even if I let him have it, he wouldn't last six months."

"Campbell doesn't agree. He says he could salvage it."

"This isn't Christmas, Mrs. Haig. No stockings hung by the chimney with care. No gifts."

"A three-year note," she said, trying desperately to remember just what it was Campbell had said, "three years at prime."

Messenger laughed. "The man's a fool."

"He's not. If he says three years then he means it."

There was a decanter and glasses on a table.

"May I?" she asked.

"Of course. And pour me one."

He made no move to get up. He was establishing their relative positions from the start.

Alex went to the table, aware of how the peignoir flared out from her legs when she walked. Messenger watched her. She poured the brandies and went to him. He motioned her to put his down next to him.

"Go ahead," he said. "I'll have mine in a bit."

She drank off half the glass. It burned going down. But good. She was standing just in front of him now. His deep chest was heaving under the robe.

"You hate newspapers like the *Mail*," he said, drawing out the tension, perhaps trying to calm himself.

"Yes."

"But you'll do this thing?"

"For him," she said.

He reached out a big hand, one pudgy finger extended, just touching the loosely tied sash.

"And to get him his three years, you're prepared to do just what?"

"Do I have your word?"

"Oh, you have my word, Mrs. Haig. My intention is to hurt your husband painfully. Letting him play his silly games with *The New York Mail* is a small concession."

She sipped at the brandy more slowly as his finger tugged gently but purposefully at the sash. The robe fell open.

"And you, Mrs. Haig, you'll keep your word?"

She stood motionless. "Yes," she said, the word nearly a gasp.

Charlie Messenger nodded. "Excellent," he said.

"Just tell me what you want," she said.

He nodded again. And then he told her.

53

Publishers do not like to see newspapers die, to see other press lords fail. There are two thousand daily newspapers in this country, and in the death of any one of them the survivors sense the uneasy intimation of their own doom. Newspaper proprietors are no more fond of the bankruptcy courts than lesser men. Neither were they overly enamored of Charlie Messenger.

But this fellow Haig. Surely he had embroidered the tapestry of his own destruction. Arrogant, egotistic, a loner, no respectable dues-paid member of the club, a troublemaker and a common scold, a sensationalist whose sheets seemed better suited to the racks at supermarket checkouts than to the kiosks and carrier boys of more seemly papers.

There was fellowship among the press lords. But Haig? Well, Haig was different. His defeat by Messenger elicited few tears. "Too damned bad about Haig" went the conventional wisdom. "Too damned bad Charlie didn't strip him bare!"

None of them knew just how bare Charlie Messenger had stripped Haig. No one knew, only Haig's wife.

Although she had choreographed her own daughter's degradation by Messenger, irrationally certain that by driving a wedge of jealousy

387

between Alex and her husband she could destroy both their marriage and his career, Nora Noyes had not yet been informed as to the events in California. Instead she was puzzled and disappointed to learn of Haig's reprieve. She had expected Messenger to ruin Haig, to take away *The New York Mail,* to leave him beached and bleeding for his sins. Why had Charlie displayed such inexplicable charity toward an enemy?

It was the season for opening her cottage at Newport, a normally pleasant spring task involving the crisp issuance of orders and the expectation they would crisply be carried out. Nora found herself snapping pettishly at servants and even at the season's first resident cleric. She had tried to be so helpful to Messenger, seeing in him a rich man of her own class, a potential ally, even a future and far more suitable husband for Alex than this boorish outlander Haig.

Nora had inspired Messenger's Gothic strategy of punishing Haig by seducing his wife. At the appropriate time, under the appropriate circumstances, Charlie intended to let Nora know just how well her scheme had worked. Nora would find ways and means of letting Haig know about Alex's infidelity. For if Haig never knew, then where was the pain?

But Messenger had fallen unaccountably silent. Nora did not know about California. She knew only that Messenger had not destroyed this man she so hated. She could not understand his generosity. Messenger did not bother to justify himself. Savoring the memory of Alex Haig's lovely face as she knelt before him in the bedroom of his Malibu mansion, remembering the feel and that smell and the taste of her body, he concluded it would be even more amusing, more satisfactory to keep their complicity secret. Perhaps Alex would play again. He was more strongly drawn than he could ever have imagined. He would reserve comment to Nora for the moment and concentrate instead on some more permanent liaison with this shatteringly desirable young woman.

It would be, he intended, an arrangement in which Haig played no part.

Even after all these months of intimacy Haig loved to look at his wife's body. There was in him, he supposed, something of the voyeur. And the Calvinist in him disapproved. Which did not so much deter him as add the delight of the forbidden. Alex understood this. And there was in her a complementary exhibitionism, unrestrained by Catholicism, and an enthusiasm for bed and for the preliminaries that went with it.

Except now. Now that they were home again in New York with the lawyers haggling over details of Haig's corporate defeat and of Charlie Messenger's astounding last-minute concession, the bone of a *New York Mail* tossed carelessly into the cage of the sorely wounded loser. Now that they were back in their house an explicable reticence had taken hold of Alex. That first night he had tried to make love to her, the awful two days with Messenger and the long flight behind them.

He lay on their big bed smoking, willing the fatigue to ooze out of his bones, mentally jotting notes for Gideon, for Farrell, for the advertising people. He was to have his three years, it seemed, at usurious rates. But he *had* it. The paper was still his.

"Ours not to reason why," he said, watching Alex empty a suitcase and hang rumpled clothes.

"What?"

"Why Charlie let up. When he had me under his foot, all ready to twist and squash like something that crawled."

She said nothing, tossing underwear and stockings into a small, soiled pile of flimsy on her chaise.

He was sensitive to her moods. "He didn't say anything to you? While I was phoning Gideon?"

She shook her head. "Nothing. We hardly spoke. It wasn't a very relaxed situation."

He lighted another cigarette from the stub of the first. He rarely smoked like this. "That's what gets me. He hates my guts, hates the *Mail.* Guess I can't blame him all that much. That story we ran the day of his brother's funeral . . ."

She turned now. "That was a cruel story, Campbell. Cruel and unnecessary."

"News."

"By that definition you can justify anything. People make mistakes. They get into trouble. They do stupid things. Do they all deserve to be plastered all over the front page for their families to read?"

"Warren Messenger wasn't just 'people.' You know that. Your father was a public figure. So is your mother. You're intelligent enough to make the distinction."

She slowly folded a slip. "Suppose I did something bad. Something scandalous."

He tensed. "You don't do such things," Haig said.

"Ha," she said, the sound conveying little humor, "what about that night in the Village? When you had to come and—"

Haig swung his feet off the bed and stood. "You made a mistake. You had too much to drink and you were upset. That isn't the same."

"You feel worse about that night than I do, Campbell," she said, cutting across the flow of his words, "and you know why? Because you have me right up there on your little pedestal. Your wife! How could Alex Haig do anything stupid? Isn't she the great Campbell Haig's *wife?*"

He drew then on his self-control, not wanting the thing to escalate, not wanting either of them to say more, to say things that might be difficult later to forget.

In silence they went to bed. She had undressed in the bathroom and when his hand moved toward her in the big bed she stiffened. And pulled away. Campbell said nothing but turned and tried to sleep. California, he reasoned, had been as hard on her as it had been on him. She'd seen him brought low. Time would take care of it, he thought hopefully. Just don't do or say anything now that will leave scars.

Finally he slept. But she did not.

Why do I feel so dirty, so filthy, so cheap? she asked herself. After all those bars and motel rooms in the years before Campbell, those meaningless, empty, rotten nights with men who didn't even know my name? Messenger at least knew that. He knew what he wanted. I was the price that had to be paid for the *Mail.* All right, the price has been paid, the deal has been closed, Campbell has his newspaper, and Charlie Messenger had Haig's wife. She stifled a groan, remembering that huge, gross, hairy body, those fat hands, those little, eager, daring eyes. She'd done things before, in motel rooms. Oh God, had she done things! Crazy things, perverted, sordid, kinky things. The Greenwich Village bar—the hands of those women, touching her body, pawing her, the sound of their voices, rasping, avid, wheedling, pouring filth into her ears. She had nodded, yes, yes, yes, and meant it, until Campbell came, a ridiculous knight errant with a yellow cab for a charger.

None of it made her feel as dirty as she now felt about Charlie Messenger. But that was because Messenger had paid. He'd bought her with *The New York Mail.*

I've lost my amateur standing, she thought. And made Campbell her unknowing pimp.

When at last it came, her sleep was restless, nightmarish, waking her twice in a night sweat so intense she rose twice to strip off her gown and towel her body before returning to their bed.

Haig threw himself into the task of saving his last big newspaper. Twenty years it had taken to build his chain. He had lost it in a few weeks. But there was no time for regret, for recrimination, for analysis. Messenger had won, Messenger had unaccountably given him a second chance. Let us be duly grateful.

His relations with Sean Farrell were formal and distant. With Gideon he was more relaxed. But lacking was the easy congress of earlier years. Benaud continued to shoulder an inordinate share of his financial blundering. Not true, Haig shouted, you warned me. Warned me every step of the way, shook computer readouts under my nose and told me what was coming. And I didn't listen! It's my name on the building, not yours, Gideon. These are my failures, my vices, my sins.

Ah, said Gideon, taking counsel with himself, these Calvinists and their rapture with suffering and guilt!

It was a good season for news.

The local teams were winning, the Moslems were sacking embassies and taking hostages, the casinos in New Jersey were proving a Sodom and Gomorrah of corruption to the grand juries, a hero cop was murdered, a film star was "telling all" in an especially messy divorce case, an expelled student shot his math teacher, a nun declared her pregnancy, naming as father the Holy Spirit.

Violence, money, sex: These were what sold tabloid newspapers, or so held Joseph Medill Patterson of the *Daily News* fifty years ago, so held Campbell Haig today. Of course the news columns of Haig's *Mail* touched, lightly, on other matters. But rarely heavily or effectively on the still-fresh administration of Lenny Sparg, the boy-mayor who had destroyed Judah Wine and giggled through foam-speckled lips at the dismemberment of Haig's empire by Charlie Messenger.

Sean Farrell urged swift and terrible retribution. "The *Mail*'s given him his honeymoon. Let's crack down on him now. No more Mister Nice Guy."

Farrell was in his usual posture, sprawled over one of Haig's couches in the publisher's office. He knew this annoyed Haig. But Haig did not react. He knew how formidable had been Farrell's performance running the paper while he, Haig, was distracted, try-ing to fend off Messenger and disaster.

"Let's get him," Farrell said. "Let's get Lenny Sparg."

Haig shook his head. "Too soon. You can't bring down an ad-ministration until it's begun to put together a record. A bad one. Lenny hasn't done a damn thing so far."

Farrell bounced off the couch. "Arresting Judah? Arranging his destruction? Framing Ben Cork on that phony drug charge? You call that not doing a damn thing? To say nothing of the pattycake he played with Messenger these last few months."

Haig was patient. He was too relieved at having salvaged the *Mail* to permit Farrell to lance his joy.

"I'm not forgetting any of those things. But let's maintain a little perspective here. Ben's been dealing drugs for years. You know that, I know that. As for Judah the arrest was trumped up. But a homosex-ual is vulnerable."

Farrell grunted, unsatisfied. "We have a madman in City Hall. I think it's this paper's solemn responsibility to bring him down."

Haig regarded him narrowly. "This paper's responsibility is to keep the public informed. Not to mount vendettas."

Farrell was up and pacing now, the indolent pose shattered by anger.

"Do you always have to be right? Isn't there anything you don't know, anything you can't do better than anyone else?"

"Of course there are things I can't do. And don't know. But I think I know better than you what's right for the *Mail*."

Farrell cursed. "I'm talking about what's right for seven million people. For New York!"

"We're journalists," Haig said, "not campaign managers or the fair elections practices committee or the Goddamned conscience of the country. My job is to put out a paper that people will buy and will want to read. Entertain them, inform them, pique their curiosity. Oratory belongs in Congress. Sermons are for church. Newspapering is a business, not a religion."

Farrell's face reddened. "You make it sound like canning tomatoes," he said scornfully.

"Get off your soapbox, Farrell. I feel as strongly as you do about Lenny Sparg. In time, when he gives us the opening, the *Mail* will do a job on Lenny. But we're not going off half-cocked on another Children's Crusade. You sound like Peter the Hermit. 'Come follow me and we'll defeat the Saracens!' And instead of liberating Jerusalem the kids ended up in the brothels of Anatolia. Grow up, Farrell!"

Sean growled. Haig thought he was about to throw a punch. Haig was right. Instead Farrell clenched his big fists and turned his back, facing toward the window and the river but not seeing either.

Under other circumstances, Farrell thought, he and Haig might have been friends. They both loved the newspaper, they were both consummate professionals, they were both men of an age and a time and a craft.

At first there was resentment because Haig had bought the newspaper that Farrell had been sufficiently naive to think belonged not to its proprietors, Meg or Haig or . . . anyone! but to the talented men like Farrell who wrote for it, whose names appeared daily in its pages, whose words and ideas and inspiration spilled out across its blank pages like printers ink. When you loved something, you put your name on it. Farrell had done that. For nearly ten years.

Yet it belonged to Haig.

Then he fought with him for bringing in the guards, for exacerbating *l'affaire* Brasky to its ridiculous, tragic climax. He knew, in some dark instinctive corner of his mind, that Haig was wrong, that his insistence on militancy would destroy . . . someone.

The "someone" had turned out to be Sissy.

Sean sat in a bar, on a slim afternoon, sipping a slow drink, feeling sorry for himself, regretting things beyond regret, as the Irish do.

"Another?"

"Sure."

The barman measured out a bored drink. It was a joint on First Avenue: salesmen cheating on their time, advertising people out of work, a few housewives restlessly waiting for six o'clock.

"Where I belong," Farrell told his mirrored image. The image made no reply, and so he thought again of Campbell Haig, refreshing resentment.

He'd taken Alex. *Bought* her. No, that was bullshit. Alex was as rich as Haig. You didn't buy women like Alex.

But he'd taken her!

Why had Haig anointed him editor? He must have known he and Farrell were destined to compete. An uneven combat, he realized that, but worth the try. The *paper* made it worth the try.

He and Haig would never understand each other. He could no more accomplish Haig's financial juggling than Haig could write one of his columns. Yet they had shared the *Mail*.

They had shared Alex.

That was finished. Now there was Sissy. Why, then, did he know he had to see Alex one more time? Why was he phoning to insist they meet?

54

Alex met Farrell in one of his hangouts, a coffee shop marginally in Greenwich Village. He had wanted to do it properly, a lunch at the Four Seasons, a drink at "21."

"Is that such a terribly good idea?" she'd asked when he phoned, declaring it was vital that he talk with her.

"No," he'd said, sulking a bit, the way he did, "now that you're Mrs. Haig I suppose it isn't."

He'd emphasized the "Mrs." She understood. He had never quite forgiven her betrayal. She had never considered it as such; he clearly did.

The waitress brought them steaming coffee in thick mugs without saucers. The ketchup bottle was crusted over and a halo of drowsy flies hovered above it.

"I wanted you to know Sissy and I are getting married."

"Why, Sean, that's wonderful. For both of you. I hope you'll be very happy."

She meant it. Farrell nodded, unsmiling.

"She's a great girl. I'm trying to get her to go back to work. She's first rate, you know. Even if old Meg hadn't been her grandmother she would have been."

"Sean, you don't have to sell me on Sissy. She and I have been friends for a long time."

"Well, I wanted you to know."

There was something final and pugnacious about the words, about the set of his jaw, like the sentence that ends a cheap detective novel.

"I'm glad. Glad for you. Glad you've told me."

This is stupid, she thought, all this mouthing of banal courtesies over coffee in a luncheonette. Was this what friends were reduced to simply because they had decided, or one of them had, that they were not in love? Could he possibly still want *her* and not Sissy?

"It's okay to tell Haig," he said. "It'll be announced in a few days."

"He'll be happy," she said, "for you both."

The coffee was still too hot to drink. She wished the cup were already empty so she could thank him and shake hands and get up and get out of there. It was an awkward time. And Farrell wasn't making it any better.

"You think it's right, then?"

Oh, she thought, taut as greyhounds and still very much under the pressure of California and the guilt of Charlie Messenger, what the hell does he want me to say?

"Of course I think it's all right." Then, unable to resist, she asked, "Don't you? Are there any doubts?"

He stiffened. "Of course not. I don't marry women I don't love."

"No," she agreed. But she was not so sure.

His hand moved rapidly, knocking against the cup, sloshing coffee over the table.

"You think I'm doing this on the rebound from you?"

"Sean, are you trying to pick a fight? No, I don't think that. Not at all."

"Well," he said, not looking at her but down at the table, slick and glistening from the spilled coffee, "I just thought I'd tell you. I wasn't going to go off mysteriously the way you did with him."

She made one last stab at avoiding anger.

"Sean, that was wrong of me. It happened so fast. Then I didn't know what to say to you, how to explain."

He shrugged. "No explanation necessary. You loved him. You didn't love me. Those things happen. I'm a big boy."

Are you? She waited until he spoke again.

"You and Haig getting along all right?"

"Sean, we're married. I love my husband. Why shouldn't we be getting along?"

Close to the surface of her response was California, Messenger. Had there been talk? Oh, my God!

"No reason. I'm just making conversation, I guess."

Her cup was still nearly filled but she pushed it away.

"Well, thanks for telling me, Sean. I'll call Sissy."

"Yes," he said glumly, "I'm sure you will." There was a nasty edge to the last words.

"Look, Sean, I'm getting a bit fed up with this bout of temperament. What do you want me to say? Do you need some sort of assurance that you're doing the right thing in getting married? Is that what you want? Because, believe me, I'm not in the counseling business these days. I have enough to do running my own life without playing 'Dear Abby' to you or anyone."

"You probably think I feel sorry for her."

"That's a rotten thing to say. And a worse thing to think."

"Well?"

"Sean, five minutes ago I was very happy for you. For both of you. Right now I'm not so sure. Does Sissy know you've got all these doubts?"

"What doubts?"

"Come on. I know you. All this crap about marrying on the rebound and whether people think it's because Sissy lost her arm and you feel sorry for her. My God, that's hardly an auspicious way to start a married life together."

He was brooding now, very much the moody Irishman, sensitive and hurt.

"I was in love with you," he said hopelessly.

"You were infatuated. We had fun together. We liked one another. We were good in bed. That isn't love. I hope to hell you have more than that with Sis."

"I love her."

"Good, then forget all this other stuff."

"But you were important."

"Oh, Sean, you were going through your star-fucker period. I wa
a name in the newspapers and we went to bed together."

His anger flared. "Star-fucker! Is that all you thought of me then
Is that what you think?"

"Yes, I guess, part of it." She was glacial now, giving him th
rough edges.

The waitress came over. "More?"

Farrell shook his head and the girl tore off a page from her littl
pad and placed it facedown in the spilled coffee.

He pushed himself back in the seat, ready to stand.

"Sissy's got only one damned arm," he said cruelly, "and she'
more complete than you'll ever be. You and Haig are a match mad
in heaven. Who else would have either of you?"

He slid out of the booth and left, his straight back communicatin
contempt.

Well, she thought, if he still had a crush on me, that tore it
Sometimes being bitchy was to perform a kindness. She hoped Siss
would understand.

Farrell had forgotten to pay. Alex put a dollar on the table in th
spilled coffee.

Farrell knew before the cab had swerved toward him, answerin
his hail, that he had been wrong. Alex was right, he had tried to pic
a fight. What the hell was it? A lingering desolation over having los
her to Haig, a sneaking suspicion that in Sissy he was settling fo
second best, the curling edge of self-honesty that told him he wa
marrying the girl to make up for her arm? Any of these things o
all of them?

He told Sissy, unable not to. "You don't love me," she said, voic
dull and bitter. "You pity me."

"I pity myself," he said miserably.

They sat—it was her apartment—in chairs that faced but with
eyes turned away. It was the pivotal instant, they both knew. H
could walk out now and it would be ended. I hope he does, Siss
thought. Praying that he wouldn't.

Farrell got out of his chair, moving quickly, as he always did. He
right hand jerked involuntarily toward her mouth. She willed it t
halt. She would not again be destroyed, never again would sh

crumble and fall apart. He's going and I will not beg, I will not plead.
I will not cry!

He did not go. He turned toward her, reached out and pulled her
up and to him. His other arm snaked around her waist and drew their
bodies together.

"Come on," he said.

"Yes," Sissy said.

They went into the bedroom and he began to undress her. They
had made love before. But this would be the first time they would
make love just after he had been alone with Alex. In Sean Farrell,
resentment of Haig, a lingering desire for Alex, doubt about his
motives, still gnawed at consciousness.

Blinded by sexual hunger, excited by a love for Sean that went
beyond bodies, Sissy didn't care. It was enough that he was there.
She would give him no more choices. He must love her. He must!
As she loved him. She had the strength now, the passion, the deter-
mination. She would fight and plot and tease. She would do anything. She would never let go.

Late that night, as he slept curled close to her, she looked into his
tough little boy's face, and smiled. She knew this was a competition
she would win.

Roy Sheldon loved guns. He was a city boy but the army had
taught him about them, had awakened within him a vaguely defined
passion that except for a summary court-martial was the only remarkable thing about his three-year hitch. The court-martial derived from
the beating he had given a German girl in Wiesbaden.

One entire wall of his cheerless basement apartment was covered
with them, serried rows of dully gleaming, carefully hung, tenderly
polished and lubricated rifles, shotguns, revolvers, automatics, one
Browning Automatic Rifle. Once a week Sheldon went to a gun club
in Westchester to fire his licensed weapons. He wished there were
some way he could soundproof the basement so he could fire the
others. Firing his weapons always excited him. He had no girl but
there were bar pickups, and when one of them coincided with an
evening on which he had fired the range, the sex was always better.
In bed he would think about guns.

Guns excited him. He loved them as he loved few other things.

He was a man with many hates and few enthusiasms. And one of his hates was the newspapers.

Roy Sheldon hated Haig for the wrong reasons. He knew all about how cozy the *Mail* and its publisher were with the Jews and the niggers and the spics and everyone else causing trouble, the welfares and the drug addicts and the queers. Sheldon knew better than anyone else where evil dwelt, where vice resided. The newspapers! Peddling their filth, coddling the criminals, applauding abortion. No wonder there was so much divorce, that teenagers were hooked on dope, that the family was breaking down. Newspapers!

It was not known to Sheldon that Haig's *Mail* had campaigned against government-funded abortions, for stronger drug laws, against welfare fraud, for tougher sentencing, that on most issues the *Mail* and Sheldon were at one.

Sheldon had spent the evening in his local bar, an anonymous storefront on an anonymous little street off Queens Boulevard, drinking draft beer and watching a ball game on television, an angry, empty man looking for something to hit out at, frustrated not to have targets. Lean as wire, drawn fine with hatred, with only a modest beer belly punctuating his length, he slouched on a stool, ignoring the banter of men around him, the casual flirtations with a waitress. Now even the ball game forgotten, he stared at the long rows of bottles behind the bar, at the mirror image of his own face fragmented here and there between them.

A dog-eared copy of that day's *Mail* lay folded thick under his right elbow, padding it against the cold slop of the hardwood bar. His upper weight bore down on that elbow, and his right hand held his beer glass. But the newspaper held out no comfort beyond that. On page one and then again on pages four and five, the headlines, the words, and the pictures told another, too-familiar story of violence and death, yet another child raped, yet another liquor store held up, yet another cop gunned down in a bloody shootout. Niggers! Addicts! Welfares! The words and the pictures tore at him like barbs. And Sheldon saw the joy in the headlines, the glee in the lead paragraphs, the relentless support the *Mail* gave to the daily horrors. Even more than the politicians, the niggers, addicts, and welfares, Sheldon hated the *Mail*. The *Mail* was the source of the sullen anger on which Sheldon fed.

And to top it off the *Mail* had the balls to print one of those pious
ittle sermons that passed for editorials on this very day, demanding
tiffer new restrictions on the ownership of guns by ordinary citizens.
Vhat a sick joke! As if it were hunters and gun-club members and
cared grocers who were killing cops and shooting delicatessen clerks.
\s if the hoods and the pimps and the addicts would tamely turn
n their weapons and apply for licenses to bear arms. These were the
eal criminals, the commies and the queers who wrote such drivel,
he men who made their money on the sale of newspapers, who
lourished on the blood money of the raped and bleeding decent
itizens of this crummy Goddamn town. It was the newspaper
ditors who should lie dying in the gutters, the people who wrote this
hit about gun control while they coddled the Goddamn muggers
nd killers.

People like this Haig who owned the *Mail*!

It so happened that Roy Sheldon was confused. That afternoon's
Mail had carried the news reports and photos of the latest criminal
ampage. It had been that morning's *News* that ran the gun-control
ditorial.

But in Roy Sheldon's fevered mind such fine distinctions were
lurred by hatred.

Roy Sheldon was the man who caused Hearst and Pulitzer and
Gordon Bennett to sweat and tremble. It was for Sheldon they built
heir moats, barred their windows, hired Pinkertons, and investi-
ated the stopping power of barbed wire and tear gas. For Sheldon
·as the beast, the mob, the unthinking, unknowing animal their
.ewspapers aroused from sluggish sleep. Men like Sheldon neither
·rooded nor speculated nor thought. They simply . . . felt. And a
·an for whom emotion substitutes for reason is not a man but an
·nimal. He is the always feeling, never thinking, irrational, frus-
·ated, envying, hating beast. He is the mob.

And now Roy Sheldon, angry for all the wrong reasons, was about
· do that which Gordon Bennett and Pulitzer and Hearst always
·ared. He would mistake the newspaper for the news. And in his
·uddled, inarticulate rage, he would strike at the man whose name
·ocked him from atop its masthead.

55

Campbell Haig had finished his critique of the *Mail*'s metro edition
circling errors and awkward layouts and dull headlines with a large
emphatic grease pencil and handing it to a copyboy for remakes or
the second edition. Benaud would scream, as he always did, about
the cost. Even with these new electronic typesetting consoles it cost
money to make minor corrections. But Gideon's name was not atop
the masthead on the editorial page. Haig's was. And not even the
crushing burden of his debt to Messenger was going to make him
put out a slack newspaper. He picked up another, unmarked copy
of the first edition.

BROOKLYN GANG
SLAYS HERO COP

The headline, big and black, stared out at him. He knew what his
critics said about such headlines, what even Alex thought of them
how she had voiced her objections.

"But they're scary, Campbell. All that violence and disaster and
vice all over the front page. The more degrading the story the bigger
the headlines. There's something about the *Mail* that's scary."

He had looked at her and nodded. "These are scary times, Alex."

She had paused for an instant, and then, very quietly, she had asked, "And you never consider the possibility that you could be wrong?"

He had seemed genuinely confused by the question. "Why, no, not when it comes to newspapers. No."

That was how it had gone during that curious, depressing passage of time following their trip west, following Messenger's unpredictable, wildly generous concession. A barrier had come between them, unaccountable, solid, tangible. And it was still there.

"Farrell?"

They were in Sean's office, not as grand as Haig's, but with big old dark-brown leather Chesterfield couches and the same view of Brooklyn and the river, only two floors lower. The foreign editor, a pansified and very competent former correspondent with a transatlantic accent, had just finished his assessment of the latest Middle East mess. Sean was behind the desk, his eyelids half descended, the dozing appearance not fooling anyone. Haig perched on an arm of one of the couches, restless, always moving, anxious for the next edition, the next headline, the next story.

"Nothing from me," Farrell said at last.

Damn you, Haig thought. Sulky Irish brute!

"Keitler?"

The entertainment editor embarked on a long and pointless yarn about a television star who was opening in her first Broadway play and on whom he thought they might, just might, do a feature. "It looks promising," he droned, "you see, her agent told Barnes that . . ."

Jesus, Haig thought, remembering that the entertainment editor had been a member of the Pulitzer jury a year ago. No wonder the Goddamn Pulitzers went to the wrong people!

"Sports?"

The sports editor, a little banty rooster of a man with the black hair and the cheekbones of an Indian, had something possible. Two of the Yankees gotten into a brawl in an East Side bar the night before and—

"Then why isn't it in today's *Mail*?" Haig snapped.

The sports editor looked pained. "It *is*, Campbell. Second inside sports page. A brief. We got a statement from the bartender at home this morning and we're going outside with it in the second edition."

Haig grunted. It was as close as he ever came to an apology. Sports bored him. But that didn't excuse his missing a story. He must be getting slow. His morning with Alex . . .

The city editor, Donovan, had unearthed yet another ghetto grammar school where not only were the children illiterate, but the principal.

"We're reproducing the letter tomorrow, Campbell. You've got to see it to believe it. He wrote to some parent, misspelling everything, including the 'truely yours.' "

Haig nodded. "Good, let's do an editorial too. Blame it on Lenny Sparg."

Farrell's eyes widened. "The schools' chancellor isn't Lenny's man. He's a holdover from the last regime."

"I know that," Haig snapped. "Pin it on Lenny anyway. He's the mayor. Give him the heat, not this poor bastard of a principal."

"Okay," Farrell said, voice thick with dislike.

Haig shrugged. They didn't have to love him, just put out his paper. Everything else, everything beyond the *Mail*, shriveled and wasted into trivia. The newspaper was the thing. This next edition and the next and the first tomorrow morning.

"Get that headline bigger," Haig grumbled, as the editorial meeting broke up and the half-dozen men drifted out of Sean's office onto the floor of the city room on their errands of greater or lesser urgency. Haig alone remained behind.

Still perched on the couch arm, he waited until the door had closed behind the last of them, had watched them through the glass wall as they scattered through the city room, and then turned to Farrell.

"Well?"

The editor looked up at him, the eyes still sleepy, the thick legs still spraddled atop the desk, Farrell's entire posture still one of insolent defiance.

"Well, what?"

"You're sulking again, Farrell."

"The masthead carries my name as editor," Farrell said. "You put

t there. But ever since that Messenger business you've been playing
editor yourself. I'd think that entitles a man to an occasional sulk."

Haig nodded. It was a point. "Yes, I *have* been editing the paper.
don't blame you for feeling resentment. But I'm doing the job
because I think it has to be done. Circulation hasn't gone anywhere
with you in the chair."

"Cover price increases hardly ever boost circulation."

"If you give them a newspaper they have to have, they'll pay fifty
cents for it. They'll pay a buck! And if newsprint prices keep going
up, they will. But you've got to edit the paper," Haig said, shaking
his head. "You've got to turn out a paper they'll line up for, that
they'll buy day after day after day."

"And I'm not putting out a good paper?" Farrell asked, the edge
in his voice for the first time audible.

Haig considered pulling back. Instead he said quietly, "No, not
as good as it *could* be. If you didn't have the ability, I'd either replace
you or leave you alone to work under me. But you have the stuff. And
that's what annoys me. That you aren't working at it."

"You seem to have a theory about everything, Haig. What's your
theory on that?"

Haig paused. Then he said, "I think you're dogging it. Dislike for
me. Something personal. Or maybe you'd rather be running another
kind of newspaper."

"Sure I would. I'd like to be running the *Times* or *The Washington Post.* Care to call Punch or Kay Graham and recommend me?"

"The *Mail* isn't good enough? Too blue collar? Too loud? The
headlines a bit black for your taste?"

Farrell got up then, flushed, angry. But he said nothing.

"Haig, this is scumbag journalism. Raunchy, sensational, steal-
the-picture-off-the-grieving-mother's dresser. Is that what it has to
be? Can't we be better than that?"

"You're fighting me, Farrell," Haig said. "You're fighting the
Mail. The kind of paper the *Mail* has to be today. I've told you a
thousand times but you fight it. You're dealing, Farrell, with a
generation of people who can't read, who get their news from Dan
Rather in twenty-two minutes every night. They're impatient,
they're busy, they don't have the leisure to ponder and they don't
give a damn about your precious style. They want it fast, they want

it simple. That's what the *Mail* does. That's its genius. That's why
it exists, for the poor bastards who don't have the capacity to cope
with the *Times*! That's our job, to give them the news, give it
straight, without the phony bullshit, in plain type and with the best
pictures and the clearest headlines we can write. And if you don't
understand that, or can't live with it, then maybe you better go back
out to Hollywood and write movies."

He turned now, to face Farrell once again.

The editor stared at his employer. "You really believe that, don't
you, Haig?"

"Why, yes, I do." Haig nodded. "It's why I bought the *Mail*. It's
the job I have." He looked toward the door of Farrell's office, toward
the bustling city room beyond. "I believe in this newspaper and in
what I do. You don't. That's the difference between us."

"It's more than that," Farrell said coldly.

"What is it, Farrell?" Haig knew this was not just some vague
conflict over publishing philosophy, over the size of the headlines.
It was more than that.

Uncharacteristically, Farrell fell silent. Haig drove in on him.
"You always thought you knew better about running a paper than
I did. The editorials we ought to be running. The typefaces, the story
selection, the promos we run on TV." He shrugged. "Okay with me.
I never did give a damn for a man who didn't have his own ideas,
who wasn't absolutely sure he knew better than the boss. You're a
bright boy, Farrell. Good editor. I don't know who taught you about
words but whoever it was did a job. I wish I could write the way you
do."

Sean still said nothing. Haig's tone changed.

"But my name is on the building. The *Mail* belongs to me. If it's
a bad newspaper, blame me. But don't go around whining that I
didn't level. I told you from the start the hard decisions were mine,
not yours. Well, didn't I?"

Unable to stop himself, Farrell nodded. "You did. You warned
me, I'll give you that, Haig."

Haig exhaled, exasperated. "Then what in hell is eating at you?
You've been at me since the day I bought the *Mail*. Why? What
is it about me?"

Farrell got up. "You're wrong, Haig. Not since the day you bought
the *Mail*."

"No?"

Farrell, feeling the pulse of anger, knew he should not say it. He went ahead, suspecting he was wrong, unable to stop himself.

"No," he said, "since the day you bought Alex."

Haig was shocked into momentary silence. Then: "I don't know what you mean by that," he said, his voice low and dangerous, his mind, his entire body as tense as when he had stalked his father's killers twenty years before.

"Before you ever met her, Alex and I were lovers."

Haig had selected and very carefully picked up one of the yellow pencils on Farrell's desk. To retain control now was again to demonstrate his superiority. Farrell's words shattered the attempt. The pencil splintered in his grip and he threw it down.

"You bastard!" Haig shouted, lunging at Farrell, once again a little boy, head down, arms windmilling, charging at the enemy.

Sean Farrell, who had learned to fight on the coast of Brooklyn, coolly waited until Haig had reached him and then, quite competently, smashed a big fist into his employer's face and watched as Haig sank slowly, almost gracefully, into an unconscious heap at his feet.

Looking down at the body Farrell said quietly, "I'll get out now." And left, hating Haig and hating himself.

Well, thought Campbell Haig, that tore it. This was what he hadn't wanted. God knows, he hadn't wanted this!

A copyboy had seen him hit, and fall, and one of the older editors nervously had fetched a wet cloth. Haig had sat there on the floor for a few moments after they revived him.

"I never was much of a boxer," he said wryly, more to himself than to the half dozen of his employees who had gathered around. Then he got up and went upstairs to his own office, leaving behind him the inevitable brushfire of office gossip there was no way to damp down.

Miss Mayhew looked at him oddly and in his bathroom Haig could understand why. His face was red, swollen under the right eye, and there was still some blood trickling from one nostril.

It had been stupid of him to go at Farrell. Not so much that Farrell would be the better fighter and that Haig would have to lose. But for giving any credence to that crazy boast that he and Alex had been lovers. Farrell must have been mad to think Haig would believe that!

He did not. He trusted his wife. It was as simple as that. Alex had told him everything else, about the bars and the motel rooms and the casual pickups. She would have told him about Farrell. He bathed his face and forcibly reasserted control. Icy cold, that was what was needed now. No emotion. He didn't need additional problems. Messenger's loan terms and the plight of the *Mail* were sufficient of a burden without this, the necessity of finding a new editor or having it all over town that Sean Farrell had punched his boss and stalked out. Damn! If only Farrell hadn't let resentment and the argument over Lenny Sparg make him so emotional, so mulish, so frantic that he would dredge up the moronic lie about Alex!

If only he, Haig, had been less rigid, less . . . in love.

There had been other confrontations that had not ruptured their professional relationship. "I don't want you to love me," he'd shouted more than once at Farrell. "Don't even like me! Just give me a great newspaper every day."

And now, he added, but to himself, "And don't tell a man you've fucked his wife."

Before he went home that night he had convinced himself there was nothing in it. Farrell's punch would be explained away as a bitter argument over publishing philosophies. Thinking of his beloved Alex, he consoled himself with the pleasantly superior conclusion that the Irish were more useful in the moving of heavy loads than of heavy thought.

Farrell had bragged. To hurt a man he resented. That was all there was to it. Nothing more!

56

A lovely spring morning, promising later heat but now still cool and dry and coming alert with the noises of the street and of a bird that clung precariously to that spindly tree reluctantly blooming just outside their bedroom windows. Campbell had stirred first, and half asleep, moved instinctively toward his wife's warmth under the light summer blanket. Just as instinctively she curled toward him. The nightmare of Charlie Messenger was fading, gradually the barriers she had guiltily erected between Campbell and herself were crumbling. What she had done she had done for him. Why then this stupid guilt? Campbell knew who she was, knew of her nocturnal ramblings of the past, had dragged her half-conscious from a den of lesbians. Why should the night with Messenger loom so terribly?

Because now she was Campbell's wife and in saving his newspaper she had risked destroying their marriage. And more than their marriage.

"I hate the *Mail*. I *hate* it!" So ran the litany of her remorse, so had it run for too long.

On the Madison Avenue flank of what used to be the Hotel Biltmore stands the old Men's Bar, shuttered now, dusty and for lease, a victim of raised consciousness. The women, having liberated it, went on to do their drinking elsewhere, and the men, in shock, drifted away, leaving behind them only the ghosts of martinis long drunk, commuter trains long gone. In the great lobby, where soldiers used to meet their girls under the clock, where college boys gathered and, when necessary, threw up in the potted ferns, Japanese businessmen hurried through in their cautious little suits. Farrell watched them hurry by and was depressed. New York, like the rest of America, retained no reverence for the past, no seemly nostalgia for better times than these. It was eight o'clock on a Monday morning and Campbell Haig had summoned him to a summit meeting over breakfast. He would be coming in to Grand Central on the early train from Rhinecliff and he wanted to see Farrell away from the office. Breakfast in a shop near the old Biltmore had seemed a sensible compromise.

Haig had told his wife little of his brief, inglorious battle with Sean Farrell, dismissing it as a violent difference of opinion about the newspaper. She was all too willing to accept the evasion. Her own, bitter last confrontation with Farrell was still so fresh she had no desire to talk about him or his muddled motivations. Poor Sissy, marrying a man still going around muttering lovesick nonsense about another woman. Well, Sissy was demonstrating a resourcefulness Alex would not have believed she possessed a year ago. Perhaps she could still make something of her love for Farrell.

Then, that weekend at Mayfair, their first in a month, Campbell shocked her. He intended to make peace with Farrell.

"But, Campbell. The man hit you. In your own office. . . ."

"His office, not mine."

She waved aside the distinction. "But why? I don't understand."

Haig grinned. He was a man who could make mistakes, often did, but he was also a man who understood the essential priorities. Alex was his again, whatever shadow had passed between them in the wake of Malibu was gone. Their love was once more intact, unblemished. And he still had the newspaper. Only barely, but he had it. Given these two facts, his wife and his work, everything else was unimportant. Even the fact that one of his employees had babbled nonsensically of some imagined flirtation with Alex, even that devastatingly crisp Farrell punch to the face, tended to fade into insignificance.

In the West of Haig's early empire building it was not unknown for punches to be thrown, for reporters and editors to settle grammatical differences with their fists instead of with Fowler's *Modern English Usage.* Men who grew up in towns like McAllen respected direct action, even if it sometimes resulted in bloodied noses and loosened teeth. Gideon Benaud, trained by Max Aitken, assured Haig that a punch thrown by the Irish had no more significance than an arched eyebrow among the British. Farrell, to do him credit, had played within the rules during those first days after he hit Haig. He refused interviews with reporters from the media departments of *Time* and *Newsweek,* stayed away from Costello's and the Lion's Head, issued no statements critical of the *Mail* or of his former employer. Haig matched his restraint. And now, after a week of circling one another cautiously, like warring alley cats, they were about to meet again.

Nor was Farrell as pugnaciously eager for the final break as he had thought he was a week earlier. Sissy had welcomed his decision. Enthusiastically, which was understandable. She hated Haig and with reason. But how the hell was he to live without a job? And he was damned if Sissy was going to support him.

Farrell knew he was right in his mind about Sissy now. He could credit her for that, her good sense and her amazing new sexual power over him. He was staying in her flat now. For more than a week they had been together and the intimacy, the exuberance of her joy had at last sluiced away the last vestiges of his jealousy, his forlorn desire for Alex.

Haig had taken the train alone. Alex would drive down later to the city. He paged through the *Times* and *The Wall Street Journal* during the two-hour ride, wondering what he was going to say to Farrell, what Farrell would say to him. It was a good sign that the editor had agreed to meet with him. If there did not exist at least some marginal hope for professional reconciliation, Farrell would simply have turned down his invitation.

Haig's train rattled past the sealed-up windows of burned-out

Harlem and plunged with a roar into the tunnel beneath Park Avenue.

Farrell was waiting. He offered the first important gesture.

"About Alex," he said, "that was crude of me. Rotten. It was all a long time ago. Finished. She's your wife and I'm going to marry Sissy Valentine and that's it."

Haig nodded. "Good," he said. "I'm glad for you. For both of you."

Without any further preamble or even a courtesy nod at the hovering waiter, exuding a confidence and self-assurance he did not altogether feel, Haig began. "I am an optimist. I believe in the *Mail.* I believe in myself. I want to believe in you and I think that I can."

Farrell sat back, saying nothing.

Haig continued. "I believe in this newspaper, believe in what I'm doing, how I run it. Two years ago, before I bought the *Mail,* I was a lot richer, I didn't work as hard, I had fewer enemies, I didn't owe a son of a bitch like Charlie Messenger more money than I used to think existed outside of federal deficits. And even if it could all be undone, I wouldn't do a thing differently except for your girl. There is no city in the world like this one, there is no other place worth the gamble I've taken. I'd rather have tried in New York and failed than never to have tried here at all.

"You're needed at the *Mail,* Farrell. I need you. And New York needs the *Mail.* There's need for the kind of paper we know how to run.

"And do you know why? Because I think there are a couple of million people out there who aren't Alex Haig or Sissy Valentine, who never went to college, who lack the social graces, who love this newspaper as I do. As I think you do. It's their nickels and dimes and quarters that pay you and me, and I think we owe them something. We owe them a hell of a lot, in fact. Every day we owe them a simple, exciting, entertaining window on the world.

"There's a need for stories about potholes in Queens and crooked councilmen and people in old-age homes and muggers and girls in trouble and auto accidents and subways with brakes that fail and chorus girls who make it and how Eighth Avenue pimps recruit those Minnesota blondes. Seamy? Corny? Sensational? Sure it is. But, by God, it's real! We're the meat-and-potatoes paper, Farrell.

We're the people who one day are going to catch Mayor Sparg without his built-up shoes and we'll run that picture as large as it can go on the front page and we'll laugh that murderous little delinquent right out of town."

He paused, absentmindedly picked up Farrell's half-filled coffee cup, and then slammed it down into its saucer, sloshing coffee over half the table.

"I need you to help me do that, Farrell. I don't care if you hate my guts. I don't care what your girl thinks of me. I don't, God forgive me, care what my own wife says. I want to get this paper back into the black and to pay off Messenger and to keep *The New York Mail* the same ornery, awkward, embarrassing, loud, abrasive tabloid it is now. You let Messenger or some son of a bitch like him take it over and it will end up the bland New York outlet for canned wire-service features and puff pieces about Messenger's high-blown society friends. I won't permit that. They're going to have to carry me out of the *Mail* to get hold of it. I've pawned everything I had, damn near, to keep it out of Messenger's hands. I don't intend to let him have it. Ever."

Haig stopped.

"Well?" he said.

Farrell's face took on that pugnacious look.

"All right," he said. "I'll come back."

Haig was buoyant.

"Good," he said. "Fine."

Farrell did not smile. "One thing, Haig. No one, not even you, is ever going to get me out of that chair again. Understood?"

Haig smiled. Maybe they could be a team, after all.

57

Now, on a summer morning three thousand miles east of her shame, Alex Haig slowly woke, knowing it was time for an end to withdrawal, that whatever she felt about his newspaper, whatever his obsession with it had done to her, she loved the man who would be the father of her child.

As slowly as she woke, in the cool, dim light of their bedroom in Manhattan, she just as slowly snaked a round arm under Campbell's neck and pulled his head toward her.

Sensitive to her slightest signal, Haig's heart seemed to move within him. Not only was there no resistance, no strange restraint, but for the first time in so long there was the eager pull of her sensuality. He stared down at her face, sulky with sleep, the wide mouth slightly opened, the familiar grin faintly blurred by passion, the strong chin, the blue-gold eyes, the thick chopped blond hair mussed and damp. As his mouth descended toward hers her face melted out of focus, becoming a soft blend of blonds and pinks and reds, the eyes clashing, and then their mouths met and melded, even the morning taste of her tongue clean and young and fresh.

His mouth broke away. "I love you, Alex."

"I know," she said sleepily. "That's why I'm here."

She pulled herself half upright and in a swift, efficient motion stripped off her T-shirt and tossed it aimlessly from her.

How young she was, how beautiful. He never tired of seeing her breasts, the pale aureoles circling the pink nipples, the incredible high lift of them, the creamy smoothness against the faint bikini tan of California, the erotic counterpoint of shape and weight and skin tone. Just as he could stare forever at the dancing blue and gold of her eyes, the dramatically thick brows, and the laughing, cockeyed grin that until this past month forever played around the generous proportions of her wide mouth and framed those teeth, milky white as children's.

Her legs, those solid thighs that so bedeviled her, those sturdy calves, twined now with his and his hand dropped to cup her vagina, his fingers began to plumb her opening, quickly damp, seeking the clitoris, seeking her.

"Oh, yes," she said, her voice a murmur, her arms pulling him closer. "Oh, yes, Campbell."

Her belly moved under him and then her hips and then their mouths were again one and smoothly, wetly, he entered her as man might first have entered Eden.

Two hours later he was in the limousine driving south on the FDR Drive and she was showering and dressing. They were to lunch together, a small, ad hoc celebration of nothing at all, but before that there was the eleven-o'clock appointment with her gynecologist. She was certain she was pregnant but it would be unfair to Campbell to tell him until there was official confirmation. By her own reckoning she was well into her second month. California had been four weeks ago. Surely a child would wipe all of that out, flush away the memories and the guilt.

She was glad she had conceived before the night with Messenger, as if the fact of carrying Campbell's child had rendered her less vulnerable, though she had not known of her pregnancy at the time.

Suppose the child had been Messenger's! She shuddered at the thought. Then, more sensibly, remembering in cruel detail the things she had done with Charlie Messenger, she knew there was no danger of that. Messenger had forced her to do everything but the one thing that might have caused conception.

By noon it was official. The doctor had said so. By one Campbell

would be at La Grenouille and he would know it too. Striding
downtown along Madison Avenue she tried to imagine the baby
within her, tried to feel it—no, him!—and then tried to imagine
Campbell's joy. On the busy, sunlit street, this sturdy, healthy young
woman ignored the questioning, admiring, puzzled looks of pass-
ersby and hugged herself with both arms.

How beautiful everything is!

For Haig, who knew nothing of his child but only that Alex's love
for him was once again intact, it was also a morning of pleasure, of
total contentment, of the deepest satisfaction he had known since
his defeat by Messenger. Circulation was booming, retail advertising
was showing signs of recovery, Farrell was working hard and effectively in the editor's chair. Even Gideon's old face bore less of a
resemblance to the more sorely put-upon of the biblical prophets.
They were going to make it with the *Mail*, by God! And Alex had
come back to him.

He bounded out from behind Meg Valentine's old desk, glanced
through one of the picture windows toward the river and a coastal
tanker, rust-streaked and riding empty and high on the tide, passing
swiftly under the bridge to the sea, and after a moment's reflection
he crossed the great room to the hall and the elevator bank. As he
went he nodded absently at the women's-page editor, a tiny, frightened woman who scuttled crabwise through hallways, her back always against the wall, lest she be taken by surprise and carried off
to rapine and worse. Campbell shoved his hands into his pockets and
when the elevator arrived leaped into it, nearly colliding with a
workman carrying a package, looking about in some confusion. The
man got out and looked vaguely up the corridor. The elevator door
closed.

The morning meeting went well. Brophy had a source who promised great things on a burgeoning little municipal scandal they all
hoped would eventually lead to Lenny Sparg. Haig lazed on the
windowsill of Farrell's office, smoking a cigarillo and enjoying the
play of words by intelligent men, men who knew their jobs and who
understood the great city beyond. He tossed in a question or two,
was satisfied by the answers, gave Farrell a brief grin of approbation
over a front-page headline suggestion.

When the men stood up Haig turned to Farrell.

"Long lunch today, Farrell. I may not get back. Phone me at ome if there's anything."

"Sure."

Haig nodded briskly and followed the others from the office.

The city room smelled as it always did, stale smoke, the stink of offee gone rancid in cardboard containers, the musty smell of tacked newspapers, and through the windows the oily, fishy smell f polluted rivers. Somewhere a wire service machine clattered, hones rang, men and women talked. The staccato click of typewriters underlay the dialogue and the occasional shout of "copy!" Paint eeled from the walls, sunlight flickered bravely through windows dull with dust and dead flies, the institutional gray of the steel desks mposed a monochromatic severity on the cluttered chaos of the big oom. Haig drank it all in.

"God, but I love it," he told himself.

He paused to read some wire copy at the city editor's desk. Watching from the office, Farrell could see his face brighten, see his mouth form into a quick, instinctive laugh. Then Haig turned and walked toward the corridor and the bank of elevators, a lean, hurrying figure of a man, moving as he always did, as if he were late for some vital appointment.

Roy Sheldon, the "workman" with the package, was waiting for him at the elevator bank.

58

Those first hours after her husband was shot crawled slow as years for Alexandra Noyes Haig. They had come for her at La Grenouille in that loveliest of all Manhattan dining rooms, and the pleasant, placid anticipation of a meal, a glass, a tranquil, loving hour with the man she loved had suddenly shattered into shards of taxi horns, of solicitude and morbid curiosity, of contradictory assurances and premature sympathy, of the antiseptic stink of hospital corridors.

He was at Bellevue, the hospital nearest to the newspaper. Gideon Benaud turned her away at the doors of the intensive care unit.

"Alex," he said, his wise old face shocked and sad, his long arms wide and embracing. She let him enfold her, and the old man could feel her strong, flat back under his hands. She was breathing rapidly, but no sobs shook her frame.

"How bad is he? Can I see him?"

Benaud knew her too well to lie. "He's got a chance. But it's bad. They're operating now. I don't think you ought to go in there. They probably won't let you anyway."

Gideon took her arm and walked her down the corridor. Nurses and orderlies passed in a blur. Benaud steered her into an unoccupied office on the same floor. She sat down in a swivel chair behind a desk and he lighted her cigarette. She asked no questions. Thinking to take her mind from the tragic drama of the operating room, he told her what he knew.

"They caught the man."

"Who was he?" she asked dully.

"He wasn't anybody," Gideon said, awe in his voice, "he was just . . . nobody."

She nodded. Her lovely face was pale and empty, reflecting none of the coiled energy, the intensity of life Benaud was accustomed to seeing there. Good, he thought, she's in shock, none of this is really registering, none of it is really hurting yet.

"Is there anyone you want me to call?" Benaud asked.

She shook her head.

"His mother?"

"Yes," she said then, "phone his mother."

He did not want to leave her but he did not want to make the call where she could hear him. He stood there, an old man and sad, confused.

Alex stubbed out the half-burned cigarette in a jar lid on the battered desk.

"I'm carrying his child, Gideon."

"Oh," he said, "that's fine, Alex. That's good."

She shook her head. "He doesn't know. I was going to tell him at lunch."

"You'll tell him later. It'll be the best medicine he could ever want."

"Sure," she said, "sure."

They waited and then Gideon went to check once more. And still she did not cry.

In intensive care a man in a green cotton gown and surgical cap came up to Gideon: "Mr. Benaud? Dr. Sachs. I can tell you that everything is being done; there is no time to consider other avenues of treatment, of course. You may call in any other doctor you want but the time is past for consultation. You want to know his chances. He has none. A shotgun wound in the chest and upper belly at close range leaves no chance. Please understand that. We are keeping him alive but he is going to die. Tonight, tomorrow, in a week. One lung,

arteries, part of his shoulder are shot away. I'm going back now." He
left Benaud immediately. The old man had listened with no change
of expression, but his red face had gone a deathly gray.

Gideon went back to Alex in the office where she waited. Some
one had brought her tea in a foam cup; the teabag string hung out
an indecency; the tea was still seeping in milky water. She had drunk
half of it and smoked half of three cigarettes.

"What do they say?" she asked.

"He's coming along fine," Gideon said, his great-chested voice
carrying all the amazing conviction of which it was capable.

On the day Roy Sheldon shot Campbell Haig, *The New York
Mail* had recorded other acts of violence.

In Bedford-Stuyvesant a policeman named Sabbatino was shot to
death during the holdup by four men of a Washington Avenue social
club.

On West Forty-sixth Street in Manhattan a visiting Parisian
restaurateur was shot to death by two men after he refused their offer
of drugs. His female companion reported that he lay wounded on
the sidewalk for nearly an hour before anyone would respond to her
cries for help.

Two blocks away, on West Forty-fourth Street, a Baltimore cabi-
netmaker was killed by a twenty-pound cinder block tossed from a
rooftop by parties unknown.

In the East Village two members of a motorcycle gang were
choked to death after having been tortured with a soldering iron.

In Brownsville a Hasidic Jew died following injuries suffered in a
street altercation with local youths.

A Nassau county policeman shot his wife, a Park Avenue doctor
and his ailing wife committed suicide, two dealers were shot to death
in Harlem, and in Jamaica a nineteen-year-old unwed mother put
her year-old child in an oven "to cleanse him of the devil."

All these stories were in all editions. The attack on Campbell Haig
had come too late for even the final edition, the Wall Street
close.

For those next few days as he clung to slender life, several people
pondered the potential convenience of Campbell Haig's death.

It took a stern lecture from Mavis Sparg to moderate her husband's glee at Haig's shooting. She had found Lenny capering in ecstasy around his office at City Hall.

"The son of a bitch," Lenny kept saying, "someone shot the son of a bitch."

"Lenny," his wife said soberly, "now isn't the time to score points off Haig. Right now send flowers to Haig's wife."

The reactions of his rival press lords were more seemly. They, after all, were as vulnerable to mindless violence as the rebel Haig. Ponderous editorials sounded the theme, solemn as the loose drums of a requiem march. The First Amendment was duly cited. Peter Lenger's tenuous links to *The New York Mail* were briefly noted. The public comments of the nation's great publishers were most seemly. Privately, they were somewhat different.

Nora Noyes heard the news at her cottage in Newport. Immediately she phoned her daughter, and when there was no reply she telephoned one of her priests.

"You will say a mass for him, won't you, Father?"

"Of course."

"Good," she said, "it will so comfort poor Alex."

And when she had put down the phone she fantasized about reclaiming an estranged daughter. "If only he'll do the decent thing and die."

Junior Valentine was ecstatic, but he still worried. That son of a bitch was just mean enough to survive.

Charles Messenger wondered whether Haig's death would please him. There was a certain poetic symmetry in having Haig killed just a year after Warren's death. But Charlie had gone to a great deal of trouble, to say nothing of expense, to get Haig into the vulnerable position into which he had now been backed. And yet . . . and yet, there was always Alex Haig to consider, a bereaved widow with debts, badly needing a patron. Charlie was still remembering the smell, the feel, the taste of Alex.

Farrell vacillated.

Haig was a man. And a journalist. A good one, a damned good

one. Whatever Farrell thought privately of his headlines and h
prejudices and his mulishness, they had made peace. And Haig love
Alex. Of that Sean harbored no doubts.

For Roy Sheldon, muddled and resentful in his cell, for Haig t
live would strip the act of its grandeur. Whoever remembered th
names of men who had fired and missed? No, for Sheldon's plac
in history, for his consolation in this dreary pen, full of niggers an
spics, Haig would have to die. Or else where was justification for th
act?

"Guard!" he cried out, and when the man came, tired and impa
tient: "Is he dead yet? Did he die?"

That night or the next, time had begun to telescope, Alex too
a taxi downtown from the hospital to the waterfront across th
cobbled road from the old *Mail* building. Unable to sleep, drive
by memory, she walked out onto the rotting wharf to listen to th
passing river, to watch the harbor traffic, to stare across at th
lights of Brooklyn. She had no desire to enter the newspaper the
owned but in some strange way she wanted to look out again a
that view that so pleased Campbell. She had no idea that she wa
reenacting his own optimistic vigil on that dawn he bought th
Mail, no idea that across there in Brooklyn the crippled Roeblin
had lain, staring back at the Manhattan his bridge would one da
reach.

A warm night. Bums slept curled against the bulkheads of th
wharf, two or three hopeful fishermen cast lazy lines out into th
black current. Somewhere, in the loom of warehouses and freigh
depots, a drunk sang his mournful dirge, silenced now by the rum
bling of a BMT subway train hurtling over another bridge to th
north. Behind her, the night sounds of the city, a siren, a truck'
backfire, the grinding of a garbage compactor, the *wah-wah-wah* o
an ambulance, the *whir* and *whoosh* of automobiles rushing over
head on the FDR Drive. Behind her, high above, the lighted win
dows of the financial district, cleaning women at work; behind her
at street level, the dimly lighted window of a workman's bar, grimy
sullen, and still. Not the sort of place Campbell would have patro
nized; perhaps, she thought with a shudder, the sort of place sh
might once have gone in her wild, nocturnal roamings.

Only not now. Not now and not ever again. Not the mother of Campbell Haig's child. . . .

She was back at his side that morning.

When the nurses had left the room she spoke to him, telling him of her love for him, of a life stretching buoyantly, exuberantly before them, of happiness yet to come, of the child she now carried within her strong, young body, *his* child, surely his son, the gift of his love.

Once, knowing it was silly, that there was nothing there he could feel, she gently lifted his right hand, with all its tubes, and placed the palm of it on her belly.

"Your son, Campbell, your son is here."

That night, exhausted from her vigil at Campbell's bed, she could not sleep. She went down into the kitchen to brew a pot of tea. On the counter was the day's mail, stacked there by the cleaning woman. Waiting for the water to boil she skimmed idly through the stack. A handwritten envelope bore her name. She slit it open.

It was dated three days before.

> I think it's time for us to get together again, Alex. I know this was not part of our 'arrangement' but I confess not being able to forget how you looked, how you felt, and what we did that night in my bedroom. I will be in New York next week. Please make the necessary arrangements. You can consider my coming as pleasure, or, if you prefer, as a payment of interest on my loan to Haig. Either way, I do not really care. But when I arrive, I want you to be there. I am sure you understand. I would hate to be forced to say anything unpleasant about a wife to her husband.

It was unsigned.

The kettle was boiling but she did not hear its whistle as she tore the letter in half and then in half again.

A madman's bullet had saved her from Messenger's sordid blackmail.

59

There was no pain, which puzzled Haig. He was aware of other tactile impressions, the tubes in his nose, in one arm, but little else. He knew this was a hospital. He knew Alex and Gideon had been there, several times, and that others, presumably doctors and nurses, had been there. They were the ones with the different voices. Not that he discerned words, only sounds and murmurs, indistinct but distinguishable by tone. He could see but he did not look. His eyelids were too weighty to lift. And he did not talk. The task of framing words, of coalescing thought, was beyond him. There was, above all, a drain, a vacancy, an emptiness, as if the essence of him was flowing out and away.

Alex was there again, murmuring, and then she was gone. Or had he imagined her? He thought that it might simply be imagination because his father had also visited the room and he knew his father was dead. Beaverbrook was dead as well. So was that foolish boy, Sissy's brother, who stole and whose name he had forgotten. Meg was dead as well. And Warren Messenger. Judah? No. Judah lived. He was clear on that. So many deaths, so long a casualty list. Perhaps he should never have come here, should have stayed in McAllen, running a country newspaper in the company of neutral men with-

out ambition. But if ambition had not gnawed at him, brought him
to New York, he would never have found Alex.

Most of the time he slept. He did not know this. His sleeping
dreams, his waking fantasies, his brief, occasional passages into conscious reality all tended to blur into one amorphous, dim awareness.
He suspected this meant he was dying, balanced precariously on that
chalk line between life and whatever went after. It did not frighten
him but there was, faintly because every emotion was now faint, a
ripple of regret. Nothing passionate. He lacked the strength for
passion. For hatred. In hate's place was only a vague curiosity about
the man who had shot him, who he was and why he had done it.
He remembered Sheldon's face, the sound of his voice as he called
his name, the clumsily wrapped package he carried, the emerging
black snout of the gun. Haig had raised one hand toward Sheldon
in a gesture of restraint. Then, the sound, the shock, a sense of
falling, tumbling, the footsteps running, and nothing more. Until he
was here. How much time had passed? What day was it? Who was
the man and why had he shot him?

There were moments when he confused Sheldon with Charlie
Messenger. Certainly Charlie had reasons. So too, he freely admitted, did others. There were always motives for shooting a newspaper
publisher. There was never a single edition of a great city paper that
did not carry within its columns the seeds of violence. Angry resentment, scandal, perversion, criminality, the excesses of the wealthy,
the despair of the impoverished, the mistreatment of children and
the discarding of the aged, the smooth peculations of confidence
men and the immoral self-serving of the elected, they were all
recorded every day in every newspaper, driving the sullen and the
disaffected and the marginally sane to murderous rage.

Which story, he wondered, had touched the man who shot him?

He drifted. There was the prairie and the river. New York and
McAllen. A dusty street where his father died and Roebling's bridge
and the rented flat beyond. There was Alex's golden body and his
mother's dry hand in the summer heat. A suite in Paris that night
so long ago when the *Mail* first beckoned and a bar in the Village
where Alex had cried out to him. There was Messenger's snarl
and Gideon's benediction. Farrell's ridiculous claim on his wife and

Ben Cork's deep laugh. There was Judah and there was old Meg.
Why was his father's desk not there?

"Alex, Alex," he shouted in silence.

She knew he had called, though she had heard nothing. He was
paler now than ever, pale and shrunken and still. But then, for an
instant, not still. His right hand seemed to tense, tried to move. He
wants something, she thought desperately, but I don't know what.
The nurse, perhaps the nurse would know. Alex reached for the pull
button. But she never touched it. His hand moved again, tried to
lift its own ponderous weight from the sheet.

Then she knew. Alex reached out and once more took his lean
right hand and placed it against the gentle curve of her belly, next
to where their child lived.

"He knows!" The words burst from her joyously.

At eight o'clock in the morning, seven days after he was shot,
Campbell Haig died.

"There never really was a chance," the chief surgeon informed
Gideon Benaud, as if the very inevitability of his death made it more
palatable.

Gideon nodded solemnly. Then, moving slowly with grief and
heavy with years, he went to the telephone.

"It's all over, Alex. About twenty minutes ago."

She thanked him and hung up.

She wandered, quiet and alone, though the house, *their* house,
her hand straying occasionally to that nearly flat belly within which
he still lived, to the chair where he liked to sit, to the pictures he
loved to look at, to the bed where they slept and loved one another. She did not cry. Later she would permit tears, later in the
lonely nights.

Delia Haig had flown north a few days earlier. Alex telephoned
the old woman. First a husband, now an only son, violently dead.

"I wish there was something I could say, my dear, something I
could tell you that would make it better. There isn't. Believe me,
there just isn't."

"I know," Alex said, "I know."

At the *Mail* Farrell called in the two associate editors. There was

Haig rule that, except on the masthead, "where it belongs," the owner's name was not to be mentioned in the newspaper. They had broken that rule when he was shot. Now they broke it again.

"What the hell," Farrell said, "what can he do now? Fire me?"

The second edition, the one that hit the streets at eleven in the morning, carried the front-page headline:

CAMPBELL HAIG DEAD

Nora Noyes, concelebrating Newport with her priests, got through on the telephone that afternoon. As a Catholic, she prayed for his soul. As Nora, she hoped he would burn in hell. Now, with a restrained sob in her voice, she offered to come to the city or to fly Alex to Newport, giving her daughter shelter "from those horrid, prying journalists."

In a righteous fury she hung up when Alex said, "Fuck off, Mother."

Lenny Sparg proposed lowering city flags to half staff.

"Lenny," said wise old Mavis Sparg, "this was a newspaper publisher. Not Albert Schweitzer."

Charlie Messenger flew East. It was a funeral he did not want to miss. With a man like Haig you were never sure until they shoveled in the dirt.

Sissy Valentine, to her own surprise, wept. Perhaps she was mourning her brother and herself. Had it been only two years since Haig had come to New York? She and Willie had been young and untouched and whole. Haig had changed all that. Now he was dead. She could not understand why she was crying, unless it was for Alex, who now had no one, while Sissy had Sean.

Gideon Benaud mourned. This could have been another Beaverbrook and now he was gone. The Beaver had had his ninety years, Campbell less than half that. A waste. Gideon mourned, too old a dog to find another master.

Sean Farrell got drunk that night at the Lion's Head and punched a man who had said, "That fucking Haig, he got what he asked for."

Somehow, Alex Haig got through the funeral.

Three days later Charles Messenger requested an audience Gideon Benaud, the red hair graying, the huge body bent, sat at her side like some court chamberlain, some loyal old retainer.

"They don't lose any time, do they?" he asked, as they waited in Alex's living room for Messenger to come.

"No," she said, "not when you owe them money."

Messenger was solicitous.

"Mrs. Haig," he said, observing the proprieties in view of Gideon's presence or Alex's black dress, "I'm not sure precisely how much Campbell told you of our . . . arrangement."

"He told me," she said crisply, "a three-year loan at one percent over prime."

"Why, yes," he said, startled to find her so businesslike.

"And?" she asked.

He made motions with his big, knobby hands, those hands she knew so well. "Well, I just wanted to assure you that I will be more than patient. That perhaps in view of . . . events, after you and Gideon have had a chance to review the situation, if you wish to discuss it with me, I would be more than glad—"

"If there is any change, Mr. Messenger, I will inform you through Mr. Benaud."

How cold she is, Messenger thought, as an awkward silence stilled the room. If I didn't know better I'd think she was as frigid as her mother.

The Messengers were not accustomed to being dismissed. "Perhaps if you and I could chat informally—" he resumed.

"Mrs. Haig has asked me to be here," Gideon said, formal, forbidding.

Alex reached over to pat his arm. "No, Gideon, it's all right. I'll phone you later at the office."

When they were alone Messenger said, "Alex, I want the *Mail.* And more than that, I want you."

She half smiled. "We have our three years' grace, Mr. Messenger."

and I don't think you possess quite the same leverage you did that night in California."

"No," he said, "I don't."

"Good, then we understand each other."

He shook his head. "That wasn't what I was proposing, Alex. I want to marry you."

She stood up, struggling for control. Then: "Mr. Messenger, the newspaper is not for sale. Neither am I!"

A maid ushered him out.

She spent that weekend alone, at Mayfair, the great house empty and silent above the black Hudson flowing inexorably, eternally toward the sea. How Campbell had loved to sit there on the lawn staring out at it, how he had dreamed and planned and wondered, how he had talked to her for hours of their lives, their future, their tomorrows. Gone now, all gone, swept thoughtlessly downstream like chips tossed in the river, lost in the swift current that would carry them to the unknowing ocean.

There was an inevitability about the river. As inevitable, she supposed now, with a tranquility she knew she should not feel, as his death. How often he had told her of Pulitzer and Hearst and the others, of how they feared the mob their own newspapers had created. They had feared the mob and had died old men. Campbell knew about the mob and cavalierly had dismissed it. Perhaps that had been his fatal flaw. If only he had been afraid. . . .

She knew that now she too should be afraid, that fear would bring prudence, maturity, the good sense to recognize when the fight is lost. There must come a time when you raise the white flag.

But she knew that if he had been afraid he would not have been Campbell. She knew, also, that with Campbell's child growing within her, neither could she be afraid. To surrender was easy. To battle on, against the Messengers and the Spargs and the Roy Sheldons, whoever he was, was more difficult. But necessary.

She had known and loved and would bear the child of a great man. A great man, from that night when he was twenty and had fought in the bar outside McAllen, had driven his old car over the marking stakes and the white strings of the developers' land, the land someone had stolen and had killed Sam Haig to keep.

Oh, God, she thought, the words strangling in her throat, Camp
bell, Campbell, we *need* you!

The "we" was coming more naturally now. She was no longer
alone.

Ten days later, a week before her twenty-seventh birthday, the
same age at which old Meg Valentine had been left a widow,
Alexandra Noyes Haig summoned the company limousine and was
driven downtown to *The New York Mail.* It was midmorning, fresh
after a night rain, the city clean and showered and vigorous. To her
left, as the big Cadillac tooled south along Franklin Roosevelt's
elevated driveway, the East River swept powerfully toward the upper
bay and the ocean beyond.

How he loved this drive, she thought. And how I loved him.

At Forty-fourth Street they sped past the United Nations. The
chauffeur, as instructed, had placed the *Times* and *The Wall Street
Journal* on the back seat. She ignored them, concentrating instead
on the great and vibrant city her husband had wanted to impress and
to understand. And that had killed him. To the left, across the river,
was Long Island City, smokestacks and warehouses and the satellite
plant where they printed *The Daily News.* Pepsi-Cola signs and Con
Ed smokestacks, wharves and church steeples, and then, as the car
continued south, the Gowanus Canal and vast Brooklyn, miles and
miles of row houses, churches and chimneys, more piers and wharves
now, the navy yard, an aircraft carrier cradled tenuously in dry dock,
and clustered about it lean gray ships.

New York! Like Venice a city floating on the sea. A city that had
always and would always draw men like Haig, men from the West
and the prairie and those dusty, square states beyond the Mississippi.
Why did they come here when they knew it would, in the end,
destroy them? She knew the answer. Like Everest, it was there. To
be climbed and conquered.

The big car swung right off the drive onto the potholed shunt of
South Street, past the project houses and the Puerto Rican kids
playing in the puddles along the curb, past the loading platforms
and the trucks and unfathomable Chinatown and Little Italy beyond. He had not understood the city, not fully, nor had the great
city understood him. Like the muscular, sweating antagonists of

me ancient arena, man and city had jousted, bled, and battled.
ne had fallen.

Miss Mayhew, alert and competent, met her at the door.

The lift, big as a freight elevator, stopped at every floor to admit
en and women with cardboard cups of coffee. Embarrassed, they
odded hello. At the sixth floor she did not wait but led Miss
layhew down the long hall to Campbell's office. How familiar and
t how alien it seemed!

There was the big desk, Meg's desk and then Campbell's,
rangely bare now, lacking the fallen leaves of copy paper, computer
rintouts, circulation reports, tear sheets, copies of each of that day's
litions. Dully, through her thin-soled shoes, she could feel the
resses roll, could sense the great animal strength of the newspaper
rowling beneath her, pulsating, grinding, roaring. It was this build-
g, those machines, that had torn out Sissy's arm, that had elected
residents, that had changed the fate of small nations, that had, in
e end, killed her lover, her husband, the father of her unborn child.

Alex circled the desk once and then, hesitantly, she sat down. Miss
layhew, pad poised, waited, uncertain and tactful.

Alex swiveled toward the river. A coastal tanker was beating its
ay north against the current, pennants flying bravely in the morn-
g breeze. Alex watched it for a moment and then turned back to
e secretary.

"Please get Mr. Farrell on the line."

When the connection had been put through, when she heard his
ice, close and familiar, Alex said, with a crispness that surprised
liss Mayhew:

"Mr. Farrell, I want you to stay on as editor of the *Mail.* Do you
gree?"

There was an instant's hesitation.

"Well?"

"Yes," he said, "yes, Mrs. Haig, of course I'll stay on."

"Good."

She hung up the phone and turned again to the secretary, still
oised there with her pad, her patient anticipation.

"Miss Mayhew," Alex said, her voice steady, almost calm, "please
ave Mr. Benaud come up."

"Yes, Mrs. Haig."

"And take this memo for all employees."

"Yes?" The pencil hovered over the steno pad.

"Mrs. Campbell Haig," Alex began, "announced today that sh will become publisher of *The New York Mail*, succeeding her hu band, Campbell Haig, who . . ."

Beyond them both, beyond this room, the river ebbed toward th sea.